Barcelona

Cadogan Guides
3rd Floor, West End House, 11 Hills Place,
London W1R 1AG
cadoganguides@morrispub.co.uk
Distributed in the USA by
The Globe Pequot Press
246 Goose Lane, PO Box 480, Guilford,
Connecticut 06437–0480

Copyright © Dana Facaros and Michael Pauls 2000

Book and cover design by Animage

Cover photographs: John Ferro Sims
Chapter title page pictures
from photographs by Mary-Ann Gallagher

Maps © Cadogan Guides, drawn by Map Creation Ltd

Editorial Director: Vicki Ingle
Series Editor: Linda McQueen

Editor: Claudia Martin
Proofreading: Linda McQueen
Indexing: Hilary Bird
Production: Book Production Services

UK ISBN 1-86011-948-4
A catalogue record for this book
is available from the British Library

Printed and bound in the UK by
Cambridge University Press

The author and publishers have made every effort to ensure the accuracy of the information in the book at the time of going to press. However, they cannot accept any responsibility for any loss, injury or inconvenience resulting from the use of information contained in this guide.

About the Authors

Dana Facaros and Michael Pauls have written over 30 books for Cadogan Guides, including all of the Spain series. They have lived all over Europe but recently hung up their castanets in a farmhouse in the Lot valley surrounded by vineyards.

About the Contributor

Mary-Ann Gallagher is a travel writer and editor. She has lived in New York, Japan and London and has written and updated five titles for Cadogan Guides.

Authors' Acknowledgements

We would like to extend our heartfelt thanks and sloppy kisses to Mary-Ann Gallagher, tango queen and dogsbody extraordinaire, as well as a major contributor to this book. Also, a big thank you to Claudia Martin, whose fast and furious editing got it out on time.

Contributor's Acknowledgements

I would like to thank Giray Ablay for sound advice on crossing roads, and Danni, José and especially Tito at the Hostal Eden for many kindnesses.

Contents

Around the Edge 193–212

Museums and Monuments 213–18

Day Trips 219–24

Food and Drink 225–38

Where to Stay 239–48

Entertainment and Nightlife 249–54

Shopping 255–61

Further Reading, Language 262–72

Index 273–81

Maps and Plans

Barcelona is something else, isn't it? There you have the Mediterranean, the spirit, the adventure, the high dream of perfect love. There are palm trees, people from every country, surprising advertisements, Gothic towers, and a rich urban tide...

Federico García Lorca (1926)

At last, on one living point of the earth, modern times have found an asylum.

Le Corbusier (1932)

Introduction

Observe Barcelona, and you may begin to wonder just what kind of asylum Corby meant: this is a city that goes about its business and its pleasure with such ballistic intensity that it's hard to tell whether it's insanely serious or seriously insane. A glance at the record, however, shows that such outbursts of energy are a recurring feature in a city whose fate has been to be bottled like a genie for long stretches of history. Its most recent bottler of course was Franco, and when its most recent liberator, the Grim Reaper, came on 20 November 1975 to carry the old man to his reward it was to the tune of a million corks popping off every bottle of *cava* in the city. Barcelona then rolled up its sleeves and channelled its pent-up energy into making up for four decades, but with such geyser-like force that it has not only caught up but shot into the vanguard to become the hippest city in Europe, fizzing and sparkling and doing whatever it takes to make itself too big to get stuffed in a bottle ever again.

All cities are unique, but Barcelona manages to be extra unique. Cradle of Spain's industrial revolution, it sees itself as the southernmost city of northern Europe and northernmost city of the south, with a hard Protestant nose for making piles of money, sweetened by Mediterranean colour and spontaneity. Yet the city it resembles the most is New York, with its gung ho capitalism and financiers; its cosmopolitan airs; its mania for design and fashion; its art galleries, publishers, theatres; its lack of modesty and love of strutting its stuff—with two World's Fairs under its belt, the Olympics and, coming in 2004, an event it cooked up called the Forum of Cultures to promote world peace. Barcelona has the restless can-do spirit of the New World; grandiose projects and utopian schemes run like golden threads through its very woof and warp. It is a city of strong will, a work of art and, like Paris, the shop front of a nation.

1

Only this nation isn't Spain. Barcelona is no mere second city trying harder (although it is that too): it's also the capital of Catalunya, a long-submerged nation which now takes the palm as Spain's wealthiest autonomous region. The Catalans have their own language, traditions and quirks, but, above all, they do what they do with intensity. For fun they stand on one another's shoulders to build human castles, and play with fireworks, 'fat heads' and dragons. They dote on choral music, opera and Barça. They slurp down red peppers stuffed with pork and squid, and salt cod with honey. Their unique medieval and Modernista architecture has left Barcelona looking like no other city in the world. Franco was only the most recent centralizer who tried to kill off their language and culture, but he only made the Catalans all the more determined to revive them. So while cutting a splendid dash on the international stage, Barcelona is cementing its language and customs in place, with a non-racial inclusiveness that could be a blueprint for other nationalities struggling to keep heart and soul intact in a multi-cultural world. The symbol of all this is the continuation of Gaudí's Sagrada Família, a project so big and eccentric and so essentially Catalan that anyone trying to bottle up the Catalans in the future will have a pretty hard go of it.

Pat today's Barcelona on the back for being so innovative, so successful and so much fun, but take off your hat to the risky high-wire act that made it all possible. On the edge of living memory, this was a city so divided that rich and poor were mowing each other down in the streets. Only two churches in Barcelona were never set ablaze by Barcelonans (and that was only thanks to armed guards). It is the only city in the West ever ruled by Anarchists—until the Communists clobbered them, before Franco's Fascists clobbered them in turn. A lesser city, so badly wounded, might have scratched its scabs until they festered into infections and permanent scars; another city with Barcelona's money-grubbing instincts might have sacrificed its personality once and for all on the altar of Mammon. The Barcelonans, who like all Catalans pride themselves on their *seny* (an untranslatable word that means wisdom, practicality, common sense), willed otherwise. Rather than fester, their city fermented and matured, and emerged from Franco's bottle with character, consensus and tolerance. Beneath all the hype and glitter, Barcelona's—and Spain's—skill in pulling the transition off so smoothly is the coolest thing of all.

Travel

Getting There

By Air

Barcelona's international airport is **El Prat de Llobregat**, 12km to the south. There are three terminals: **A** for international flights, **B** for domestic and some European flights, and **C** for shuttle flights between Spain's major cities. For flight information, the general number is ✆ 93 298 38 28.

Air France	✆ 93 379 74 63
British Airways	✆ 93 379 44 68
Delta	✆ 93 478 23 00
easyJet	✆ 90 229 99 92
go	✆ 90 133 35 00
Iberia	✆ 90 240 05 00
KLM	✆ 93 379 54 58
TWA	✆ 93 215 81 88
Virgin Express	✆ 90 046 76 12

From the UK

There is an astounding variety of flight options these days to Spain from the UK: **British Airways**, ✆ (0345) 222 111, *www.britishairways.com*, operates direct services from Heathrow, Gatwick, Manchester and Birmingham to Barcelona. Spain's national airline, **Iberia**, ✆ (020) 7830 0011, *www.iberia.com*, operates on many of the same routes.

A number of low-cost airlines have begun operating in the UK in recent years, offering scheduled flights at near-charter prices. **Go**, ✆ (0345) 605 4321, *www.go-fly.com*, a subsidiary of British Airways, offers return flights from Stansted to Barcelona for as little as £80; **easyJet**, ✆ (0870) 600 0000, *www.easyjet.com*, flies from Luton to Barcelona with prices starting at around £90; and **Virgin Express**, ✆ (020) 7744 0004, *www.virgin-express.com*, flies to Barcelona from Heathrow and Gatwick via Brussels with prices starting from £90. Note that the cheapest prices are only available if booked well in advance. Last-minute fares are, in fact, not much cheaper than those of the major carriers.

charter flights

These can be incredibly cheap, and offer the added advantage of departing from local airports. Companies such as **Thomson**, **Airtours** and **Unijet** can offer return flights from as little £80. Check out your local travel agency, the Sunday papers and TV Teletext. In London, look in the *Evening Standard* and *Time Out*. Remember, there are no refunds for missed flights—most travel agencies sell insurance, so that you don't lose all your money if you become ill.

Campus Travel: 52 Grosvenor Gardens, London SW1 OAG, ✆ (020) 7730 3402, *www.campustravel.co.uk.*

STA: 6 Wright's Lane, London W8 6TA, ✆ (020) 7361 6161, *www.statravel. co.uk.*

From the USA and Canada

There are numerous carriers that serve Spain. Most regular flights from the USA or Canada are to Madrid or Barcelona. **Iberia,** the Spanish national airline, offers fly-drive deals and discounts. From anywhere in the USA and Canada, you can use Iberia's toll-free line, ✆ (800) 772 4642.

Iberia offices in the USA include:

New York: 655 Madison Avenue, New York, NY 10022, ✆ (212) 644 8797.
Los Angeles: 4227 Wilshire Bd, 3209, Los Angeles, CA, ✆ (323) 692 2965.

Airlines with direct routes to Spain include:

American Airlines	toll-free ✆ (800) 433 7300
Continental Airlines	toll-free ✆ (800) 231 0856
Delta	toll free ✆ (800) 241 4141
United Airlines	toll-free ✆ (800) 538 2929
Air Canada	toll-free ✆ (888) 247 2262, *www.aircanada.ca*

Airlines with routes to Spain via Europe include:

British Airways	toll-free ✆ (800) 247 9297
KLM	toll-free ✆ (800) 777 5553
Lufthansa	toll-free ✆ (800) 645 3880
TAP Air Portugal	toll-free ✆ (800) 221 7370
Virgin Atlantic	toll-free ✆ (800) 862 8621

Currently a charter from New York to Madrid varies between around $400 and $600, depending on the season. You may want to weigh this against the current price of transatlantic fares to London, from where in most cases you can get a low-cost flight to Barcelona departing within a day or two of your arrival. The Sunday *New York Times* has the most listings.

Major charter companies and consolidators include:

Council Travel: 205 East 42nd Street, New York, NY 10017, toll-free ℭ (800) 743 1823, *www.counciltravel.com.*

Spanish Heritage Tours: 116–47 Queens Bd, Forest Hills, NY 11375, ℭ (718) 520 1300; uses Air Europa.

TFI: 34 West 32nd Street, New York, NY 10001, ℭ (212) 736 1140, toll-free ℭ (800) 745 8000.

Transport to and from Barcelona Airport

Trains link the airport with Barcelona's Plaça de Catalunya and Estació de Sants every 30 minutes from 6.08am to 10.38pm. The more frequent **A1 Aerobús** connects both domestic and international terminals with Plaça de Catalunya, Estació de Sants and Plaça d'Espanya (*Mon–Fri 5.30am–11.15pm every 15 minutes; Sat and Sun 6am–11.20pm every 30 minutes*).

By Train

London to Barcelona is a full-day trip, changing trains in Paris and at Port Bou/San Sebastián/La Tour de Carol or Toulouse.

The TGV service from Paris to Bordeaux can cut some hours off the trip if the schedule works right for you. Time can also be saved by taking the **Eurostar** (ℭ (0990) 186 186) through the Channel Tunnel to Paris. Services are frequent and take just under three hours from London (Waterloo) to Paris (Gare du Nord). Fares are lower if booked at least 14 days in advance.

EU citizens over and under the age of 26 and non-EU citizens who've been resident in Europe for six months are all eligible for the three-zone **InterRail** pass (currently £269 if you're over 26 or £195 if you're under 26). Passes entitle holders to a month's unlimited travel across Europe, plus 30–50% discounts on trains to cross-Channel ferry terminals. **Contact:** Rail Europe, 179 Piccadilly, London W1V 0BA, ℭ (08705) 848 848, *www.raileurope.co.uk.* The equivalent North American **EurRail** pass can be bought in the USA, for 15, 21, 30, 60 or 90 days; it too saves the hassle of buying numerous tickets, but it will only pay for itself if you use it every day, everywhere. It's not valid in the UK, Morocco or countries outside the European Union. Two weeks' travel is $388 for those under 26; those over 26 can get a 15-day pass for $554, a 21-day pass for $718, or a month for $890. **Contact:** Rail Europe US, ℭ (1 800) 438 7245, *www.raileurope.com.*

Bookings: Rail tickets to Spain from England, or vice versa, can be obtained from **Rail Europe**, 179 Piccadilly, London W1V 0BA, ℭ (08705) 848 848, *www.*

raileurope.co.uk, or from their North American office, ✆ (1 800) 438 7245, *www.raileurope.com*. Take your passport. Tickets for local Spanish services can be obtained from certain UK travel agencies.

By Coach

One major company, **Eurolines**, offers departures several times a week in the summer (once a week out of season) from London to Spain; the journey to Barcelona takes 24 hours. Single fares are about £80; return fares around £110. Peak-season fares between 22 July and 4 September are slightly higher. There are discounts for anyone under 26, senior citizens and children under 12. In the summer, the coach can be the best bargain for anyone over 26; off-season you'll probably find a cheaper charter flight.

Information and booking: Eurolines, 52 Grosvenor Gardens, London SW1, ✆ (020) 7730 8235.

By Car

From the UK via France you have a choice of routes. Ferries from Portsmouth cross to Cherbourg, Caen, Le Havre and St Malo. From any of these ports the most direct road route takes you to Bordeaux, down the western coast of France to the border at Irún. An alternative route is Paris to Perpignan, crossing the border at the Mediterranean side of the Pyrenees, then along the coast to Barcelona. Both routes take an average of a 1½ days' steady driving. You may find it more convenient and less tiring to try the ferry from Plymouth to Santander operated by **Brittany Ferries**, ✆ (08705) 360 360 (high-season tickets for a car and four people from £750), which cuts out driving through France and saves expensive *autoroute* tolls.

Customs and Entry Formalities

passports and visas

Visitors from the UK or other EU countries must present a valid passport. Holders of US, Canadian or New Zealand passports can enter Spain for up to 90 days without a visa. Holders of Australian, South African or other passports will need a visa, available from any Spanish consulate either at home or in Europe.

If you intend to stay for more than three months, you must apply for a community resident's card (*permiso de residencia*) at the Foreign Nationals Office (*Oficina de Extranjeros*) at the **Delegacion de Gobierno**, Avinguda Marques de l'Argenteria, ✆ 93 483 05 44; for appointments call ✆ 93 482 05 60.

Those arriving direct from another EU country do not have to declare goods imported into Spain for personal use if they have paid duty on them in the country of origin. You are allowed to bring in, duty paid, up to 800 cigarettes, or 400 cigarillos, 200 cigars or 1kg of tobacco; plus 10 litres of spirits, 90 litres of wine and 110 litres of beer.

Those arriving from outside the EU are allowed to bring in duty-free 200 cigarettes, or 100 cigarillos, 50 cigars or 250g of tobacco; plus 1 litre of spirits (or 2 litres of fortified wine or other spirits under 22% alcohol); plus 2 litres of wine.

Tour Operators

General Tour Operators

The following offer straightforward city breaks and accommodation in Barcelona (some catering to a special interest as well).

in the UK

Abercrombie and Kent, Sloane Square House, Holbein Place, London SW1W 8NS, ℗ (020) 7730 9600, ℗ (020) 7730 9376. Flights and hotels, also information on a range of high-quality special-interest tours

Accommodation Line, 1st Floor, 46 Maddox Street, London W1R 9PB, ℗ (020) 7409 1343, ℗ (020) 7409 2606. Wide range of 1–4-star hotels (no flights).

American Express Europe, Destination Services, 19–20 Berners Street, London W1P 4AE, ℗ (020) 7637 8600, ℗ (020) 7631 4803. City breaks and fly-drive holidays.

British Airways Holidays Ltd, Astral Towers, Betts Way, London Road, Crawley, West Sussex RH10 2XA, ℗ (01293) 722718, ℗ (01293) 722702. Holidays including fly-drives.

Elegant Resorts, The Old Place, Chester CH1 1RB, ℗ (01244) 897777, ℗ (01244) 897770.

Fly Sky Travel, 46 Victoria Road, Surbiton, Surrey KT6 4JL, ℗ (0208) 390 5343, ℗ (0208) 390 3331. Last-minute charter flights.

Kirker Travel, 3 New Concordia Wharf, Mill Street, London SE1 2BB, ℗ (020) 7231 3333, ℗ (020) 7231 4771.

Magic of Spain, 227 Shepherd's Bush Road, London W6 7AS, ℗ (020) 7533 8888, ℗ (020) 7533 8830.

Mundi Color, 276 Vauxhall Bridge Road, London SW1 1BE, ℗ (020) 7828 6021, City breaks and flights only.

Page & Moy, 135–140 London Road, Leicester LE2 1EN, ✆ (01162) 507000, ✉ (01162) 507123.

Room Service, 42 Riding House Street, London W1P 7PL, ✆ (020) 7636 6888, ✉ (020) 7636 6002. Accommodation service.

Solo's Holidays, 54–8 High Street, Edgware, Middx HA8 7ED, ✆ (020) 8951 2800, ✉ (020) 8951 2848.

Thomson Holidays, Greater London House, Hampstead Road, London NW1 7SD, ✆ (020) 7387 9321, ✉ (020) 7387 8451.

Time Off (Thomas Cook), 1 Elmfield Park, Bromley, Kent BR1 1LU, ✆ (020) 8218 3537, ✉ (020) 8218 6363.

Trailfinders, 194 Kensington High Street, London W8 4QY, ✆ (020) 7937 1234.

Wallace Arnold, Gelderd Road, Leeds, West Yorkshire LS12 6DH, ✆ (0113) 263 6456, ✉ (0113) 231 0749. Coach tours.

Worldwide Journeys Plc, 243 Euston Road, London NW1 WBU, ✆ (020) 7383 3898, ✉ (020) 7383 3848.

in the USA

Marketing Ahead Inc., 433 Fifth Avenue, New York, NY 10016, ✆ (212) 686 9213, ✉ (212) 686 0271, the leading hotel and *parador* agents in the USA.

Specialist Tour Operators

The very helpful **Spanish Tourist Office** is located at 22–3 Manchester Square, London W1M 5AP, ✆ (020) 7486 8077, ✉ (020) 7486 8034, *www.tourspain.es*, brochure requests ✉ (0891) 669 920 (45p per minute). They stock brochures and leaflets on most main towns and cities in Spain as well as information on a variety of holiday options.

cultural tours

Martin Randall Travel, 10 Barley Mow Passage, Chiswick, London W4 4PH, ✆ (020) 8742 3355, ✉ (020) 8742 7766. Cultural tours accompanied by a lecturer.

Page & Moy Ltd, 136–40 London Road, Leicester LE2 1EN, ✆ (0116) 250 7000. Cultural guided tours: *Catalonia and Barcelona* and *Barcelona, Madrid and Seville*, all fully escorted and staying in 3- and 4-star accommodation.

Plantagenet Tours, 85 The Grove, Moordown, Bournemouth BH9 2TY, ✆ (01202) 521895. Changing programme of historical tours.

Prospect Music and Art Tours, 36 Manchester Street, London W1M 5PE, ℭ (020) 7486 5704, ✆ (020) 7486 5868. Art and cultural breaks, plus tours of the big museums.

Specialtours Ltd, 81a Elizabeth Street, London SW1W 9PG, ℭ (020) 7730 2297. Fully escorted cultural tours.

Voyages Jules Verne, 21 Dorset Square, London NW1 6QG, ℭ (020) 7616 1000, ✆ (020) 7723 8629. Changing programme of escorted cultural tours.

special-interest holidays

Arblaster & Clarke Wine Tours, Clarke House, The Green, West Liss, Hants GU33 6JQ, ℭ (01730) 893344. Wine tours, visiting Barcelona with excursions to Tarragona vineyards.

Bike and Sun Tours, 42 Whitby Avenue, Guiseborough, Cleveland TS14 7AN, ℭ (01287) 639739, ✆ (01287) 638217. Bike and motorbike tours throughout Spain.

Don Quijote UK, 2–4 Stoneleigh Park Road, Stoneleigh, Epsom, Surrey KT19 0QR, ℭ (020) 8786 8081, ✆ (020) 8786 8086. Language courses plus accommodation.

Languages Abroad (CESA), Western House, Malpas, Truro, Cornwall TR1 1SQ, ℭ (01872) 225300, ✆ (01872) 225400. Language courses in group classes, with accommodation in college residences or with host families.

Spanish Study Holidays, 35 Woodbrook Road, Loughborough, Leics LE11 3QB, ℭ (01509) 211612, ✆ (01509) 260037. Language courses, with local accommodation arranged.

Getting Around

By Bus

Barcelona's public transport authority, **TMB** (ℭ 93 318 70 74), is efficient, cheap and user-friendly. Its buses run until 11pm—the 14 main lines also have special afterhours 'Nitbuses' (night, not lice)—and at each stop their routes and timetables are clearly posted. You can pay the 150 pts fare on board; the Nitbus is more expensive. If you're using one of the day/multiple day passes listed below, put it in one of the machines behind the driver to be date-stamped.

By Metro (Ⓜ)

The city also has five underground **metro** lines with Muzak pumped into the stations, and a sixth underground line operated by the **FGC** out of Plaça de

Catalunya. As stylish as Barcelona is, its metro is not, but it is certainly fast and cheap: trains run until 11pm, or 1am at weekends, and cost 150 pts a ride.

For either the city buses or metro you can save money by purchasing a **T-1 pass** in the metro stations, which offers 10 single rides on the metro, buses or FGC for 825 pts. A **T-10/x2 pass** also offers 10 single rides with the added bonus of a free transfer within an hour; this pass costs 1,325 pts. There are **one-** (625 pts), **three-** (1,600 pts) and **five-day** (2,400 pts) **passes** valid on the metro, buses or FGC. If you are planning a longer trip, a **T-50/30** pass, costing 3,500 pts, lets you make 50 single journeys in 30 days, and a **T-Mes** is a monthly pass with no restrictions and costs 5,550 pts.

By Tram and Funicular

TMB also operates the **Tramvia Blau**, a pretty, refurbished old-fashioned streetcar, running from Plaça Kennedy to Plaça Dr Andreu (250 pts one way; *running 9am–9.35pm, weekends only in winter, daily in summer*), and Barcelona's **funiculars**. One funicular runs from Plaça Dr Andreu to Tibidabo (350 pts one way; *running end March–April and end Sept–Oct, Sat, Sun and hols 12–5; May, Sat, Sun and hols 12–5 and Thurs 10–6; June, Wed–Fri 10–6, Sat, Sun and hols 12–5; July and Aug, Mon–Thurs, Sun and hols 12–10, Fri and Sat 12–1am; early Sept, Mon–Thurs 12–8, Fri–Sun 12–10*). Another funicular goes from metro Paral.lel to Montjuïc (215 pts one way). From the latter, you can continue to the Castell de Montjuïc on the **Teleférico de Monjuïc** (225 pts one way; *open June–mid-Sept, Mon–Fri 11.15–8, Sat–Sun 11.15–9; mid-Sept–Oct daily 11.30–2.45 and 4–7.30; Nov–May weekends only*). Services grind to a halt on weekdays out of season; ring TMB for schedules, © 93 443 08 59.

By Tourist Bus

TMB operates the **Barcelona Bus Turístic**, which has two loops, a red/north one and a blue/south one, taking in the best-known sights of the city. The buses run every 20 to 30 minutes, allowing you to get off and on at will, on either route. A one-day ticket (purchase it on the bus) is 2,000 pts, two days (consecutive) 2,500 pts, and children cost 1,700 pts a day (under-fours go free). You get a number of discounts with the ticket (the Poble Espanyol, for instance, is half-price) that can make it excellent value (and you don't have to use the discount vouchers on the same day).

A special bus service for serial shoppers, the eerily named **TombBus**, plies between Plaça de Catalunya and Plaça Pius XII on the Avinguda Diagonal; normal metro/bus passes are not valid on this service, which runs *Mon–Fri 7.30am–9.30pm, Sat and Sun 9.10am–9.20pm.*

By Taxi

Taxis are ubiquitous and reasonable. If you can't find one, call ✆ 93 357 77 55/ ✆ 93 490 22 22/✆ 93 300 11 00; for cabs with disabled access, ✆ 93 358 11 11.

By Bicycle

Hire a bicycle from **Un Cotxe Menys**, 3 C/ Esparteria, ✆ 93 268 21 05 (Ⓜ Barceloneta), who also arrange guided tours on bicycles; or from **...al punt de la trobada**, 24 C/ Badajoz, ✆ 93 225 05 85 (Ⓜ Barceloneta), who also have tandems if you want to re-create Ramón Casas' famous painting in Els Quatre Gats. Or there is **Los Filicletos**, 38 Passeig de Picasso, ✆ 93 319 78 75 (Ⓜ Barceloneta), near the Ciutadella.

By Balloon

This new venture, begun in 2000, takes you up to 150m, to sway over the city for 15 giddy minutes. For information, call ✆ 93 423 18 00, ✎ 93 423 26 49.

Practical A–Z

Spain has the lowest birth rate in Europe, but children are omnipresent in Barcelona. This is not so much to do with some demographic quirk as the fact that children aren't regarded as a race apart: you'll find them up until the wee hours in bars and restaurants, having a good time as their parents blithely sit and chat away into the night with a group of friends. Barcelona is a fairy-tale city with whimsical buildings that have pointy roofs like witches' hats and scaly façades like dragons but, if all that palls, there are plenty of other child-friendly attractions.

watery fun

Cheapest and easiest is going to one of the six **beaches** around Barceloneta and the Port Olímpic, all spruced up for the 1992 Olympic games, with lots of cafés, bars and restaurants. There are more beaches up and down the coast if you are prepared to get on a train or hit the road with thousands of others. All get packed in summer, particularly at weekends. The city council organizes children's sports and activities on the beaches between March and May, culminating in the Festa de la Platja in May. The tourist office can supply all the details (*see* pp.23–4). The **Aquarium** (*see* p.144) has an enormous central tank full of sharks and a new interactive centre, Planeta Aqua, with three levels: the first has exotic fish and jellyfish from the ocean depths; the second has creatures from the coldest seas, including penguins; and the third has caimans and piranhas from tropical rivers.

Illa Fantasia at Vilassar del Dalt, 24km from Barcelona (*©* 93 751 45 53; regular buses from Estació-Sants), is one of Europe's largest waterparks, and becomes a water disco in the evenings. Between Barcelona and Tarragona, **Aqualéon Safari** at Finca les Basses, 65km from Barcelona (*©* 97 768 57 76), is a combined water and safari park with tigers, eagles and parrots as well as wave machines, water slides and dolphins.

museums

Most kids and teenagers can spend a happy few hours with the hands-on science exhibits at the **Museu de la Ciència** (*see* p.203), even though explanations are only in Catalan and Spanish; there's a special section for the under-fives. Any football-crazy kid will love the **Museu del Futbol Club Barcelona** (*see* p.209), and nearly all would enjoy the **Museu Marítim** (*see* p.142), which has an entertaining virtual-reality show, with English-language headphones. The **Museu d'Història de Catalunya** (*see* p.146) has enough touchy-feely exhibits to make up for its Catalan-only policy, while the **Museu de Cera** (*see* p.76) is a pretty dull wax museum but might keep the little squirmers pacified for an hour on a rainy day.

Barcelona's **Zoo** is in the Parc de la Ciutadella (*see* p.120) and offers dolphin shows, a farm area and Snowflake the albino gorilla. On Barcelona's highest mountain, the **Tibidabo Parc d'Attraciones** (*see* p.204) is great fun; getting up there is fun too if you take the Tramvia Blau and the Tibidabo funicular (*see* p.11). While you are up there, visit the **Torre de Collserola** (*see* p.204), a high-tech telecommunications tower with a glass lift up to the observation deck. The **IMAX cinema** at Port Vell (*see* p.144) shows kid-pleasing nature shows and rock concerts. After dinner, take in the aquatic ballet of the **Font Mágica** (*see* p.182).

Outside Barcelona, suckers for roadside attractions will like **Catalunya en Miniatura** in Torrelles de Llobregat (take the Oliveras bus from Plaça d'Espanya; *open winter 10–6, summer 10–7; adm exp*), with models of the 170 best monuments of Catalunya; a mini-train does the rounds. The Catalans were so miffed when Paris won Disneyland Paris that they built their own theme park, **Port Aventura**, near Salou, but with much scarier rides, including Europe's biggest roller coaster, but there's plenty for little kids too (© 977 77 90 90; 75 minutes by train from Passeig de Gràcia or Sants—the park has its own station; *open Mar–Oct daily 10am–8pm, late June–mid Sept daily 10am–midnight*).

parks

The **Park Güell** (*see* p.199) is a favourite with kids, as is the **Parc de la Ciutadella** (*see* p.120), with a mini boating lake and pretty picnic spots. Other good ones are the **Parc de la Creueta del Coll** (*see* p.202), which has a lake for boating and swimming and a little artificial beach, and the **Parc de l'Espanya Industrial** (*see* p.212), with another lake and popular playground. There are pony rides and miniature-train rides at the **Parc del Castell de l'Oreneta** (bus no.60 or 66), not far from the Monestir de Pedralbes. The glorious **Parc de la Collserola** (*see* p.205) has nature trails and picnic spots.

Climate and When to Go

Barcelona is very much a year-round destination, so much so that there's not really such a thing as an off season; in the last few years the hotels have been booked full all year round. The climate is Mediterranean, fairly temperate but often quite humid: July and August are the hottest months, but the sea breeze often comes to the rescue to keep it from being stiflingly so. In the winter you'll want a nice warm coat. Wettest months are September and October, but you may need an umbrella any time up to June; spring in particular tends to be changeable. January can be surprisingly sunny. In August many shops and restaurants close altogether. If you can pick and choose, May, June or September are usually the most delicious months weatherwise, and June and September have the added attraction of festivals (*see* 'Festivals and Calendar of Events', opposite).

Average maximum/minimum daily temperatures in °C (°F):

Jan	April	July	Oct
17 (63)/7 (44)	25 (77)/7 (44)	33 (91)/16 (61)	24 (75)/10 (50)

Consulates

Most of these are open only Monday to Friday mornings, so it's best to ring first. Outside office hours, you'll be given an emergency number to ring.

Australia: 98 Gran Via Carles III (Ⓜ Maria Cristina), ✆ 93 330 94 96.

Canada: 77 Passeig de Gràcia (Ⓜ Passeig de Gràcia), ✆ 93 215 07 04.

Ireland: 94 Gran Via Carles III (Ⓜ Maria Cristina), ✆ 93 491 50 21.

New Zealand: 64 Travessera de Gràcia (FGC Gràcia), ✆ 93 209 03 99.

UK: 477 Avinguda Diagonal (bus no.41 or 66 from Plaça Catalunya), ✆ 93 419 90 44.

USA: 23 Passeig Reina Elisenda (FGC Reina Elisenda), ✆ 93 280 22 27.

Cybercafés

Barcelona abounds in places with Internet access. Several cafés have coin-operated Internet machines, as do some hostels and a couple of the *bureaux de change* on the Ramblas. The easyJet empire will shortly be opening up a branch of its cheap Internet cafés on the Ronda Universitat. Here are a few other options:

El Café de Internet, 656 Gran Vía de les Corts Catalanes (Ⓜ Passeig de Gràcia), ✆ 93 412 19 15, has a café, snack bar and printing service; 250 pts for 30mins.

Interlight, 106 C/ Pau Claris (Ⓜ Passeig de Gràcia), ✆ 93 301 11 80, is one of the nicest Internet cafés, with a pleasant atmosphere and very helpful staff on hand; 500 pts for 30mins.

La F@ctoria, in the Von Till snack bar, Plaça Universitat (Ⓜ Universitat), ✆ 93 451 08 33, has computer terminals at tables so you can get a burger or a salad while you surf the Net. There are a dozen terminals at the back of the café if you don't want to eat, and the prices are very reasonable; 260 pts for 40mins.

Among the dozens of other places offering Internet access without a café are the two branches of **inetcorner**: the first is near the cathedral at Plaça Ramón Berenguer II, 1st Floor, *inetcorner@catedral*, and the other is near the Sagrada Família, 21 C/ Sardenya, *inetcorner@sagradafamilia*. Or you could try **Picking Pack**, 276 C/ Consell de Cent (on the corner of C/ Balmes), ✆ 902 20 23 20, a print shop, with a fax and photocopying service, PCs and Macs for use, and an Internet café.

Disabled Travellers

Barcelona is far from paradise, but things are slowly getting better. All newer museums have wheelchair access; older ones may have limited access. Ring ahead (for numbers, *see* **Museums and Monuments**) to find out what's what. Most hotels (but not the cheap ones) have at least a few accessible rooms, and restaurants are rarely a problem. *Aerobúses* from the airport are wheelchair-friendly, and, on average, one out of three buses on the most popular routes have access. Although taxis are required to transport wheelchairs, many are small and awkward; to book a special mini-van (*Taxi Amic*) ring Taxi Ràdio Móvil, © 93 358 11 11, or Barnataxi, © 93 357 77 55. Few metro and FGC train stations have lifts. For advice on building access, contact the city's bureau for the disabled: the **Institut Municipal de Persones amb Disminució**, 161 C/ Llacuna, © 93 291 84 00, © 93 291 84 09 (**Ⓜ** Glories, bus no.56, 60 or 92), *open mid-Sept–mid-June Mon–Fri 8–8, mid-June–mid-Sept Mon–Fri 9–3.*

Electricity

The current is 225AC or 220V, the same as most of Europe. Americans will need converters, and the British will need two-pin adapters for the different plugs. If you plan to stay in the less expensive *hostales*, where the current may still be 125V, it may be better to leave your gadgets at home.

Festivals and Calendar of Events

Barcelona takes its festivals seriously. Traditional events, especially the *festes majors*, are occasions for a very specialized battery of Catalan folklore and traditional music. In the daytime you'll find processions of *gegants* (tall figures of wood and papier mâché, supported by a man in the skirts) and *capogrossos* (demonically grinning 'fat heads', made of the same materials), and the daring construction of human towers by *castellers* who climb on each other's shoulders to the eerie music of the *grolla*, attaining eight or even levels. At night, the big event is the *correfoc*, or 'fire-running', when terrifying dragons (a bit like Chinese ones, made of teams under canvas and wood) spit fireworks into the crowds, chased by devils brandishing fireworks (a bit dangerous). Tourist offices (*see* p.23) and websites will have additional information and precise dates.

1 Jan   The new year is brought in with big public parties and the custom of gulping down a grape for each chime of the bell at midnight, for luck.

5 Jan	The Three Kings arrive in Barcelona by sea and join a parade through the streets, hurling sweets to the children as they go.
17 Jan	Beginning of a week-long *festa major* in the Barri Sant Antoni.
Carnival	Barcelona has an opening parade, and private parties during the carnival season.
March	Festival of the Guitar, in the Palau de la Música Catalana.
23 Apr	The festival of *Sant Jordi*, Day of the Book and Rose (*see* p.65).
late Apr	*Feria de Abril*, ten days of Andalucian flamenco and carousing.
May	Popular International Comics Fair, held in the Estació de França; *Festival de Flamenco*, at the Centre de Cultura Contemporani.
late May	Corpus Christi, once the city's biggest festival, now reduced to mere displays.
early June	*L'Ou com Balla*, festival of the 'dancing egg', in fountains around Barri Gòtic, especially the cathedral cloister and Casa de l'Ardiaca.
June	*Trobada Castellera*, a grand meeting of Catalan *casteller* groups in Plaça Sant Jaume; *Sonar*, a three-day Festival of Advanced Music and Multimedia Art.
21 June	*Festa de la Música*, a French initiative celebrated in Barcelona since 1996, with free concerts in the streets.
23 June	*Nit del Foc*, the 'Night of Fire', the maddest night of the year in Catalunya. There are only a few small fires tolerated in the city, but non-stop fireworks shake Barcelona all night as everyone downs *cava* and sweet cakes called *cocas de Sant Joan*. It's followed by a public holiday.
late June– mid Aug	*Festival del Grec*, a wide-ranging programme of theatre, music and dance in the Teatre Grec and Mercat de les Flors.
late Aug	*Festa Major de Gràcia*, a giant party that draws thousands; there are wonderful street decorations. The *Festa Major de Sants* follows on its heels.
11 Sept	*Diada*, Catalan National Day, with flags, speeches and rallies.
23 Sept	Barcelona's week-long *festa major*, dedicated to Nostra Senyora de la Mercè, with all the ingredients on a huge scale, as well as concerts (including the BAM alternative music festival) and races, culminating in a frenzied *correfoc*.
late Sept	*Festa Major de Barceloneta*, with more carousing.
Oct	Festival of Contemporary Music, in venues around town; also World Music Festival, sponsored by the Funació la Caixa.
Oct–Dec	International Jazz Festival.

8–24 Dec   *Fira de Santa Llúcia*, the big Christmas market in front of the Cathedral, with a great choice of *cagoners* (*see* pp.62–3).

Health and Emergency Services

Medical emergencies: ✆ 061; **police**: ✆ 091; **fire brigade**: ✆ 080.

In a **medical emergency**, go to the nearest *hospital de la seguretat social*, all of which have 24-hour casualty (*urgències*) departments. Two are Clínic, 170 C/ Villarroel (Ⓜ Hospital Clinic), ✆ 93 227 54 00, and Santa Creu i Sant Pau, 167 Avinguda Sant Antoni María Claret (Ⓜ Hospital de Sant Pau), ✆ 93 291 90 00.

There is a standard agreement for EU citizens, entitling you to a certain amount of free non-emergency medical care in the public health centres, but it's not straight-forward. You must obtain a form E111 before you leave; if you aren't staying long, you may find it easier to buy **travel insurance** and go to a private clinic. Non-EU travellers should check with their policies at home to see if they're covered in Spain, and judge whether it's advisable to take out additional insurance. Be sure to save all doctors' and pharmacy receipts (you'll have to pay cash on the spot).

If the complaint isn't serious, go to a **pharmacy** and tell them your woes. Pharma-cists are highly trained and, if there's a prescription medicine that you know will cure you, they'll often supply it without a doctor's note. Local newspapers list *far-macías* that stay open all night; alternatively, outside the door of most pharmacies you'll find the rota listing the nearest ones on duty, or ring ✆ 010 or ✆ 098.

Lost and Found

The city's lost property office, the **Servei de Troballes**, in the Ajuntament, 9 C/ Ciutat (Ⓜ Jaume I), ✆ 93 402 31 61 (*open Mon–Fri 9–2*), is where items found on the street, and in buses, metros and taxis should end up.

Media

Since 1881, *La Vanguardia* has been Barcelona's leading **newspaper**, politically conservative but not rabidly so. It has a reputation for the best classified ads. It has recently been kicked off its perch as Catalunya's circulation king by the tabloid-style *El Periódico de Catalunya*, published in Castilian and Catalan editions. The Socialist *El País* is Spain's biggest and best national paper, and provides a special local Barcelona section, though circulation remains painfully low. Other big papers are *El Mundo* (the middle-of-the-road challenger that revealed many of the Socialist scandals that *El País* daintily overlooked), which has a Catalan edition; and *Avui*, the first post-Franco Catalan paper, strongly supportive of Jordi Pujol's party. Major for-eign newspapers are easily found in the kiosks along the Ramblas. The free monthly

English-language *Barcelona Metropolitan* has features, good listings and classified ads, and can be found in bars, cinemas and bookshops frequented by ex-pats.

As for **TV**, Catalan-language programming has made huge inroads: TV3, the original Catalan station, sponsored by the Generalitat, is one of the most watched (especially the Catalan soap operas and football), and there's also its artier offspring Canal 33. The Ajuntament has its own station, BTV, with local happenings and a popular 9pm newscast. The mainstream Spanish channels TVE1 and TVE2 now have a host of private, satellite and cable stations for competition. The nation watches more TV than any other in Europe (except, of course, for Britain).

Money and Banks

Spanish **currency** comes in notes of 1,000, 2,000, 5,000 and 10,000 pesetas (pts), all in different colours, and coins of 1, 5, 10, 25, 50, 100, 200 and 500 pts. On 1 January 1999, the euro became the official currency of Spain (at the rate of 166.386 pts to the euro), although peseta notes and coins will continue to be used until 30 June 2002, after which they will be worthless. The introduction of euro bank notes is slated to start on 1 January 2002.

Most banks in Barcelona will exchange money, or traveller's cheques from a major company, for a certain and often hefty commission. Look for the *cambio/ canvi/ change* signs; for traveller's cheques, bring your passport. **Banking hours** are Mon–Fri 8.30am–2pm, and Sat 8.30am–1pm only from Oct to April.

American Express offices can be found at 259 C/ Rosselló (Ⓜ Diagonal), ℂ 93 217 00 70 (*open Mon–Fri 9.30–6, Sat 10–12*), and at 74 La Rambla (Ⓜ Liceu), ℂ 93 301 11 66 (*open April–Sept daily 9am–midnight; Oct–March Mon–Fri 9am–8.30pm, Sat 10–2 and 3–7*). For **traveller's cheque emergencies**, freephone ℂ 900 99 44 26.

Exchange offices are conveniently open when banks are not and charge no commission, although the exchange rates are usually poor. There are handy ones in the airport (*open daily 7am–11pm*) and at Estació-Sants (*open daily 8am–10pm*).

Your best option in Spain is usually to draw money out of an ATM (*Telebanco*) with a **credit card**. ATMs are everywhere, and instructions for use are in English. Most hotels, shops and restaurants take credit cards as well (just look for the little signs in the window). But don't rely on hole-in-the-wall machines as your only source of cash: if, for whatever reason, the machine swallows your card, it can take up to 10 days to retrieve it. If this or some other mishap occurs, there are English-speaking 24-hour helplines:

American Express: ℂ 91 519 60 00.

Diner's Club: ℂ 91 547 40 00.

MasterCard: ℰ 900 97 12 31.

Visa: ℰ 91 519 60 00.

Opening Hours

Shops in Barcelona open on Monday to Saturday between 9 and 10 am, and close between 1 and 2pm; on Monday to Friday they reopen between 4.30 and 5.30pm and close by 8 or 9pm. Larger shops stay open all day, and some, like book and record shops, may be open on Sundays. The larger **churches** roughly keep shop hours, while the smaller ones are often only open for an hour or two a day.

Museums tend to follow shop opening hours, though abbreviated in the winter months; nearly all close on Mondays. Seldom-visited ones have a raffish disregard for their official hours, or open only when the mood strikes them; it's best to ring ahead to avoid disappointment.

For bank and post office opening hours, *see* 'Money and Banks' and 'Post Offices'.

Police Business

Police: national, ℰ 091; municipal, ℰ 092.

Violent crime is relatively rare in Barcelona, but pickpocketing, bag-snatching and general preying on gullible foreigners happens with enough frequency in crowded areas for you to be on your guard. The Ramblas and other tourist haunts and the metro are prime hunting grounds. Walking around at night is safe—primarily because everybody does it—although you should steer clear of the dark alleys of the Barri Xinès. To report a crime, go to the **Turisme-Atenció**, 43 La Rambla (**Ⓜ** Liceu), ℰ 93 301 90 60/317 70 16 (*open Sun–Thurs 7am–midnight, Fri–Sat 7am–2am*). This polyglot police office specializes in helping tourists, especially in filling out the statement (*denuncia*) essential for your insurance claim.

There are several species of police. The Policía Nacional are dressed in dark blue; their duties largely consist of driving around in cars and drinking coffee, although they are also chiefly responsible for investigating serious crime. Their headquarters (*always open*) is at 49 Vía Laietana, ℰ 93 290 30 00. The Guàrdia Urbana, in navy and light blue, are generally responsible for law and order and traffic, although gradually the Generalitat's police, the Mossos d'Esquadra, in similar colours (with added red braid), are sharing some of their duties.

Post Offices

The main post office is a very grand building on Plaça d'Anton López (at the south-eastern end of Vía Laietana), ℰ 93 318 35 07 (*open Mon–Fri 8–10, Sat 8.30–10*).

Here you can pick up your post restante, using the address Lista de Correos, 08070, Barcelona, Spain. You can send or receive faxes from any post office. Postboxes, marked *Correos y Telégrafos*, are yellow; collections are generally Monday to Friday only. Most tobacconists sell stamps and they'll usually know the correct postage for whatever you're sending.

Public Holidays

On public holidays, banks, offices, shops and many restaurants close, while most museums and public transport go on to Sunday schedules.

1 Jan	*Cap d'Any*	(New Year's Day)
6 Jan	*Día des Reis*	(Three Kings)
March/April	*Divendres Sant*	(Good Friday)
March/April	*Pasqua Florida*	(Easter Monday)
1 May	*Festa del Treball*	(Labour Day)
May/June	*Dillluns de Pasqua Granada*	(Whit Monday)
24 June	*Sant Joan*	(St John's Day)
15 Aug	*L'Assumpció*	(Assumption)
11 Sept	*Diada Nacional de Catalunya*	(Catalan National Day)
24 Sept	*La Mercè*	(Our Lady of Mercy)
12 Oct	*Día de la Hispanitat*	(Columbus Day)
1 Nov	*Tots Sants*	(All Saints' Day)
6 Dec	*Día de la Constitució*	(Constitution Day)
8 Dec	*La Imaculada*	(Immaculate Conception)
25 Dec	*Nadal*	(Christmas Day)
26 Dec	*Sant Esteve*	(St Stephen's Day)

Sports

Barcelona's newly discovered vocation as a Mediterranean resort means you can now take the metro to the beach and swim without catching a disease. The long promenades by the sea between Barceloneta and the Vila Olímpica are a favourite of joggers, and there are places that hire out bicycles and roller blades if you want to slip along on wheels. The city is also well supplied with inexpensive municipal sports centres and pools, and any local can direct you to the nearest one.

Although Barça's Camp Nou is the biggest football stadium in Europe, season ticket holders have nearly all the seats. If you're determined, ring the club (© 93 496 36 00) to find out exactly when tickets go on sale and get there early to join the queue (the office is on Travessera de Les Corts Catalanes), or commune with one of the ticket touts who cluster nearby.

Telephones

Like most of the rest of Europe the national monopoly has recently broken up, and competition is bringing prices down while confusing everyone. Most phone boxes are still run by Telefonica, and these accept coins, credit cards or phone cards (sold in *estancos* and post offices), and usually contain complete dialling instructions (in English). All local numbers (20 pts) in Barcelona now have nine digits; if you see a seven-digit number, it usually works if you put a '93' in front of it. Freephone numbers begin with 900; mobile numbers begin with a 6; 902 numbers are toll calls. For international directory enquires, call ℗ 025. National directory enquiries are on ℗ 1003. Phones in bars and cafés usually charge 50 per cent more than street phones. Expect to pay a big surcharge if you do any telephoning from your hotel or a phone in a public place that does not have a coin slot. The international cheap rate is from 8pm to 8am Monday to Saturday, and all day Sunday and public holidays.

For calls to Spain from the UK, dial 00 followed by the country code (34), the area code and the full number. For international calls from Spain, dial 00, wait for the higher tone, and then dial the country code (e.g. 00 44 for the UK, 001 for the USA).

Time

Spain is always one hour ahead of Greenwich Mean Time, and generally six hours ahead of Eastern Standard Time in the USA.

Tipping

Tips in Barcelona are welcome but not really expected. For taxis it's common to tip five per cent, or ten per cent if the driver's friendly and helpful. In bars and restaurants leave five per cent. It's common to leave 300 pts a night for the chambermaid in a hotel.

Toilets

Apart from in bus and train stations, public facilities are rare in Barcelona. On the other hand, every bar on every corner has a toilet; don't feel uncomfortable using it without purchasing something—Spaniards do it all the time.

Tourist Information

Australia   203 Castlereagh Street, Suite 21A, PO Box A-685, Sydney South NSW 2000, ℗ (2) 264 7966, ✉ (2) 267 5111.

Canada   102 Bloor Street West, Toronto, Ontario, M5S 1M8, ℗ (416) 961 3131, ✉ (416) 961 1992.

UK	22–3 Manchester Square, London, W1M 5AP, ✆ (020) 7486 8077, 📠 (020) 7486 8034.
USA	8383 Wilshire Boulevard, Suite 960, Beverly Hills, California, 90211, ✆ (213) 658 7188, 📠 (213) 658 1061.
	665 Fifth Avenue, New York, NY 10022, ✆ (212) 759 8822, 📠 (212) 980 1053.

Barcelona's tourist offices distribute excellent detailed maps, transport maps, and a little booklet with useful telephone numbers and addresses called *See Barcelona*. There is an excellent website at *www.barcelonaturisme.com*, and a city site at *www.bcn.es*.

Plaça de Catalunya: located underground on the Corte Inglés department store side of the Plaça, ✆ 906 30 12 82; *open daily 9–9*. This has an accommodation booking service (for the same night only, ✆ 93 304 32 32), a bank, a gift shop and coin-operated Internet access.

Palau Robert: 107 Passeig de Gràcia, ✆ 93 238 40 00,*www.gencat.es/probert*; *open Mon–Fri 10–7, Sat 10–2.30*. This has information on all of Catalunya.

Estació de Sants: *open Oct–May Mon–Fri 8–8, Sat and Sun 8–2; June–Sept daily 8–8*.

Ajuntament: Plaça Sant Jaume; *open Mon–Sat 10–8, Sun and hols 10–2*.

Airport: ✆ 93 478 47 04/05 65; *open Mon–Sat 9.30–8, Sun 9.30–3*.

Palau de la Virreina, 99 Ramblas, ✆ 93 301 77 75, and **Palau Moja**, 7 Ramblas. Both specialize in city cultural information.

Other kiosks are open in summer only in Plaça de Catalunya, Passeig de Gràcia, by the Sagrada Família, Vila Olímpica and Port Vell. In summer, a team of 'Red Jackets', based near the Sagrada Família and other tourist sites, give on-the-spot information in several languages.

discounts and walking tours

The **Barcelona Card** is valid for 24, 48 and 72 hours (2,000 pts, 2,500 pts and 3,000 pts respectively) and offers discounts at several shops and restaurants, and many of the main attractions, but, best of all, it gives you unlimited use of the metro and bus system. A list of where you can get discounts comes with the card. It is sold at tourist information offices.

The tourist office organizes **walking tours** of the Barri Gòtic; they are very popular and you would be well advised to book early. Tours in English begin at 10am on Saturday and Sunday; in Catalan and Castilian, they start at noon. The Museu d'Història de la Ciutat organizes a series of tours through the Barri Gòtic; for information call ✆ 93 315 11 11.

History

Before AD 711: Founded neither by Hercules nor Hannibal, Barcelona makes its shy debut on the stage of history

In later years, when this poncing peacock of a city felt the lack of a foundation myth, Barcelona's literati would summon up no less a personage than Hercules to play the role of city father. Hercules would have passed this way on his tenth Labour, while driving the cattle of Geryon back to Greece. He had already founded Cádiz and built the Pillars of Hercules, and the Barcelonans thought they could sneak their town on the list too. A different story, based on the similarity of the names, credited a leader of the most prominent and powerful family of Carthage with the founding—**Hamilcar Barca**, father of Hannibal.

If Barcelona was indeed a Carthaginian settlement, no archaeological evidence has yet been unearthed to prove it. As far as anyone can tell, the first Barcelonans were the Celto-Iberian **Laietanos**, who lived in scattered villages on the rich plain, gathered oysters from the shore, and had a citadel or religious centre on Montjuïc. In 15 BC, in the reign of Augustus, the Romans founded **Colonia Faventia Julia Augusta Paterna Barcino** on a low hill between two small streams, just north of Montjuïc. Although surrounded by fertile, well-watered land, Barcino lacked a good harbour, and it never became half as important as Tarraco (Tarragona), the major city of northeastern Spain. Roman Barcino, a typical walled, rectangular *castrum* of the sort found all over the Empire, covered what is now the core of the Barri Gòtic. It was a tiny town, at its greatest extent no more than 500 yards long; the modern Plaça Sant Jaume probably marks the site of its forum, and stretches of the Roman walls still stand; an impressive slice of Roman foundations, still intact under the medieval city, can be visited by way of the Museu d'Història de la Ciutat.

In AD 262, Barcino suffered a sacking at the hands of the Franks, in a raid that was a prelude to the Germanic invasions that would overwhelm the western Empire a century and a half later. The Franks did far more damage to Tarraco, and after the Roman legions regained control of the situation Barcino, with a rebuilt and strengthened set of walls, seems to have gradually supplanted it as the most important town in the region. The walls failed to keep out the **Visigoths** in 415 but, rather than rape and pillage, they moved in and briefly made Barcelona the seat of their court. In a peculiar footnote to history, an important child was born here in 715—the son of the Visigothic King Ataulf and Galla Placidia, who was the first-born daughter of the Roman Emperor Honorius. Galla Placidia had been taken hostage when the Visigoths sacked Rome five years previously; while accompanying Ataulf on his people's migrations, somehow the two had managed to fall in love. Their partnership created the intriguing possibility of a reconciliation between Roman and barbarian, but Ataulf was murdered in Barcino the same year, probably by agents of the enraged Honorius, and their son died soon after. Galla Placidia returned to Italy, where after Honorius' death she presided over the last years of the dying western Empire.

Barcino was keeping its name in the headlines as late as 431, when another Visigothic King, Amalaric, was murdered there. With the Franks mounting continuous raids from across the Pyrenees, the city was no longer a tenable capital, and the Visigoths established themselves in Toledo, leaving behind nothing except perhaps their name. Some historians say that Catalunya, which previously had never been recognized as a distinct region, comes from 'Castellania', for its many castles, though another tradition says the name was originally 'Gothalanda'.

711–1000: Caught in the middle between Franks and Moors, the Catalans find an opportunity to become masters in their own house

The Visigothic Kingdom of Spain, after a promising start, slowly went to pieces amidst the ambitions of its barons, religious bloodymindedness and economic disarray. The Franks might well have eventually gobbled it up, had not a bigger and fiercer foe come out of nowhere to beat them to the job. This foe was the Arab-led army of Islam, which had rolled over all the Middle East and North Africa in less than a century since the death of Mohammed. Their invasion of Spain began in 711, and two years later, when the Moors destroyed Tarraco, Barcelona took note and surrendered without a fight. Although the Moors briefly seized parts of France too, the Franks gradually pushed them back over the Pyrenees, leaving Barcelona as one of the furthest outposts of the new state of al-Andalus. Its Moorish governors, generally left to their own devices, allied themselves with the Franks or the Emirs at Córdoba as they found convenient. Meanwhile, up in the safety of the Pyrenees on both sides of the current French–Spanish border, a population that included many refugees from the Moorish conquest was developing a distinct language and cultural identity. They were becoming the Catalans.

In 801, Charlemagne's son Louis the Pious reconquered northern 'Gothalanda'. Barcelona was an important walled fortress, and in 874—a year of clashing coiffures—the Frankish King Charles the Bald made the Catalan baron **Guifré el Pilós**, or 'Wilfred the Hairy', its first count. According to legend, this Wilfred was hairy down to the soles of his feet. And the legends about him are numerous, for later Catalans did their best to make him into a nearly mythological founding hero (*see* **Topics**). The historical Guifré seems to have got his job by disposing of a Frankish baron who was on the outs with Charles. Guifré brought much of what is now Catalunya under his control, and he endowed Barcelona and the region with churches and monasteries. As Frankish power decayed after Charlemagne's death, Catalunya was increasingly left to its own devices. In 985, when Barcelona was attacked by the great Al-Mansur of Córdoba, the Franks failed to respond to requests for aid. Count Borrell II declared his county's sovereign independence, and the Franks could do nothing about it.

1000–1213: A trading city and a feudal kingdom forge a partnership, and it proves delightfully profitable for them both

Barcelona faced the new millennium with a population of probably little more than a thousand. Over the next two centuries, however, this insignificant town would quite suddenly and startlingly grow fat and rich. It isn't entirely clear how they managed it. Though unique in Spain, Barcelona's career parallels that of the emerging merchant towns of Italy and northern Europe. Its main economic assets were the two most useful gifts a medieval town could ask for: iron and wool. From an early date, the town seems to have become a centre of cloth manufacture, while up in the Pyrenees the Catalans found a little iron ore and discovered an advanced technique for smelting it; the product of these Catalan forges found its way to the city, to be made into prized swords and armour. Yet more profit came from the produce of the surrounding farmland, and from the booty acquired by Barcelona's counts in the wars of the Reconquista against the Moors. The pennies were piling up, and the city invested some of its surplus wisely, building ships and developing maritime links across the Mediterranean, just as Venice, Genoa and Pisa were doing. By the 1030s Barcelona had the first stable gold currency in western Europe.

Those Italian cities, run as free republics, faced a constant fight with their nominal overlords, the Holy Roman Emperors, to hold on to their freedoms and their money. Barcelona had an easier time of it. The business interests of the city and the ambitions of the counts found a happy symbiosis and, as both grew in power, trade and the flag went hand in hand. Under **Ramón Berenguer I** (1035–76), Barcelona extended its control as far as Carcassonne and Montpellier in Languedoc. After him, with typical Catalan peculiarity, rule was shared by twin brothers named **Ramón Berenguer II** (1076–82) and **Berenguer Ramón II** (1076–97); the only way to tell them apart was that the first was called 'the Towhead' until the second was nicknamed the 'Fratricide', for which crime he was eventually forced into exile.

The twins and their successors continued to direct their efforts at expansion towards the north. To the west and south lay Zaragoza and Valencia, defended by El Cid, and they couldn't beat him; the Cid in fact captured Berenguer Ramón twice. Berenguer Ramón was succeeded by his twin's son **Ramón Berenguer III** (1097–1131). He suffered the last Moorish raids, but eventually prevailed, acquiring new lands which put him into contact with the growing inland kingdom of Aragón. The third Ramón Berenguer also did much to bring the rest of Catalunya under Barcelona's control, adding lands over the Pyrenees in what is now French Catalunya, or Roussillon.

The marriage in 1137 between Barcelona's Count Ramón Berenguer IV and the heiress of Aragón, Queen Petronila, brought the city the Crown of Aragón and all the prestige and patronage of royalty. Now the counts were '**count-kings**', and rulers of the second most powerful and populous kingdom on the peninsula. The unusual title is a hint of just how important Barcelona continued to be in the new state; it also reflects the Catalans' ancient tradition of rights and privileges, codified as the *Usatges* in the time of Ramón Berenguer I. Their count-king ruled not by divine right, but on a down-to-earth contractual basis, evident in the people's famous oath of allegiance: 'We, who are as good as you, swear to you, who are no better than we, to accept you as our king and sovereign lord, provided you observe all our liberties and laws; but if not, not.'

The new state continued to rack up successes. **Alfons II** (1162–96) absorbed the rest of Roussillon. **Pere I** (1196–1213) took part in the greatest victory of the Reconquista, the 1212 Battle of Las Navas de Tolosa that resulted in the fall of all of al-Andalus, save only the Kingdom of Granada, to Castile. The next year, however, found Pere over the Pyrenees, in support of the Catalans' Languedocien and Provençal cousins, terrorized by the French armies of the Albigensian Crusade. The Battle of Muret, in 1213, was one of the turning points of medieval history. If the Aragonese and their allies had beaten Simon de Montfort, the Midi might eventually have become Aragonese instead of French; certainly, it would have grown closer to Catalunya, to which it was far more closely related, linguistically and culturally, than to the Parisians. Instead, King Pere's own carelessness threw away a battle in which he had superior forces, and he lost his life.

1213–1355: Catalunya rules the waves

If the Battle of Muret closed off the chance of expanding their influence to the north, the Aragonese and Barcelonans were happy to take the ample opportunities that still existed over the seas. **Jaume I the Conqueror** (1213–76) led Barcelona into what the Catalans consider their Golden Age, beginning its new maritime empire with the acquisition of Valencia and the Balearics, previously Muslim-held islands full of merchants and pirates who presented a major obstacle to Barcelona's commerce. Jaume's descendants, by way of conquest, treaties and marriage, expanded this empire across the Mediterranean.

In many ways, it was a remarkably advanced and progressive state. Barcelona's trade, and nearly everyone else's, was regulated by a maritime code called the *Llibre del Consulat del Mar*, written under Jaume I in 1259; it became as widely used in medieval Europe as the maritime code of Rhodes had been in ancient times. In Barcelona, Jaume organized the merchants into a kind of guild called the Universitat de la Ribera, which functioned practically as a city within the city. The same king gave Catalunya a parliament, the **Corts**, in 1249, and a permanent governing body, the **Generalitat**, and to govern the city of Barcelona he instituted the **Consell de Cent**, made up of a hundred citizens, in which even the smaller merchants and artisans were represented.

For now, the merger of commercial city and the feudal Aragonese kingdom was proving to be one full of synergy; the commercial strategy of the Barcelona merchants and the dynastic ambitions of the house of Aragón went hand in hand. Jaume I's will divided his kingdom in two parts: **Pere III** (1276–85) got Catalunya, Aragón and Valencia, while his younger brother **Jaume II** ruled the trans-Pyrenean possessions and Majorca as his vassal. Although hardly suitable to Pere, as long as these two were alive the arrangement worked out well. Later Majorcan and Catalunyan kings, though cousins, often had as hard a time getting along as Ramón Berenguer and Berenguer Ramón. Occasional tiffs did little harm to Aragón or Barcelona—they were out building an empire in the Mediterranean together. Sicily had fallen into their hands in 1282, after the revolt of the Sicilian Vespers. The Sicilians had thrown out the usurper Charles of Anjou and his French, and, as the rightful heir to the throne by marriage was the Aragonese king, they appealed to Aragón for protection.

Next came Sardinia, which seemed a perfect base from which to harass Barcelona's chief commercial rivals, Genoa and Pisa. The Aragonese helped the Sards get rid of their Genoese and Pisan overlords, and then tried to seize the place for themselves in 1324. It took them nearly a century to finish the job, in the face of a determined national revolt of the Sards. The conquest of Sardinia, besides exposing the darker side of Aragonese imperialism, proved to be their first bad investment. For all the trouble and time it cost them, the island never amounted to anything more than a constant worry and a drain on the royal treasury.

In a short time, the ambitions of Barcelona had spread across the Mediterranean. The '**Catalan Companies**' of merchant adventurers controlled much of the Mediterranean trade, and the city maintained over 120 consulates abroad. The Catalan Companies ruled parts of Greece for over 80 years, including Athens after 1311. While having a hand in all the intrigues of the Levant, they weren't particular about their choice of allies. In 1355 they ferried the Ottoman Turks, who hadn't yet built a navy, across the Sea of Marmara, and so helped to begin the Turkish conquest of the Balkans. For all that, the biggest part of the city's trade, and the source of most of its wealth, was in the western Mediterranean, and particularly north Africa, where the Barcelonans had a virtual monopoly.

1300–1479: Great ambitions lead to a great fall, and Barcelona loses everything, including its freedom

By 1300, Barcelona's population was up to 50,000, making it by far the largest and richest city in northern Spain. Under Jaume the Conqueror the city was forced to begin an extensive (and expensive) new circuit of walls to fit them all in. Under **Jaume II the Just** (1291–1327), **Alfons III** (1327–36) and **Pere III the Ceremonious** (1336–87), the Gothic city's most important and splendid monuments appeared.

For all its wealth and spectacular exploits overseas, however, things were not necessarily going well at home. While the great merchants prospered from a large area of relatively free trade, smaller ones and manufacturers became increasingly beset by competition, especially from Majorca and Valencia. Like a modern American city, Barcelona in the midst of its opulence became a discontented and dangerous place plagued by unemployment, poverty and crime. The city's poor even knew recurrent famines, beginning in 1330 when the merchants' affairs were booming. Epidemics were also common. The **Black Death** arrived in 1348, killing off a third of the population (as elsewhere in Europe), and it returned in increasingly less virulent reprises over the next century.

Along with hard times came increasing factional strife and, with the help of the Church, a spell of ethnic hatred Barcelona had never before known. The city was home to some thousand Jews, who had contributed much to the city's economic and cultural life. Fire-eating preachers, mostly Dominicans, had been making the rounds in Spain and stirring up anti-Semitism since the 1260s. Increasingly, the kings of Aragón were no longer able to protect the Jews from forced conversions, robbery and murder. The first serious pogroms came in 1391, with massacres all over Spain; almost half the Jewish population in Barcelona was slaughtered.

With the Jews dead or in hiding, Barcelonans still had each other to torment. Gang warfare seems to have been common throughout the 14th and 15th centuries, and no sane person would venture out of their house after dark. Social disorder was expressed on a slightly more elevated level in the bitter struggles of the city's two political factions, the Biga and the Busca—the 'Beam' and the 'Splinter'. The solid, conservative Biga was the party of the biggest merchants; it believed in free trade, sound money and the continuance of the great disparities of wealth that made life in Barcelona so interesting. The Busca, though not really a popular party, was interested in tariffs to save the smaller firms and manufacturers who were being killed by the Biga's precocious medieval version of economic globalization.

The Biga usually had the better of the fight, even after its economic vision started to fall apart in the 1380s, to the music of a resounding wave of bank crashes. There was some relief by 1401, when the city organized a municipally run bank to sort out the debts, but by this time it was clear that Barcelona's strangely modern experiment in capitalism was running out of steam. With the plagues, the hinterland was in a bad way too, no longer able to feed the capital or supply it with resources. The booming city itself had already sucked away most of the countryside's life and population and, now that the boom was over, the streets of Barcelona offered little employment for the migrants.

After 1400 Barcelona's population started to decline, so much so that it was surpassed in size by its archrival Valencia. And as if the city did not have enough troubles, it was losing its bread-and-butter trade in the western Mediterranean to the Genoese, who had developed more efficient ships that were twice the size of Barcelona's; Genoa captured the trade of Christian Seville and Moorish Granada, which gave it an opening into North Africa. The Atlantic coastal trade was growing, but there Barcelona found itself completely blocked out by the Portuguese and the Basques.

If Barcelona was sinking, however, it was not apparent to the city's leaders. All through the troubles of the 14th and early 15th centuries, they continued to embellish the city as if they were on top of the world. Some of the great church-building projects went on even during the plague years, and even after 1400 new palaces were built, while the Catalan school of painting reached its height. Meanwhile, the city's fortunes continued to decline along with its political cohesion. In 1410, when **Martí I the Humane** died without an heir, the influential future saint of Valencia, Vincent Ferrer, helped give the throne to a Castilian house, the Trastá-mara. The first of the Trastámara kings, **Ferran I** (1412–16) and **Alfons IV** (1416–58), showed a greater interest in Castilian and foreign affairs than in Aragón's—Alfons gained the throne of Naples, where he is better known to history as Alfonso the Magnanimous, and he spent most of his time there.

These new rulers broke the final tie of mutual interest that had held Catalunya-Aragón's delicately balanced system together. Popular revolts in Barcelona in 1436 and 1437 were only the prelude to worse struggles to come. In 1453 the Busca finally, but briefly, took control of the Consell de Cent. The motives and alliances of the various parties involved become extremely complex at this point—all of Spain was in political turmoil—but the great revolt that began in 1462 was essentially a struggle between Barcelona's ruling class and King Joan II. Ten years of civil war followed, finally ending with the surrender of a city under siege by its own king. Barcelona was ruined. 'Today no trade at all is practised in this city,' the *consellers* recorded in 1473. Joan's son was Ferran II to the Catalans, but he would have preferred to call himself by his Castilian name, Fernando. He had been married to Isabel of Castile in the middle of the wars and, when his father died and he assumed the throne in 1479, Castile and Aragón were effectively united. Spain was one, and Catalunya was suddenly a small corner of a very large kingdom; its capital was an exhausted, bankrupt metropolis that had no prospects, and no friends.

1479–1714: Under the Spanish thumb, Europe, History and God forget all about Barcelona

At first, Barcelona entertained some wan hopes that Aragón's union with powerful, thriving Castile would supply a much needed transfusion of money and vitality into the kingdom. What happened was quite different. The union of Spain was soon revealed as an outright annexation by Castile. The Castilians tended to see the Catalans as troublesome hotheads, always insisting on the ancient rights set down in their *Usatges* in order to shirk their share of the increasingly heavy national burden. The Catalans, on the other hand, saw Castile as a fat bloodsucking parasite. Historians, especially if they are Castilian, tend to give **Fernando and Isabel**, *los Reyes Católicos*, much better reviews than they deserve. This most grasping, brutal and bigoted couple were far too interested in squeezing all they could out of Catalunya to finance their own imperial ambitions; their only gift to the region was the Inquisition, which arrived in 1487. Not only were the new rulers entirely uninterested in helping Catalunya get back on its feet, but they took steps to make sure it would have no share in the new opportunities open to Spain. A codicil in Isabella's will specifically prohibited Catalan merchants from trading with the New World.

Not content with ruining its economy, Madrid treated Catalunya as just another of its colonies, and ruled it through a viceroy, like Peru or the Philippines, and a Supreme Council of Aragón dominated by Castilians. A lesser city than Barcelona might have disintegrated altogether, but the city's merchants showed remarkable resilience. They hung on in their old palaces, taking whatever limited chances were available to them and occasionally selling off a little of the furniture. They merrily argued over their ancient rights and privileges with absolutist kings as if it were still the Middle Ages. If a king came to visit, they would throw impressive spectacles that they could not afford in his honour, but they would refuse to take off their hats to him—the *Usatges* said they didn't have to. In spite of everything, they endured.

For Spain in its 'Golden Age', power and decadence went hand in hand, as Madrid strove to extend its power on three continents, while driving the nation to moral, intellectual and economic bankruptcy at home. The Castilian heartland suffered as much as any part of the nation, but Catalunya, beyond the loss of its trade, had the added burden of being on the front lines of the long wars between Spain and France. The government quartered troops on the populace, and the soldiers distinguished themselves more in pillage and robbery than fighting the French. That, along with the continued assaults on Catalan liberties and institutions, sparked off a revolt in 1640 that Catalans call the **Reapers' War**, the *Guerra dels Segadors*, as it began with a riot by a mob of labourers who were gathered in Barcelona looking for employment on the harvest. They caught the Spanish Viceroy, Santa Coloma, hiding in the Drassanes shipyards and tore him to pieces.

Managing a successful rebellion in a region packed with soldiers was something that could only have happened in the grand *Decadencia* of 17th-century Spain. The Catalans allied with the French, and named **Louis XIII** as their new count-king. He sent down an army, which defeated the Castilians in a battle underneath Montjuïc, but the affair was hardly settled. The Catalan leaders managed it badly, and their region lapsed into anarchy through 12 years of inconclusive struggles before the French finally betrayed them. Barcelona, left on its own, was besieged and starved into submission in 1652. In the final treaties France got to keep northern Catalunya, Roussillon.

This bad memory led Barcelona to line up against the French in the next act of the drama, the pan-European commotion called the **War of the Spanish Succession** (1701–14). When the Catalans backed the claim of the Austrian Archduke Charles against French Bourbon Philip V, it was a costly bet on the wrong horse, and a hopeless one once their English allies abandoned them and made peace with France. In the end, the Catalans were alone again and Barcelona came under siege once more—by James Stuart, Duke of Berwick, the bastard son of the deposed James II of England who was now in the service of the Bourbons. After 15 months of resistance the city fell in November 1714, and down with it, this time, went Catalunya's *Usatges*, its institutions and the last vestiges of its autonomy. The Catalan leaders were drawn and quartered, and a large number of die-hard resisters were buried in a mass grave near Santa Maria del Mar. This time, the Castilians were determined to kill off whatever remained of Catalan spirit, even its language. To that end, publication of books in Catalan was forbidden, and the region's universities were closed.

1714–1830: While the Spaniards aren't looking, Barcelona begins to plot a comeback built on calico and booze

The old capital of the count-kings became just another provincial city of Spain, and Felipe punished it with the construction of the Ciutadella, a huge pentagonal fort intended to protect the city not from foreign armies, but its own people. The Barcelonans were forced to pay for it themselves, and its building meant the demolition of half of a neighbourhood, La Ribera, in a city that was already suffocatingly overcrowded. To make matters worse, Madrid decreed that no one would be allowed to live outside the walls. The city began to consume itself, expanding at the expense of its parks, patios, squares and gardens; the current maze of dark canyons in the old city is the result. For the next century and a half, Barcelona acquired taller and taller buildings, and the conditions in which its people lived became increasingly unhealthy. The new quarter of Barceloneta, built on reclaimed land around the harbour, appeared in 1753. This was originally planned to house the families displaced for the Ciutadella, except that, with typical Bourbon efficiency, it came some 40 years too late. Even then, it brought little relief, and its grid of narrow streets soon became as overbuilt and crowded as the rest of the city.

At least Barcelonans were working again. Once the Catalans had been suitably punished, Bourbon policy was never quite as black-hearted as Fernando and Isabel's. The new dynasty hoped it could eventually earn the Catalans' loyalty by giving them a chance to make a living again, and through the 1700s business in the old town started to pick up. The results were dramatic. The old instincts had never died and, like some capitalist Sleeping Beauty, the city's mercantile élite magically popped up from its 200-year slumber, full of entrepreneurial fizz and ready to make some deals. The Catalans found two very profitable new businesses. After about 1730, Barcelona specialized in the manufacture of printed cotton cloth; the empty spaces outside the walls became the *prats d'indianes*, 'fields of calico', where the cloth was hung out to dry. Catalunya's depressed farmers gave up their subsistence crops and planted vines, and Barcelona distilled their grapes into cheap brandy— *aguardiente*—and shipped it off by the boatload to thirsty Latin America.

In 1778, Madrid finally removed the last restrictions on trading with the colonies, and the long build-up turned into a boom. By 1780, the population had more than doubled since 1714, to 110,000. The first industrial cotton mill was founded the same year, and factory production soon replaced the old medieval guilds in every field, as Barcelona began its career as the 'Manchester of the Mediterranean'. The merchants returned to their exchange, the Llotja, and new palaces rose along the new promenade, the Ramblas. Barcelona was back in business at the old stand.

The **Napoleonic Wars** were a rude interruption. Britain's blockade stopped the American trade cold, and the city went into a deep depression while Napoleon's men raided and looted its churches and monasteries. As much as they hated Madrid, the Catalans had learned from experience that the French were even worse. They remained steadfastly loyal to Spain this time, and mounted a bitter and often effective guerrilla campaign in the mountains. Once, in 1808, the Catalan irregulars even defeated a French army in a pitched battle near Montserrat.

The French were chased out in 1814, but Barcelona's recovery would not happen overnight. Epidemics of yellow fever and cholera hit the overcrowded city in 1821—only the worst of many. The year 1823 brought another unpleasant surprise: four more years of French occupation, when Britain and Austria directed a French army to suppress Spain's liberal revolution of 1820. The wheels of Barcelona industry didn't get back to full speed until the 1830s.

1830–88: Everything to make a modern capitalist city is complete—booming industry, a thriving culture, a World's Fair and continuous battles in the streets

One habit that the new Barcelona had in common with its medieval counterpart was treating its workers like dirt. Barcelona's industrialists, Spain's politicians and the Church connived to squeeze them to the limit; working conditions were appalling, especially for the women and children, who generally worked 15 hours a day. To these, home was slums so unhealthy that epidemics raged and mortality rates were among the highest in Europe. Dissent or attempts at organization were ruthlessly suppressed. Anger was not limited to the workers. Barcelona's progressive middle classes had complaints of their own about the reactionary regime that King **Fernando VII** (1814–33) brought in after Napoleon's defeat. Between the two, the city became a hotbed of radical ideas, and it boiled over in increasingly violent **revolts**.

The first outbreak, in July 1835, brought the burning of the most of Barcelona's monasteries and convents after a poor bullfight spilled over into mob rage. Regular riots and Luddite attacks on factory machinery enlived the next two decades. The biggest riot was a revolt called the *Jamancia* in 1842, in which the rebels took control of the city but were bombarded into submission by the cannons of Montjuïc castle; over 400 buildings were destroyed or damaged. In 1855, the city's workers mounted their first general strike. To the industrialists, these were relatively minor irritations. They kept making money, and the city was rapidly modernizing. In 1848, they built Spain's first railway, from Barcelona to Mataró.

Bursting at the seams, Barcelona finally got permission from Madrid in the late 1850s to demolish its walls and expand outside them. Through the 1860s, the fields of calico disappeared under the great grid of the Eixample, designed by Ildefons Cerdà. One of the most ambitious planning schemes of 19th-century Europe, it nearly quintupled the size of the city. Later, new, wide streets, Passeig de Colom and Via Laietana, were driven through the old town, following the example of Baron Haussmann's transformation of Paris. Traffic and sanitary considerations were only part of the reason. As in Paris, Barcelona's rulers were thinking of the ever present menace of revolt: their new streets would make barricades difficult and facilitate cavalry charges.

Of course, they also made wonderful boulevards for the new rich to promenade along and show off their carriages. Their new, modern, up-to-date city, with its impressive expansion, its pride and growing cosmopolitanism, evoked comparisons with Barcelona's medieval golden age, and fostered a new pride in things Catalan. The **Renaixença**, or Renaissance, began with a movement to redeem and re-establish the Catalan language, long submerged by the forced Castilianization of Madrid. As with the Czechs, the Irish and many other peoples, language was the key element of a new nationalism. Catalan dictionaries and grammars first appeared under Napoleon's occupation. By the 1830s, Barcelona journals were printing new poetry on Catalan patriotic themes. The medieval poetry competitions, the *Jocs Florals*, were revived in 1859, and the literary crusade was carried on by Catalunya's finest 19th-century poets, **Jacint Verdaguer** (1843–1902) and **Joan Maragall** (1860–1911), who led the way in bridging the Catalan of the troubadours and the everyday language still spoken by the people. From there, the *Renaixença* grew into a fervent nationalist cultural movement in all the arts, from music to architecture.

In this heady climate, under dynamic mayor Francesc de Paula Rius i Taulet, the city put on the **Universal Exhibition** in 1888, set in the new park where the recently demolished Ciutadella had stood; it showed the world, in the mayor's words, that the Catalans 'were the Yankees of Europe', and it saw the beginnings of Barcelona's distinctive Modernista architecture. The Queen of Spain came to open the exhibition and she was welcomed as 'Countess of Barcelona' by the main nationalist organization, the Lliga de Catalunya, which also presented her its agenda for greater political autonomy.

1888–1923: Between Anarchist bombs and Modernista buildings, Barcelona becomes the liveliest, edgiest corner of the Mediterranean

By the end of the 19th century, Barcelona had one of the most developed economies of Europe, based on iron, textiles and trade, just as it had been in the Middle Ages. Prosperity, however, brought little improvement in the conditions of working people, and the issues that caused all the trouble in the 1830s were still unsettled. For a while, boom times papered over the growing discontent, but in the 1870s the city was ready to explode once more, and this time the heat would be turned up by the new ideology of Anarchism (*see* p.60). Odd as it may seem, Anarchism found in Spain its strongest support anywhere in Europe, among two very different but equally desperate groups: the impoverished peasantry of Andalucía and the modern industrial workers of Catalunya.

The movement grew rapidly in Barcelona, and continued to do so even after it was driven underground in 1874. It gave an ideological home to those workers—increasingly, a majority of them—who were willing to meet the violence of the army and the employers' gangs of thugs with violence of their own. The two sides battled through the streets intermittently for the next three decades, while Barcelona became the bomb capital of Europe: in 1893, anarchist bombs killed 20; the next year, one exploded into the expensive seats at the Liceu; and in 1896, they blew up the religious procession of Corpus Christi. Usually the police were unable to find the perpetrators, and would simply round up likely suspects from the Anarchist cafés, and a few would be tortured and sentenced to the garrotte.

While bombs and bullets flew, Barcelona was paradoxically enjoying its most creative era. In the 1890s, Catalan culture flowered impressively, with the painters Ramón Casas and Santiago Rusinyol and their circle—which included the young Picasso—at the café Els Quatre Gats. Everything in the city's arts was converging on a style, and this acquired a name, **Modernisme**. Its painting and poetry would not make much of an impression outside Catalunya, but in architecture the Modernistas were about to astound the world. **Antoni Gaudí**, the greatest among them, began work on the Sagrada Família in 1883, and built La Pedrera on the Passeig de Gràcia in 1905. The Modernistas' buildings set the tone for the rapidly developing Eixample, giving the city a new look, almost a new identity, while back in the old centre Barcelona's Bohemians were perfecting the louche *demi-monde* life of the Barri Gòtic.

The **Spanish-American War** of 1898 was an earthquake for all of Spain. Many among Barcelona's élite had started by amassing fortunes in the colonies in tobacco, shipping or slaves; they were called *indianos*. The loss of Spain's last important colonies closed off considerable trade opportunities, and the end of the war filled the city with tired, disgusted ex-soldiers with little or no chance of employment.

Barcelona smouldered for another decade, and by 1909 the city was a tense, dry tinderbox, ready to ignite. The conscription of young Catalans for an unpopular imperialist war in Morocco provided the spark; as the unwilling recruits boarded ships, the Anarchists and Socialists staged protests by the port and confronted the police. Even the most conservative bourgeois supported them, as good Catalans once more defying Madrid. Emotions ran high and, with the calling of a general strike on 26 July, the Barcelonans lost all track of their *seny*, their famous common sense. The strike turned into a revolt, barricades went up, arsenals were raided for weapons, and a leaderless mob took over the city. Though discouraged by lack of support from the rest of Spain, the Barcelonans still turned the revolt into a head-on collision with the army. At the end of what was called the **Setmana Tràgica**, or Tragic Week, 116 people were dead and 80 buildings torched, 70 of them churches or monasteries. Barcelona had confirmed its role as the most radical city in Europe, 'Anarchism's rose of fire', and its workers gained considerable sympathy afterwards, as the army's execution of even moderate leaders, and its torture of Anarchist leaders in the fortress of Montjuïc, shocked Europe.

Spain's neutrality in the **First World War** brought more boom times, as exports to the belligerents soared and the city's industrialists diversified and modernized to meet demands. Rural Catalans, impoverished by wartime inflation and seeking jobs, moved into the city; the population doubled between 1910 and 1930 as

Barcelona became the largest city in Spain. In the same period the city was rocked with over 800 strikes. Workers' conditions only grew worse; by 1919, the Anarchist workers' union of Catalunya (the CNT) had over 50,000 members in Barcelona alone, but remained unrecognized by the employers even after a devastating, two-month-long general strike. The violence spiralled, as employers hired thugs to kill unionists and the workers lashed back in kind. The chaos and the rising body count gave Spain's rightists the excuse to close down parliamentary democracy. The Captain General of Barcelona, **Miguel Primo de Rivera**, declared a military dictatorship and the 'abolition of the class struggle' with the approval of King Alfonso XIII.

1923–39: Through dictatorship and Civil War, Barcelona undergoes its trial by fire, and in the end the city is humbled yet again

The dictatorship of Primo de Rivera was proof, if the Catalans needed any, that nothing had really changed since the time of Fernando and Isabel. Spain still looked on Catalunya and its exotic, excessive capital with a mixture of contempt and fear, and was prepared to do anything to suppress it. The dictator banned the CNT, and attempted to do the same to the Catalan language and its nationalist symbols, but he did promote Barcelona's **International Exhibition** of 1929 to show his version of Spain to the world. This initiated another building boom, one that included the city's first metro line. It also gave it its first great wave of immigrants from other corners of Spain, especially from Andalucía, Murcia and Galicia. Those who couldn't find places to stay in the slums ended up in new shantytowns on the periphery. Barcelona needed them, but once the metro was dug and the fair was over many Barcelonans wished very much that they would go home. Catalan Republicans, taking a less bigoted view, began to teach them Catalan in night classes.

The old dictator retired the next year, and in 1931 Spain voted a left-wing landslide in municipal elections that provided a dramatic renunciation of the old order, leading to the abdicaton of Alfonso XIII and the birth of the Republic. In Catalunya, the big winner was the popular old ex-colonel **Francesc Macià**, head of the left-wing Republicans (Esquerra Republicana), who declared the 'Republic of Catalunya', although three days later he agreed for the sake of the young Spanish Republic to limit this to autonomy under the rule of a revived Generalitat. The outraged, outgoing mayor declared he would resign only under force. The amiable Macià gave him the most gentle of pushes with his hand and asked if that were force enough, and it was.

The other patricians and their Lliga de Catalunya did not lose so gracefully. Barcelona had always been theirs, and they were not about to support Macià's mix of Republican leftists, CNT Anarchists, professors, and trade unionists; many of them would later collaborate with Franco. For the moment, they were happy when the elections of 1934 brought in a right-wing national government, inciting an insurrection that resulted in the jailing of both leftist and Catalan leaders, including **Lluís Companys**, the liberal trade union lawyer who succeeded Macià as head of the Esquerra Republicana.

After two uneasy years, the left-wing coalition regrouped as the Popular Front and won again in the national elections of 1936, in Catalunya with the CNT as the biggest party, followed by the Bloc Obrer Camperol, which later became POUM, the Workers' Party of Marxist Unification. Lluís Companys became president of the Generalitat. The elections were followed within a few months by **Franco**'s coup and the outbreak of the **Civil War**. In Barcelona, the success of the workers and loyal Republican troops in defeating the rightists and army forces revolutionized the city; churches were set alight and fifth columnists and Falangist supporters rooted out and summarily shot, while the anguished Companys tried desperately to contain the impassioned mobs. Wearing a tie on the streets became a provocation, and many bourgeois left the country or escaped into the zones conquered by Franco.

The left was hardly unified: the Esquerra Republicana wanted to control the situation to avoid intervention of state and loss of Catalan autonomy; the rapidly growing Communist party, the PSUC, wanted to win the war before the revolution; while POUM and the Anarchists believed that the revolution and war were inseparable. As Franco's army made major gains across Spain in 1937, Barcelona became the theatre of a left-wing war-within-a-war, recorded for history by George Orwell in his *Homage to Catalonia*. The Republican army and the Communists, the most serious and best-organized group on the Republican side, sorted out the Anarchists once and for all, saving Franco the trouble later. Refugees filled the city; the Italians based in Mallorca bombed it throughout 1938, and half a million Republicans fled towards France in January 1939 as it surrendered. Franco took particular delight in humiliating the city, executing and imprisoning thousands in reprisals. Barcelona was put on notice: 'Spain has arrived', and all things Catalan were banned; through the 1940s, even speaking Catalan in the street was risking jail. The burghers of Barcelona put their suits and ties back on, and went back to work.

1939–75: Four stultifying decades with Francisco Franco, in which Barcelona is sat in the corner and told to be quiet

Business was rotten. The next two sad and impoverished decades saw food, electricity and everything else in short supply; in 1947 the city came very close to famine. Other parts of Spain were suffering more; immigrants flocked to the city, and Franco did everything to encourage them, hoping a tidal wave of poor Andalucíans would dilute Catalanism into a harmless eccentricity. The exhausted, broken city already faced a housing crisis before they arrived. Unlike earlier immigrants, the new arrivals didn't integrate, but lived together in their shanty-towns and ghettos; the banning of Catalan meant they never learned the language.

To the dictatorship and its supporters, Barcelona was the 'anti-Spain', the city of immorality, separatism and communism, and masses were ordered to expiate its sins. It was clear to Franco (who was always known here as Paco Rana, or 'Frank the Frog') that he was never going to win the Catalans' hearts and minds, and he never tried. In 1951, an increase in tram fares led to the biggest protests since the Civil War; this time, however, overt repression was avoided, as part of the new image the dictator was trying to project. In the atmosphere of the Cold War, Franco was able to make the deal with the democracies that would ensure his survival. In 1952, the Catalan language was tentatively decriminalized, at least in songs, in a few books and at a poetry contest, in which the prize was given out by Cardinal Spellman of New York, symbolic of the new friendship with the USA. The following year saw the US–Spanish military pact, and the beginnings of American aid.

By 1960, Franco had given up his attempt at national self-sufficiency, and a new generation of economists and technocrats was tooling up the country for its impressive industrial take-off of the next two decades. Spain's new-found vocation for mass tourism brought in hard currency, and for many of the tourists Barcelona was the first stop. The city's appointed mayor, **José Maria de Porcioles**, presided over a building boom of soulless, sprawling high-rise housing projects and factories on the outskirts, and disfigured old Barcelona with massive car parks and roads. Never mind that nearly every city in the world was doing it in the 1960s, or that Franco's planners did the same to Madrid: Porcioles remains one of Barcelona's favourite villains. As in Paris, they also paved over all the cobblestones to make it impossible for protesters to build barricades.

The 1960s were a strange time for Barcelona; many people look back on it with a shudder: the philistine tastelessness of a new bourgeoisie interested only in 'peseta pragmatism', happy with their SEAT 600s and their first television, caught between *seny* and the urge to protest, between forgetting and remembering. Still, shoots of new life were poking up through the cracks of the Castilian concrete. In 1960, future Catalan president Jordi Pujol was arrested and imprisoned for two years after devising a protest at Palau de la Música—singing the *Song of the Catalan Flag* at a concert while a delegation of Franco's ministers was in the audience. Not long afterwards, Barcelonans formed their first neighourhood groups. These were seeds of a new participatory democracy, and they became very active by the mid-1970s, leading most of the protests of the period, demanding basic services, better public transport, complaining against exploitation and siting of factories.

Cultural resistance too was slowly being reborn, in an atmosphere of underground Catalan poetry readings and *samizdat* publishing of works on Catalan literature and history. The upper classes that had welcomed the stability Franco brought were becoming disillusioned by the regime's torture, exile and imprisonment of protesters and university students. Anarchists and communist cells and trade unions began to regroup clandestinely. In the last decade of Francoism, while both the regime and the dictator were slowly losing their faculties, a half-hearted machine of repression was increasingly unable to contain the alternative and critical culture that was emerging in the streets. Thinly veiled protest songs became widely heard, from a movement called the *Nova Cançó*, led by group called the Setze Jutges (17 judges). Even the censored newspapers became more openly critical. Many Barcelonans had gone to Paris in May 1968 for an exiles' Festival of Catalan Culture, just in time to witness the great student revolt, which sent them home impressed, and more frustrated than ever.

1975 to the present: the happy ending

When Franco finally died, on 20 November 1975, every single bottle of *cava* in Barcelona was emptied. The morning after, like the rest of Spain they started wondering what would happen next. As it became clear that their new king, **Juan Carlos**, was moving them towards democracy with a steady hand, the Catalans kept their cool and did nothing to make it more difficult for him. Many had feared that all the passions and hatreds of the 1930s would explode again, but 40 years of mostly silent opposition to Paco Rana was enough to wear off many of the sharp edges, in Catalunya as in Spain as a whole.

When the king's appointed prime minister, **Adolfo Suárez**, won the first elections in 1977, he invited Josep Tarradellas, Catalunya's long-time president-in-exile, to return and restore the Generalitat. The next year the Socialists under Narcis Serra won control of the city government, the Ajuntament, and they have kept it ever since. From 1982 to 1997 the mayor was the popular **Pasqual Maragall**, grandson of the poet, tireless improver and promoter of his city. The first regional elections in 1980 gave the presidency of the Generalitat to **Jordi Pujol** of the nationalist CiU (Convergènicia i Unió) party, and he has been just as securely entrenched, though he narrowly survived a challenge by Maragall in the 1999 elections.

The Catalan virtue of *continuitat* is remarkably tenacious in the region's politics. If they had had free elections in the 14th century, or the 18th, the pattern would probably have been much the same. Now, the two very different parties of the conservative villages and the radical city work well together, showing what Catalans like to call 'creative tension' while competing to further the region's interest—and to take the credit for its successes. In national politics, the Catalans had the best of all possible worlds. Jordi Pujol's CiU held the balance of power in Madrid, allied first with Felipe Gonzalez's Socialists and then with the Partido Popular. Whatever measures any government wanted to push through, they had to clear them with the Catalans—and naturally there were always strings attached, in the form of more autonomy or more treats for Catalunya. In the ultimate sign that things have really changed for ever, the conservative prime minister **José Maria Aznar** can be seen making statements on Catalunya's regional television in passable Catalan. Today, Aznar's Partido Popular finally holds a majority in parliament without having to form a coalition with the feisty Pujol, which has taken some wind out of his sails (the rest of Spain thinks it's about time, too).

By any measure, the accomplishments of Maragall, Pujol and company over the past 20 years have been remarkable; their creative channelling of 40 years of pent-up energy and Catalan quirkiness have made Barcelona the most dynamic city in southern Europe. Currently, the population is over four million; by 2020 it is projected to reach seven million. Even in an economy that has modernized as spectacularly as Spain's, Catalunya has managed to stay in the lead. Pujol has been pushing to make the region a high-tech paradise; in the Vallès, Japanese capital is financing what he hopes will be Catalunya's Silicon Valley. All the designer tinsel of Barcelona's obsessive hipness is only the shop-window dressing of a city that works hard for its living, and knows how to sell itself. The real Barcelona runs on metals and machine industries, textiles and chemicals. It also outranks Madrid as the world's biggest publishing centre in the Spanish language (not to mention Catalan). There is a busy stock exchange, and an annual trade fair, the Feria de Barcelona on Montjuïc. Not the least of the Catalans' achievements has been defusing the little time bomb Paco Rana left for them, the hundreds of thousands of poor immigrants from southern Spain. This they managed with an effort towards good faith and fairness, and by compromising their nationalism enough to define a Catalan as anyone who wanted to be one (and who learned the language).

For all that, it has been the tinsel that gets the world's attention. As they demonstrated conclusively at the opening and closing ceremonies of the 1992 Olympics, no city in Europe does tinsel better. If you dig deep enough, you will not find a lot of difference between Barcelona's Olympic inspiration and Atlanta's. Both are up-and-at'-em metropolises that desperately wanted to break into the ranks of the 'world cities', and both hoped to effect a substantial physical regeneration in the process. Barcelona managed it with infinitely more style. The games were no isolated effort, but rather another example of Catalan *continuitat.* The city had in fact applied many times for the Olympics, and never won the prize. In 1936, they created a 'People's Olympics' in opposition to the games over which Adolf Hitler was presiding in Berlin; it was to have opened on the very day the Civil War began.

Mayor Maragall, with a bit of help from Olympics czar Joan Antoni Samaranch, a Catalan, won the 1992 Olympics for the city and used it as a vehicle to push through a six-year-long building programme, which for the third time radically transformed the city, giving it a fresh orientation towards the sea, restoring its monuments, cleaning up its seedier quarters and gentrifying others, filling its squares and new parks with sculpture. The Olympics are long over, but the process shows no sign of stopping. People here are always thinking, always waiting for the next show. Their next project, under Maragall's successor, Socialist mayor **Joan Clos**, is the *Forum Global de les Cultures* in 2004. Clos is a rare politician who believes that Europe's immigration problems are not the fault of the poor immigrant, but Europe's attitude—so it could be interesting. At the time of writing (mid-2000) no one outside Catalunya had even heard of the planned event, but knowing Barcelona the odds are that, four years from now, the city, a show-off of Daliesque proportions, will be back where it loves to be: up front, centre stage, in the limelight of the entire world.

Architecture and Art

Roman, Visigothic and Romanesque (3rd century BC–12th century AD)

In spite of the continuous occupation of the old city for the last 2,300 years, some of the **Roman walls and towers** remain remarkably intact, surviving in much better nick, in fact, than any of the later city walls. A few columns from the **temple of Augustus** show that Barcino was keeping up with Rome's other colonies, and the excavations under the **Museu d'Història de la Ciutat** evoke everyday life in ancient Barcino. The **Museu Arqueològic** has mosaics, sculpture and other artefacts, but nothing outstanding, nothing foretelling Barcelona's future greatness.

Through the Dark Ages, civilization's candle was flickering at least a little more brightly in Spain than it was in France or most of Italy. Spain's Visigothic rulers did their share of building, but here only a few capitals from columns have survived, recycled into Barcelona's later Romanesque churches, of which only a few remain (**Sant Pau del Camp** is the best of rather slim pickings). What Barcelona does have is a fabulous collection of 6th–12th-century Romanesque murals in the **Palau Nacional** (Museu Nacional d'Art de Catalunya), brought here from churches in the remote valleys of the Pyrenees. Their eccentric style and use of bold flat colours and patterns would exert a powerful influence on Barcelona's greatest 20th-century painter, Joan Miró.

Catalan Gothic (13th–15th centuries)

Catalunya first developed a true national style in the late 13th century, with a Gothic architecture unlike any other. Not for the Catalans the dizzying heights, pointed arches, pinnacles, flying buttresses and flamboyant pageantry of northern Gothic: their Gothic is restrained almost to the point of plainness, the austerity broken only by thin bands of decoration around doors and windows, and geometric hexagonal towers. What fascinated the Catalans was width and mass, and in their conquest of horizontal space they were as daring as the masters of Chartres. Nowhere is the style more striking than in Berenguer de Montagut's **Santa Maria del Mar**, with its fortress-like exterior hiding one of the most breathtaking interiors of any church in Spain. **Santa Maria del Pi** is a fine example on a smaller scale, with the typical wide single nave.

Some secular buildings are just as solid after some 650 years of service. The open, elegant spaces of two important seats of the city's medieval government, the **Saló Tinell** by Guillem Carbonell and **Saló de Consell de Cent** by Pere Llobet in the Ajuntament, are simple and striking, divided into bays by semicircular transverse arches—including the widest masonry arches ever built in Europe. The **Drassanes** shipyards (now the Museu Marítim) with its huge naves, the **Antic Hospital de la Santa Creu** (now the National Library of Catalunya) and the **Llotja** by Pere Llobet all have remarkable interiors that must once have seemed especially spacious in the dense fabric of the old city. One trademark is the builders' mastery of the shallow Catalan vault; the **cathedral crypt** by Jaume Fabre is one of the finest examples.

Barcelona's Gothic palaces usually present massive stone façades to the street but open up to reveal courtyards with elaborate stairs and galleries, often supported by the daintiest of columns, so thin they seem to be made of cast iron: you can see them in the merchants' palaces along **Carrer Montcada**, in the **Generalitat** and also in the cloister at the **Monestir de Pedralbes**, the best surviving Gothic religious complex in the city. The medieval Barcelonans were also gifted ironworkers, famous for their elaborate armour, weapons, locks, keys and tools, a tradition that survived intact into the 19th century to add brio to many a Modernista building. There is an important collection in the **Museu Frederic Marés**.

In the 13th and 14th centuries, Catalan painters and sculptors tended to follow international trends, with a strong influence from the painters of Siena. Even so, the painters come close to a national style, one that displayed a careful attention to anecdotal detail and narrative, with a naturalism of expression and gesture. The founder of the school was the court painter of Pere III the Ceremonious, **Ferrer Bassa**, whose frescoes (1346) in the Capella de Sant Miquel at the Monestir de Pedralbes are among the finest works of the century. The studio of his successor, **Ramon Destorrent**, produced the **Serra brothers** (active 1357–1405), Jaume and Pere, who often worked together, producing altarpieces of lavish colour and detail, including the first large-scale altarpieces, or *retables*, in Catalunya.

Their workshop, however, fell out of favour as Virgins grew blonder and blonder and International Gothic became the vogue, reaching Barcelona in the late 1380s by way of the papal court in Avignon and Violante de Bar, the Provençal wife of Joan I, who introduced the Court of Love and the *Jocs Florals* poetry competition to Barcelona. **Lluís Borrassá** (d. 1424) was the Catalan pioneer in the new painting, known for his elegant gestures and richly attired figures, followed by the very courtly painter and miniaturist **Bernat Martorell** (active 1427–52), who has recently been identified as the 'Master of St George' of the famous altarpiece in the Chicago Institute of Art; one of his best works is in the cathedral. His student **Jaume Huguet** (1412–92) became the leading painter in Barcelona; his love of natural detail typical of the Renaissance (especially in his faces, where he was capable of great subtlety) is combined with a love of gold-embossed backgrounds and lavish textiles that gave his patrons their money's worth in fashion. He left a great *retable* in the Capella de Santa Àgueda (now part of the Museu d'Història de la Ciutat) and a series of altarpieces in the Palau Nacional. In the late 15th century, Hispano-Flemish realism made its appearance in Catalunya with **Bartolomé Bermejo** of Córdoba, who settled in Barcelona and left the city two singular masterpieces, one in the cathedral museum and the other in the Palau Nacional.

In the early 14th century, the Pisano-trained sculptor of Santa Eulàlia's sarcophagus in the cathedral inspired other local sculptors: the chief names are **Marc Safont**, who also worked as an architect in the Generalitat; **Pere Sanglada**, creator of the choir and tomb of Sant Oleguer in the Cathedral; and **Pere Joan**, who carved the Generalitat's rondel of St George.

Intermission (16th–mid-19th century)

Barcelona continued to build in its three-century period of decadence, though little that was exceptional or distinctively Catalan. The best buildings of the 17th century are the **Casa de Convalecencia**, attached to the Antic Hospital de la Santa Creu, and the **Palau Dalmases** on the Carrer Montcada. Of the Baroque churches, the Jesuit **Betlem** has the best façade, while **Sant Sever** is the only one that didn't have its innards incinerated in later episodes of church-burning. In the 18th century, neoclassical palaces went up along the then new Ramblas, including the monumental **Palau de la Virreina**, although the most congenial and atmospheric legacies of the Enlightenment era in Barcelona are the aristocratic **Parc del Laberint d'Horta** up in the hills and the popular **Barceloneta** quarter, built on landfill down by the sea. Within the city walls, the most welcome improvements were in spaces provided by the first wave of church and convent burning in 1835: the **Plaça Reial**, the **Boqueria** market, and the **Liceu** opera.

Catalans began to paint in earnest again, inspired by the international success of **Marià Fortuny** (1838–74), a Romantic stylist who used short, shimmering brush-strokes verging on Impressionism. He was also the first to find his way to Paris, then the art capital of the world; a few Bohemian years in Montmartre would become a *rite de passage* for all painters from Barcelona to soak up the latest -isms.

Modernisme (1880–1910)

> *That is what Modernisme is, a great movement of enthusiasm and liberty in search of beauty.*
>
> Juan Ramón Jiménez

As Barcelona burst outside its walls into the new Eixample in 1860, it did so with feelings of ambivalence. Now that they had room to build at last, how should they build? Tired neoclassical forms and pastiches could hardly express the spirit of the cultural reawakening of the *Renaixença*. Catalan architects looking for answers studied the French medievalist Viollet-le-Duc; they agreed with Ruskin that 'ornament [was] the origin of architecture'; and they liked William Morris' 'totality' of design integrated with decoration. But what struck the loudest chord was a book called *Der Stil* (1861–3) by German architect Gottfried Semper. Semper described how architecture derived from its original functions (the shelter, warmth and defence of the cave) and evolved according to need and society, and that a building and its decoration should express its function. To mimic historical styles, as the medieval revivalists were doing, was repulsive. It was essential to be modern, and Modernisme, as the city's new style came to be known, used the latest technologies while keeping in mind Semper's dictum 'Originality is a return to origins'.

Barcelona's Modernista triumvirate of architects would respond to all these often contradictory currents in surprisingly different ways. What they did have in common, however, was their fervent nationalism (Domènech and Puig were also politicians), a trait they shared with Barcelona's newly assertive bourgeoisie, who had piles of money to spend and the empty streets of the Eixample to fill up. Although part of the arts and crafts movement of the later 19th century, Modernista architecture has little of the drooping tendrilly melancholy of the slightly later Art Nouveau or Jugendstil, no aesthete *fin de siécle tristesse*; it is vigorous, bold, colourful and often playful. The Modernistas and their clients were optimists who felt that Barcelona at long last was on her way again.

The first great Modernista, Lluís Domènech i Montaner (1849–1923), was a well-travelled Renaissance man who adored Shakespeare. He took Semper's 'return to origins' as a return to brick and iron, combining traditional Catalan craftsmanship with new technologies. In 1877, as an assistant professor of architecture, he wrote an article called 'En Busca d'una Arquitectura Nacional' (In Search of a National Architecture) which became the Modernista manifesto, and three years later he showed what he meant in the proto-Modernista **Editorial Montaner i Simón** (now the Fundació Antoni Tàpies). Domènech's use of the latest technologies and his talent as a master organizer saved the bacon of the 1888 Universal Exhibition and made him the city's darling when he orchestrated the building of a massive hotel in only 59 days. This and his other fair buildings were demolished, except for the **Castell dels Tres Dragons** (now the Museu de Zoologia). His masterpieces, the **Palau de la Música Catalana**, the **Casa Lleó Morera** and the **Hospital de Sant Pau**, are remarkable for their complete integration of decoration and often for their technological daring.

Josep Puig i Cadafalch (1857–1956) was the most historically minded of the big three, an archaeologist and scholar who wrote a definitive book on Catalan Romanesque, and also a successful nationalist politician. For him, Semper meant an imaginative re-interpretation of Gothic. He did a good deal of work outside Barcelona but left the city some highly individualistic works: **Casa Amatller**, **Els Quatre Gats**, **Casa de les Punxes**, **Palau Macaya**, **Palau Quadras** and the **Fábrica Casarramona**. In the 1920s he modified his style to fit into the prevailing Noucentista currents, and his last buildings, for the 1929 International Exhibition, border on the Baroque. He went into exile at the end of the Civil War, and returned in 1943, but was never allowed to build or politick again.

By far the greatest genius of the international Art Nouveau movement, Antoni Gaudí i Cornet (1852–1926), went beyond the others into uncharted territory; his return to origins was a return to the forms and structure of nature herself. The son, grandson, and great grandson of coppersmiths in Reus near Tarragona, he had grown up watching his father make cauldrons from flat sheets of metal, a hands-on creating of volumes. Gaudí would approach architecture in the same way. He was more a sculptor and poet than an architect, and improvised as he went along: 'He didn't make plans,' said Miró. 'He made gestures.'

Gaudí's life and career are a remarkable study in paradox and contrariness (*see* **Topics**, p.58). Although he shared the Modernista fascination with Gothic and other historical forms, the ideal of total integration of decoration and architecture, and their nationalism (spiritually and often crankily, but not politically), Gaudí never liked to be called a Modernista, because as a good Catholic he didn't believe in Modernism. He was a reactionary, yet he went far beyond any architect of his time into the realms of pure imagination; while others drew on Gothic, his goal was to take it to a higher stage of evolution. Convinced that 'the straight line is man's creation; the curved line, God's', he was a mediocre student, having little interest in his trade's age-old tools, the compass and T-square and the Euclidian geometry that had been the vocabulary of buildings since antiquity. Nature and God didn't build that way, so why should he? He did, however, spend time poring over architecture books with illustrations from around the world, studying Moorish and Hindu designs that he would later combine with Gothic, natural forms and his own imagination in the **Casa Vicens**, the **Pavilions Güell** and the **Palau Güell**.

Gaudí's creation of new forms and his integration of decoration, which was as essential to the structure as the walls or roof, went far beyond anything built by his colleagues. No architect ever studied nature more intently: in his buildings, stone became organic, sensuous, dripping; iron was beaten into whiplash ribbons, palm fronds, kelp and spider's webs; the old Muslim art of covering surfaces with a rippling mosaic skin of tiles (*trencadis* in Catalan) was given a new vibrant meaning, reaching an epiphany in the playful **Park Güell**. In the Park Güell, and the other masterpieces of his mature style (**Crypt Güell, Casa Battló** and **La Pedrera**), he completely freed himself from the past. To make his buildings stand up required mind-boggling mathematics in those pre-computer days. He also had the luck to draw on a highly skilled craft base to give his imagination substance.

No modern architect has marked a city the way Gaudí has Barcelona, and the most visible proof of this is the **Sagrada Família**, the longest-running work in progress in Europe. Paris prides itself on its 'world-record-breaking spirit'—which London has tried to capture with its big dome—but Gaudí, who envisaged this church and the private religious society which is actually building it, will slam dunk them both.

By the time Gaudí died, he was ignored by the art establishment, but the people of Barcelona came out 10,000-strong to his funeral.

The Modernista Big Three tend to overshadow a host of other fine architects. Some who collaborated with Gaudí in particular built some astonishing buildings in their own right, especially Josep Maria Jujols i Gibert (1879–1949), 'one of the most subtle, original, unprejudiced and provocative personalities of contemporary art', as Carlos Flores called him. His best-known works are associated with Gaudí—the serpentine bench at the Park Güell, the balconies of La Pedrera, the roof of the Casa Battló—but he also built a number of unique buildings, including **Casa Planells**. Joan Rubió i Bellvé (1871–1952), from Reus, built some of the city's most imaginative brickwork, in his **Casa Golferichs** and **Casa Roviralta** (or Frare Blanc), and continued building in Gaudí's manner into the 1930s in the **Universitat Industrial**. Gaudí's closest collaborator, his 'right hand' Francesc Berenguer (1866–1914), was also from Reus. He left a charming legacy, mostly in Gràcia. Some suspect his contribution to Gaudí's work was as important as it was unpublicized.

While Modernista architects concentrated on revitalizing Catalan building with references to history, nature and myth, Modernista painters were keen to modernize Catalan society itself and open it up to the artistic trends in Paris. Their work never rose to the level of the architects but at the start of the 20th century they nurtured a young Andalucian named **Picasso**. The most talented Barcelonan was **Ramón Casas** (1866–1932), the 'Catalan Toulouse-Lautrec' (and the first man in Barcelona to own a car), who in his youth painted a handful of bold, almost photographic, large political paintings, but he later turned his fine technique to churning out beautiful slush, society portraits and advertisements that put him in great demand in America. His great friend, the high-spirited **Santiago Rusinyol** (1861–1931), was an amiable morphine addict now better known for his amusing writings than his pretty landscapes and genre scenes; his legendary Modernista festivals at Sitges flirted with Symbolism in art and literature. One of the most original figures to come along was **Isidre Nonell** (1873–1911), who painted poor gypsy women in simplified forms, inspiring Picasso's Blue Period, and who moved close to abstraction before he died. The Museu d'Art Modern has a representative selection of their works, while Picasso gets his own museum, with many works from his Barcelona days.

Rodin was the strongest influence on Modernista sculptors. The expressive **Miquel Blay** (1866–1936) worked on the Palau de la Música Catalana, along with the delightful and prolific **Eusebi Arnau**, who supplied many of the nymphs, dragons and saints on the Modernistas' buildings. The most Rodin-like was **Josep Llimona** (1864–1934), author of the popular. His masterpiece is the greatest of all Modernista public works, the startling **Monument to Dr Robert**.

Noucentisme, International Modernism and the Avant Garde (1910–39)

The inevitable reaction to the extremes and individualistic eccentricities of Modernisme set in, in a style known as Noucentisme, 'nineteen-hundredism', which sought balance and order in a return to Catalunya's Mediterranean roots: Brunelleschi was the new hero, but the result was usually a tepid neoclassicism. In architecture, however, Gaudí's influence kept Modernisme popular among the patricians, although it was heavily criticized by Noucentistas, who despised its 'disorder'. The Primo de Rivera dictatorship made the 1929 International Exhibition a riot of pompous pastiche (the **Palau Nacional** and the **post office** in Vía Laietana), although some attractive Noucentista buildings did get built: the **França station** and **Graphic Arts Palace** (now the Museu Arqueològic).

Cézanne was the model for the Noucentista painters, who were led by **Joaquim Sunyer** of Sitges (1874–1956), whose best work also has something of Matisse's line, and in sculpture by **Josep Clarà**, whose solid nudes (the *Goddess* in Plaça de Catalunya) recall Aristide Maillol. Another painter from Barcelona, the virtuoso monochrome muralist **Josep Maria Sert** (1874–1945), who painted the Ajuntament's Saló de las Cròniques, is in a category all his own. **Pau Gargallo** (1881–1934) began working with Domènech on his massive hospital project, and decorated the Montjuïc Noucentista stadium, while developing his own playful style.

Even while Noucentisme held forth in the 1920s, new things were happening, in part because of Picasso's interest in the city. Cubists were first exhibited at Dalmau Galleries in 1912, and Picasso also introduced Barcelona to Diaghilev's Ballets Russes and Eric Satie. During the First World War the city became a favourite refuge for artists: Picabia came and started the Dadaist magazine *391*; Duchamp and Schönberg spent time here; and Stravinsky, Trotsky and Einstein passed through. Andrè Breton's Surrealist manifestoes were signed by **Joan Miró** (1893–1983) in 1924 and **Salvador Dalí** (1904–89) in 1929. Although Dalí became the most famous Surrealist, in part due to his unparalleled talent for self-promotion, Miró always remained true to its principles of seeking inspiration in the unconscious mind freed from reason and logic; his *Dona i Ocell* has become one of the symbols of the new Barcelona and his Fundació Joan Miro has a fine collection of his works. Catalunya's age-old tradition in ironwork was re-invented in the imaginative sculptures of **Juli González** (1876–1942), who met Picasso in Barcelona; his iron sculpture *Montserrat* was displayed alongside *Guernica* in the 1937 Paris exhibition.

International Modernism (not to be confused with Catalan Modernisme) came to Barcelona with **Mies van der Rohe**'s Pavelló Barcelona in the 1929 exhibition, which provided a home for Mies' famous 'Barcelona chair', an icon of Modernist design. It inspired young **Josep Lluís Sert** (1902–83) to follow Le Corbusier for a few years.

The Republican government was keen to remake and rationalize Barcelona: the Macià plan wanted to re-use built-up space, standardize hospitals, recover beaches and parks, and construct public housing. Architects of the GATCPAC group campaigned to open up the dense and impoverished neighbourhoods in the old city and let in light and air. Two projects that were actually completed, each a model of the social vision of the Republic, were the **Dispensarí Antituberculós** in El Raval, and a huge, barracks-like workers' housing called **Casa Bloc** (Passeig de Torras i Bages) by Sert and Josep Torres Clavè, who died in 1938 on the Ebro front. One of the most interesting buildings of the period, the **Clinica Barraquer** (1936), has kept its late Art Deco charms—a style that never really caught on in Barcelona. In the other arts, the culturally diverse **Amics de les Arts Noves** (members included Miró, Dalí, Sert and Torres Clavè) saw art as public patrimony, and sponsored concerts, excursions, and poetry readings by Lorca.

The Franco Years (1939–75)

For the new regime, one of the first priorities was to get rebellious students out of the city centre and into a new **university city** along the upper Diagonal; plans were made in 1940 but a lack of cash delayed the first bricks and mortar until 1955. This area of the city would see an important share of Barcelona's building; psychologically, the most important structure was **Camp Nou** stadium (1957), much of it paid for by supporters for the joy of watching Barça occasionally beat Franco's Real Madrid. Otherwise, some of the best building of the 1950s and 60s was by José Antonio Coderch de Sentmenat (1913–84), although his support for the regime kept him from leading Barcelona's architects in any coherent way. His **Casa de la Marina** (1951–3) was one of the first Modernist buildings in Franco's Spain. In 1960 he designed the famous **Casa Tàpies** in Sant Gervasi (57 Carrer Saragossa), windowless on the outside but magically lit within from an interior courtyard, and in 1968, when business followed the university up the Diagonal, he contributed the rather beautiful **Torres d'Oficines Trade**.

Art in the 1940s in Franco's Spain was uniformly monotonous, dull and derivative; in 1948 the Dau al Set (the 'seven-spot die') was founded in Barcelona to shake things up. The originators included **Joan Ponç** (1927–1984), **Modest Cuixart** (b.1925) and **Joan-Josep Tharrats** (b.1918), who drew from the French Surrealists in poetry, art and literature, and embraced dreamlike states and psychic automatism. **Antoni Tàpies** (1923–94), an early member, emerged in the 1950s as one of the leading artists in Spain; after Franco's death he carried out a number of public projects, including his startling *Homage to Picasso* (also see the Fundació Tàpies). Another favourite in Barcelona, **Joan Brossa** (1919–98), composed poem-objects and sculpture poems dotted around the city. The leading sculptor of the time was **Josep M. Subirachs** (b.1925), who created a number of public works in a rough, textured style (including the city's first public abstract sculpture, in 1958), but the work he'll be remembered for is his controversial Passion Façade of the Sagrada Família, begun in the early 1980s.

Barcelona's housing crisis became urgent as the Spanish economy took off in the 1960s and flooded the city with a new wave of immigrants, who were housed in superblock suburbs thrown up around the city perimeter (of course many cities without the excuse of a dictatorship built equally ghastly projects). Speculators in the Eixample not only disfigured many Modernista buildings, but demolished some altogether. At the same time, however, more thoughtful architects strove to re-create Barcelona's architectural panache in contemporary terms, even while concentrating on down-to-earth affordable housing. MBM—Josep Martorell (b.1925), Oriol Bohigas (b.1925) and Englishman David Mackay (b.1933)—emerged in the late 1950s as the most successful experimenters, their early achievements culminating in the **Escola Thau** near the university. In 1962, Ricardo Bofill (b.1939) founded his multidiscipline Taller de Arquitectura, building apartments using Catalan brick and ceramics; his controversial co-op **Walden 7** (1975) in the nearby suburb of Sant Just Desvern was inspired by the bio-fascist theories of B. F. Skinner. Bofill is one of the last of the authoritarian master architects, those who would squeeze peoples' lives to fit the Avant Garde buildings so graciously bestowed on them. His work and the theology behind it impressed the French, who would keep him employed on increasingly monumental and increasingly neoclassical housing projects in Paris and Montpellier, while Walden 7 has been literally falling apart since the day it was built.

Josep Lluís Sert, who went into exile after the Civil War and served as Gropius' successor at the head of Harvard's School of Architecture, returned to design his best building in Barcelona, the luminous white **Fundació Joan Miró** in 1972. But as Antoni González and Raquel Lacuesta wrote in their *Barcelona Architecture Guide*: 'A number of architects had already found a sanctuary in the laxity of the "gauche divine", and there was a general move towards a relaxing of social commitment and a taking refuge in the vicious circle of design.'

Barcelona, Make Yourself Pretty (1975 to the present)

In the late 1970s, Oriol Bohigas, now in charge of the city's culture and planning, teasingly declared: 'To set Barcelona back on course, everything built under Franco would have to be demolished.' Of course no one took him literally, but all agreed there was serious work to be done. Barcelona's post-Franco rulers have been Socialists, but they were also solid bourgeoisie who, like the generations that preceded them, wanted to make their mark on the city. They certainly have, in an explosion of building financed by a continuing economic boom and pushed forward by an insistent Catalan cultural imperative. They've rivalled the Paris of Mitterrand and

Chirac, and the new Berlin will find them hard to beat. Their vindication has been in the throngs of visitors who come to pay homage to 'the hippest city in Europe'.

In architecture, the 'vicious circle of design'—the parade of fashionable architects and designers constantly upstaging each other to be the boldest, the newest, the hippest— has been at best a mixed blessing. The fact that the Royal Institute of British Architects awarded its 1999 Gold Medal to the city's redevelopment effort *in toto* was taken by many as a warning sign that something in Barcelona has probably gone very wrong. Much of the work that attracted RIBA's recognition, however, is a thoroughly admirable effort at historic preservation, one of the most comprehensive anywhere. Barcelona claims to have the strictest historic preservation rules in Europe. Starting with a limited budget in the 1970s, the city has continued to oversee innovative conversions of historic buildings, a trend that had begun with the Museu Picasso back in 1963. The 70s also brought the first initiative to encourage owners to restore and polish up façades in the *Barcelona posa't guapa* (Barcelona, make yourself pretty) campaign.

The next programme, begun in the 1980s, was far more ambitious: a series of new squares and parks around the city—nearly a hundred of them—with the idea that creating new open spaces, rather than new buildings, would be a more dramatic and less expensive way of giving the city a new look, while providing landmarks and focal points for anonymous, jerry-built postwar neighbourhoods. Leading artists and designers were invited to contribute designs. The programme became internationally trendy, and it gave the city a mix of the good, the bad and the ugly. Urban design, a simple and gentle art that is always defeated by cleverness, has had a rough time in this new Barcelona; it's a mystery how a city with such delightful exemplars as the Ramblas, the Plaça Reial and the squares of Gràcia should be so at a loss to create spaces where buildings and people get along and enjoy each other's company. One of the first and most successful of the new spaces was the **Parc de la Creueta del Coll** by MBM, with big art supplied by Eduard Chillada and Ellsworth Kelly. No doubt the most horrific attack on the fabric of the city has been the **Plaça de les Glòries Catalanes** on the Diagonal, an isolated park enclosed in a gigantic elevated motorway roundabout.

The programme did stir up a lot of public debate, with a continuing controversy between partisans of urban 'hard squares' and more parklike 'soft squares'. One of the most influential turned out to be the brutal 'hard square' **Plaça dels Països Catalans** (1983) by Estació Sants, by Albert Viaplana and Helio Piñón. This team, before it split up in 1998, unsuccessfully converted the convent of **Santa Monica** into an art centre; they did better with the **Casa de la Caritat** (1993; now the Centre de Cultura Contemporani) conversion, and became the toast of the town with **Maremagnum** (1995) in the Port Vell, a glorified shopping mall that heaves with shoppers and revellers day and night.

Maremagnum is just the noisiest aspect of the plans developed in the 1980s to reconnect the long-neglected waterfront to the city, with big projects that have been nearing completion in recent years. Being awarded the 1992 Olympics in 1986 fit right in with the city's plans, as the shore north of the centre was selected as the site for Olympic-related redevelopment.

There are times like these when fate and politics conspire to give a city a new start, and it sets to work transforming itself, full of faith and bravado and confidence. Rome was like that in the decades after Italian unification, and the result was some of the most pitiful monumental gigantism ever seen in Italy. Many European cities felt the same way after the destruction of the Second World War: trapped in the Modernist delirium, they inflicted damage on themselves that will take a century or longer to redeem. Post-Franco Barcelona has not been quite so masochistic, but its experience has demonstrated once again that the result of good intentions and manifestoes is often a force-fed architecture that tastes like hothouse tomatoes.

The **Vila Olímpica**, built by a score of award-winning architects under the charge of MBM, is a prime example of that bland aftertaste. Then there's Ricardo Bofill, who still gets commissions here. His scheme for the Parc Miró was rejected by Miró himself, who hated his 'dead' neoclassical design that reminded him of Franco, but he built the **Airport Terminal** (1992) and a pair of neoclassical temples (the **Institut Nacional d'Educzcio Fisica de Catalunya** on Montjuïc, and the new **Teatre Nacional**, in 1999). A rare (but fashionable) Madrileño to build in Barcelona, Rafael Moneo, contributed the **Auditori** (1999) and the Brobdingnagian **L'Illa** on the Diagonal (1993), typical of the blank, chilly postmodernism that has been transforming the city's business districts.

Rare exceptions have come from the engineer-architect Santiago Calatrava of Valencia, creator of the technically advanced **Pont Felipe II** (1987), and the **Torre de Telefònica** (1992) on Montjuïc, which are both so popular they are best known by his name. Some of the most striking works have come from outsiders: Arata Isozaki's **Palau Sant Jordi** (1990), Norman Foster's **Torre de Collserola** (1992), the **Museu d'Art Contemporani** (1995) by Richard Meier, and the new **World Trade Center** by I. M. Pei (2000).

Topics

Gaudí means 'delight' in Catalan, and the remarkably innovative architecture of the man who bore that name often lived up to it. Yet as late as the 1960s, he was regarded by most people as eccentric; hippies and Surrealists loved him, but rationalist architects and other respectable folk gave him a wide berth. But you don't have to be in Barcelona long to realize that his reputation has not only undergone a sea change but now fuels an industry of its own: you can take an all-Gaudí tour, purchase models of his benches in Park Güell, or build your own little Casa Batlló from a paper kit. The opera *Gaudí*, by Joan Guinjoan and Gaudí scholar Josep M. Carandell, premiered at the Liceu in 2000. The year 2002, the 150th anniversary of his birth, has been designated the International Gaudí Year, with exhibitions and events organized all over the world.

Gaudí, however, would not have been world-famous had he not caught the eye of the richest man in Barcelona, Eusebi Güell. Güell's father Joan had a knack for making money, as an *indiano*—a 19th-century merchant in Cuba—and investing in textiles, cement and nearly everything else. Eusebi had a privileged son's knack for spending, and fancied himself the Lorenzo de' Medici of Barcelona, the city he adored. Perhaps he and Gaudí were destined to meet all along, but the actual conjunction occurred at the Paris Exhibition of 1878, when the 31-year-old Güell saw an extraordinary 10ft-high glass, iron and mahogany display case for a Barcelona glove company. It was love at first sight. Güell tracked down the 26-year-old who designed it and, when his father-in-law, the tycoon Marquis de Comillas, needed a chapel for his summerhouse, Güell suggested Gaudí. He never looked back.

Gaudí at the time was something of a dandy. He had been a sickly, precocious child in Reus. As a teenager he and a friend had proposed restoring the then ruined Romanesque monastery at Poblet, one of the lodestones of Catalan nationalism, with revenues from tourism (this was 1870, mind, before there was such a thing as mass tourism). Once he got his diploma, his first jobs were working with Fontserré on the Parc de la Ciutadella and building a workers' cooperative in Mataró (1878), his one socialist fling. He spent his money on well-cut suits, went to the theatre, became the man about town; he was witty, but had a quick temper. '*Gent de camp, gent de lamp*' (country people, lightning-bolt people) is an old Catalan saying.

He was in fact ripe to be patronized by the wealthiest families in Barcelona. His interest in Oriental and Arab architecture fed their fantasies (El Caprichio in Comillas, Casa Vicens in Barcelona), and when Eusebi Güell gave him his first major commission, for the gate, lodge and stables for the Finca Güell in 1884, it gave him his first chance to work on a theme (Verenguer's Catalan epic, *L'Atlàntida*). Güell was so pleased that two years later he asked Gaudí, by then a close friend, to build him a mansion, money no object. The result was fit for a Renaissance prince, a remarkable monument to the passions of Eusebi Güell—his love for Wagner and Shakespeare, his nationalism and morbid piety.

Gaudí was always proud to be the son of a craftsman, but in the circle of Güell he became increasingly anti-democratic and authoritarian, while turning into the worst sort of neo-medieval religious crank. He told friends that he saw himself as God's humble servant in a world made of punishment and pain. And that was just Catalunya, which he rarely left; the rest of the world simply wasn't real. He was convinced that irreconcilable differences separated Catalans and Spaniards, but handled them with his very own brand of Catalan nationalism: 'We cannot say "Death to Spain",' he wrote. 'Because we are Spain (Hispania Citerior, or Tarraconense); those of the Centre are outside of Spain, they are of the Ulterior. The name is *ours*.' Take that, Castilian impostors!

One might expect someone with Gaudí's crabbed views to build dungeons for a Catalan Inquisition, but the crankier he got, the more wonderfully he built. His next project for Güell, the church for the Colonia Güell in Santa Coloma del Cervelló just south of Barcelona, was the first time he cut loose completely from historical eclecticism and soared into the realms of pure imagination, creating one of the most remarkable spaces of the 20th century. His work never went further than the crypt, but it stands as a revolutionary architectural sculpture, a cave held together by mathematics and Catalan craftsmanship. Eusebi Güell's aims for his Colonia Güell, however, were the opposite of revolutionary: he hated unions, socialists and above all calls for the abolition of child labour—they seemed unpatriotic, when Catalunya had to compete with the likes of France, England and America. He hoped that, by moving his textile workers into a paternalistic pseudo-cooperative in the country, he could more peacefully exploit them.

Güell's next project was the Park Güell, which was ostensibly a residential colony for the rich, although Josep M. Carandell, in his *Park Güell: Gaudí's Utopia* (1998), suggests Gaudí and Güell had another agenda: the park would be the secret garden of their beliefs, Catholicism spiced with an esoteric *garam masala* of Masonry, Gnosticism, Rosicrucianism and alchemy. These ideals of 'labour and philanthropy' can be seen in *Garraf*, a poem based on Güell's writings by his secretary Picó i Campanar, and in clues left by Gaudí in his buildings—even his signature two-sided Greek cross is more Masonic than Catholic. Another inspiration was Thomas Moore's *Utopia*, translated into Catalan by another Güell secretary. According to Carandell, Güell and Gaudí saw Catalunya as Utopia and the Park Güell as their *al fresco* lodge and a Delphi for the Catalan people.

Gaudí reached his pinnacle of fame in 1910, with the Casa Milà. Güell took an exhibition of Gaudí's work to Paris and showed it in the Grand Palais. Gaudí was asked to build a hotel in New York. But the next year he nearly died of fever, and afterwards he worked exclusively on the Sagrada Família. His reclusive tendencies (he never had a serious love interest, or gave interviews or posed for photos) increased as the few people close to him died—his niece Rosa in 1912, his collaborator Francesc Berenguer in 1914, Güell in 1918.

Since his death, Gaudí's more pious followers have been clamouring for the Church to canonize him; the Association for the Beatification of Antoni Gaudí was founded in 1992 by a group of architects and artists, and in March 2000 the Vatican announced that it would open the case. Now his followers have to prove that he performed miracles. They have got time, though: there are another 3,464 candidates (including Princess Grace) in the queue ahead of them. And now they have another obstacle in Carandell, who in view of Gaudí's Freemasonry, pride and bad temper has come out publicly against the whole thing.

The Rose of Fire

Within every Catalan there is an Anarchist.

Joan Maragall

Catalans consider *seny*, 'common sense' or 'practical wisdom', as their principal virtue. It makes them rich and sets them apart from the rest of Spain, or at least old romantic Spain, run by a creaky nobility that regarded commerce with distaste. *Seny*, however, has a Catalan counterpart: *rauxa*, or 'uncontrolled passion'.

While Güell and his cronies sought Utopia in Modernisme and modernization, their workers sought theirs in Anarchism. The bourgeoisie sublimated their *rauxa* in Wagner, architectural excess and exotic sex (at least judging by the bills of fare at Barcelona's bordellos), while the Anarchists expressed their *rauxa* by erecting barricades. Engles, in his *Bakuninites in Action*, noted that Barcelonans were better at constructing barricades than anyone. But there was *seny* on the Anarchist side as well; their magazine *Acràcia* was well written and carefully thought out. The one thing that the Anarchists and bourgeoisie shared was a resentment of central authority. For the latter, it was Madrid, especially after the bumbling government lost Cuba and the Philippines, both Catalan cash cows, in 1898. For the Anarchists, of course, authority was anyone who lorded it over the brotherhood of man, be it Church, government, army or capital, all of whom made man evil by assuming he was so.

The history of the class struggle in Spain began in the Bonoplata factory, the country's first steam-powered plant; in 1835, during Barcelona's first spate of church burnings, Luddite saboteurs set it on fire, too. Things became serious in 1855, when the government banned trade unions and Barcelona responded with

Spain's first general strike. At that time it was estimated that a family of four living in the city needed a minimum of 4,000 *reales* a year to live; an unskilled labourer made less than 2,500. And no matter who was in charge—19th-century Spain was a banana republic without the bananas—nothing changed. Like Pirandello's characters in search of a play, Barcelona's frustrated workers were in search of a belief.

It arrived by train in October 1868 with Giuseppe Fanelli, an apostle of Bakunin. He spoke only Italian and French, but he had some newspaper clippings of Bakunin's speeches and pamphlets, and they were enough. In that same year, the Anarchist paper *Solidaritat Obrera* was founded, and gave meaning to the sporadic uprisings among Catalan farm labourers, and workers in the mills of Sants and Poble Nou. The Anarchists staged strikes, inevitably lost, and after each defeat became more radical, lashing out in impotence. Fervent believers drifted into political terrorism. Even the peaceful-minded majority were political innocents, and their actions tended to be irrational and spontaneous. The police and city didn't know how to cope, and after a political crime rounded up and tortured not only Anarchists but moderate trade unionists and people suspected of any kind of progressive ideas.

This being Barcelona, there was the added ingredient of Catalanism. The Anarchists found it irrelevant, but it coloured the other, smaller workers' parties. The Socialists, in spite of their internationalist view of the class struggle, were emotional Catalans, as were the Republicans, and both groups resented the Bourbons and the Spanish state. The Radicals, led by Alejandro Lerroux (a paid agent of Madrid), were as anti-clerical as the Anarchists, but openly fomented anti-Catalanism among workers, by equating the bourgeoisie with Catalan nationalism; he found ready listeners among immigrant workers. As Gerald Brenan wrote, Barcelona 'became the scene of extraordinarily complicated and unscrupulous manoeuvres: radical Republicans contested elections with the secret support of Conservative Madrid, gangsters were taken into the pay of the Government, Anarchists were provoked or egged on, and the police themselves laid bombs at the doors of peaceful citizens in an endeavour either to intimidate the Catalan Nationalists or to produce a state of affairs in which the constitutional guarantees could be suspended.'

After a spontaneous orgy of *rauxa,* the *Setmana Trágica* (Tragic Week) of 1909, Anarchists dubbed Barcelona *La Rose de Foc*, the Rose of Fire. Two years later, the Anarchist trade union CNT was founded, and 80 per cent of Barcelona's workers joined. The employers wanted it banned. Noucentisme architecture, seeking classic harmony and balance, was Barcelona's new fashion, and industrialists such as Güell became fond of quoting Goethe's 'injustice is preferable to disorder'. Between 1910 and 1923, 800 strikes rocked Barcelona while the bosses made a killing out of the First World War, selling to both sides. Manufacturers backed the dictator Primo de Rivera, and made a witch's pact with the Spanish army because they realized that the police alone could not keep workers down. Unfortunately for them, when Franco declared his coup in 1936 the police stayed loyal to the Generalitat and joined the Anarchists in the battle for the city.

The CNT would run Catalunya for the remainder of 1936 and part of 1937, making Barcelona unique in Europe as the only city to have been governed by millennial Anarchists. The revolution began at once, exalting unbridled individualism and the brotherhood of man against bureaucrats, bosses, politicians and priests. Factory owners vamoosed, and the bourgeoisie who stuck around carefully disguised themselves as workers. Shops and cafés became collectives; progressive schools were established; women's rights and healthcare were seriously addressed for the first time in Spain; servile and ceremonial forms of speech were abolished; large buildings seized by workers were given rent-free to the poorest of the poor. There were no more private cars; even one-way signs were regarded as oppressive. Many workers were as naïve as they were idealistic, and they ignored the darker side of organized Anarchism, the *patrullas de control,* with its death lists and old scores to settle. Many who had volunteered to be *patrullas* left in disgust at the massacres of clergy, who were especially singled out for the Church's long-standing support of the propertied classes.

Typically, the CNT lost its hold on Barcelona in chaotic circumstances—Orwell, who was there, was hardly the only one who was confused. On 3 May 1937 Lluís Companys, at the time president of Catalunya only in name, but supported by the Communists, ordered a takeover of the telephone company from the CNT. The Anarchists rose one last time, supported reluctantly by the Trotskyist POUM, built barricades and won the streets, but true to their name they didn't follow through and take political control. It was suicide. In three days at least 1,500 people were killed in the bitter fighting, and no sooner had the Anarchists laid down their arms for the sake of the Republic than the Loyalist Army and the Communists started to round up members of the CNT and POUM; those who weren't shot often found themselves imprisoned in the same cells as Falangists. In the confusion at the end of the war, the Generalitat left enough incriminating documents behind for Franco's reprisal squads to have little trouble finishing them off.

Seven Obsessions

I: The Catalan Crapper

While attending mass one day in Barcelona in 1959, Luís de Galinsoga, the pro-Franco director of the city's leading newspaper, *La Vanguardia*, couldn't stand it any longer. He stood up in church and memorably shouted: '¡*Todos los catalanes sono un mierda!*' (All Catalans are shit!). Enough protests were raised, and enough people boycotted the paper, for Franco to sack the newspaperman personally. Barcelonans didn't have much to laugh about that year, but Galinsoga's fate must have evoked at least a few smiles. They probably weren't even as miffed as they let on. Just as Brussels has its Mannekin-Pis, Barcelona has a jolly fixation with Number Two.

It may be because the medieval city grew up between two torrents, the Cagallel and the Merdança, 'turd taker' and 'shit stream'. Both were buried centuries ago, under the Ramblas and the Rec Comtal, only to become scatological streams of consciousness. 'Every Barcelona street has its underground shadow, its indecent other self, just as every life casts a shadow of death...underground waterfalls are formed...of excrement from the petty bourgeoisie and the proletarian immigrant; fat from rare fillet steaks and from numberless chorizo sausages and red peppers,' writes Manuel Vázquez Montalban in *Barcelonas*. He goes on to suggest: 'Just as in the past pedagogues advised their students to complete their education by visiting the leper colonies and morgues from time to time, regular visits to today's sewers would act as a perfect counterbalance to the conceit of urban man.' You can actually do this at the Museu del Clavegueram and learn about the father of Barcelona's modern sewers, Pere Garcia Fària, an engineer who wrote about Anarchism and in 1922 published a book called *Spain's Primary Social Problem is its Sanitation*.

But older even than dreams of sewers is the *cagoner,* or Christmas crapper, a figurine with bare buttocks suspended over a lovingly carved pyramid of poo, an essential figure in any Barcelona Christmas crib since the 1500s, placed just downwind from the main event in the manger. Not even Christmas-crib-mad Italy has anything like a *cagoner*: pizzerias, plates of spaghetti, elephants, camels and Turks, yes; crappers, no. Catalunya squats alone. Ethno-psychoanalysts wonder: is the *cagoner* the fertility symbol of an obsessive anal retentive race? An expression of down-to-earth reality—the Messiah may have come, but the duodenum pushes on? The embodiment of Catalan opposition to central authority, even divine authority? Most *cagoners* wear traditional costume, with floppy red Catalan cap, but there are variations for collectors—Sherlock Holmes, policemen, movie stars and even nuns. All wear beatific smiles.

The value of a good crap is brought home to the young in another tradition, the *Tió*, or 'Uncle', Christmas log, which the children beat with sticks, shouting, *'Caga, Tió, caga!'* (Shit, Uncle, shit!) until Tió excretes sweets. On Epiphany, the Three Kings bring naughty children sugar-coated turds made of dried figs. Catalan nationalism used to be recalled each time a schoolchild went to the 'Felipe', a universal euphemism in honour of the detested Bourbon conqueror Felipe V. After all, as cookbook writer Josep Canill de Bosch wrote in *La Cuyna Catalana* (1907): 'Regular body functions make nations strong. Strong nations lead the pack, and eventually become masters of the world.'

II: The Four Bars

Not four drinking holes, but *les quatre barres* of the *Senyera*, the red and gold stripes of the Catalan flag which appear as often in Barcelona as Guinness signs do in Dublin (well, almost). The Catalans claim it pre-dates the flag of Denmark, which is supposed to be the oldest national flag in the world, and have a good story to explain its origins: the Count of Barcelona, Guifré el Pilós, or Wilfred the Hairy, was called up by the Frankish King Charles the Bald to aid him in fighting the Normans in *c.* 898, and Guifré arrived in the nick of time to turn the tide of the battle (the original tale had Guifré aiding Louis the Pious in his siege of Moorish Barcelona, although Louis was dead before Guifré was born; this is the historically corrected version, which is just as doubtful). But it really doesn't matter: the essential thing is that Guifré is mortally wounded in battle and, when the king, be he Bald or Pious, comes to visit the valiant warrior in his tent, Guifré confesses that his one regret is that he is dying without having earned a coat of arms to wear on his golden shield. The king responds by dipping his fingers in Guifré's blood and running them down the shield, and *les quatre barres* was born. Actually he dipped his thumb as well, and there were five stripes until Jaume I suppressed one so that the four could represent the provinces of Catalunya: Barcelona, Girona, Lleida and Tarragona.

III. Dragons

The bull—that passionate, earthy archetype of fertility and death—may be the totem beast of Iberia, but he has little place in Barcelona. One bullring has closed for lack of interest, and the other only holds sporadic *corridas* for the Andalucian diehards. No, the creature the Catalans hold to their hearts is more fiery, more dangerous and quirky. Ever since 1229, when Count-King Jaume I had a vision of St George (Jordi) lending a hand at the siege of Mallorca, the most chivalric of saints has been the patron of Catalunya, and his encounter with the dragon, which according to the old hagiographies happened in Syria, was in the Catalan mind transported to Montblanc near Tarragona. In 1285, Count-King Pere III climbed up the Catalans' sacred mountain, Canigou (now in the French Roussillon), and he found a dragon up there too.

The legend of Jordi and his dragon was seamlessly grafted on to Catalunya's favourite 9th-century dragon saga. It seems that the Moors, realising they couldn't defeat the counts of Barcelona, decided to play dirty and brought a baby dragon over from North Africa and set it loose. When it began to grow fat on the surrounding peasants and the boldest knights, the father of Guifré the Hairy had the Christian derring-do to slay it at last. It was skinned and displayed on feast days, the grandpappy of the dragons who come out to play during Barcelona's *festes*, who spew fireworks in the pandemonium of the *correfoc*, or fire-running.

Modern Barcelona is filled with dragons. A few are medieval, but the majority date only from the 19th century, when they made a big comeback in poetry and art. Puig i Cadafalch and Gaudí were obsessed with them; the latter's Casa Battló is a dragon masquerading as a house. The newest one is in the Plaça de l'Espanya Industrial, a benign creature who doubles as a slide for the local kids. Most of the others are on the small side, compared with Jordi's, not much bigger than dachshunds. Very few, in fact, pretend to be threatening. In 1456, the Generalitat made George's Day (23 April) the Festival of the Rose, the equivalent of Valentine's Day, when men would give their love a red rose, just as George gave his princess the rose that sprang from the dragon's blood. Rilke perhaps understood dragons best: 'All the dragons in our life could be princesses who hope to see beauty and courage in us. Things which terrify us are helpless and hope that we will help them.'

IV: The *Sardana*

As with so much that the Catalans do, they go about their national dance, the *sardana*, with a gravity that the rest of us reserve for getting our cars out of the pound. Especially the older people: watch them in front of the cathedral on Sunday at noon, or in the evening in Plaça de Sant Jaume when the *cobla* of musicians gather and play, all as serious as accountants. Their coats and bags are placed in a pile in the centre, hands are joined to form a ring, and everyone steps intricately to the right, then to the left—slowly or more vigorously, depending on the rhythm. The feeling that this is a communal rite is always there, an affirmation of Catalan identity and unity, of gracefully tapping Catalan feet gently awakening Catalan earth—it's all as far from the wild, pounding goblin of flamenco as you can get. The dance is harder than it looks but, if you want to give it a go, don't go off about: 'To dance the *sardana* imperfectly is to commit a sin against art; it is to insult Catalunya,' according to Aureli Capmany. Franco, needless to say, banned it.

The Catalans learned the *ballo sardo* during their unwelcome occupation of Sardinia and, as the Sards claim their circle dance is Neolithic, the *sardana*'s roots are very deep indeed. So what comes as a surprise, seeing the serious faces, is the music, which is nothing like the Sard or any other folk tune you've ever heard, but rather in the vein of spritely boulevard melodies; nearly all *sardane* were composed in the mid-19th century by one Pep Ventura. There's an occasional melancholy strain, but it never lasts long; sometimes the tempo picks up, and the younger circles work up a bit of a sweat.

V: The New Fish

In Barcelona, if you're not seeing a dragon or the *quatre barres*, you're probably looking at a submarine. On a recent trip we counted at least six: one outside the

Museu de la Ciència, one on the Moll d'Espanya, one in the Parc de les Aigües, another at 341 Avinguda Diagonal, and two inside the Museu Marítim.

One thing that long irked Barcelona's entrepreneurs was the dearth of home-grown Catalan gadgets: they knew how to sell stuff better than anyone in Spain, but had to resort to industrial espionage in Manchester to get their textile mills rolling, and they lacked the inventions that gave the Yankees such an edge in the business world. One hall in the 1888 Universal Exhibition was famously filled with Catalan ideas that never got off the ground; this was their last chance to catch someone's eye, and they failed. The great exception was the *Ictineo,* the 'new fish', built in 1859 by Monturiol to help the coral fisherman of Cadaques. It went down to a depth of 20m and survived 54 trips. Its success interested the military-minded, and an *Ictineo II* was built by private subscription, equipped with a 10cm canon that could fire underwater. It worked fine. In 1868 it was sold as scrap and forgotten.

VI: Eleven Men with One Ball Between Them

Barça…mes que un club ('More than just a club')

First there were a few bored Englishmen getting up a game on turnip fields on the outskirts of town. Then they formed clubs, as expats do: the Hispania Football Club and the Barcelona Football Club, or Barça, founded by English and Swiss residents. The Barcelonans were intrigued and began to play, too, encouraged by the news from the city's hygienists that football was good therapy for the ills caused by the Industrial Revolution. Hispania (now Espanyol) was supported mainly by pro-Hispanic residents of Barcelona (nicknamed the *periquitos*) but Barça became linked with Catalan nationalism. Immigrant workers were fairly impervious to the choral societies and the *Renaixença* of Catalan verse, but most of them adored football, and Barça became the prime vehicle for them to identify with the Catalan cause, to become *culés*, or arses, as fans are known—shades of the *cagoner* (*see* p.62).

Politics, as usual, was never far, and in times of trouble matches turned into mass political rallies. In the 1920s, after the *culés* had had the affront to laugh at a royal procession, Les Corts was closed by dictator Primo de Rivera. In 1936 the president of the club had the misfortune to be in Castile, where he was caught and executed by Franco. When Barcelona was occupied in 1939, Franco ordered that the club be purged—directly after it had been infiltrated by the Communists, Anarchists and Catalan Nationalists.

In spite of a Spanish Football Federation run by Falangists, Barça won five football cups in the early 1950s. They offered the best alternative to the invincible machine of Real Madrid, a club pumped full of money by the stodgy old dictator until it became the best in the world. Supporting Barça became an act of protest against the regime. It was the 'unarmed army' of the Catalans, forbidden even to speak their own language, and one of the few outlets available to express any kind of national unity. To this day, Barça remain incredibly popular, with more members scattered around the world than any other club. They performed the rare trick of winning three cups in Barcelona's great year of 1992, and they still rule, in spite of much discontent with the current manager and players.

VII: The Totality of Design

> ...in the 1980s Barcelona was also flooded with a peculiarly
> nitwitted and lighthearted mode of design, growing from a juncture
> among disco, comics, fashion, PoMo theory (or what passed for it),
> and Memphis mannerisms. This is the stuff with franchising clout
> and media appeal, and it ramps over the city like kudzu.
>
> *Barcelona*, Robert Hughes

If it ever occurred to God to ask Barcelona to update the Bible, the Gospel of John would start 'In the beginning there was the Design.' The idea of 'total design' was adopted from William Morris by the Modernistas—Gaudí designed everything down to the doorknobs of his buildings—and their contemporary heirs, with inborn Catalan flair and capitalism, leave nothing untouched. Birthday cakes are designed. Toilets are designed. Street cleaners wear designer uniforms emblazoned with designer Bs. In the 1980s the rage was designer bars, inspired by the latest science fiction films or post-industrial chic. The most famous one, the Torres d'Avila, by Javier Mariscal and Alfredo Arribas, has 'more design per square metre' than any bar anywhere, introducing a novel concept of design so oppressive that the atmosphere has been compared with a museum or even a morgue. Are Mariscal and Arribas the two tailors of the emperor's new clothes? Are the clients supposed to know that they know that they know? Enquiring minds don't give a monkey's toss.

If you are a popular designer you may be forgiven anything. Take Mariscal, for instance, whose career was nursed by design guru Fernando Amat of Vinçon. He began with comic strips, which led to the Torres d'Avila, which led to the Olympic mascot, a goofy non-referential dog-cat thing called Cobi; no one liked it, especially the nationalists, who had been hoping for a dragon. Fed up, Mariscal went back to his native Valencia and in an interview called Jordi Pujol a dwarf and said that Catalunya would be better off without the Catalans. Called to account by the Barcelonans, Mariscal squirmed in front of the cameras and the temperamental artiste was forgiven. Meanwhile, Cobi launched Mariscal on the international stage. His 'nitwitted and lighthearted' style has been linked to much that is trendy about Barcelona, and he has indeed spread like kudzu, even beyond the city; Mariscal has since been commissioned to design Italian furniture, a logo for the

Swedish Socialist Party, an aquatic park in Nagasaki and 'Twipsy', the mascot for Hannover's Expo 2000.

One suspects that what so many find appealing about Mariscal and lightheartedness in general is that serious these days is usually a flop. In many ways lightheartedness has been a commercial success. Barcelona has yet to engender a great playwright, yet the contemporary theatre scene is palpitating, and wows audiences around the world with its playful multimedia energy that crosses all language barriers. Enjoy it while it lasts.

The setting is so ripe that someone would have founded a city here soon or later. Barcelona occupies a plain between the rivers Besòs and Llobregat that gently descends to the sea, wrapped in an amphitheatre of mountains that shield it from the north winds. At the southern end of the port rises the city's oldest landmark, a smooth-humped mountain called **Montjuïc**, now Barcelona's pleasure dome, studded with museums and parks, and since 1992 crowned with the Olympic 'ring'. On the landward side, the highest peak in the Sierra de Collserola is **Tibidabo**, with its priceless views and amusements.

Old Barcelonans may have bewailed their eclipse during the days of Imperial Spain, but moderns may be thankful that their lack of prosperity has left intact the old quarters of the **Barri Gòtic** and **La Ribera**, containing one of the greatest concentrations of medieval architecture in Europe. The **Ramblas**, Barcelona's showcase promenade, divides the Barri Gòtic from **El Raval**, which despite determined clean-up moves remains the city's most piquant neighbourhood, with the remnants of the old red-light district, the **Barri Xinès**, co-existing with a new, vibrant art scene.

The enormous **Plaça de Catalunya**, the bustling heart of the city, is the big revolving door between the dense hive of the old city and the part of the map

Orientation

that looks as if it has been stamped by a waffle iron. The waffle is the **Eixample**, the 19th-century extension that coincided with the careers of the Modernista architects, whose brilliant buildings brighten the monotonous blocks. Beyond the Eixample, the city has digested the once independent towns of **Gràcia**, **Sarrià** and **Pedralbes** and spread as far up the hills as gravity permits.

Meanwhile, Barcelona has turned its attention to its long-neglected seafront: next to **Barceloneta**, a planned working-class neighbourhood from the 18th century, the **Port Vell** (old port) has been transformed into an urban play-ground, complete with aquarium and tremendously popular shopping mall, while on the other side of Barceloneta the **Vila Olímpica**, founded to house Olympic athletes, is sweating urban hormones to become a swank address.

Note on maps: *For convenience's sake, and to fit it on a map, Barcelona is inevitably treated as if the Mediterranean were south of the city rather than southeast. If you ever need to be reminded of the true compass points, Avinguda del Paral.lel and Avinguda de la Meridiana are the city's only true east–west and north–south streets: hence their proud names in an otherwise tilted, or, as some might say, permanently disorientated, town.*

Note on text: *The abbreviation C/ is used throughout for Carrer (meaning 'street').*

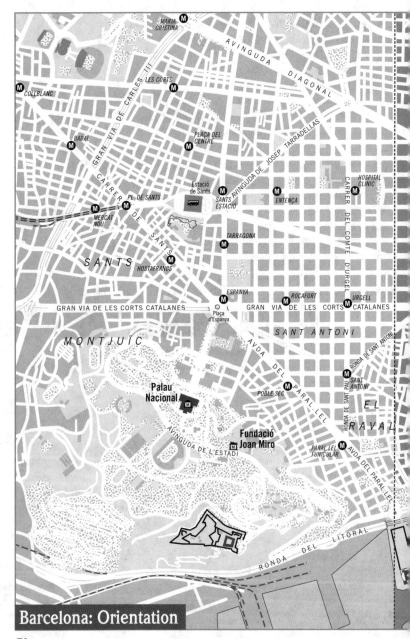

MARIA CRISTINA Ⓜ

AVINGUDA DIAGONAL

Ⓜ COLLBLANC

LES CORTS Ⓜ

GRAN VIA DE CARLES III

Ⓜ BADAL

PLAÇA DEL CENTRE Ⓜ

AVINGUDA DE JOSEP TARRADELLAS

CARRER DE SANTS

CARRER DEL COMTE D'URGELL

HOSPITAL CLINIC

Estació de Sants 🚌

Ⓜ SANTS ESTACIÓ

AVINGUDA DE ROMA

Ⓜ ENTENÇA

PL. DE SANTS Ⓜ

Ⓜ MERCAT NOU

SANTS

HOSTAFRANCS Ⓜ

TARRAGONA Ⓜ

ESPANYA Ⓜ

ROCAFORT Ⓜ

URGELL Ⓜ

MONTJUÏC

GRAN VIA DE LES CORTS CATALANES

Plaça d'Espanya

GRAN VIA DE LES CORTS CATALANES

SANT ANTONI

AVDA DEL PARAL·LEL

RONDA DE SANT ANTONI

Palau Nacional Ⓜ

POBLE SEC

RONDA DE SANT PAU

Ⓜ SANT ANTONI

EL RAVAL

Fundació Joan Miro Ⓜ

AVINGUDA DE L'ESTADI

PARAL·LEL FUNICULAR Ⓜ

AVDA DEL PARAL·LEL

RONDA DEL LITORAL

Barcelona: Orientation

70

Barcelona: Ten Essential Sights

1 **The Ramblas**: A colourful stage for the city's life since the 18th century. The Ramblas is every Catalan's choice for the Most Beautiful Street in the World; visitors are often willing to concede the point. *See* pp.73–82.

2 **The Sagrada Família**: Barcelona's symbol, and a building site with works in progress for well over a century now. Gaudí's unmistakable toffee towers loom 300ft over the city, but they're miniatures compared to what's in store for Barcelona as the most startling church in Christendom creeps towards completion in 2026. *See* pp.169–73.

3 **Palau Nacional**: The perfect aperitif to Barcelona's art feast. It's nothing less than the world's greatest collection of Romanesque painting, full of astonishing surrealist vigour. *See* pp.182–5.

4 **Museu Picasso**: A fantastic museum devoted to the artist, who spent his formative years in Barcelona. This biographical collection contains both his earliest and latest works, and a blow-by-blow account of his sparkling duel with a 17th-century master—Velázquez. *See* pp.113–15.

5 **Park Güell**: Antoni Gaudí's most delightful construction, and by any measure one of the seminal works of the 20th-century imagination. (Yet the visionary architect used to walk about his park separating couples who snuggled on his famous serpentine bench.) *See* pp.199–201.

6 **Fundació Joan Miró**: A superb collection in a lovely setting on Montjuïc. Joan Miró, the playful Catalan Puck, cast a spell of primary-coloured priapic glee over his native city. *See* pp.188–90.

7 **Santa Maria del Mar**: The finest monument to the city's remarkable career as a medieval mercantile metropolis. Catalan Gothic was Barcelona's first great adventure in architecture, and this is its epiphany. *See* pp.117–18.

8 **Passeig de Gràcia**: The glittering catwalk of Modernista architecture. Its 'Mansana de la Discòrdia' contains work by the three greats, Gaudí, Domènech and Puig. The grand finale is La Pedrera—Gaudí's work of sculpture masquerading as a building. *See* pp.156–62.

9 **Palau de la Música Catalana**: A theatre that has become the national holy-of-holies. Do Catalans come from another planet? Lluís Domènech i Montaner's masterpiece of Modernisme not only defies description but settles that question once and for all. *See* pp.108–11.

10 **Snowflake**: Once upon a time there was a city that became great, and prided itself on its own cleverness, never suspecting that it owed all its fortune to a lucky charm in the form of a camera-mugging albino gorilla. He's the only one in the world, and Barcelona belongs to Snowflake. *See* p.122.

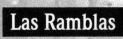

Las Ramblas

It's the first place everyone heads for, one of Europe's most truly urbane thoroughfares, the 'most beautiful street in the world', according to Lorca. It is also one of the busiest: day and night the Ramblas (there are actually five connected streets in a mile-long string) are crowded with natives and visitors from every continent. Kiosks sell newspapers in every conceivable language; cafés, hotels, burger stands and magically tacky souvenir stands have sprouted up along its length; the street's become a stage for Catalan Elvis impersonators, unicyclists, puppeteers, flamenco buskers and dozens and dozens of posing 'human statues'. If not the real Barcelona, the five Ramblas have a big share of Barcelona's extrovert soul.

Ramla means 'sand' in Arabic, and long ago this is what it was: a sandy gully of the river that drained the Collserola mountains, and eventually so many less pleasant effluents that it became known as the Cagallel, the turd-taker. In the 13th century, when Jaume I built the first set of medieval walls, they went up to the edge of the Cagallel and used it as a moat. In the dry season it became a thoroughfare, where butchers had their stalls, where employers came in search of day-labourers, and where the gallows bore their strange fruit. By 1366, what had become a clogged sewer was completely filled in and, at the end of the 18th century, trees were planted and benches installed; cast-iron streetlights, kiosks and flower stalls were added in the 19th century. In 1859 the first plane trees thrived to such an extent that Barcelonans say something 'grows like a tree in the Ramblas' when they mean it grows like weeds. For places to eat and drink along the Ramblas, *see* pp.227–8.

Rambla de Santa Monica

From the 15th to the 18th centuries this leafy, lowest section of the Ramblas lay under the pall of foundries. Catalan ironworking derring-do, so prominent in the work of the Modernistas, in fact has a long history. In 1463, Barcelona cast a colossal 35,420lb cannon named 'Santa Eulàlia', the biggest ever, but it blew into smithereens the first time it was fired. Emperor Carlos V in his endless wars showered so much business on the dozen foundries here that he called them his 'twelve apostles'.

Not so very long ago the Rambla de Santa Monica was more seedy than sooty, shared by sex shops and prowling prostitutes, but like the rest of the post-Olympic city it has been tidied up. At the weekend the entire length of this *rambla* is taken over by arts and crafts stands. The focal point of the big clean-up, the bleakly

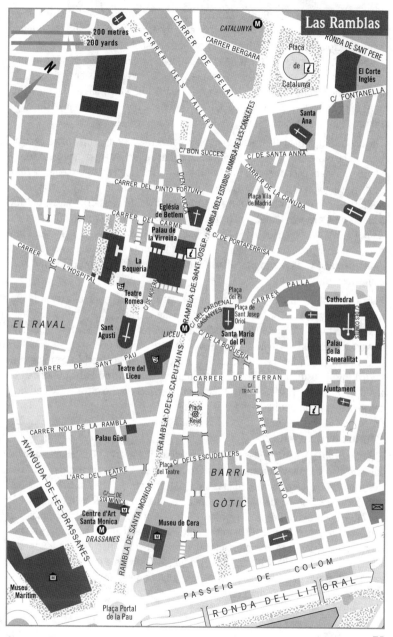

Las Ramblas

CARRER DE PELAI

CARRER BERGARA

CATALUNYA

Plaça de Catalunya

RONDA DE SANT PERE

El Corte Inglés

C/ FONTANELLA

200 metres
200 yards

CARRER DELS TALLERS

CARRER DE PELAI

Santa Ana

N

C/ BON SUCCES

C/ DE SANTA ANNA

CARRER DEL PINTO FORTUNY

C/ DEN XUCLA

RAMBLA DE LES CANALETES

CARRER DE LA CANUDA

Plaça Vila de Madrid

Església de Betlem

CARRER DEL CARME

Palau de la Virreina

RAMBLA DELS ESTUDIS RAMBLA DE SANT JOSEP

C/ DE PORTAFERRISSA

CARRER DE L'HOSPITAL

La Boqueria

Teatre Romea

CARRER DE PALLA

Plaça del Pi

Plaça de Sant Josep Oriol

C/ DEL CARDENAL CASANYES

CARRER

Cathedral

EL RAVAL

C/ DE MORERA

Sant Agustí

LICEU

Santa Maria del Pi

Palau de la Generalitat

C/ DE LA BOQUERIA

Teatre del Liceu

CARRER DE SANT PAU

CARRER DE FERRAN

C/ TRINITAT

Ajuntament

Plaça Reial

RAMBLA DELS CAPUTXINS

CARRER DE AVINYÓ

Palau Güell

CARRER NOU DE LA RAMBLA

L'ARC DEL TEATRE

Plaça del Teatre

C/ DELS ESCUDELLERS

BARRI

AVINGUDA DE LES DRASSANES

C/ DE STA MONICA

GÒTIC

Centre d'Art Santa Monica

DRASSANES

Museu de Cera

RAMBLA DE SANTA MONICA

Museu Marítim

PASSEIG DE COLOM

RONDA DEL LITORAL

Plaça Portal de la Pau

modern **Centre d'Art Santa Monica**, at No.7 (*open Mon–Fri 9.30–2 and 3.30–7.30, Sat 10–2; adm free*), was created by Albert Viaplana and Helio Piñón from the cloisters of the 17th-century monastery of Santa Monica, in an uneasy fusing of old and new; the soaring arches built to awe have been divided up into cramped cubes in order to create hanging space. The centre has been eclipsed by the sleek new contemporary art museum (*see* p.130), which has also scooped up most of the cash, but it can still pack a few surprises. Beneath it is one of the city's cultural information centres, with free entertainment guides and leaflets.

The brainchild of the city executioner, Nicomedes Méndez, is rather more popular. Noting the crowds that gathered to watch famous Anarchists meet the *garrotte vil*, Méndez, a quiet bachelor who lived with his pet rabbit, sought to prolong the thrill by displaying waxworks of its victims. The city vetoed this in a spirit of civic pride (although it found nothing wrong with other cities' famous criminals), but the **Museu de Cera** was under way (*open winter daily 10–1.30 and 4–7.30, summer daily 10–8; adm exp*). Housed in a bank building of 1867, at the end of a short passage, the original languid neoclassical statues now share the cornice with Superman and C3PO from *Star Wars*; within, Nixon, Franco and Pinocchio keep company with the British royal family.

Back out in the Rambla is a pretty fountain made of four graceful caryatids supporting a dome, one of twelve donated by the English philanthropist Richard Wallace to mark the 1888 Universal Exhibition. Only five Wallace fountains have survived; if they look familiar, you've been to Paris, another recipient of Wallace's largesse. Just up from the wax museum, at No.30, the old Hotel Falcon was converted into housing for Barcelona's new university, **Pompeu Fabra**, founded by the Generalitat in 1990 to bring higher learning back to the city centre and help rehabilitate the slum with fresh-faced students.

Rambla dels Caputxins

The next *rambla*, Rambla dels Caputxins, defines the heart of Barcelona's original theatre district, of which the recently refurbished **Teatre Principal** (1850s), designed by Francesc Daniel Molina, is the oldest survivor. This, in fact, is the heir of Barcelona's first wooden playhouse, built on this site in 1579 by the Hospital de la Santa Creu, after Felipe II granted it a monopoly on dramatic spectacles in Barcelona to raise revenue. Opposite, in the **Plaça del Teatre**, stands a charming monument of 1900 to Frederic Soler (known as Serafi Pitarra), 'the founder of Catalan theatre' (1839–95), who is seated nonchalantly on a giant marble 2, decorated with volutes and seaweedy forms. Just a block down from here, at 8 C/ dels Escudellers, the **Grill Room** (1902) has retained much of its delicate Modernista decor inside and out.

Just a few steps off the Rambla to the left, at 3 C/ Nou de la Rambla, is Gaudí's Modernista masterpiece, **Palau Güell** (*see* p.136), while another slight detour, on C/ de Colom to the right, leads into the arcaded oasis of the **Plaça Reial**, Barcelona's only square designed as a set piece and the only one 'twinned', with Plaza Garibaldi in Mexico City. It replaces a Capuchin convent that had the dubious distinction of being the first to be burned in the first church-burning uprising of 1835. This was sparked by a disappointing bullfight held to celebrate Queen Isabel II's birthday. The angry crowd dragged the last dying bull to the Capuchin convent, where orators whipped them into a frenzy with tales of wicked plots by Carlists and priests. When the rubble was cleared away, the land was auctioned off, and Francesc Daniel Molina won the competition to design a square, taking advantage of the new space in the chaotic jam-packed city. He enclosed it in harmonious neoclassical residences with shops and cafés on the ground floor, on the model of Madrid's Plaza Mayor, decorated with terracotta reliefs of busts of great navigators and discoverers of America. After hitting rock bottom as an outdoor parlour for muggers, addicts and prostitutes, Plaça Reial was given a face lift in the early 1980s, when its tall palms were planted. Yet even in its most desperately grotty era the square hosted a Sunday-morning stamp and coin market, as it does to this day; among the merry hordes who descend on Barcelona there is still a minority of philatelist tourists, and this is their Sagrada Família.

The palms chaperone the late 19th-century iron **Font de les Tres Gràcies** splashing in the centre and two flamboyant Modernista **lamp-posts**. These are Gaudí's earliest (1878) known works, designed in his student days and covered with emblems of Hermes, the god of commerce. The square still has a slightly raffish edginess; street musicians, tourists, eccentrics (including a man on the bicycle with a sidecar for his dog), narrow-eyed chancers and wide-eyed backpackers from the *pensions* all gather on the café terraces to watch the world go by. New benches designed by Oriol Bohigas, Barcelona's grand poobah of urban design, allow space for only one bottom each. In the northeastern corner, the Café-Restaurant Taxidermist was until recently filled with stuffed animals instead of stuffed tourists; Dalí, who once ordered 200,000 ants and a rhinoceros, was one of the shop's best customers. One shop that has survived intact is just a step away in Carrer del Vidrea: the antiquated **Herborista del Rei**, founded in 1823 and still selling teas and soaps under the watchful eye of a bust of Linnaeus.

Back on the Ramblas there is a pair of Barcelona's oldest hotels, the **Oriente** (converted in 1882 from a Franciscan college; the lobby is built around the cloister), where Hans Christian Anderson, Maria Callas and Errol Flynn checked in (and Antonioni filmed part of *The Reporter*); and the **Quatre Nacions**, which has Liszt, Einstein, Stendhal, Chopin and George Sand in its guestbook. The latter described the Ramblas of a schizophrenic Barcelona still squeezed inside its walls during the First Carlist War in 1833, when the Ciutadella was a fortress manned by what seemed like an army of occupation:

> *Beyond three lines of cannons, isolated from the rest of Spain by ban-*
> *dits and the civil war, Barcelona's carefree youngsters took the sun on*
> *the Rambla, a long avenue, bordered by trees and buildings like our*
> *own boulevards. Beautiful, amusing, coquettish women seemed con-*
> *cerned only with the folds in their linen and with wafting their fans.*
> *The men passed the time smoking and laughing, teasing the women,*
> *discussing the Italian opera without worrying, apparently, about what*
> *was happening on the other side of the walls. But once night had fallen,*
> *once the opera was over, the guitars were muted and the city's security*
> *entrusted to the night watchmen on their vigilant strolls, nothing could*
> *be heard above the noise of the sea except the sinister cries of the*
> *guards and the explosions, which, even more sinisterly, could be heard*
> *at uneven intervals from different places, short and sharp or contin-*
> *uous, sometimes near, sometimes far, always until the first light of*
> *dawn. Then everything was silent for one or two hours and the bour-*
> *geois seemed to sleep soundly while the port stirred and the sailors*
> *arose. If in the hours of recreation, someone dared to ask what those*
> *strange, frightful noises had been the night before the Barceloneses*
> *replied, smiling, that nobody was interested and that it was prudent not*
> *to try to find out.*

At the head of the Rambla dels Caputxins stands an institution that Barcelona is especially proud of: the **Gran Teatre del Liceu** (*open for visits 9.45am–11am, last admission 10.15; adm; information office Mon–Fri 2–8.30*), inaugurated in 1847 in place of a Trinitarian convent burned after the same inept bullfight in 1835. Ethical concerns were voiced about replacing a holy site with a secular frivolity, and the curse of the Trinitarians has brought it a string of disasters. Gutted by fire in 1861, it was rebuilt by Josep Oriol Mestres on an even grander scale, with 4,000 seats (second only to La Scala in Milan). As a symbol of the élite, it was the target of the most notorious of all the city's Anarchist attacks, on 7 November 1893, when during the second act of *William Tell* two bombs were hurled from the upper gallery into the orchestra—a bull's-eye strike on the bourgeoisie. The final toll was 22 dead and 50 wounded; in the chaos that followed, the perpetrator, Santiago Salvador, calmly stood by the front door and watched them carry out the bodies. Justice caught up with him in Zaragoza and he was executed the next year, singing the Anarchist anthem as the executioner tightened the garrotte. A century later, in 1994, the Liceu burned to the ground during last-minute work on the set for *Turandot*. A campaign to replace it began immediately and, by late 1999, the prima donnas were once again tickling the ears of Barcelona's opera mavens.

The new theatre is a clone of Oriol Mestres' much loved old building, as well as a vast improvement on what had become rickety and squeezed. Some of its former eccentricities have been surreptitiously ironed out: sightlines and acoustics are much improved, the stage area has been almost tripled and a computer system installed to handle all the stage machinery (including a very thick fire curtain). A new extension envelops a sleek rehearsal hall and foyer. The lobby has the opulent grandeur of yore and a wide marble staircase leading up to the dazzling Salon of Mirrors, the fashionable meeting place of late 19th-century society. Plump green and gold columns and glittering chandeliers are reflected endlessly in gilt-edged mirrors, while simpering muses and allegories of music scamper overhead amid florid musical slogans. The auditorium, one of the largest in Europe, is a great whirl of gilt and red velvet; the theatre's signature red velvet chairs reappear in the fantastical ceiling paintings, created by the brilliant Catalan artist Perejaume, forming ranks of undulating mountains fading into stormy skies.

When the Liceu was rebuilt, it necessitated the moving of Spain's oldest perfume shop, the **Perfumeria Prat**, founded in 1847 and now carefully reconstructed across the street at 68 Las Ramblas. Farther up, the **Pla Boqueria** (or Pla de l'Os), with its colourful ceramic mosaic by Miró (1976), marks the spot where the Cagallel met a stream coming down from Sarrià (now C/ de l'Hospital). The *pla*, or flat space, that the rivers formed became the medieval gate of Santa Eulàlia, where fairs and markets took place in the shadow of the gallows. The farmers and traders were replaced a century later by cardsharps and gamblers, and there are still a few around, hoodwinking the innocent with the shell game or three-card monte. Also here, at No.82, a bank occupies the most exotic building on the Ramblas, **Casa Bruno Quadros** (1896), a former umbrella-maker's, studded with bright Oriental parasols and defended by a swirling dragon holding a brolly, designed by Josep Vilaseca. Opposite, at No.77, is Enric Sagnier's tall, narrow **Casa Doctor Genové**, with its mosaic-framed clock (1911), and the lavish Modernista **Antiga Casa Figueras** (1902), selling luscious Escrivà cakes and chocolates. By now you'll probably have received a flyer for the **Museu Eròtica**, 96 bis Las Ramblas (*open daily 10am–midnight; adm; under-16s admitted only with an adult*), a private collection of rare and campy erotica from around the world (with a special Barcelona section, and a unique 'pleasure chair') in a seedy old-style Ramblas setting.

Rambla de Sant Josep

Pla Boqueria marks the beginning of the Rambla de Sant Josep, which has also been known as Rambla de las Flores ever since the first flower stalls sprang up during the

Corpus Christi celebrations in 1853. Once, the flower girls themselves were as much of an attraction as their wares: the Modernista painter Ramón Casas was surely not the first or last to have fallen in love with, and married, one. On the left, a large Modernista neo-Gothic arch beckons you into the lively Mercat de Sant Josep, better known as **La Boqueria** (*open Mon–Sat 8am–8.30pm*), founded on the ruins of the old monastery of Sant Josep. It had the first permanent stalls in the city, and was roofed over in 1914. It is still the place to find the greatest choice of food in Barcelona. Skip past the front stalls and delve into the interior, where prices haven't taken on tourist dimensions and the dizzying range of produce can be fully appreciated, from succulent palm roots and heavenly wild mushrooms (available year round from Llorenç Petras at stall 870, who sells nothing else) to glistening sea creatures from Jacques Cousteau's more bizarre films.

Just up from the market, the imposing neoclassical **Palau de la Virreina** was built in 1778 by the Viceroy Manuel Amat of Peru with the loot he skimmed off the fabulous silver mines of Potosí. The viceroy laid on the marriage of the century when he wed a young girl of Gràcia, but in 1782 he dropped dead, leaving everything to his 19-year-old widow, the Virreina Maria Francesca, who became a fixture of Barcelona society for the next 50 years. The city has converted the palace into an exhibition space and cultural information centre, with an excellent bookshop on the ground floor (*open Tues–Sat 10–8.30, Sun 10–2.30; call ahead © 93 301 77 75 to see the palace's Catalan **national coin collection**). Within the courtyard is a glassed-in display of a family of wood and papier-mâché giants, including that of Jaume I and his queen Violante of Hungary, the latest in a line of enormous characters who have appeared in Carnival, Corpus Christi processions and *festas* since at least 1320. There's an eagle and even a new *gegantona* called Laia, a 4th-century girl who 'represents the brave, caring spirit of Barcelona'.

Rambla dels Estudis and Rambla de les Canaletes

The next *rambla*, the Rambla dels Estudis, was named after L'Estudi General, the university that once stood here, founded by Martí the Humane and moved 100km to Cervera in 1714 by Barcelona's nemesis Felipe V; nowadays the promenade is full of the whistles and chirps of its permanent bird market. Monuments on this segment include the recently cleaned 18th-century Jesuit **Eglésia de Betlem**, with a fancy Churrigueresque portal, its once equally lavish Baroque interior incinerated in 1936. Next to it, the old Jesuit College was replaced in 1880 with the **Philippines Tobacco Company** (No.109), dressed with allegorical figures representing Commerce and Overseas Trade. This was run, like much else in Barcelona, by Eusebi Güell, and supplied most of Spain's cheap smokes.

Güell's father-in-law, the Marquis of Comillas, lived opposite in the arcaded 18th-century **Palau Moja**, now the Generalitat's department of culture. The marquis, with huge business interests in Cuba and the Philippines, was a Catalan robber baron of the first water, but he was also patron of Catalunya's greatest 19th-century poet, the priest Jacint Verdaguer, who after the success of his *L'Atlàntida* (1878) and *Canigó* (1885) spent much of his time in a private apartment here as family chaplain and distributer of alms. Verdaguer was a son of humble peasants, and all the acclaim he received as the 'Catalan Homer' had a dismal effect on him—he stopped writing altogether and fell into a guilt-ridden depression. He gave away the marquis' money so lavishly that there were daily queues at the palace's back door. Under the influence of a quack priest who convinced him that the down-and-out were infested with devils, he spent every spare moment performing exorcisms. He sold the rights of his literary estate for peanuts to a family of con artists who convinced him that their daughter was the mouthpiece for the Virgin Mary. Concerned about his erratic behaviour (and lack of new poems), the marquis intervened with the bishop, and Verdaguer was suspended from the priesthood, a crushing blow that led the poet to defend himself in the press, until the bishop relented and re-frocked him in 1898. When he died four years later, Barcelona showed it hadn't forgotten him: 10,000 mourners attended his funeral.

Farther up, on the left at No.115, the Royal Academy of Science and Art was founded in 1796. The ornate façade of 1883 bears Barcelona's **official clock**. The two small towers were used for meteorological and astronomical observations. The academy was converted into the **Teatre Poliorama** in 1910 and recently restored. George Orwell was positioned in one of its towers in 1937, during the bitter fighting between the CNT, POUM and the Communists; shot through the throat, he stayed with his wife in the nearby **Hotel Continental**, undergoing therapy and lying low while his POUM militia was being ruthlessly purged by the Communists.

The top little segment of the Ramblas, the **Rambla de les Canaletes**, is named after a magical **fountain** dispensed beneath a four-headed streetlight that promises that all who drink of it will stay or return to Barcelona. The water is supposed to be the purest in the city, and there are tales of Barcelonans who become very fond of visitors, going out of their way to make sure they drink from the Canaletes, or alternatively going to extraordinary lengths to make sure they don't get anywhere near the place. The fountain also functions as an informal debating platform or Speaker's Corner, especially for football supporters, and was one of the few such outlets under Franco; jubilant F. C. Barça fans still come here to celebrate after a victory.

Plaça de Catalunya

At the top of the Ramblas stretches the Plaça de Catalunya, once an open prairie beyond the walls and now a prairie corralled by big buildings. As squares go, it's up with blockbusters such as Piazza San Pietro in Rome, although Red Square in Moscow is larger by a sixth. There was always a longing to do something grand to this space, but disappointment with Cerdà's plan of the Eixample and procrastination killed it; in the meantime, huge private mansions went up in the middle and there were more delays as their owners were taken to court. Finally, the square, as designed by Francesc Nebot, was inaugurated in 1927. In the centre are two illuminated fountains and Subirachs' **monument to Francesc Macià**, Republican president of the Generalitat in 1931, a large upside-down stair on a pedestal which seems to be a curious way to remember a man affectionately known as 'Grandad'. This Piranesiesque hulk looks ready to crush the *Goddess,* an older, wistful sculpture by Josep Clará. In the same Noucentista mold is Pau Gargallo's stone *Shepherd Playing a Flute* and the rather dopey *Barcelona* by Frederic Marés, an allegory of industry (Mercury) and maritime trade (a woman on a horse holding a ship).

Although the planners and designers don't like it much, Plaça de Catalunya stubbornly remains the hub of human and pigeon life in Barcelona. Nearly all the city buses, metro and FGC lines converge here, and a fleet of department stores occupies the fringes: **El Corte Inglès**, a cross between a ferry boat and a radiator; the new, dull **Triangle shopping mall** (which is redeemed by a huge FNAC); and a spanking-new **Marks & Spencer**. Banks take up much of the remaining space. During the Civil War, the Banco Español de Crédito was the Hotel Colón and headquarters of the Socialist PSUC, draped with enormous portraits of Lenin, Marx and Stalin. When Franco's troops took the city in 1939 it was with a military parade that ended here. The offending portraits and all the other signs were stripped, and the square was renamed Plaza del Ejército, or Army Square. Thirty-eight years later, on 11 September 1977, it was the focus of the first official post-Franco Catalan National Day celebration, attended by an estimated 250,000 people, in one of the largest public demonstrations in Spanish history.

Barri Gòtic

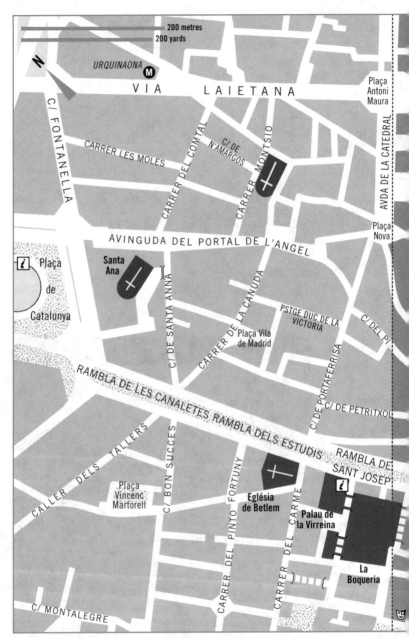

200 metres
200 yards

N

URQUINAONA M

V I A   L A I E T A N A

Plaça Antoni Maura

C/ FONTANELLA

CARRER LES MOLES

CARRER DEL COMTAL

C/ DE N'AMARGOS

CARRER MONTSIO

AVDA DE LA CATEDRAL

Plaça Nova

AVINGUDA DEL PORTAL DE L'ANGEL

Santa Ana

Plaça de Catalunya

C/ DE SANTA ANNA

CARRER DE LA CANUDA

Plaça Vila de Madrid

PSTGE DUC DE LA VICTORIA

C/ DEL PI

C/ DE PORTAFERRISA

RAMBLA DE LES CANALETES RAMBLA DELS ESTUDIS

C/ DE PETRITXOL

RAMBLA DE SANT JOSEP

CALLER DELS TALLERS

C/ BON SUCCES

CARRER DEL PINTO FORTUNY

Plaça Vincenç Martorell

Església de Betlem

CARRER DEL CARME

Palau de la Virreina

La Boqueria

C/ MONTALEGRE

84

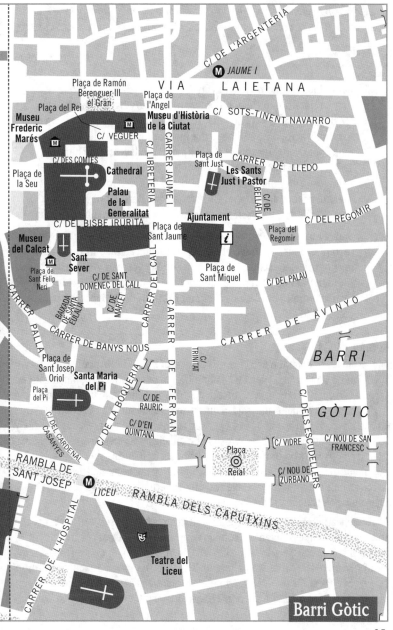

C/ DE L'ARGENTERIA

Ⓜ JAUME I

V I A   L A I E T A N A

Plaça de Ramón
Berenguer III
el Gran

Plaça de
l'Angel

C/ SOTS-TINENT NAVARRO

Plaça del Rei

Museu
Frederic
Marés

Ⓜ

Museu d'Història
de la Ciutat

C/ VEGUER

C/ DES COMTES

Plaça de
la Seu

Cathedral

Palau
de la
Generalitat

Plaça de
Sant Just

CARRER   DE   LLEDO

Les Sants
Just i Pastor

C/ DE BELLAFIA

C/ DEL REGOMIR

Ajuntament

C/ DEL BISBE IRURITA

Plaça de
Sant Jaume

ⓘ

Plaça del
Regomir

Museu
del Calcat

Ⓜ

Sant
Sever

Plaça de
Sant Felip
Neri

C/ DE SANT
DOMENEC DEL CALL

Plaça de
Sant Miquel

C/ DEL PALAU

C/ DE MARLET

BAIXADA DE SANTA EULALIA

CARRER DE BANYS NOUS

CARRER   DE   AVINYO

C A R R E R   D E   A V I N Y O

Plaça de
Sant Josep
Oriol

Santa Maria
del Pi

Plaça
del Pi

C/ DE LA BOQUERIA

C/ DE FERRAN

C/ DE
RAURIC

C/ D'EN
QUINTANA

C/ VIDRE

C/ NOU DE SAN
FRANCESC

Plaça
Reial

C/ NOU DE
ZURBANO

C/ DELS ESCUDELLERS

B A R R I

G Ò T I C

C/ DEL CARDENAL
CASANYES

RAMBLA DE
SANT JOSEP

Ⓜ LICEU

RAMBLA DELS CAPUTXINS

CARRER   DE   L'HOSPITAL

Teatre del
Liceu

Barri Gòtic

85

> *Barcelona is the only city in the world whose centre looks like this.*
> *It is the only city in the world which was powerful in the fourteenth*
> *century and not afterwards.*

Colm Tóibín

If you look on the map, you can see it at once: the 'egg yolk' of Roman Barcino, in the loop between the curving C/ Banys Nous, C/ d'Avinyó and Vía Laietana. Its gentle hill of Mons Tàber was Barcino's acropolis, and here the institutions of medieval Barcelona took root over the ruins of their Roman predecessors. Then in the 1870s, when the city gravitated out into the Eixample, it left behind a time capsule, the heart of the most extensive Gothic neighbourhood in Europe. Christened the Barri Gòtic in the 1920s, Barcelona's egg yolk remains remarkably intact and sunnyside up.

Sunday morning is an ideal time to visit the Barri Gòtic. If it's the second or fourth Sunday of the month, you can take in the guided tour of the Generalitat, but on any Sunday you can visit the Ajuntament and watch the Barcelonans dance the *sardana* in front of the cathedral. For places to eat and drink in the neighbourhood, *see* pp.228–30.

Roman Walls

The ideal way to enter the Barri Gòtic is by way of **Plaça de l'Àngel**, at the corner of C/ Jaume I and Vía Laietana (Ⓜ Jaume I). Just outside the city's main gate, or Portal Major, it was originally the Plaça del Blat, or 'wheat square', where all the city's grain was bought and sold. During the 9th-century translation of Santa Eulàlia's relics from Santa Maria del Mar to the cathedral, the body suddenly became too heavy to carry here, whereupon an angel appeared and pointed accusingly at an official, who confessed that he had pocketed Eulàlia's toe. He replaced it and the procession continued. An obelisk topped by the accusing angel, erected in 1616, stood here until the anti-clerical city government of 1823 toppled it; the angel now points from a niche in the façade of No.2.

The streets around Plaça de l'Àngel have Barcino's best-preserved **Roman walls and towers**, some as high as 46ft, making cameo appearances in a mesh of medieval building, especially along C/ Sots-tinent Navarro; one tower was discovered only in 1968. More walls, just up Vía Laietana in the **Plaça de Ramón Berenguer III el Gran**, overlook Josep Llimona's equestrian statue of the count who married Barcelona to Aragón in 1137 and brought the city a royal crown.

The Home of the Count-Kings: Plaça del Rei

From Plaça de l'Àngel, take C/ Llibreteria, the old Roman road into the city. Along it stands the city's oldest shop, the **Subirà Cereria**, founded in 1761 and moved here in 1847 with the building of Vía Laietana; its gilded woodwork, plaster torch bearers and frescoes make it a unique place to buy a candle. Turn right here, at C/ del Verguer, into little **Plaça del Rei**. This handsome ensemble was originally the courtyard of the Romanesque-Gothic **Palau Reial Major**, a palace begun in the 10th century for the counts of Barcelona and expanded when they became the kings of Aragón. The square would make a perfect setting for an opera—and is often used for summer performances—but at least once its picturesque fan of steps saw real drama, when Fernando the Catholic (never a favourite in Barcelona, after he wed Isabel and subjected Aragón's interests to Castile) narrowly escaped having his throat cut by a disgruntled peasant. Like most squares in Barcelona, it has a new work of art: Eduard Chillada's bronze ***Topos*** (1985). It looks like a giant safe.

Museu d'Història de la Ciutat

> *Open Oct–June Tues–Sat 10–2 and 4–8, Sun and hols 10–2; July–Sept Tues–Sat 10–8, Sun and hols 10–2; closed Mon; adm includes 30min virtual-reality tour in English.*

On the edge of the square you'll find the entrance to the Museu d'Història de la Ciutat. This is in a 15th-century Gothic merchant's palace, painstakingly moved to Plaça del Rei in 1931 from C/ de Mercaders to make way for the new Vía Laietana. While digging its foundations, workers uncovered a surprise: houses of Roman and Visigothic Barcino, stretching beneath the modern C/ de los Comtes, complete with a 4th-century baptistery directly under the cathedral. These layers of the ancient city —the largest underground excavations of any ancient city in Europe— have remained remarkably intact; it is possible to tread the ramparts in the footsteps of Roman sentries, and look down on roads marked by wheel ruts gouged out two millennia ago. Traces of indigo dye still stain the stone vats of the laundry and dying workshops, which fell into disuse and later were incorporated into the baths, equipped with a gymnasium and massage rooms. Further evidence that Barcelona was born industrious awaits in the tidy and still faintly pungent remnants of the factory where salted fish and *garum* (fish sauce) were prepared for export. Circular fermentation vats are pocked with the grape skins and pips of Laitania, a simple, cheap wine popular in the 1st century BC, when the average Gaius knocked back around three-quarters of a litre a day. The distinctive amphorae that Laitania was shipped in have been found as far away as England.

In the 4th century, when Christianity became the religion of the empire, a prestigious Roman family donated their property for the city's first Christian basilica and episcopal palace; note the pretty floor mosaic from their house that survived in the church. For these early Christians, baptism required complete immersion; the remains of the deep 4th–8th-century font are topped by the words '*Iubet Renuntiare Inimicum Dominus*', chanted to renounce the devil during the rite. When the Visigoths established their court in Barcino before relocating to Toledo, relations with the families of Roman descent remained cordial as everyone went about the real business of making money. After the Visigoths converted, Ugnes, the bishop, presided over the Council of Barcelona in 599. In order to host it, the episcopal palace was given a facelift, and a secret hollow for storing relics was hidden in the altar. Even back then one's fellow Christians were not entirely to be trusted.

Other exhibits in the museum proper include models, diagrams and photos, such as the 14th-century *Llibre Verd*, the book of Barcelona's privileges, and two crude 16th-century wooden statues of the hirsute Fray Garí and the baby who identified him, in the arms of his nurse (*see* p.104). A flight of steps, flanked by busts of unknown Romans who now resemble prize fighters with their chipped or missing noses, leads up into the Palau Reial itself. This was renovated in the 14th century, when the magnificent **Saló de Tinell** was added (*may be closed when an exhibition is being mounted*). Begun in 1359 by Guillem Carbonell, architect to Pere the Ceremonious (who insisted on a number of astrological calculations before laying the first stone), its six huge rainbow arches cross a span of 56ft, with wooden beams filling in the ceiling between; viewed from the corner of the hall, the arches appear to magically radiate from a single point. In the antechamber, a detached fresco shows a procession led by a king and bishop (*c.* 1300). Banquets, funerals and even parliaments were held in the Saló de Tinell; in 1493 Fernando and Isabel received Columbus here after his first voyage, and later the Inquisition held its trials here, so dreaded that the stones in the walls were said to move if a suspect told a lie. After 1714, the room was baroqued over as a church for Clarisse nuns who had been displaced by the Ciutadella, and everyone presumed the original Saló de Tinell was lost for ever, until someone dug under the plaster in 1934 and *voilà*.

The hall is linked to the apse of the lofty and narrow **Capella Palatina de Santa Àgueda**. Begun in 1302 by Jaume II and his queen Blanche of Anjou, the chapel was re-dedicated to St Agatha by Papal Bull in 1601, thanks to a precious relic: the stone where the breasts of St Agatha were laid after Roman soldiers snipped them off in Catania, Sicily. The chapel's glory is the golden, lavish *Retablo del Condestable* (1466), the masterpiece of Jaume Huguet. The vestry holds an enormous bell-tower clock, made in 1575 and the largest of its kind in the world; after keeping the Barcelonans on time for three centuries, it was restored in 1986 and can be visited by request.

A narrow, almost hidden, staircase leads out to the curious skyscraper which rises over the square—five storeys of galleries built by Antoni Carbonell in 1557 and anachronistically named the **Mirador del Rei Martí** after the popular humane king, to hide the unpleasant truth that it was really a spy tower for the hated viceroy, or Lloctinent, a position set up by Fernando the Catholic; it bears an uncanny resemblance to Mussolini's skyscraper in EUR just outside Rome. The last building in Plaça del Rei, to the left of the royal palace, is the **Palau del Lloctinent**, also by Carbonell. This once held the Archives of the Crown of Aragón, one of the world's greatest collections of medieval documents, dating back to 844, but these were moved in 1994 and the building is now closed. Walk outside Plaça del Rei to C/ de les Comtes to peek into the fine courtyard with a magnificent coffered ceiling over the stair.

Museu Frederic Marés

Open Tues–Sat 10–5, Sun and hols 10–2, closed Mon; adm.

Nearby, in Plaça Sant Iu, is the Museu Frederic Marés, occupying the part of the royal palace that King Fernando gave to another of his popular gifts to Barcelona, the Inquisition. It later became the Reial Audiència, or Royal Law Courts, and then a convent for the Clarisse. Incredibly, as big as it is, it contains only a fraction of the collections of the sublime and ridiculous amassed by sculptor and hoarder extraordinaire Frederic Marés (1893–1991). On the ground floor, armies of tiny Iberian ex-votos, each figure touchingly distinct, are followed by the largest collection of sculpture in all Spain: an astonishing array of 12th–14th-century polychrome wood sculptures of sweet-faced Virgins and room after dizzying room of stylized crucifixes that seem to erupt from the walls simultaneously in a Daliesque nightmare. The goriness continues on the first floor, with flayed and bleeding medieval saints punctured with arrows (and one of the best pieces, a 12th-century relief of the *Vocation of St Peter*), and then on to the 19th century, when the Baby Jesuses have real hair and dolly faces, all intermingled with Spanish masterpieces, a famous collection of Catalan iron, Montserrat memorabilia and colourful plaques of the Dance of Death, showing the Grim Reaper reeling with ladies, monks and peasants.

Your brain will reel if you venture upstairs, into the 16 rooms of Marés' 'Museu Sentimental' swollen with scissors, fans, giant cigars, little lead Moorish and Christian soldiers and every kind of 19th-century flotsam and jetsam from sea shells to door knobs. On the top floor, the Entertainment Room, despite its enticing title, holds dolls and early bicycles. Marés' study has been left just as he liked it, although now it too is crammed with his sentimental sculpture. In the cool, vaulted courtyard by the entrance, orange trees fill the air with scent in spring, next to a charming outdoor café, perfect for dizzy museum victims.

The Cathedral: La Seu

Open daily 8–1.30 and 4–7.30.

Opposite the Museu Marés in C/ de los Comtes is the side door to Barcelona's huge Gothic cathedral, La Seu, the third church to stand on the site. The 4th-century original visible in the Museu d'Història de la Ciutat was flattened in Al-Mansur's raid in 985; of the second, a Romanesque church built from 1046 to 1058 by Ramón Berenguer I, only a doorway remains. The current model was begun in 1298 by Jaume II, and, rather unusually, the first thing that went up was the right transept and this **portal of Sant Iu** (St Ives); the carvings up on the left show St George and Barcelona's first count, Wilfred the Hairy, fighting a dragon and griffon, respectively. Originally a bridge over the street here allowed the count-kings to go to mass without rubbing elbows with their subjects.

The **façade** of the cathedral provides a fine backdrop to the *sardanes* danced here at noon on Sunday (*see* p.65), even if it doesn't look quite right for such a venerable church—perhaps because it was only begun in 1882, by Josep Oriol Mestres with funds provided by banker Manuel Girona. Mestres followed the plans of 1408 by French master Charles Galtés, or Carlí in Barcelona. Although it has little to do with the Catalan style, it's not as bad as some of the 19th-century façades pasted on other Gothic cathedrals (Florence, say), but it nearly got something completely different: during a moment of power in 1820, anticlerical Liberals proposed engraving the blank wall with the Catalan Constitution and Civil Code.

Inside, La Seu is Catalan Gothic at its most lavish and grandiose. It has only three aisles, but the architects made it look like five. One of the very few churches in Barcelona to escape the Anarchist firebugs (thanks to armed guards from the Generalitat), the interior is rich and atmospheric, a dazzling accumulative effect of a thousand details. The first chapel on the right, the star-vaulted **sala capitular**, contains the lucky crucifix borne by Don Juan on the mast of his flagship at the Battle of Lepanto in 1571; the S-shaped twist in Christ's body came about, they say, from dodging a Turkish cannon-ball. Underneath lies Pere Sanglada's effigy of St Olegario (d. 1137), Bishop of Barcelona and advisor to the counts; his body lies below like Sleeping Beauty, in remarkably good nick after 860 years. The **baptistery**, to the left of the door, has a plaque that records the baptism here of the first six native Americans, brought over by Columbus, in 1493; its beautiful stained-glass scene of the *Noli me Tangere* is based on drawings by Bartolomé Bermejo.

The **choir** is enclosed in the middle of the nave, behind a beautiful Renaissance screen by Bartolomé Ordóñez (*open Mon–Sat 9.30–12.30 and 2.30–4; adm, the ticket also includes the lift to the roof*). The richly sculpted stalls of the 14th to 15th century were given fancy canopies and painted in 1514 with the arms of the

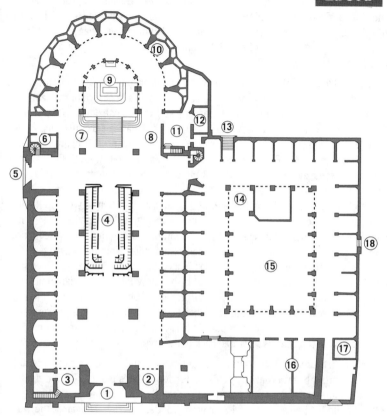

1 Main entrance
2 Sala capitular
3 Baptistry
4 Choir
5 Portal of Sant Iu
6 Lift to the roof
7 Crypt of Santa Eulàlia
8 Tomb of Ramón Berenguer
9 Presbytery
10 Chapel of Sant Joan Baptista i Sant Josep
11 Sacristy
12 Treasure
13 Portal of La Pietat
14 Fountain of Sant Jordi
15 Cloister
16 Cathedral museum
17 Chapter archives
18 Portal of Santa Eulàlia

kings of France, Portugal, Poland, Hungary, Denmark and England, when Carlos V summoned them as Knights of the Golden Fleece to Barcelona, a proto-session of the United Nations before all were plunged into war; you can see Henry VIII's seat directly on the emperor's right, facing the altar. Hunting and other profane scenes decorated the lower parts of the stalls, and the fanciest carving of all, by Pere Sanglada, is on the **pulpit** (1403).

The choir faces the elegant, daringly low-vaulted **crypt** with an enormous key-stone, designed by the Mallorcan Jaume Fabre, who was in charge of the cathedral works from 1317 to 1339. It holds the relics of the co-patroness of Barcelona, Santa Eulàlia, who lies in a beautiful 14th-century alabaster **sarcophagus**, attrib-uted to Pisan sculptor Lupo de Francesco, a follower of Giovanni Pisano. Hagiographers suspect Eulàlia is the same as Merida's more famous St Eulàlia, who died at the same age in the same year (303), but Barcelona vehemently denies it as mere coincidence. The story goes that Eulàlia, the Christian daughter of a mer-chant of Sarrià, threw dirt on the altar of Augustus and refused to worship Rome's gods, and the scenes on the tomb show the 13 grisly trials designed to change her mind, including being thrown naked into a vat of starving fleas and a seduction attempt by the handsome son of the Roman commander. Nothing swayed her, and her martyrdom ended when her torturers lopped off her breasts and crucified her. Thirteen, her age when all this happened, is somehow Eulàlia's special number: to gain her special protection at sea, a mariner was obliged to visit her tomb 13 Fridays in a row. The rest of the crypt has been curiously arranged to resemble theatre boxes—you almost expect poor Eulàlia to get up and perform. Her original 9th-century sarcophagus is set in the back of the crypt.

After the virtuoso crypt, the **altar** is an anticlimax, supported on two Visigothic capitals, with a bland bronze Crucifix by Frederic Marés behind. To the right of this, the founders of the Romanesque cathedral, Ramón Berenguer I and his wife Almodis, lie in the painted velvet-covered wooden sarcophagi against the wall. The door here leads into the sacristy and the **treasury** tucked behind (*not always open*); holding pride of place here is a late 14th-century gold and silver gem-encrusted monstrance, in the form of the throne of Martí I, with a tower and royal crowns, along with a silver-plated processional cross by Francesc Villardel, of 1383.

Of the chapels radiating from the **ambulatory**, the fourth one on the right, dedi-cated to Sant Joan Baptista i Sant Josep has the best art: the recently restored and minutely detailed altarpiece of the *Transfiguration* by Bernat Martorell (1450). On the far left side of the ambulatory you'll find the lift to the **roof**, with grand views over Barcelona.

The Moor Under the Organ

Until recently, there was a Moor's head called the *carcassa* under the cathedral's ornate 16th-century organ. The story goes that it represented the head of Ali Baba, the defeated admiral at Lepanto, and on feast days it vomited forth sweets for the children. It may also have been a reminder of the Templars, who were a major force in medieval Catalunya. Count Ramón Berenguer IV the Great joined the Templars in 1131 in response to an emissary sent by the founder of the order, Hugues de Paynes (Hug de Pinós, himself probably a Catalan), whose shield bore three Moors' heads, symbolic of knowledge and understanding—hence the Baphomet, the brass head the Templars were accused of worshipping. The Moor's head later pops up throughout the Mediterranean in places claimed by the Catalans, notably the islands of Mallorca, Corsica and Sardinia. The Templars counselled and trained the kings of Aragón (Jaume I the Conqueror was their star pupil), until Jaume II, builder of this cathedral, banned the order at the end of the 13th century, not long before the pope dissolved it on charges of heresy.

What people tend to remember most fondly about the cathedral is the charming green oasis of the **cloister**, begun in 1385 (but currently half-hidden by scaffolding). Its iron-grilled chapels were once dedicated to the patron saints of Barcelona's guilds ('Our Lady of Electricity' is still going strong) and many leading guild masters are buried in the floor; the capitals are covered with intricate carvings although they're hard to make out. A pretty pavilion holds the **Fountain of Sant Jordi**, with a figure of St George rising from a mossy green blob. At Corpus Christi—until the 19th century, the biggest holiday in Barcelona, when guilds competed to make the most elaborate or alarming floats—flowers are wound around the fountain and a hollow egg is set to dance in the jet of water (*l'ou com balla*). Nor does anyone have to look far for an egg, because 13 white geese natter away next to the fountain, with their little houses and pond. They have been there since anyone can remember, symbols of Santa Eulàlia's virginity or a memory of the geese that saved Rome, or (most likely) just because. Also note the **Romanesque doorway** that leads back into the church, the only surviving bit of Ramón Berenguer I's cathedral, cobbled together of ancient Roman stones and capitals.

One chapel in the cloister houses the **Cathedral Museum** (*open daily 10–1; adm*), with retables and reliquaries retired from duty, starring a *Pietà* (1490) by Bartolomé Bermejo, his masterpiece and one of the first oil paintings in Spain; a beautiful altarpiece by Jaume Huguet, painted for the guild of the Esparto workers; and the organ cabinet door paintings (1560) by a Greek painter, Pere Serafí, whose nickname was 'Peter of the Seven Ps' for his Peter Piper slogan '*Pere Pau pinta portes per poc preu'* ('Peter Pau paints doors for bargain prices').

Around the Cathedral

More art, this time garnered from the diocese, has been pensioned off to the left of the cathedral in the **Pia Almoina**, headquarters of one of Europe's oldest charitable foundations, founded in 1009. The current building, incorporating part of a Roman tower and its prophylactic head of Medusa, dates from 1423 and has recently been restored to house the excellent but often overlooked **Museu Diocesà** (*open Tues–Sat 10–1.30 and 5–8, Sun 11–2, closed Mon; adm*). Among the treasures are the striking Sienese-inspired *Taula de Sant Jaume*, by Arnau and Ferrer Bassa; a beautiful letter from the royal bureaucrat Felipe II, in Latin; a reliquary of Sant Cugat (1312); a tormented *Crucifixion* from the 13th century; and Romanesque frescoes of the *Apocalypse* from the apse of Sant Salvador de Polinyà (1122), a precursor of Picasso's *Guernica* and a preview of the treasures in the Palau Nacional. The *Custodia de Santa Maria del Pi* (1587) by Llàtzer de la Castanya is a masterpiece of the goldsmith's art, and there are retables by Bernat Martorell and the Portuguese Pere Nunyes. There's a startling 15th-century anonymous retable of *Sant Bartolomeo*, a candidate for the goriest in Barcelona (although it has plenty of competition), in which the saint, peeled of his skin, goes right on talking until his indignant persecutors lop off his head. Upstairs are alabaster virgins, including one by Pere Joan, and Gil de Medina's huge *St Christopher* (1545).

On Thursdays, a flea market takes place in front of the cathedral in **Plaça Nova**, which also hosts the Christmas market, where discriminating shoppers can find the finest array of *cagoners* (*see* p.62). Plaça Nova's **Collegi d'Arquitectes** (1962) is a poor ad for the architectural trade, but its otherwise dreary façade is decorated by a sketchy frieze of popular celebrations (including the giants who feature in so many Barcelonese festivals) by Picasso—he sent the designs from France for his only piece of public art in Barcelona. Opposite, heading back into the Barri Gòtic, are two Roman towers, renovated in the 12th century, that guarded Barcelona's northeastern gate. The niche in the left-hand one held a statue of Sant Roch, to ward away plague. In front of this, an arch of the Roman aqueduct was reconstructed in 1958. Huge iron letters spilt across the concrete, erected by the poet Joan Brossa in 1994 when the square was given its last makeover, spell out 'Barcino'.

Walk up between the towers, and to your left is the 12th- to 14th-century **Casa de l'Ardiaca** (of the Archdeacon), now home to the city's most important archive of newspapers and magazines, going back to 1792 when the city's first paper, the

Diari de Barcelona, was founded. In 1902, when the Casa de l'Ardiaca was owned by the lawyers' college, Domènech i Montaner was called upon to install a postal slot. Domènech refused to damage the ancient door, but built a Modernista slot on the side that expressed his opinion of lawyers with a swallow and a tortoise—the swallows, he explained, with wings to soar into the realms of truth, the tortoise plodding along at the pace of court procedures. He also created a charming tiled courtyard draped in wisteria, with its lofty palm and pretty Gothic fountain, which is also put into service for Corpus Christi Day egg-dancing. Opposite is the Romanesque **Capella de Santa Llúcia** (1268), founded by Bishop Arnau de Gurb, whose tomb is within; Lucy's feast day, 13 December, is the official opening of the Christmas market. Long straight C/ del Bisbe Irurita separates the Casa de l'Ardiaca from the medieval **Palau Episcopal**, the bishops' palace, built on the Roman wall. Although it's off limits, you can look into the elegant Romanesque courtyard with its pretty arcade, another work of Bishop Gurb.

Plaça de Sant Felip Neri

The lane next to the episcopal palace, C/ Montjuïc del Bisbe, leads back to one of the Barri Gòtic's prettiest squares, the nearly enclosed **Plaça de Sant Felip Neri**, its melancholy perhaps derived from its former role as burial ground of the executed, whether prisoners or heroes. Its components are simple: one fountain, two trees and a church of **Sant Felip Neri** (1751), with a severe façade and a big Baroque altar inside. During the Civil War a bomb went off here (you can still see scars on the church), and in the 1940s, when the square was rebuilt, two handsome but excessive buildings that the city didn't know what else to do with were relocated here: the Renaissance **Casas del Gremi de Calderers**, once headquarters of the coppersmith guild, and the **Casa del Gremi dels Sabaters**, the shoemakers' guild, under the sign of their patron St Mark. This now contains the little **Museu del Calçat** (*open Tues–Sun 11–2, closed Mon; adm*), a delightful journey into the history of shoes, from repros of Roman sandals to 17th-century toe pinchers and a precious, dainty hand-painted silk slipper. There are celebrity shoes, owned by famous Catalans (Pau Casals and Everest-climber Carles Valles); a shoe 'without any sewing!'; tiny ones for Lilliputians; and, biggest of all, the brogues made for the statue of Columbus for his wedding to New York's Statue of Liberty.

If you retrace your steps to C/ del Bisbe Irurita and turn right, you'll find **Plaça Garriga i Bachs**, a dusty little square facing the cathedral cloister, dedicated to five heroes of 1809, who attempted to take the Castle of Montjuïc from the Napoleonic occupiers; three ended up hiding in the cathedral organ for three days before they were caught and hanged or garrotted. The church on the corner, **Sant Sever** (*open Tues and Thurs 1–2.30*), was, like the cathedral, protected from Anarchists by armed guards during the Civil War, and is one of the few to preserve its frothy

Baroque interior, with an altar in a *trompe l'œil* setting by Jeroni Escarabatxeres. The continuation of C/ Sant Sever, **Baixada de Santa Eulàlia**, is named for the saint's descent naked in a barrel full of broken glass that was rolled up and down the street 13 times; a tabernacle in the street tells the tale.

Plaça de Sant Jaume: The Generalitat and Ajuntament

Just beyond Sant Sever, C/ del Bisbe Irurita passes on the left C/ de la Pietat, where you can see the last and most striking cathedral door, the **Portal del Pietat**, with a strikingly angular Pietá by late 15th-century German artist Michael Lochner. After this, C/ del Bisbe Irurita under a picturesque **Bridge of Sighs**, a much maligned pseudo-Gothic touch added in 1928, when the city was busily rediscovering its roots. What sighs, if any, are exhaled on the bridge are by President Jordi Pujol as he leaves his official residence, the 16th-century **Casa de los Canónigos** (the former canons' house), on his way to work in the **Palau de la Generalitat**, seat of the Catalan autonomous government (*guided tours second and fourth Sundays of each month, in English at 11am, free but bring ID and arrive early to sign up*).

Created by Jaume I in 1249, the first Generalitat was made up of representatives of the three Estates (Church, military and civilian), and in 1359 it assumed fiscal responsibility for the realm, making it Spain's first parliament with clout. This palace, made out of several Gothic mansions, was adapted in the early 1400s to give the Generalitat a permanent seat. When Felipe V abolished it in 1714, the palace became seat of his Reial Audiencia, which rubberstamped Madrid's policies. But such is the Catalan virtue of *continuitat* that no one ever forgot the real Generalitat: in 1931, it became the seat of the autonomous government of Catalunya, and since 1977 it has again resumed its function—not something many secular medieval buildings get to do. Jordi Pujol is the 115th president, since 1359.

The façade on C/ del Bisbe Irurita, designed in 1416 by Marc Safont, has some of the best gargoyles and modillions in Barcelona—many proto-caricatures, before Annibale Carracci officially invented them in the 16th century—topped by a superb **rondel of St George** by Pere Joan, a work that so pleased the Generalitat that they paid the sculptor double the agreed price. The **Gothic courtyard** is especially lovely, with a carved exterior stair ascending on a daring stone arch to a gallery with a slender colonnade, the whole crowned with pinnacles and remarkable gargoyles that for the world look like medieval Barcelonans. The **chapel** is entered by way of Marc Safont's Gothic portal (1436), flamboyant, vertical and ornate in a town that usually prefers its Gothic unadorned and broad in the beam. This of course is dedicated to Catalunya's patron, Sant Jordi, or George, and on his feast day, 23 April, thousands queue up to see the magnificent displays of red roses in the courtyard for the Festival of the Rose and the Book—men traditionally give their women a rose, and since 1926 women have given their men a book, in honour of Cervantes and Shakespeare, who both died on 23 April 1616 (these days, it's less proscribed: women give roses, men give books, many give both). The chapel's magnificent altar frontal of 1451, now hanging on the wall, shows George and the dragon in a landscape littered with leftovers from previous meals, all stitched in gold and silver thread. On the altar is a handsome silver statue of Sant Jordi (1430) in articulated Milanese armour tickling a baby crocodile of a dragon with his lance.

When the Generalitat was enlarged in 1526, it added the orange-tree courtyard, the **Pati dels Tarrongers**, and beyond that the ceremonial **Golden Room**, named for its remarkable 16th-century gilt ceiling. Here Flemish tapestries on the triumphs of Petrarch replace the Noucentista frescoes by Torres Garcia, which fell out of favour in the Primo de Rivera dictatorship (his detached works are now displayed in another room). Jordi Pujol and his ministers meet in the **Sala Antoni Tàpies**, with the eponymous master's painting based on the four medieval chronicles of Catalunya. A plaque commemorates the return of president-in-exile Tarradellas from France on 23 October 1977 ('*Ja sóc aquí!*'—'Here I am now!'—were his famous words, which he repeated so often that it became a joke). The Generalitat is also proud of its 40-bell carillon, which sounds every hour between 8am and 8pm, and plays a full concert of traditional Catalan melodies once a month.

C/ del Bisbe Irurita ends in **Plaça de Sant Jaume**, where the Generalitat displays an inoffensive Roman Renaissance-style façade of 1617, complete with another statue of Jordi (1860) by Andreu Aleu. This square, where Barcelonans come to dance the *sardana* on Sunday evenings from 7 to 9, has been the heart of civic life since it served as Barcino's forum, at the intersection of the *cardus maximus* (C/ da la Llibreteria) and *decumanus* (C/ del Bisbe Irurita). A warren of medieval streets filled the space until the 1840s, when the forum became a forum again with the building of C/ de Ferrán, providing an ongoing, face-to-face dialogue between the Generalitat and Barcelona's City Hall, the **Ajuntament** (*open Sat and Sun 10–2; bring ID*). Jaume I sowed its seeds at the same time as the Generalitat, first by appointing a committee of 20 peers in 1249; by 1272 this had evolved into an annually selected Consell de Cent (Council of a Hundred), who ruled the city until 1714, proving itself to be one of Europe's most successful examples of representative government. Its flexibility was unusual: tradesmen as well as patricians served, and the number 100 was not set in stone, but varied as circumstances saw fit. To keep biases to a minimum, names of approved candidates were chosen by lottery.

The Ajuntament's neoclassical **façade**, added in the 1840s, is cold potatoes, but like the Generalitat it preserves a Gothic façade, on C/ de la Ciutat, watched over by Santa Eulàlia. The oldest part of the Ajuntament, the **Saló de Cent** by Pere Llobet (1372), has round ribs reminiscent of Saló de Tinell; it was restored by Domènech i Montaner in the 1880s, and Gothic bits were added in 1914. The **Saló de las Cròniques** is lined with bravura golden murals on the great moments of Catalan history, by Josep Maria Sert (1928), who went on to decorate New York's Waldorf Astoria and Rockefeller Center (over Diego Rivera's murals) before becoming, as Robert Hughes called him, 'the Tiepolo of the dictatorship'.

From the Plaça de Sant Jaume, narrow C/ Paradí leads to the summit of Mons Tàber, marked by an ancient millstone in the pavement; here, just inside the handsome Gothic courtyard of the **Centre Excursionista de Catalunya**, are four impressive Corinthian columns and part of the podium from the 1st-century AD Roman **Temple of Augustus**, trapped like an exotic orchid in a hothouse. The Centre Excursionista was founded in 1876 as a cultural probe into Catalan roots, interested in art, history and science; Jacint Verdaguer, Santiago Rusinyol, Domènech and Gaudí were members and would go on excursions into the countryside to ponder Romanesque churches, caves, mountains or woods. In spite of being steeped in nationalism, it was the one and only Catalan organization tolerated under Franco. One of the first things the *excursionistas* did after the old dictator's death was climb Mount Everest to plant a Catalan flag.

Another Catalan institution came into the world near Plaça de Sant Jaume. A few yards down C/ de Ferrán, a shopping street with streetlamps that hang like earrings, a plaque at No.42 marks the spot where Joan Miró was born in 1893, in an arcade called **Passatge del Crèdit**. Miró's dad, a jeweller, did all he could to thwart his only son's desire to paint, forcing him to attend school until he had a nervous breakdown. His parents then bought a farm at Montroig and took young Joan there to recover, and when they returned to Barcelona they let him use part of the house as a studio; it was so cramped that Miró had to crawl in on his hands and knees (and he wasn't that big: one old friend described him as 'an antediluvian glow-worm'). On this same side of the Ajuntament, facing its eyesore annexe (1969), in Plaça de Sant Miquel, is the lavish **Palau Centelles** (1514); at Baixada de Sant Miquel 8 you can step into its charming Gothic-Renaissance courtyard.

Around Plaça de Sant Jaume: El Call

In the Middle Ages, the entrance to Barcelona's ghetto (*El Call*, from the Hebrew *qahqal*, or 'meeting place') was just to the left of the Generalitat, on modern C/ del Call. No one knows when the first Jews moved to Barcelona, although the Visigoths bear the ignominy of passing Spain's first anti-Semitic law, in 694, which made all Jews slaves. By the 11th century, the Call was a well-organized community within a community that was also the intellectual centre of Catalunya, home to its finest schools, hospitals, baths, translators, poets, astronomers and philosophers.

The Universitat Judía was the only institution of higher learning in the land for centuries. It was here that the mystic Moshe ben Nahman debated the divinity of Christ with Dominican monks at the famous 'Disputation of Barcelona' in 1263, so impressing Jaume I the Conqueror that he gave the rabbi a handsome reward.

In 1243, however, the same count-king had ordered that the Call be walled off and so set apart from the rest of the city, and that Christians not be allowed to enter except when goods were displayed for sale in the streets; Jews were also compelled to wear long, hooded cloaks with red or yellow bands. Much of this segregation was said to protect Jews from increasing persecution by rustic Reconquista fanatics; Jews expelled from other territories in Spain, especially Navarre and Castile, were made welcome here by the count-kings, who depended on the community as the bankers to the Crown, ambassadors and interpreters, especially to Arab courts, and offered royal protection and favours in exchange.

El Call began to incite a dangerous amount of envy. In 1391, a group of Castilians in Barcelona spread rumours that the Black Death had been brought by Jews from Navarre, inciting riots and the looting of the Call. The Consell de Cent had 10 of the Castilians arrested and condemned to death; when the news hit the streets, the mob raised a militia in the countryside to liberate the men and attack the Call, brutally wiping out most of the community. King Joan I had the 22 instigators put to death, but could not halt the growing tide of anti-Semitism, and in 1424, with the Castilians on the throne of Aragón, the Jews were expelled from the Call, and the stones of their synagogues and cemeteries were later quarried to build the Generalitat and Lloctinent. In 1492, Fernando and Isabel compelled all the Jews in Sepharad (the Hebrew word for Spain) to convert or leave. Five centuries later, in 1925, Primo de Rivera granted the Sephardim around the world citizenship and protection under Spanish consulates. Not long after, Barcelona rediscovered its role as a haven, as 7,000 Jews moved into the city in the 1930s. A synagogue was opened in C/ de l'Avenir. Franco, for all his faults, never persecuted Jews.

The main synagogue in the Call stood off C/ del Call, on C/ de Sant Domènec del Call; here No.6 is a house from the 11th century, considered to be the oldest still standing in Barcelona. Near here on tiny C/ de Marlet, one stone remains poignantly in place, inscribed in Hebrew: 'Sacred foundation of Rabbi Samuel Hassareri, of everlasting life. Year 692.'

Santa Maria del Pi and Around

C/ de la Boquería, the continuation of C/ del Call, leads into one of the first medieval *vilanovas* built outside the Roman walls, the Barri del Pi; its name comes from a majestic pine that once stood in front of **Santa Maria del Pi**, just to the right off C/ de la Boquería. One of the best-loved churches in Barcelona, it was founded in the 10th century. Rebuilt beginning in 1322, the church is a textbook example of Catalan Gothic, austere and wide, but with a rose window said to be the largest in the world. The interior was gutted during the Civil War—hence the rather garish replacements of most of the stained glass. But take note of the choir in the back, built on a stone arch even shallower than the vault in Santa Eulàlia's crypt in the cathedral, then rebuilt in the 19th century. One hopes it will last, because no one remembers how to build the like.

The intimate squares surrounding the church, **Plaça del Pi** in front with a commemorative pine tree, and **Plaça de Sant Josep Oriol** on the side, were originally cemeteries, and are now filled with cafés and frequent markets (*see* p.260). At 3 Plaça del Pi, the former retailers' guild has the oldest surviving *esgrafiado* decoration in Barcelona, from 1685, and at the corner of C/ de Petritxol stands the ominous-sounding **Casa de la Sang**, or House of Blood, home of the confraternity of the Puríssima Sang, founded in 1342 to comfort prisoners condemned to death, accompanying them to the scaffold dressed in long black robes with conical hoods; Michelangelo belonged to a similar order in Rome. C/ de Petritxol is a pretty street, lined with old houses and garden balconies and tile decorations; the **Sala Parès**, at No.5, is the oldest art gallery in the city (1884), once owned by the son of poet Joan Maragall. Ramón Casas, Isidre Nonell and a 20-year-old Picasso all had exhibits here.

Plaça de Sant Josep Oriol is named after a 17th-century priest of Barcelona, who performed a miracle during the celebration of his canonization held here in 1806, when his namesake, the architect Josep Oriol i Mestres, with a physique like Humpty Dumpty, fell off a footbridge high above and landed here, not only in one piece but without the slightest damage to his person. A marble plaque commemorates his famous fall. Nearby, the seated bronze figure glancing over his spectacles is Àngel Guimerà (1849–1924), a playwright who lived in C/ de Petritxol. He edited the newspaper *La Renaixença* and in 1877 became a *Mestre en Gay Saber*.

The *Jocs Florals*

A *Mestre en Gay Saber*, *or* 'master of joyous knowledge', was a troubadour, and if it seems peculiar that there was one running around Barcelona in the mid-19th century it's because of the overwhelmingly nostalgic nature of the *Renaixença*. The first Jocs Floral, or Floral Games, a poetry competition between troubadours, took place in Toulouse in May 1324. In 1388, Queen Violante de Bar, a devotee of the Courts of Love, brought the games to Barcelona, where the third prize was a silver violet, the second a golden rose, and the first prize a real rose, because, like the greatest poetry, a rose can never be successfully imitated—as the winning poem would presumably endure for ever, no poet could ask for a greater reward. Much medieval Catalan verse, especially by the great Ausiàs Marc (1397–1459), is powerful pithy stuff. In 1490 the genre went out with a bang with Joanot Martorell's *Tirant lo Blanc*, Europe's first prose novel, an epic mix of chivalry and satire. The heroics may well have been based on the 'White Knight', the Romanian-Hungarian Turk-crushing hero John Hunyadi, but the bawdy, ribald bits are pure Catalan. It was one of Cervantes' favourite books.

After dying out in the 15th century, the *Jocs Florals* were revived by the Ajuntament in May 1859 as a way to promote the writing of, and a readership for, Catalan verse, which had all but died out. 'Fatherland, Faith and Love' were the mottoes, and the subject of most of the poems. A jury selected the winner, and the first prize once again was a real rose. A poet who earned three was a *Mestre en Gay Sabor*. The *Jocs* were a great success and eventually even produced some good verse; Joan Maragall and Jacint Verdaguer, other *Mestres*, are still read today. In the other arts, the *Jocs Florals* and their twee quaintness were perhaps most important for the impatient reaction they provoked in the 1890s: Modernisme.

From Plaça de Sant Josep Oriol, C/ de l'Ave Maria leads into **C/ de Banys Nous**, a street that follows the curve of the Roman walls and was named after its 'new' Jewish baths, new in 1160 at any rate; this, and its extension, C/ de la Palla, are chock-a-block with antique shops. Turning right in Banys Nous, you'll pass one of the city's landmarks, its oldest and most atmospheric wine *bodega*, the brick-vaulted **El Portalón**, founded in the 1860s. Farther down, Banys Nous returns to C/ de Ferrán; to the right here, the little church of **Sant Jaume** was built over a synagogue in 1394 by a confraternity of converted Jews and dedicated to the Trinity. In 1876 it was re-dedicated to St James the Moor-slayer, and topped in 1876 with a strikingly late relief of the same; the 14th-century retable inside was commissioned by Pere III for the cathedral.

South of Plaça de Sant Jaume

Leaving El Call behind at C/ de Ferrán, C/ de Banys Nous continues south as **C/ d'Avinyó**, where several old palaces were converted into brothels around the start of the 20th century. The 19-year-old Picasso had a studio nearby at C/ dels Escudellars Blancs, and he had the ladies in mind when he painted *Les Demoiselles d'Avignon* (1907), his unfinished manifesto of Cubism, a painting that was so incomprehensible even to other artists that it wasn't displayed publicly until 1937. In an interview in 1933 Picasso explained the name:

> Les Demoiselles d'Avignon! *How that name gets on my nerves! It was coined by Salmon [André, poet and friend]. You know at first it was called* The Brothel of Avignon. *You know why? Avignon has always been a familiar name for me, a name connected with my life. I lived only a few steps from the Calle d'Avinyó. There I bought my paper and watercolours. Then, as you know, Max Jacob's grandfather was a native of Avignon. We were always making jokes about this picture. One of the women was supposed to be Max's grandmother...*

If you walk along Avinyó, note the fine *esgrafiados* that embellish the houses at Nos.26 and 30, and the leering stone faces which dot the door lintels of former brothels. The street is now lined with some of Barcelona's sleekest cafés, bars and designer shops. To the right, C/ de N'Arai leads to a new triangular *plaça* named in homage to George Orwell.

Further down Avinyó, C/ del Comtessa de Sobradiel on the left leads into another 13th-century *vilanova*, named for a 10th-century irrigation ditch dug by Count Reg Mir; fittingly, **Plaça del Regomir** has a sculpture that resembles an exotic toilet fixture. At 3 C/ del Regomir, a 14th-century palace with an atmospheric courtyard was converted in 1988 into the **Pati Llimona cultural centre** (*open Mon–Fri 10am–10pm, Sat–Sun 10am–2pm*). This was scarcely the first conversion to happen here: the medieval palace incorporates walls and a gate of Barcino's very first precinct, raised in the 1st century BC and visible from the street behind the glass walls. The higgledy-piggledy palace also managed to swallow up a section of the second, 4th-century AD Roman wall and two towers, which you can reach through a small passageway off C/ del Correu Vell. On C/ del Regomir, the palace's little **Capella de Sant Cristofol** (1503) was given a neo-Gothic treatment in 1899. In 1907, the first cars in Spain were blessed here, and they still queue up for a little juju every 10 July.

Plaça de Sant Just

From Plaça del Regomir, C/ del Cometa (named in honour of Halley's, in 1834) leads to **C/ de Lledó**, one of the most aristocratic streets in medieval Barcelona, although unlike its rival, C/ Montcada, its once fine palaces are still mostly hidden behind later additions. The street ends in atmospheric **Plaça de Sant Just**, named after the parish church of the count-kings, **Les Sants Just i Pastor.** Reputedly this was Barcelona's first church, built in the 4th century over the Roman amphitheatre; legend has it that Catalunya's totem black Virgin was kept here before she was relocated to Montserrat for safety from the Moors. Founded or refounded by

Charlemagne's son, Louis the Pious, in 801, it is the last church in Spain to pre-serve the ancient privilege of *Testimentos Sacramentales* (Sacramental Wills) bestowed by Louis himself, which gives any citizen of Barcelona the right to make a will, orally, without a notary or writing on paper, as long as a witness appears within six months to present its contents before the altar of Sant Feliú. The present church dates from the 14th century but its austere façade (made more austere by a rusting metal door) dates from 1883. Inside, there's a fine 16th-century retable by the Portuguese painter Pere Nunyes in the Capella Sant Feliú, lovely 14th-century stained glass and Visigothic capitals, pressed into service as fonts.

The public **fountain** in the square was Barcelona's first since Roman times. It was donated in 1367 by Joan Fiveller, a merchant and councillor who lived in C/ de Lledó; in Barcelona lore he is celebrated for standing up to a king, when he forced the retinue of Fernando of Antequera to pay tax on the salt fish they consumed in the city. This was such a signal victory of Catalan *Ustages* over Castilian privileges that the Ajuntament erected his statue in place of Hercules on its neoclassical façade. Fiveller discovered a water source in the Collserola while hunting, and had the water pumped into the city. He commemorated the event by placing his falcons and Sant Just on the fountain. It was here, in 1924, during a nationalist celebration, that the 72-year-old Gaudí was arrested and spent a night in the clink for speaking only in Catalan to a cop; perhaps the officer would have been less touchy had he known that the old man had done exactly the same when he was introduced to King Alfonso XIII, causing much royal befuddlement.

There are two important palaces here: the elegant late 18th-century **Palau Moxió**, adorned with *esgrafiados*, and behind it, in a cul-de-sac, the **Palau Palamòs**, the grandest private address in medieval Barcelona, built in the 13th century atop the Roman wall, with a fine Romanesque-Gothic courtyard. The interior, lavishly bar-oqued in the early 1700s, has a Gallery of Illustrious Catalans; now seat of the academy of fine arts, it's open by appointment (*or on the third Sunday of each month, from 10.30am–2pm*). From Plaça de Sant Just, C/ de Dagueria leads to C/ de Jaume I and back to Plaça de l'Àngel.

Towards Plaça de Catalunya: *Vilanova* Santa Anna

By the 12th century Barcelona was too big to fit in its Roman walls and overflowed to the north and east, an area that Jaume I enclosed in his 13th-century enceint. Although the Barri di Santa Anna to the north has lost much of its medieval char-acter, there are a few sights worth picking out. From Plaça de l'Àngel, continue up wide **Vía Laietana**, a street named after Barcelona's first inhabitants and drilled through the medieval town in the name of progress in 1907, much to the horror of preservationists (who quickly moved to protect the rest of the Barri Gòtic from similar depredations). The intention was to create Catalunya's Wall Street, and it does have its share of office buildings and banks: there's the **Casa Cambó** (1921–5) at No.30, a cross between Noucentisme and the Chicago school, topped with a Classical penthouse and lush garden. The same architect, Adolf Florensa, built **No.31** in 1931, in the Florentine Renaissance palace style, and No.34, his Chicago- style **Chamber of Commerce** (1931–6). The monumental neoclassical **Caixa de Catalunya** (1933) at No.35 looks like an escapee from Madrid, with its elaborate rooftop sculpture and vestibule à la Art Deco, a style rare in Barcelona (as rare as Modernisme in Madrid, actually).

At No.50 stands a survivor from the past, the **Casa dels Velers** (1763), headquarters of the silk makers' guild, *esgrafiadoed* with atlantes and caryatids in the latest silks. Opposite, **C/ del Comtal** is named after Barcelona's first semi-legendary count, Guifré il Pilós, or Wilfred the Hairy, whose summer palace was here. Heading down C/ del Comtal, tiles at the corner of C/ de N'Amargós tell a story that happened in his reign.

Two Hairy Guys

Joan Garí was a nobleman who became a hermit in a cave on the Catalan holy mountain of Montserrat. His reputation for holiness led Count Guifré to come to him, seeking a cure for his ailing daughter, the peerless beauty Riquilde. Garí seduced her instead and, horrified by his crime, doubled it by murdering her and burying her secretly by his cave. In remorse, he walked to Rome to confess to the pope, who ordered him to return to Montserrat on his hands and knees and stay that way, living like an animal, until he heard that God had forgiven him. Twenty years later, after Garí's clothes had rotted away and his hair and beard had grown to cover his whole body, Guifré was hunting on Montserrat when his dogs found what looked like a bizarre beast. Guifré brought it back to Barcelona and put it in a cage here. During the feast celebrating the baptism of his infant son, Guifré had the cage brought in to see if any guest could identify the beast, and at once the baby stood up in his nurse's arms and said: 'Rise, Garí. God has forgiven you.' Garí then stood up and told Guifré his story, and took him to Riquilde's grave. Whereupon the girl was found to be alive and well, and all lived happily ever after.

Els Quatre Gats and Around

C/ de N'Amargos ends at C/ de Montsió, on which, at No.3, is the **Casa Martí** (1895), the first building by Josep Puig i Cadafalch, a Modernista fantasy combining elements of Catalan and northern Gothic. Eusebi Arnau sculpted the St George and the dragon on the corner, a motif that Puig would make his own, although this one is even more emphatic than most, with Jordi bearing *les quatre barres* of Catalunya. Arnau also carved the other sculptures, the coat of arms made of symbols of the textile trade, and the little figures in the vegetation; the equally florid wrought iron, inspired by motifs in the cathedral cloister, is by Manuel Ballarín.

The building is renowned as the home of the Modernistas' **Els Quatre Gats** ('The Four Cats', slang for 'Just a few guys', but also recalling the famous Chat Noir in Paris), the bohemian intellectual taverna that provided much of the impetus for the city's cultural life at the start of the 20th century. Founded in 1897 by four former habitués of Montmartre—painters Santiago Rusinyol and Ramòn Casas, puppeteer Miquel Utrillo (father of the Parisian painter Maurice Utrillo) and the eccentric Pere Romeu, who abandoned painting to devote himself to cabaret and cycling—it soon became the informal late-night meeting place for writers, artists, journalists and musicians. The Quatre Gats published its own art review, held Avant Garde shadow-puppet shows, presented recitals by young composers (including Granandos and Albeniz) and put on exhibitions, including Picasso's very first, while Romeu ran things after a fashion, having a screaming fit if anyone touched a cobweb. Six years later, he closed the taverna to devote himself to his bicycle, and the place, ironically, was taken over by Gaudí and Llimona's pious Catholic Cercle de Sant Lluc, founded in reaction to the blasphemous tomfoolery of Casas and Rusinyol. But now there's a new Quatre Gats, an expensive reproduction of the original décor by Puig, with copies of the original paintings (many are now in the Museu d'Art Modern), but minus Romeu's precious spider's webs.

At the end of C/ de Montsió, turn left into shop-lined Avinguda del Portal de l'Angel. Its most interesting building is the **Catalana de Gas** at No.20 (1895), an eclectic Modernista structure by Josep Domènech i Estapà; the appliance-crazed may want to ask to visit their 'museum of gas' of historic gas-run gizmos. Another landmark on the street is the **giant thermometer**, marking Cottett, one of the city's oldest opticians. The first street to the right, **C/ de la Canuda**, is named after the wife of a wealthy man named Canut. She had been his servant, they fell in love, but her father refused to let Canut wed her, arguing that marriages between unequal partners were never happy; Canut responded by giving his beloved half of everything he owned. And La Canuda in turn became famous for her kindness and generosity. Her street leads to a last remnant of Roman Barcino, in **Plaça de la Vila de Madrid**: a row of simple 2nd- to 4th-century AD **Roman tombs**, discovered under a burned-out convent in 1957. These once lined the roads out of the city, as ancient law forbade burials within the walls; you can see how much the ground level has risen in 1,600 years. This square, as the plaque says, is 'the home of Madrid in Barcelona' (an unexpected gesture: perhaps the spirit of Canut and La Canuda lingers). The building at 6 C/ de la Canuda is the **Ateneu Barcelonès**, founded in 1836 as a literary and cultural club in the 18th-century palace of the Baron de Sabassona, of which the open stair, wonderful patrician library, romantic hanging garden and murals by Catalan Baroque painter Francesc Pla on the first floor survive. The lift, still functioning, is one of the oldest in Barcelona. Usually no one minds if you have a look around and a drink at the bar (*open daily 9am–10.30pm*).

From Plaça de la Vila de Madrid, C/ de Betrellans leads to C/ de Santa Anna, where tucked like a pearl among the oysters is the simple Romanesque church and elegant double-decker Gothic cloister of **Santa Anna**, enclosing a quiet, secluded garden with a tinkling fountain (*open daily 9–1 and 6.30–8.30, hols 10–2*). Founded by the Knights Templar in the early 12th century, the church hosted the Corts held under Fernando the Catholic—the last parliament before Aragón and Catalunya were tacked on to Castile. Modified over the centuries, and further damaged in the Civil War, there's not much to see inside the church, although, outside, one of Barcelona's last surviving roadside crosses, surrounded by a circle of saints, adds a picturesque touch. At 21 C/ de Santa Anna, the **Casa Elena Castellano** by Jaume Torres (1907, now a hotel) has a floral-theme; the vestibule is a lavish garden of stucco, ceramics and stained glass. And just round the corner from here is the Plaça de Catalunya.

La Ribera

During the Middle Ages, like Carthage of old, Barcelona was lord and terror of the Mediterranean and divided, with Italy, the enriching commerce of the East and trade was not held to be a degradation as among the Castilians; accordingly heraldic decorations are much less frequent on the houses here, where the merchant's 'mark' was preferred to the armorial 'charge'.

Richard Ford

In 1907, the new Vía Laietana cut the Barri Gòtic off from its two most important medieval *vilanovas*, the Barri de Sant Pere, the centre of medieval Barcelona's textile manufacturers, and La Ribera, the old maritime and business district that grew up along C/ de l'Argenteria, the main road to the port. In those days before Barceloneta, the sea washed up to what is now Avinguda Marquès de l'Argentera, and there was a constant bustle as goods were ferried to and from waiting ships. When the Ramblas was still a sewer, the Born was the throbbing heart of Barcelona, surrounded by artisans and their shops, while medieval tycoons wheeled and dealed in the Llontja, the hub of western Mediterranean commerce in the 13th and 14th century. Then came the lean centuries, and then the traumatic amputation of half of La Ribera for the Ciutadella in the early 1700s (*see* pp.120–22). And then Barcelona spread into the Eixample and took most of La Ribera's trade with it. Today the neighbourhood hovers on fashion's back burner, with the city's most beautiful church, Santa Maria del Mar; its most beautiful medieval street, Carrer Montcada; its most popular museum, the Picasso; and its oldest and most accessible park, the Ciutadella. For places to eat and drink here, *see* pp.230–32.

Palau de la Música Catalana

A good place to start is Plaça de Urquinaona (**Ⓜ** Urquinaona), at the top of the Barri de Sant Pere and the aforementioned **Vía Laietana**, the wannabe Wall Street that has since the 1960s lost the competition to the Diagonal. But the city's first sky-scraper, by Luis Gutiérrez Soto (1936), still scrapes away in Plaça de Urquinaona, and a block down, where Vía Laietana meets C/ de les Jonqueres, Enric Sagnier's neo-Gothic **Caixa de Pensions** (1917) sprouts pinnacles and an allegorical sculpture on the virtues of saving. Imagine a building getting dressed in the dark in a secondhand clothes shop and coming outside with nothing matching, and you have the Caixa de Pensions.

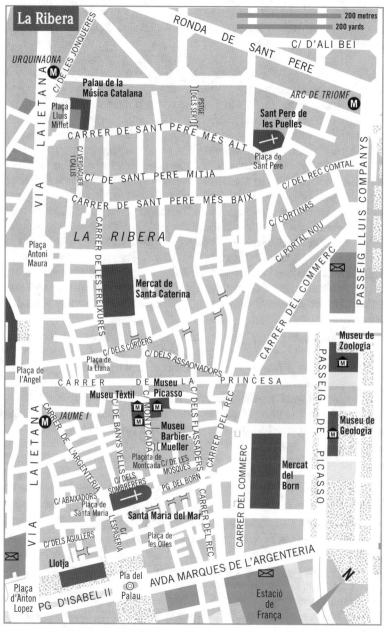

La Ribera

200 metres
200 yards

RONDA DE SANT PERE
C/ D'ALI BEI

URQUINAONA Ⓜ

Palau de la
Música Catalana

Plaça
Lluís
Millet

ARC DE TRIOMF Ⓜ

Sant Pere de
les Puelles

Plaça de
Sant Pere

CARRER DE SANT PERE MÉS ALT

PSTGE [DELS SERT]

C/VERDAGUER I CALLIS

VIA LAIETANA

C/ DE LES JONQUERES

C/ DE SANT PERE MITJA

CARRER DE SANT PERE MÉS BAIX

C/ DEL REC COMTAL

C/ CORTINAS

C/ PORTAL NOU

LA RIBERA

Plaça
Antoni
Maura

CARRER DE LES FREIXURES

Mercat de
Santa Caterina

CARRER DEL COMMERC

PASSEIG LLUIS COMPANYS

Museu de
Zoologia Ⓜ

C/ DELS CÓRDERS

Plaça de
la Llana

C/ DELS ASSAONADORS

PASSEIG DE PICASSO

Plaça de
l'Angel

CARRER DE PRINCESA

Museu
Tèxtil

Museu
Picasso

Museu de
Geologia Ⓜ

JAUME I Ⓜ

CARRER DE L'ARGENTERIA

C/ DE BANYS VELLS

C/ MONTCADA

C/ DELS FLASSADERS

CARRER DEL REC

Ⓜ Ⓜ
Ⓜ

Museu
Barbier-
Mueller

LAIETANA

Plaçeta de
Montcada

C/ DE LES
MOSQUES

Mercat
del
Born

C/ DELS
SOMBRERERS

PG. DEL BORN

C/ ABAIXADORS

Plaça de
Santa Maria

C/ DELS AGULLERS

C/ L'ESPASERIA

Santa Maria del Mar

CARRER DEL REC

Plaça de
les Olles

VIA

Llotja

Pla del
Palau

AVDA MARQUES DE L'ARGENTERIA

Plaça
d'Anton
Lopez

PG D'ISABEL II

Estació
de
França

N

109

The next left, however, C/ de Ramon Mas, will take you to something that has no relatives on this planet: Lluís Domènech i Montaner's **Palau de la Música Catalana** (*if you can't get a concert ticket, you can book a tour; open daily 10–3.30; visits by guided tour only, with tours departing every 30 minutes in English, Spanish and Catalan, and lasting for 50 minutes—they begin with a tedious, if hilariously adulatory, 20-minute video; adm*). There's an old joke: one Catalan starts a business, two start a corporation, and three start a choral society. No one can deny that this archetypically gruff, taciturn, capitalist tribe has a musical soul, and in the *Renaixença* fervour of the 1850s an ardent Republican named Josep Anselm Clavé founded the first workers' choral groups. There were 85 of them by 1861. The most important, the Orfeó Català, was founded in 1891 by Clavé and Amadeu Vives, and soon became an important representative of Catalan ideals and culture in Spain and abroad. Flushed with success, in 1904 the Orfeó gave Domènech a brief to create a 'Temple of Catalan art, a palace to celebrate its renaissance'. The idea warmed the cockles of Domènech's nationalist heart, and he delivered in spades, subcontracting the most accomplished artists of the day to create a Modernista garden of delights. The project was plagued by financial sticky patches; Domènech took a 20 per cent cut in his fee but still hadn't been paid when the doors opened only three years after the foundation stone was laid. He was too cheesed off to attend the opening, but his masterpiece was a glittering success.

From the narrow streets, the Palau resembles a bouquet stuffed in a cupboard: the site simply wasn't big enough, but it was important to the Orfeó that it stay in the neighbourhood close to its members, and it was the best they could do. The decoration is a rapturous allegory of Catalan music and the music Catalans loved. Busts of Wagner (a big local favourite), Beethoven, Bach and Palestrina by Eusebi Arnau decorate the second floor. Miquel Blay, a disciple of Rodin, sculpted the huge corner group that projects like a figurehead on a ship, with a knight and damsel emerging from a cloud of legendary figures that celebrate Catalan popular song. Mosaics by Lluís Bru along the top of the façade show the Orfeó performing in front of the Catalan Mount Sinai, Montserrat. The lavish lobby is a cleaner's worst nightmare, the ceiling decorated with a ceramic trellis adorned with plump clusters of roses; the banisters are encased in smoky topaz glass and surrounded with blooms and vines, in honour of the Orfeó's co-founder, Amadeu Vives, who loved flowers.

The starring role goes, of course, to the main auditorium, an epiphany of stained glass and ceramics, brighter than ever now that the church next door has been demolished. The small size of the plot convinced Domènech to bring in as much light as possible, dematerializing the walls Gothic-style, but with modern technology and a steel frame, making this the first curtain-wall building in Spain—the technique had been invented for skyscrapers in 1888 with the Tacoma building in

Chicago. Rainbow-coloured sunlight streams in through Antoni Rigalt's huge stained-glass skylight, filling the jewel-like glass box. Intricate mosaics fan out across the ceiling like the splayed tail feathers of a peacock, amid a profusion of roses. The permanent hemicyclical stage set is composed of 18 unforgettable half-tile, half-3D-ceramic maidens by Eusebi Arnau in a background of *trencadis*, each brandishing a musical instrument. The proscenium is dramatically marked by flowing pumice sculptures designed by Domènech, executed by Didac Masana and finished by Pau Gargallo: Beethoven and galloping, wild-eyed Valkyries confront Josep Clavé smiling serenely under a tree, while maidens below him act out his perennial choral hit song, *The Flowers of May*.

A bust of Amadeu Vives solemnly surveys the glassed-in room in the front of the palace. This was originally open to the street, so patrons could be dropped off without getting wet, although the clatter of their cars and carriages always drowned out the end of any performance. The chandelier is a copy of one spotted in a medieval French castle, and flowers are everywhere, incorporated into the fittings, whether wood, iron, stone, glass or on the mosaics on the columns just outside. Less than a dozen years after the palace won the city's prize for the best building of 1907, opinion had swung violently against it and Noucentista architects were calling for the destruction of the 'ostentatious monument', the shame of Barcelona, the 'Palace of Catalan Junk'. Needless to say it survived all these insults, but some remodelling has been necessary over the years, the most recent a sympathetic restoration and extension in the 1980s by Oscar Tusquets. No one has managed to really fix the famously bad acoustics.

Barri de Sant Pere

The Palau de la Música overlooks **C/ de Sant Pere més Alt**, one of three parallel streets that define the old Barri de Sant Pere. This neighbourhood grew up in the 11th century on land owned by the convent of Sant Pere de les Puelles, and from the beginning was devoted to textiles. In the 18th century, when the city couldn't ship enough calico to Spain's colonies, much of the medieval fabric was replaced with factories and housing for merchants and workers. It didn't happen all at once: at No.27, a neoclassical palace was converted in 1924 into the Athenaeum Polytechnicum, where courses were held for workers. Farther down and to the left, the Passatge de Sert runs alongside an old carpet factory owned by the *família* Sert, who produced the painter Josep Maria and the architect Josep Lluís.

In Plaça de Sant Pere, **Sant Pere de les Puelles** (*open 8.30–9.30am and 7–8.30pm*) was founded outside the walls by the Visigoths, then refounded in 945 by the counts of Barcelona as a Benedictine convent. The *puelles* were the strictly cloistered young nuns, who enjoyed a great reputation for their beauty. When Al-Mansur's troops burst in in 985, the women cut off their own noses, hoping to avoid a fate worse than death; the disgusted Moors chopped off the rest of their heads. The church was rebuilt in 1147, and when the nuns left in the 19th century their cloister became a prison. After a burning in the 1909 Setmana Trágica, it was given its fortress façade; after more arson in 1936, only the Greek-cross plan and a few columns and capitals remain (the best ones are in the Palau Nacional).

The southern end of Plaça de Sant Pere funnels into the crossroads of the C/ del Rec Comtal (Creek of the Counts) and Basses de Sant Pere, streets that were built over a 10th-century irrigation ditch dug by an early benefactor, Count Mir, from the smelly old Merdança. Here too is lively **C/ de Sant Pere més Baix**, the district's shopping street, lined with medieval and 18th-century palaces. The **Farmacia Pedrell** at No.52 is the oldest in Barcelona, dating back to 1562; in 1890 it was given a Modernista facelift, with fine stained glass by Joan Espinagosa. Painter Isidre Nonell was born and died at **No.50**, in a typical artesan's house of the early 18th century. Inside the courtyard at **No.42**, you can see a rare survivor of the *barri's* old industry, the neo-Romanesque Vilumara textile mill. A 16th-century townhouse at No.7, now the Institut del Teatre, was the **Biblioteca Popular de la Dona**. Founded in 1909 by Francesca Bonnemaison, this was Spain's first public library, but exclusively for women; hot showers were another novelty in the neighbourhood. After the Civil War, it survived in the hands of the Falangist female auxiliary, although with an emphasis on home economics. The library survives on the first floor with its inscription from the great medieval philosopher Ramón Llull: *'Tota dona val mes quan letra apren'* (Any woman who learns to read is worth more).

Farther south (backtrack a bit to C/ de les Freixures) is the big neighbourhood market, the neoclassical **Mercat de Santa Caterina** (1847), at the time of writing undergoing a complete renovation according to plans by the late Enric Miralles. Like many of Barcelona's markets, it replaced a burned-out convent, leaving only the name to recall one of the city's Gothic masterpieces. Continue south on C/ de les Freixures and you'll come shortly to musty little **Plaça de la Llana**, the city's medieval wool and yarn market, just big enough for a pair of palms. The street that passes through here, C/ de la Bòria becoming C/ dels Corders, follows the route of the ancient road to Gaul, tramped by Hannibal and his 700 elephants and countless others after the Romans paved it as the Via Augusta. If you follow it a few steps up, you'll come to the **Placeta d'En Marcus** at the head of C/ Montcada, a street that belies the general shabbiness of the area; in fact it is nothing less than the finest medieval thoroughfare in Barcelona.

Carrer Montcada

This street, relatively wide and straight by medieval standards, has an unusual history. It was given in 1148 by Ramón Berenguer IV to a rich merchant named

Guillem Ramón de Montcada in return for financing the reconquest of Tortosa. Montcada sold lots to nine of his buddies, all 12th-century merchant tycoons, and they created a medieval Millionaires' Row. The presence of big money and the old Roman road led to the founding of the *correus volants*—'flying runners', the origin of the *correros*, the Spanish postal service, which is first mentioned in 1166. These early Catalan pony express riders, the *Troters*, were headquartered here, by the tiny Romanesque chapel of **Santa María d'en Marcús**, where they would ride in to be blessed before setting out. This chapel was part of a hospital, founded by a man, Marcús, after he found a buried treasure here. The hospital is long gone, as are the chapel's interior trimmings, flambéed during the Civil War. Note the Gothic windows that survived the rebuilding of the palace at 1 C/ Montcada.

Just south of here, C/ Montcada is crossed by wide **C/ de la Princesa**, a later urban improvement, from 1853, part of the link to the Ramblas from the Ciutadella to allow troops to ride straight into the restive heart of Barcelona. It enjoyed a brief fling as the city's most fashionable address. A plaque at No.37 marks the birthplace in 1861 of Santiago Rusinyol.

Museu Picasso

Open Tues–Sat 10–8, Sun and hols 10–3, closed Mon; adm.

On the other side of C/ de la Princesa, C/ Montcada comes into its own. In the 15th to 17th centuries, the descendants of the first millionaires rebuilt their palaces, with walls right up to the street, creating the current gully appearance. Most of the Gothic embellishments disappeared, but their lovely interior courtyards remained intact, hidden behind the gates. In the 19th century, when money and fashion moved away, the street went into rapid decline; in 1930 an organization was founded to safeguard it, and in 1947 it was classed as a national monument. Today, the once-secret palaces are nearly all museums or galleries, thanks to an initiative taken in 1963 to restore the loveliest of them all, the 15th-century Palau Aguilar (with a courtyard by Marc Safont) and the adjacent Baró de Castellet and Meca palaces, in order to house the Museu Picasso, the best place in Spain to see the works of a Spaniard acclaimed as the greatest artist of the 20th century. But go early: this museum vies with that of Barça for popularity and it can be tedious shuffling along with crowds.

The core of the collection was donated in 1963 by Picasso's friend and secretary Jaume Sabartés, whom he met in Barcelona in 1899. After Sabartés death it was later augmented by Picasso himself, who had a special place in his heart for Barcelona, although he otherwise refused to have anything to do with Franco's Spain. The collection begins with the drawings and doodlings of an eight-year-old in Málaga, kept by his doting mother and sister Lola, including some delightful sketches of Don Quixote and Sancho Panza and an early paper cut-out of a dog and a dove; when Picasso was young, more than one person commented that he was a reincarnated grand master. Also here is his first major academic painting, *Science and Charity*, painted in 1897 under pressure from his father to create more realist works and find himself a wealthy patron. Picasso spent almost a year in Madrid, sketching passers-by at the Circulo de Bellas Artes, and heading daily to the Prado to study the great masters, who seemed to breathe down his neck. He then spent a few months at his friend Pallarès' cottage in the village of Horta de St Jean; to the end of his days Picasso claimed that 'all that I know I learned in Pallarès' village'. He painted a number of assured, fluid landscapes, also exhibited here.

Back in Barcelona, his work becomes more eclectic and his style more personal; the exhibits include a menu *à la* Toulouse-Lautrec, his first paid commission, for Els Quatre Gats (1900), where he had his first exhibition in February 1901. Some of his paintings and sketches reveal the seamier side of Barcelona nightlife; his studio during this period was on the C/ Nou de la Rambla, on the edge of the notoriously louche and impoverished Barri Xinès. After a sprinkling of works from the Blue Period (1901–4)—the eerie *Madman* (*1904*) and the touching, helpless mother and child of *Desamperados* (1904)—and others of the Pink Period in Paris (1905), we skim forward to the celebrated *Harlequin* of 1917. By this time, Picasso was back in Barcelona, still collaborating with Serge Diaghilev and his Ballets Russes, and falling headlong for a beautiful dancer, Olga Kokhlova. It was to be the last extended period that he would spend in the city.

The collection quietly skips another four decades here, and then, just before you go to ask for your money back, explodes with the extraordinary series centred on Velázquez's *Las Meninas*, which Picasso himself donated to the museum. Between 1954 and 1962, he embarked on a series of interpretations of three major paintings (the other two were Delacroix's *Les Femmes d'Alger* and Manet's *Le Déjeuner sur l'Herbe*), but all 44 of the interpretations of *Las Meninas* are here, painted in intense seclusion between 17 August and 30 December 1956, each tiny element meticulously pored over and re-evaluated, the characters and themes becoming 'like the characters and storyline of a serial novel'. Finally, here are paintings from his last years when he lived near Cannes, and ceramics donated by his last wife, Jacqueline. The upper galleries contain a curious collection of erotic etchings entitled *La Suite 156*, conceived in his last years as a surreal combination of the erotic fantasies of an old man and a personal interpretation of the history of art, with sly digs at grand masters from Raphael and Ingres to Degas and Matisse, the same who used to breathe down his neck (take that, he seems to be saying, tickling them). Temporary exhibitions are usually very good and are held in the adjoining Palau Meca.

Picasso and the Origins of Cubism

Born in Málaga in 1881 and relocated with his family to Barcelona in 1895, Picasso was one of the first Andalucians to identify with his adopted city and learn Catalan. From 1895 to 1897 he studied at the school of fine arts in the Llontja, where his father taught, then drifted into the city's Bohemian artistic milieu headquartered at Els Quatre Gats, where his precocious talent was recognized and encouraged by Barcelona's most famous painter of the day, Ramón Casas. Even so, Picasso never had much money in Barcelona and he knew at first hand about the impoverished, outcast subjects of his first, 'Blue' Period (1901–4), revealing his 'precocious disenchantment' before he took off to settle permanently in Paris and invent Cubism. His interest in Cézanne's studies of structure and form and in African masks was the seed for his monumental break with the past, but Ellsworth Kelly hit on what may have been another inspiration behind Picasso's fragmentation and dissolution of form: the *trencadís*, or broken tiles, that Gaudí used as an integral part of his architecture. Was that Barcelona's great contribution to modern painting? Only, chances are, Picasso never saw the rooftop installations or even the Park Güell: most were not for public viewing, and he was in Paris most of the time.

Other Museums and Palaces on Carrer Montcada

Just a few steps down at 12 C/ Montcada, the **Museu Tèxtil i de la Indumentària** (*open Tues–Sat 10–8, Sun 10–3, closed Mon; adm; combined ticket available with Museu Barbier-Muller d'Art Precolumbi*) is housed in the 16th-century Gothic Palau dels Marquesos de Lliò, with a popular arty café in its attractive courtyard. Dedicated to textiles and fashion, its exhibits date back to the 3rd century and include rare embroideries from Granada, as intricate as the tile patterns in the Alhambra; a 16th-century Tournai tapestry of the Siege of Rhodes; tiny Baroque shoes (some with silver soles) and socks; sequinned flapper shifts; classic frocks by Balenciaga; and a great pair of chainmail hotpants by Paco Rabanne from the 1960s. Up in the attic, you can pick your way around heavy looms and ancient sewing machines and admire the view across the rooftops. There is also a collection of lace, another of richly embroidered *mantilla* shawls, and a series of changing exhibits in the lower galleries, which often feature young contemporary designers.

Next door, another medieval palace was painstakingly restored in 1996 to hold the **Museu Barbier-Mueller d'Art Precolumbi** (*open Tues–Sat 10–8, Sun 10–3; closed Mon; adm; combined ticket available with Museu Tèxtil, © 93 310 45 16*), an exquisite collection loaned from the museum of the same name in Geneva, each item illuminated against a black background as if on stage. The Olmecs and Mayas of Mexico, the Central Americans, the Chavín, Moche, Nazca and Inca civilizations of the Andes are all present, and their craftsmanship equals anything done in Europe at the time (2000 BC–1500 AD). There are gold ornaments, mummy masks, lip and nose jewellery, funerary ceramics, textiles and statues, some complacent and serene, others vicious and frightening, all of it powerful. One room is devoted to rarely seen works by the Amazonian islanders of Caviana and Marajó, who buried the bones of their dead in beautiful abstract vases. The shop downstairs sells a wide range of South American handicrafts.

Renovated from a Gothic original, the 17th-century **Palau Dalmases** at No.20 is the finest Baroque palace in Barcelona; don't miss the flamboyant courtyard stair, carved with the Rape of Europa, and Neptune and his Amphitrite racing up the waves in defiance of gravity. Part of the palace has been transformed into a café, the sumptuous and florid **Espai Barroc**, dripping with red velvet and candelabra, the perfect setting for the occasional Baroque music concert. Opposite, the **Galerie Maeght** occupies the 16th-century Palau dels Cervelló, with four severe gargoyles guiding the rainwater away from the solarium; run by the same people who built the Fondation Maeght in St-Paul-de-Vence, it puts on excellent changing exhibitions and has a large art shop. Other architectural leftovers from C/ Montcada's golden age include the square tower with a terraced roof and triple window at **No.23**, a combination that once characterized all the Gothic palaces on this street, and the pretty 18th-century wooden lattice-work window at **No.21**—a sole survivor of similar ones that decorated every window of the period. Near the bottom of C/ Montcada, **C/ de les Mosques**, the 'street of flies', is the narrowest in the city (40 inches wide); the flies were first drawn here by fruit stored by stallholders in the Born market, but in more recent years by its use as a late-night public convenience—complaining residents have had it closed off.

Passeig del Born

C/ Montcada runs into the wide **Passeig del Born**. *Born* means tournament and it was used as such in the Middle Ages, as well as for the Inquisition's *autos-da-fé*. At other times it was the place to see and be seen before the Ramblas stole its thunder. *Ronda el món, i torna al Born* ('Go around the world and end up at the Born') is an old saying, meaning that, no matter where a Barcelonan travels, he or she was bound to end up here; now trendy bars are bringing some of them back. Only one house, No.17, shows signs of the Born's Gothic grandeur, with turrets, solarium and mullioned windows over-restored in 1965.

There are signs (mostly street signs, to be precise) of the Born's centuries as the commercial heart of an eminently commercial city. Towards the far end of the

Born, C/ dels Flassaders, 'blanket-makers' street', is also where they minted the coin of the realm, at the **Ceca**, at No.40. One of the Ribera's oldest streets, **C/ del Rec**, follows the course of Count Mir's 10th-century canal; in the Middle Ages it was lined with water mills, and the arcaded section on Gothic pillars is one of the more picturesque corners of La Ribera. The end of the Born is closed off by the **Mercat del Born** (1876), a striking iron structure with a roof of patterned tiles, by Josep Fontseré (the designer of the nearby Ciutadella park). It served as the city's wholesale market until 1971, when like Les Halles in Paris and Covent Garden in London it was sadly relocated to the outskirts of town, depriving the district of much of its former colour and bustle. There are now plans to turn the market into the Biblioteca Provincial de Catalunya.

Santa Maria del Mar

Open daily 9–1.30 and 4.30–8.

At the other end of the Born is the apse of Santa Maria del Mar, the most beautiful of all Catalan Gothic churches. The spot has long been holy: the first church was built in the 4th century over the tomb of Santa Eulàlia. When Jaume I conquered Mallorca in 1235, he promised a temple to Mary, Star of the Sea, the patroness of his sailors, but his promise remained unfulfilled until Alfons III took Sardinia. The count-king then laid the first stone of the church in 1329 and entrusted the design to sculptor and stone mason Berenguer de Montagut, who may have had some technical assistance from the Mallorican architect Jaume Fabre.

As Catalan maritime interests expanded, so had La Ribera's population of sailors, porters, tradesmen and small merchants. Santa Maria del Mar was to be their church, and all able-bodied men in the parish donated their labour to build it, completing it in 50 years—a supersonic speed in those days, which accounts for its rare stylistic unity. In contrast to the cathedral, the church has a typical Catalan Gothic exterior, startling in its simplicity, a great, austere mass of plain sandstone masonry, softened by wildflowers sprouting from the cracks. The façade, on Plaça de Santa Maria, has a rose window framed by a pair of plain buttresses and twin octagonal towers. Other decoration is limited to a bit of tracery over the windows and door, around a simple relief of Christ, who looks like the victim of a hold-up. By the door are two small 15th-century bronze figures of the builders.

But enter, and what seemed closed and almost forbidding from without opens up to a miraculous spaciousness. In 1714 the interior was damaged in the French and Spanish bombardment; in 1936, when the Anarchists set it ablaze, its Baroque fittings burned for ten days. Yet however wonderful they might have been, no one misses them: the lack of decoration only enhances Santa Maria's sublime beauty and emphasizes the absolutely minimum of interior supports: the octagonal piers of the nave stand 42ft apart—a distance unsurpassed in any other medieval building. Two aisles, equally lofty and half the width of the nave, have only simple niches for chapels between the buttresses. The raised altar is set in a transcendent crescent of slender columns, transforming the apse into a glade in an enchanted forest. At the foot of the altar, two stone reliefs depict the longshoremen, many of whom were freed slaves, who carried the stone down from Montjuïc to build the church. The stained glass dates from every century; the best, from the 1400s, show the *Ascension* and *Last Judgement*.

Around Santa Maria del Mar

On the map, Santa Maria resembles a big beetle caught in an intricate web of streets, each bearing the name of the medieval trade concentrated there. In the days of mass illiteracy, shops would identify themselves by hanging out a model of their goods; all that remains now are the stone female faces you see here and there that marked the brothels. **C/ dels Sombrerers** along the side of the church was the realm of hatters; busy **C/ de l'Argenteria** was the silversmiths' street (if you walk up a block to C/ de Basea and turn left, you can see the tallest surviving medieval **tower house** in the city). Behind the Gothic fountain (1402) in Plaça de Santa Maria is the quaint little **C/ de les Caputxes**, scarcely altered since the 1400s, when Barcelonans came here to buy their hoods. **C/ de l'Anisadeta**, south of Plaça de Santa Maria, was named for the woman who sold anise-flavoured water; off this, **C/ Canvis Vells** and **C/ Canvis Nous** were the streets where money was changed on *bancos* (benches, hence 'bank').

C/ Canvis Nous witnessed the Corpus Christi bomb attack in 1896; the procession had just left the church (as in Ramón Casas' painting in the Museu d'Art Modern, *see* p.123) when a bomb was thrown at the rear of the procession, killing 12 poor workers and wounding many others, but missing the bigwigs in front. There were always suspicions that the bomb was tossed by an undercover agent, to justify the subsequent witch hunt of Anarchists and other suspects, who were subject to the horrific tortures, mock trials and executions at Montjuïc castle that shocked the world. Walk up **C/ L'Espaseria** for the famous view of Santa Maria's campanile. This was the street of swordmakers; their keen blades were as reputed as Toledo's—just looking at one was enough to wound, or so the Catalans claimed. From here C/ dels Asses leads into **C/ de les Dames**, ladies' street, where hopeful spinsters would gather after storms; unmarried sailors, threatened with doom, often vowed to marry the first single woman they saw on shore if they were spared. Pots and pans were the speciality in the adjacent **Plaça de les Olles**.

Along the southern flank of Santa Maria, a low wall and the fan-shaped **Fossar de les Moreres** (the cemetery of Mulberry Trees) marks the mass tomb of

Barcelonans who resisted the Bourbon troops of Felipe V in 1714. Some 3,500 bodies were brought here, and all who fought on the Catalan side were buried within a now vanished ring of mulberry trees, and all who fought for the Bourbons were buried without. The verse on the wall by poet and playwright Sefari Pitarra translates: *In the Mulberry Cemetery/No traitor lies/Even though we lose our banners/It will be the urn of honour.* This was removed after the Civil War, and reinstalled after 1977.

In 1989 the cemetery was made into a small square after the demolition of the overhead passage that linked Santa Maria to the former royal palace. The palace was the residence of Catalunya's viceroy and stood towards the sea in the Pla del Palau until it burned down in 1875. The viceroy was anything but popular in a city that once had its own count-king, and the passage was built in 1700 to allow him access to church without risk of assassination. But in one case it backfired. After the convent-burnings in 1835, Madrid sent General Bassa to reassert order, and he arrived with the provocative assertion that it would be 'either the people or me!' He didn't, however, know about the overhead passage from the church, and was surprised by a group of revolutionaries who did: they stormed over it and tossed him from his office to the crowd waiting below; he was lynched, and his body dragged to the Ramblas, where it was burned on a pyre made of the Carmelite library.

Pla del Palau

The Pla del Palau, minus the viceroy's palace, is a graceful 19th-century square; the first photograph in Barcelona was taken here in 1839. In the centre, a mid-19th-century **fountain of the Catalan Spirit** is topped with a little cherub who started life naked and has been dressed and undressed according to the sensibilities of the age for the past 150 years. The most important building on the square, the **Llotja**, or exchange, was a secular cathedral for the mercantile imperialists, and paid for by a three per cent tax on all imports and exports. It was built by Pere Arbei for King Pere III the Ceremonious in 1380, after the navy of Pedro the Cruel of Castile damaged an early, more modest building. Remodelled over the years, and slapped with a neoclassical facelift, the magnificent Gothic **Sala de Contractacions** inside was left untouched. It was the oldest continuously operating stock exchange in Europe, until Barcelona's *bourse* moved to the Passeig de Gràcia in 1996. In the 18th century, when it was the largest public space in the city, Barcelona's first operas were staged here, and later part of the building was used as a school of fine arts, where Picasso's father taught and where Picasso attended classes until he quit out of boredom. Sadly, the gates are now closed and the Llotja's future is uncertain.

Opposite the Llotja, on Passeig d'Isabel II, are the **Cases d'En Xifré** (1840), two neoclassical blocks built by Barcelona's wealthiest man of the era, Josep Xifré i

Casas (1777–1856), who made his pile in Cuba's slave-worked sugar plantations. Barcelona was in a recession at the time, and Xifré wanted to boost confidence. Outside the Plaça Reial, this was the biggest building project of the day and, when rumours began to circulate that Senyor Xifré was going bust, he had a block made of solid gold and stuck in the wall to prove it a dirty lie (he replaced it with granite once the building was completed). On the pediment, Cronos, History and a clock keep company with Urania, muse of astronomy (the Latin reads 'Urania watches the motion of the sky and stars'); on the arcades are portraits of explorers and con-quistadors, and terracotta reliefs of charming *putti* in cheerfully bowdlerized allegories of Cuban trade. One of the city's most famous restaurants, **Set Portes**, was founded as a café by Josep Cuyas when the building was new in 1840, although he died without revealing the enigma of its name (it actually has eight doors). Plaques note the various celebrities who have dined here, including Einstein and Picasso, who lived with his family in an apartment here when he was 14 and newly arrived in Barcelona.

Diagonally across Pla del Palau stands the neoclassical **Duana Vella** (the old cus-toms house, now occupied by the Guardia Civil), containing a series of murals in the Sala de Actos, portraying the reign of Carlos III, life in commercial Barcelona, and the sad adventures that befell Don Quixote in the city—where he was unhorsed and forced to give up knight errantry. Just up from here is the Nou-centista **Estació de França**, erected in 1929 for the International Exhibition. Unlike most stations, it was built on a curve in the tracks, lending the iron struc-ture an unusually sensuous beauty. Although the Estació de Sants now gets most of the trains, the station was attractively revamped in 1992 and one of its new roles is hosting the annual New Year's party and international comics fair; the entire base-ment has been converted into a popular techno club, Woman Cabellero.

Opposite the station, walk up the Passeig de Picasso to see Antoni Tàpies' ***Hom-enatge a Picasso*** (1983)—a glass cube in a pool, containing everyday household items impaled by steel bars, perpetually splashed by jets of water (added after the cube cracked in the heat). The controversial work, according to Tàpies, is based on Picasso's statement that 'A picture is not something to decorate a sitting room, but a weapon of attack and of defence against the enemy.' Local kids love it, at any rate, and use the pool to cool off in the dog days of summer.

Parc de la Ciutadella

In 1714, that bitter date in the annals of Barcelona, the besieged, isolated city fell to the troops of Felipe V after an extraordinary, heroic 11-month resistance. Barcelona knew if it fell it would lose all its rights and vestiges of independence, and so it did. But there was worse to come: half of La Ribera was wiped off the map, to construct, at Barcelona's expense, the 270-acre Ciutadella, one of the most

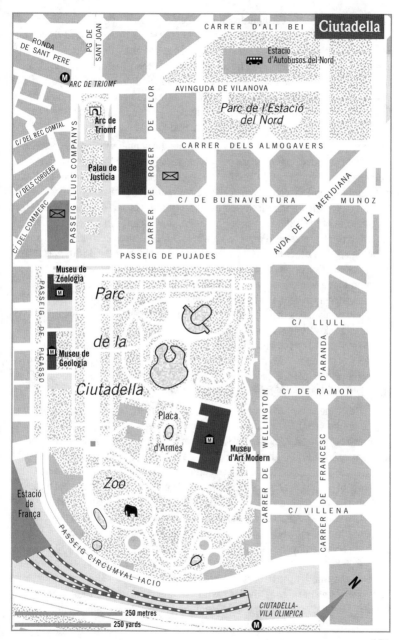

Ciutadella

CARRER D'ALI BEI

RONDA DE SANT PERE

PG DE SANT JOAN

Estació d'Autobusos del Nord

ARC DE TRIOMF

AVINGUDA DE VILANOVA

C/ DEL REC COMTAL

Arc de Triomf

DE FLOR

Parc de l'Estació del Nord

C/ DELS CORDERS

PASSEIG LLUIS COMPANYS

CARRER DE ROGER

CARRER DELS ALMOGAVERS

C/ DEL COMMERC

Palau de Justicia

C/ DE BUENAVENTURA

MUNOZ

AVDA DE LA MERIDIANA

PASSEIG DE PUJADES

Museu de Zoologia

Parc

C/ LLULL

PASSEIG DE PICASSO

de la

Museu de Geologia

D'ARANDA

Ciutadella

C/ DE RAMON

Placa d'Armes

Museu d'Art Modern

CARRER DE WELLINGTON

CARRER DE FRANCESC

Estació de França

Zoo

C/ VILLENA

CARRER DE

PASSEIG CIRCUMVAL·IACIO

N

250 metres

250 yards

CIUTADELLA-VILA OLIMPICA

121

massive fortifications ever built in Europe. Before leaving, the 5,000 evicted residents were compelled to tear down their homes stone by stone, and there was never any illusion about the Ciutadella's purpose: the army of occupation kept its cannons oiled and ready and aimed at the city. When the progressive Catalan General Prim took power with a *pronunciamento* in 1869, he gave the fort to the city, designating 150 acres for a park, and the rest to be sold off for housing to finance the demolition of the walls. Furthermore, Prim declared that the heirs of original property owners should be compensated (and many were).

A competition was held for the park's design, and the winner was Josep Fontseré, an able architect and spotter of talent (his young design team included two unknowns, Domènech i Montaner and Gaudí). The trees he planted were just beginning to make some decent shade when Barcelona's buoyant booster of a mayor, Francesc de Paula Ruis i Taulet, announced that he had secured loans in Madrid to make the park the site of the 1888 Universal Exhibition, to be opened in a mere 11 months' time. Fontseré protested, Fontseré was fired, and the project lurched full speed ahead in spite of other doomsday predictions; Barcelona in the 1880s was in the grips of another recession, and the mood was glum. But Mayor Ruis had no doubt in his mind that a world's fair was just what the doctor ordered and, although it left Barcelona deeply in debt, in hindsight city historians believe that Ruis was right, that the Exhibition was the key event that kept Barcelona from sliding irrevocably into provincial backwardness. Like all good exhibitions, it also served as a stage for innovation—think of London and the Crystal Palace in 1851, or Paris and the dazzling ironwork of the Eiffel Tower of 1889, or Chicago in 1892 and the Beaux Arts movement. Barcelona in 1888 presented the world with Modernisme. It also gave the city a Dizzy Gillespie-size taste for tooting its own horn.

The **gate** at the end of Avinguda Marquès de l'Argentera has some fancy ironwork by the young Gaudí. The **Zoo** (*open daily Nov–Feb 10–5, Mar and Oct 10–6, April and Sept 10–7, May–Aug 9.30–7.30; adm exp*) occupies much of this end of the park, at least for the time being; plans are to move the rather cramped animals out to more roomy quarters at the sea end of the Diagonal. At the entrance, the sculpture of leaping deer is not a foretaste of some of the zoo's inmates but a tribute to Walt Disney from the 1960s. The biggest crowd-puller is **Snowflake**, a rare albino gorilla with a face like a boxer, a personality like Mae West and an acute sense of his own showbiz importance. His arrival as a baby not long before Franco died was regarded by the more facetious Surrealists as a portent: Snowflake was a fallen angel come to announce doom to the smug. Within the zoo stands another symbol: the fountain that became the coy mascot of the 1888 Exhibition, the **Senyoreta del Paraigua**, 'the lady with the umbrella', by Joan Roig i Solé. Her name is Josefina, or Pepita, and like Gaudí the original Pepita came from the town of Reus, near Tarragona. When the fountain's switched on, water spurts from the top of her umbrella.

Near the entrance to the zoo is the **Plaça d'Armes**, now a formal garden with *El Desconsol* (Despair)—a copy of Josep Llimona's famous Rodinesque nude of 1907, gazing into her lily pond, slumped over by the weight of presumably sexual sin. The square has the only surviving buildings from the Ciutadella: a chapel, the Governor's Palace and the Arsenal, designed by Prosper Verboom, with trumpet-mouthed gargoyles. This was later converted into a royal residence, then into an art museum, and during the Republic, with a nice sense of irony, into the seat of the **Catalan Parliament**.

Museu d'Art Modern

Open Tues–Sun 9–7, closed Mon; adm.

The Parliament is now back in business and shares the building with the Museu d'Art Modern, although plans are to move the pictures to the Palau Nacional on Montjuïc. The contents are narrower than the name might suggest: 'modern art' in this case means Catalan art from 1850 to 1920 (the city's patricians never gave a fig for collecting paintings, so that's all there is). Arranged chronologically, it begins with Marià Fortuny (1838–74), the leading Catalan painter of the mid-19th century. The *Vicaria* is typical of his virtuoso manner that wowed them in Rome, where he spent most of his short life: exotic and mysterious, with shimmering coloured costumes. The Diputació de Barcelona sent him to Morocco in 1860 to draw battle scenes: the result was his enormous *Battle of Tetuan* (1863), full of the dust and chaos of war, honouring the 500 Catalan volunteers who fought under General Prim.

Non-idealized Realism, Courbet-style, was introduced to Barcelona by Ramon Martí i Alsina, who painted evocative street and market scenes of Barcelona. Joaquim Vayreda (1843–94), the leader of the Escola d'Olot, specialized in landscapes, rural scenes and pious farmers inspired by Millet and the *Renaixença*. By the end of the century, Realism had evolved into narrative *Anecdotisme*, which the public adored. Key figures were Romà Ribera, who had a soft touch for textures, and Joan Roig i Solé (of the umbrella lady fame) and Arcadi Mas i Fontdevila, both of Sitges, who painted bright seascapes and fishermen, and were locally believed to be in the vanguard of Impressionism; note Roig's singular *Smoking Pot on the Beach at Sitges*.

Then came the Modernistas, led by Ramón Casas. The museum has his famous *Tandem Bike Self-Portrait* painted for Els Quatre Gats—that's Casas pedalling hard in front and the buck-toothed Pere Romeu coasting behind. It also has his remarkable, almost photographic, *Corpus Procession Leaving Santa Maria del Mar*

(1898), painted two years after the Anarchist bombing. Other works are by his friend Santiago Rusinyol, who also liked to shock the bourgeoisie, but did so more in his life than his painting.

The leading Modernista sculptors—Josep Llimona, Miquel Blay and Eusebi Arnau—are represented, although the latter left his best mark on the architecture of the day. In the same vein the museum has an excellent collection of Modernista furniture that Gaudí and Puig designed for their buildings, and exquisite pieces by Gaspar Homar for Domènech's Casa Lleó Morera. A lavish Modernista private chapel built for Joan Busquets from the Casa Cendoya on the Passeig de Gràcia has been preserved, a rare survivor—most were destroyed during the Civil War.

Later Modernista painters ('the Second Generation') were more expressionist in outlook: Isidre Nonell, Francesc Gimeno, a tormented soul who produced deeply textured landscapes, and Joaquim Mir, who worked in bold patterns of colour, as in his voluptuous stained-glass screen. The Noucentista reaction is represented by a Cézanne-inspired search for structure, harmony and pure forms, in the paintings by Joaquim Sunyer of Sitges, Joaquim Torres-Garcia and in the classicizing sculpture of Josep Clarà.

The last two rooms are dedicated to artists of the 1920s and 30s, with sculptures by Pau Gargallo, a chameleon of many styles and wit, and a room of experimental works in iron 'drawn in space' by the innovator Juli González, who only turned to sculpture at age 50 after a career as a metal worker; he later taught Picasso how to weld. Perhaps most compelling of all is Salvador Dalí's *Portrait of his Father*. Dalí senior was a lawyer who supported the work of Anarchist Francesc Ferrer but hated his son's penchant for offending and shocking, a penchant that went as far as to send Franco a telegram of congratulations after he executed five prisoners in 1975. Cruel facetiousness or not, his antics completely alienated old friends like Miró and Buñuel, who stopped talking to him. This portrait, and another work here, are surprisingly the only paintings on view in Barcelona, because Dalí offended to the end, leaving his collections to the Spanish state instead of to Catalunya. Although the region does have his greatest work of all: the museum in his native Figueras.

Also in the Park

The park is well used, especially at weekends, when families come to paddle in little boats under Josep Fontseré's **Cascada**, a superbly ugly pile set in a monumental stair inspired by the Palais Longchamps in Marseille, with mythological allusions stuck here and there: four spitting dragons, Venus emerging from her half shell, and the Quadriga of Aurora. The boulder arrangements of the grotto are said to be by Gaudí. On the under-the-lindens Passeig Tilers, Fontseré redeems himself with the pretty **Umbráculo** (greenhouse for shade plants), a cast-iron building with a wooden lattice roof, while the iron and glass **Hivernacle** (a winter greenhouse, which has a very pleasant café inside) is by Josep Amargós. In between, the neo-Pompeiian **Museu de Geologia** (*open Tues–Sun 10–2, closed Mon; adm*) opened in 1882 as Barcelona's first public museum, chock full of minerals, fossils and rocks from across Spain; many of the fossils come from Montjuïc.

Best of all is the great brick **Castell dels Tres Dragons**, designed by Domènech i Montaner as the Universal Exhibition's café-restaurant, although it wasn't finished in time to sell a single *pa amb tomàquet*. This was the herald of Modernisme, with its innovative use of exposed plain brick and iron, crowned with whimsical ceramic decoration—large blue and white shields decorated with stylized motifs that run under the battlements. It was nicknamed the 'Castle of the Three Dragons' after a poem by Frederic Soler, although these days a herd of smaller creatures calls it home: it's the **Museu de Zoologia** (*open Tues–Wed and Fri–Sun 10–2, Thurs 10–6.30, closed Mon; adm*). The most dramatic exhibits—the whale skeleton suspended across the whole of the ground floor and the elephant skeleton by the back door—can be glimpsed through the windows. The displays inside (with some English explanations) are oddly absorbing in a dusty collector's cabinet sort of way: exquisitely illustrated naturalist books; a poster by Dalí (who was fascinated by scientific theories), using the double helix representing DNA as a kind of Jacob's Ladder for angels to come and go; a collection of swirling tiles from Gaudí's La Pedrera, inspired by three marine motifs (snail, octopus and algae); and, upstairs, case after case of stuffed beasts and impaled insects all silently leering at no one.

Passeig Lluís Companys and the Arc de Triomf

Outside the gate here, the broad **Passeig Lluís Companys** was designed by Fontseré as the park's salon, although all but one of his bronze statues of Catalan heroes were melted down under Franco to make the giant Virgin presiding over the dome of the church of La Mercè. An array of other monuments has taken their place: at the entrance to the park itself, there's a colourful work by Antoni Clavé, dedicated to the centenary of the exhibition, as well as the **Monument to Ruis i Taulet** (1901), featuring a bronze bust of the mayor displaying his famous whiskers—sideburns the size of propellers. On the western side of Passeig Lluís Companys, just off broad C/ del Commerç, is tiny C/ del Petons, 'kissing street', where the poor unfortunates condemned to death in the hated Ciutadella Fortress were allowed to kiss their loved ones goodbye.

On the Passeig Lluís Companys itself rise the towers of the elephantine **Palau de Justicia** (1887–1908), a Modernista work made entirely of stone from Montjuïc, by Josep Domènech i Estapà and Enric Sagnier, richly decorated inside and out. The aim was to create something solid and English in feel, as an inspiration for Spanish justice, which had yet to make a good name for itself. At the top of the promenade stands the ceremonial entrance to the 1888 fair, the **Arc de Triomf** by Josep Vilaseca. With no triumph in particular to commemorate (besides getting the exhibition ready more or less on time), Vilaseca's striking ensemble of *mudéjar*-style ceramic brickwork topped with four crowns manifests, if nothing else, the eternal Catalan longing to be different. Standing to the right, the Noucentista **Grupo Escolar Pere Vila** (1920s), by Josep Goday i Casals, has ceramic reliefs. Behind it, at 12 Avinguda de Vilanova, is Pere Falqués' idiosyncratic brick and iron-work **Central Catalana d'Electricitat** of 1897. A block beyond this is the new bus station, Estació del Nord, and the **Parc de l'Estació del Nord** (1988–91), where old train tracks have been replaced by Beverly Pepper's sinuous earthwork sculpture, defined by blue and turquoise ceramics, evoking day and night.

The one bronze statue from Fontseré's promenade that wasn't melted down was relocated in 1914, to the nearby corner of the Ronda de Sant Pere and C/ d'Ali Bei. This is the romantic and much loved **Monument a Rafael Casanova**, honouring the 54-year-old lawyer and leading member of the Consell de Cent, who grabbed the standard of Santa Eulàlia and led a charge against the Bourbons on the day before the city surrendered in 1714. The statue marks the spot where he fell wounded, and is a rallying point on the *Diada*, Catalan national day, 11 September.

El Raval

You have this Rambla, a beauty...
And there, four steps away, feverish with excess
Wider than the other, the Rambla of the poor
Trembles in the gloom of hellish light.

Oda Nova a Barcelona (1909), Joan Maragall

The *barri* of El Raval (Arabic for 'an area outside the walls') is the largest surviving section of the old city, closed in by the Ramblas, Avinguda del Paral.lel and the Rondas of Sant Pau, Sant Antoni and Universitat. Originally a *terraine vague* of orchards and gardens, the Raval found its role as a haven for the city's rejects—its unpleasant trades, its criminals, but mostly its poor and diseased. When it was joined to the Barri Gòtic by the 14th-century walls, convents and monasteries moved in to fill up the gaps. And so it marinated in its own juices until Spain's industrial revolution was born here. Workers crammed into housing around the factories, and by the 1850s the Raval (then known simply as El Quinto, the Fifth District) was perhaps the unhealthiest and most wretched neighbourhood in Europe. The average life expectancy was 40 years; criminally low pay, epidemics and illiteracy were the order of the day. Even if a man wanted to better himself, he couldn't: 120 days of the year were mandatory holidays, fuelling resentment towards the Church, which in Spain always sided with the upper classes anyway. The lower part of the *barri* became a crowded den of misery, prostitution and crime known as the Barri Xinès, Chinatown, where they kicked the gong around and where the Rose of Fire bloomed the hottest before turning to ashes.

El Raval is still poor, its population now mixed with immigrants from Pakistan and North Africa, but no part of Barcelona has received as much attention from the urban surgeons of the Ajuntament in recent years. The northern half of the Raval, always more genteel, is becoming yet more so thanks to the new contemporary-art museum, seemingly dropped from the sky like a giant white respectability magnet. Even Barri Xinès is only a shadow of its former self, although here the city's urban doctors are taking more drastic measures—the equivalent of a heart transplant. One of the chief lures of the area is its bars and restaurants, for which *see* pp.232–3.

The Old University and Contemporary Culture

Plaça de la Universitat (**Ⓜ** Universitat), at the apex of the Raval, offers a chance to have a look at the old **Universitat Central**, the heir of the Estudi d'Arts i

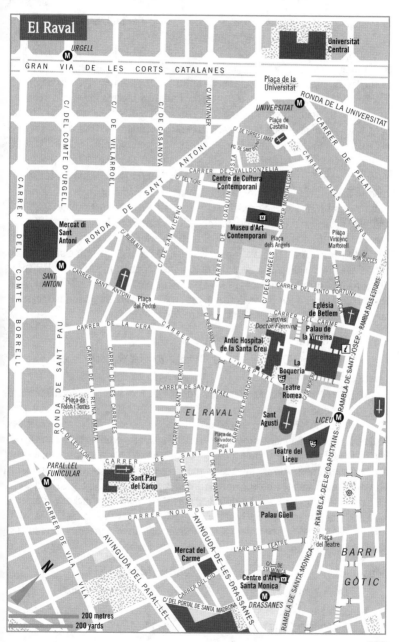

El Raval

Universitat Central

URGELL

GRAN VIA DE LES CORTS CATALANES

Plaça de la Universitat

RONDA DE LA UNIVERSITAT

C/ MUNTANER

C/ DE CASANOVA

C/ DE VILLARROEL

C/ DEL COMTE D'URGEL

UNIVERSITAT

Plaça de Castella

C/ DE TORRES I AMAT

PG DE SANT BERNAT

CARRER DE PELAI

CARRER DELS TALLERS

CARRER DE OVALLDONZELLA

C/ DEL TIGRE

Centre de Cultura Contemporani

JOAQUIM

Museu d'Art Contemporani

CARRER MONTALEGRE

Plaça dels Angels

Plaça Vinçenç Martorell

C/ BON SUCCES

CARRER DEL COMTE BORRELL

Mercat di Sant Antoni

C/ RIERA ALTA

RONDA DE SANT ANTONI

C/ DE SANT VICENÇ

CARRER DELS ANGELS

C/ D'EN XUCLA

CARRER DEL PINTO FORTUNY

SANT ANTONI

CARRER SANT ANTONI

Plaça del Pedró

CARRER DE LA CERA

CARRER

C/ RIERA BAIXA

CARRER DE L'HOSPITAL

Eglésia de Betlem

CARRER DEL CARME

Palau de la Virreina

RAMBLA DELS ESTUDIS

RAMBLA DE SANT JOSEP

Jardins Doctor Fleming

Antic Hospital de la Santa Creu

La Boqueria

CARRER DE SANT PAU

CARRER DE LA REINA AMALIA

CARRER DE LES CARRETES

CARRER DE SANT JERONI

CARRER DEL ROBADOR

CARRER DE SANT RAFAEL

Teatre Romea

CARRER D'EN ROBADOR

Plaça de Folch i Torres

EL RAVAL

Plaça de Salvador Seguí

Sant Agustí

LICEU

RONDA DE SANT PAU

C/ DE LES FLORS

CARRER DE SANT OLEGUER

PAU

Teatre del Liceu

RAMBLA DELS CAPUTXINS

PARAL.LEL FUNICULAR

CARRER DE SANT

C/ DE SANT RAMON

Sant Pau del Camp

CARRER NOU DE LA RAMBLA

AVINGUDA DE LES DRASSANES

Palau Güell

CARRER DE VILA I VILA

AVINGUDA DEL PARAL.LEL

Mercat del Carme

L'ARC DEL TEATRE

C/ DE STA MONICA

Plaça del Teatre

BARRI

GÒTIC

CARRER DEL CID

Centre d'Art Santa Monica

RAMBLA DE SANTA MONICA

C/ DEL PORTAL DE SANTA MADRONA

DRASSANES

N

200 metres
200 yards

129

Medicina, founded by King Martí in 1401. Planned and built between 1860 and 1873, the university was the first monumental building in the new Eixample, designed by Elias Rogent i Amat, a disciple of Viollet-le-Duc. Rogent used the Romanesque idiom to evoke Catalunya's roots, and reached his decorative zenith in the lavish Romanesque-Byzantine **Paranimf**, or auditorium (*open by request*). The courtyard to the left of the entrance, the **Pati dels Lletres** (courtyard of literature), with its orange trees and two-storey arcades, is especially pretty, as are the cool, lush garden and pools in the back. Like most totalitarians, Franco was keen to get students and their irritating ideas out of the city centre, and in the 1950s most of the university was relocated to the new campus in Pedralbes.

Directly across Plaça de la Universitat, **C/ dels Tallers** (street of cutters), the old road to Sarriá, was lined with slaughterhouses in the Middle Ages, when meat-cutting was banned in the city. If you walk along this, the first square, Plaça de Castella, has the rather dull Baroque church of **Sant Pere Nolasc**, formerly the church of the Mercenaris, an order dedicated to saving the souls of slaves. Behind it, C/ de Torres i Amat will take you to Passatge de Sant Bernat for the most important of the few buildings that went up during the Republic: the pale rose L-shaped **Dispensarí Antituberculosós** (1934–8), an exemplary modern clinic designed by Josep Lluís Sert and Josep Torres Clavé; the roof was made into a sun terrace and garden that offered the tubercular a chance to take the air.

Centre de Cultura Contemporani

Open Tues, Thurs and Fri 11–2 and 4–8, Wed and Sat 11–8, Sun 10–3; closed Mon; adm.

At the end of Passatge de Sant Bernat, C/ de la Verge leads to C/ de Valldonzelia; turn right and then right again for the former Casa de Caritat, at 5 C/ Montalegre. First built in 1362, it was remodelled over the centuries to do duty as a cloister for Franciscan nuns, seminary, hospital and, after 1802, as a workhouse for the poor. Then in 1987 the Maremagnum architects, Piñon and Viaplana, dipped it in a postmodernist solution, and it emerged as the Centre de Cultura Contemporani, or CCCB. The dilapidated north courtyard was replaced by a huge glass and steel block that tilts forward; the south façade was also replaced, to make way for the MACBA. The entrance is by way of the pretty 18th-century Pati de les Dones, with mosaic decoration; upstairs the CCCB hosts imaginative temporary exhibitions with unexpected urban themes, and supports local projects.

Museu d'Art Contemporani de Barcelona (MACBA)

Open Tues–Fri 12–8, Sat 10–8, Sun 10–3, closed Mon; adm.

Next door stands the glowing Museu d'Art Contemporani de Barcelona, designed by American architect Richard Meier and completed in 1995. The building almost overwhelms the collection within: all the glassed-in space in front is devoted to ramps leading between the floors (you can't help but think how the skateboarders outside in the square would love to have a go at them) and the art is crushed into second place at the back. It is a vibrant and varied gathering, nonetheless; the core includes such lights as Antoni Tàpies, Calder, Dubuffet, Barceló, Klee, Oldenburg, Raschenberg, and Christian Boltanski—don't miss his sinister bank-vault-like *Réserve des Suisses Morts* (1991). Tàpies is represented by a number of pieces, among them *Pintura Ocre* (1959), a piece of ageing, crumbling wall, scraped away to show the canvas beneath. Joan Brossa has some delightful 'poem-objects'—one is a broom, leaning against a wall, a mundane domestic object until you see that the handle is made of a string of dominoes. In Perejaume's *Postaler* (1984), the artist took a tall cylindrical frame fitted with angled slotted mirrors into different land-scapes and photographed it with all its shimmering reflections.

There are several unsettling pieces, poised between horror and laughter, including an elongated ping pong table with guns laid at each end instead of bats by Francesc Torres entitled *Taula d'Entrenament per a Comunistes Reconvertis* (1991), or 'Training Table for Reconverted Communists'. Even more bizarre is Carlos Pazos' tableau *Aquella Noche Volcí a Llovar con Bambi* (1949), a nightmarish patchwork of found materials, with grotesque creatures galloping through a carpet forest, and a huge neon deer with a pierced heart flashing. The top floor is devoted to tempor-ary exhibitions, which have become increasingly international in outlook since the present director, Manuel Borja-Villel, took over. Near the entrance, there is a very pleasant café-restaurant, and a well-stocked book and gift shop.

The back of the museum, on C/ Ferlandina, has a Keith Haring mural of 1989 called *Together We Can Stop AIDS*, relocated here from another building in the Raval that was torn down. Round the corner here, Plaça dels Àngels is named after the 16th-century **Convento de Els Àngels**, built for Dominican nuns, but later converted into a jail in 1836; in 1984 it underwent a controversial restoration as an art library. Part of it (Nos.4–6) houses the **Foment de les Arts Decoratives** (FAD), the prestigious union of architects, designers, and artists founded in 1900 and bestower of one of Spain's most prestigious architecture prizes; it often puts on contemporary exhibitions (*open Mon–Thurs 9.30–8, Fri 9.30–1.30*). At No.3, the **Centro de la Rehabilition de la Ciudad Vieja** can fill you in on the city's plans for the Raval. Farther down C/ dels Àngels, at the crossroads of C/ del Carme, stands the **Escola Milà i Fontanals** (1921), decorated with elaborate ter-racottas and one of a dozen Noucentista school buildings in the city. C/ del Carme is one of the Raval's most piquant and typical streets; a short stroll to the left will take you to the **Llenceria El Indio**, at No.24, a lovely Modernista textile shop from the early 1900s.

Antic Hospital de la Santa Creu

But backtrack a bit to the **Jardins Doctor Fleming**, benignly surveyed by a bust of Sir Alexander, inventor of penicillin, whom all Spaniards consider the greatest Scot who ever lived; nearly every city in Spain has at least a street named after him. Behind the good doctor extends the enormous Antic Hospital de la Santa Creu. This was the home of one of the oldest hospitals in the world, founded in 1024 and rebuilt here in 1401, with the intention of concentrating all the sick of Barcelona in one place. In the 16th century it had 500 beds; in the 17th century 5,000. Relocated in 1926 to Domènech i Montaner's Modernista masterpiece near the Sagrada Família (one of the last patients to die here before the final move was Gaudí), the hospital's long vaulted halls now shelter books instead of patients: the two huge Gothic arches on either side of the courtyard are the entrance to the national library of Catalunya, Barcelona's largest, with a million volumes.

The former **Casa de Convalecencia** (*under restoration at the time of writing*) was added in the 1680s as a place where patients could recuperate. The vestibule is richly adorned with magnificent *azulejos* (1682) by Llorenç Passoles, based on Rubens' *Conversion of St Paul*; others can be seen on the stair leading to the handsome Gothic chapel, which now functions as a gallery, **La Capella** (*open Tues–Sat 12–2 and 4–8, Sun 11–2; adm free; entrance on C/ de l'Hospital*), with exhibitions of young artists from Barcelona and abroad. Across the square is the surgery college, now the **Real Academia de Cirugía y Medicina**, commissioned by the progressive King Carlos III and designed by the excellent neoclassical architect Ventura Rodríguez in 1764. It has a plush elliptical anatomical amphitheatre (now a ceremonial hall), retaining the original marble dissection table that revolves so students could all have a good peek at the guts. The neglected Gothic **cloister** with its orange trees has some lively carvings to look at if you don't mind the smell of urine.

Not so Mean Streets

Narrow C/ de l'Hospital, along the southern flank of the hospital, is one of the main thoroughfares of El Raval. If, leaving the hospital, you turn left, you'll pass the **Teatre Romea**, built in 1863 and now owned by the Generalitat, although it's been upstaged by Ricardo Bofill's new Teatre National de Catalunya. A bit farther down is the woebegone, never finished 18th-century church of **Sant Agustí**, with its knobbly stone spikes colonized by pigeons. The Augustinians were relocated here when their monastery was toppled for the Ciutadella. Their church here was torched twice, in 1835 and 1936, leaving little of interest inside. It does, however, hold a place in Barcelona's heart, since in 1971 it became the birthplace of the Assemblea de Catalunya, a broad-based opposition movement that called for liberty of expression, amnesty for political prisoners, and the re-establishment of the 1932 Statute of Autonomy. When the police belatedly found out, many participants were arrested, but the die was cast for a new kind of nationalism that united everyone from Communists to Catholics. Afterwards, the authorities kept a close eye on anything that happened at Sant Agustí, most famously the funeral in March 1974 of Salvador Puig Antich, the leader of a revolutionary group called the Iberian Liberation Movement. Accused of killing a policeman, he was the last man to be garrotted under Franco, in spite of widespread protest. His funeral was attended by most of Barcelona's intellectuals and nationalists, and many boys born in Barcelona that year were named Salvador in his honour.

The street along the side of Sant Agustí leads down to C/ de Sant Pau, where just on your right you'll see the once grand **Hotel España**. In 1902–3 Domènech i Montaner redesigned the ground floor, and the friendly staff don't mind if you pop in to look at the well-preserved Modernista dining room, decorated with a mural of sea creatures and mermaids with scuba flippers by Ramón Casas (they were painted over during the prudish Franco regime) swimming over ceramic roundels representing the provinces and cities of Spain. The bar retains a wonderful, massive alabaster fireplace by Eusebi Arnau, with allegorical figures and a pussycat.

Continuing down C/ de Sant Pau is little **Plaça de Salvador Seguí**, dedicated to the famous union leader, nicknamed 'Sugar Boy', who was gunned down on this spot by hired thugs in 1923. Opposite, the **Marsella** has been owned by the same family for five generations and is one of the few Raval bars that has remained immune from change, even to the extent of serving the same old brain-draining homemade absinthe to slumming trendies. At the time of writing, the great landmark in this area is the enormous hole ripped out of its gritty heart; this will be the **Plaça de Pere Coromines** (named after an Anarchist writer of the 1890s), the centrepiece of the area, an immense, tree-lined promenade. It is the most ambitious part of the city's dogged and increasingly successful attempts to improve the area. A strange and emotional tension is apparent in the clumps of immigrants who gather, some with tatty deckchairs, to watch the old, colourful apartment blocks with their flapping laundry being noisily demolished to make way for new, mostly subsidized housing and an entirely new way of life. To see what the city has planned for the area visit the Centre for the Rehabilitation of the Old Town (*see* above).

If you're in a hurry, you can continue straight west for Sant Pau del Camp (*see* below) or turn east for the Ramblas; if not, backtrack a bit to C/ de Junta de Comerç to return to C/ de l'Hospital. To the left on C/ de l'Hospital, at No.109, is the **Farmacia Sastre Marqués**, designed by Puig i Cadafalch in 1905, with a beautiful iron lantern hanging from the corner that was knocked off by a passing truck a few years ago. A few minutes' walk leads to triangular **Plaça del Pedró** ('of the stone column'), home of the oldest monument in Barcelona, said to mark the spot where Santa Eulàlia was crucified, while the snow fell to cover her nakedness. Her statue, first made of wood, was replaced with stone by the Consell de Cent in 1673.

Whatever anticlerical sentiments were in the air, the neighbourhood never extended them to its virgin martyr, and saved the statue when the radical municipal government of 1823 wanted to turn it into whitewash. She was removed in the troubles in 1835 but replaced soon after, only to be smashed by the Anarchists in 1936 (her head was rescued and is now in the Museu d'Història de la Ciutat). Frederic Marés made the current statue, in 1951. Here too is the simple Romanesque chapel of **Sant Llàtzer**, dedicated to Lazarus, patron saint of lepers; this is all that remains of the Hospital dels Mesells, founded in the mid-1100s by Bishop Guillem Torroja, far from the city, and used as a lazaretto to quarantine sickly-looking arrivals. The brick Modernista **Carme church**, just up C/ Sant Antoni, replaces the most beautiful church lost in the fires of 1835, one that was as lovely as Santa Maria del Mar.

Mercat di Sant Antoni

Open Mon–Sat 8–2 and 3–8, Sun 9–2 for old books and coins.

In the old days, C/ Sant Antoni led to the gate that linked Barcelona to the rest of Spain, making it the scene of grand entrances and royal processions. Where the gate once stood, the **Mercat di Sant Antoni** now fills an entire square of the Eixample. Designed in 1882 by Antoni Rovira i Trias (author of the losing plan for the Eixample), this cathedral of spuds and carrots remains one of Barcelona's most impressive iron structures, shaped like an X with four long naves extending crossways to each chamfered corner. Much of the original decoration, restrained by Barcelona standards, is intact. One stand, Aviram Joana, has beautiful Modernista wrought iron and coloured glass.

From the market, Ronda de Sant Pau follows the line of the old walls down to the **C/ de la Cera**, a street named after an old candle factory and now the Raval's Romany neighbourhood, where denizens are famous for their mad bonfire leaping on St John's eve. C/ de la Reina Amalia heads south of here past the site of the Carcel Modelo (no one knows why it was called the 'model prison', but it has carried the name with it to its current location in the Eixample). A city historian could probably point out the exact section of **Plaça de Folch i Torres** that was once the Pati dels Corders, where prisoners were executed with the *garrotte vil*—the vile garrotte, Spain's 'humane' killing machine—an iron collar attached to a chair, which the executioner tightened to choke off air and crush the cervical vertebrae. As the screws were tightened on Santiago Salvador, the Liceu bomber, he sang Anarchist hymns and cried *'Viva el anarquismo!'* as long as he still had breath.

Sant Pau del Camp

Open Wed–Mon 11.30–1 and 6–7.30, Tues 11.30–12.30.

At the end of C/ de la Reina Amalia, the sturdy, squat **Sant Pau del Camp**, or 'St Paul's in the Field', is the best of the few Romanesque churches to survive in

Barcelona. Built over a Roman cemetery that was used into Visigothic times, isolated in the gardens and orchards of the Raval, Sant Pau was probably founded by the son of Wilfred the Hairy, Count Guifré-Borrell (d. 911), whose tombstone is here. Subsequently destroyed in the Moorish raids in 985 and 1115, Sant Pau was re-dedicated in 1117 by Vicounts Geribert and Rotlandis. In 1528, the monastery became a Benedictine priory linked to Montserrat. After serving as a barracks in the Napoleonic wars, it became a parish church, and survived later attempts at demolition thanks to the Catalan Excursionistas, who fought to preserve it.

Sant Pau's façade looks its age, decorated with blind arcading, strikingly archaic reliefs of the hand of God, the symbols of the Evangelists, and a wealth of bizarre little masks. The marble columns on either side of the door are made up of a mix and match assortment of 7th- and 8th-century bits. Inside, three apses are crowned by an octagonal tower—the rest was burned in the *Setmana Trágica* in 1909. Best of all is the tiny cloister with its paired columns and triple-lobed Moorish arches and garden, one of old Barcelona's most charming corners.

Avinguda del Paral.lel

Just to the west of Sant Pau lies the Avinguda del Paral.lel, the old 'Montmartre of Barcelona'. This street has had a number of official names in its career, but Paral.lel has stuck ever since 1794, when it was discovered to lie exactly on the 41° 44' parallel—fascinating to the Barcelonans, whose city otherwise refuses to square with the compass. Although the intention in the 19th century was to make the street posh and exclusive, it refused to cooperate and in 1895 launched its showbiz career with the Spanish Circus Theatre. Music halls, Flamenco *tablos* and cinemas sprouted up, creating a gaudy neon-lit fantasy land; the satirical glittering revues that took place here were the direct ancestors of Barcelona's vibrant contemporary theatre scene. The area around the Parel.lel metro was also the centre of Anarchism, where it wasn't unusual for the clubs and bars to have agitators passing the hat around 'to buy dynamite'. In 1937, when the Anarchists were in control of Barcelona, they closed down the music halls and brothels as unworthy of the revolution. When the Communists won the fight for the streets, they quickly reopened.

Two music halls have survived near the metro: **El Molino**, 99 C/ de Vila i Vilà, founded in 1909 as Barcelona's answer to the Moulin Rouge, and the **Teatre Arnau**, 60 Avinguda del Paral.lel, facing a small square dignified with a statue of Raquel Meller, a famous singer who got her start here. The nearby **Bar Español**, now blandly remodelled, was a seething nest of conspiracy in the decades before the Civil War. Down a bit, at 113 C/ Nou de la Rambla, the old **Apollo** has made the transformation from music hall to trendy club, while **Bagdad**, at No.103, once notorious for putting on the raunchiest live sex show in town, has added virtual-reality Internet sex to the menu. But Barri Xinès ain't what it used to be.

Barri Xinès

C/ Nou de la Rambla is the main street of what was once Europe's biggest red light district, the section of the Raval nearest the sea and the sailors. It became the Barri Xinès, but not because of any Chinese immigrants: a journalist named Angel Marsá, having read the lurid descriptions of Chinatowns in America, applied it to this roughest and most piquant of all Barcelona's slums, and the name has stuck around like herpes. Its huddled masses were painted by Isidre Nonell, and then by the impoverished young Picasso, who had his first studio here and used the district's poor, mad, blind and 'mothers whose milk has dried up' as the subjects for his Blue Period. Connoisseurs of the low life have immortalized it in other ways, most famously Jean Genet, who recorded his experiences as a rent boy, drag artist and thief in his *Thief's Journal*. Much to the disgust of proper Barcelona, the notoriety of the Barri Xinès brings thousands of tourists to peep up the city's skirts instead of to the Eixample, where they should be admiring its fancy dress.

Although still insalubrious and unsafe after dark, the Barri Xinès has been so decaffeinated over the past decade that neither Genet or Picasso would recognize it today. And its days are numbered. A series of nasty heroin-related deaths led to a massive clean-up before the Olympics and to the closing and demolition of the seediest flophouses. Old blocks of flats are being restored; new ones are being built. In the 1960s, Porcioles, the mayor appointed by Franco, took the first steps in cleaning up the slum by driving Avinguda de les Drassanes up from the sea to Nou de la Rambla (a project that's being continued by the Ajuntament to C/ de l'Hospital) and planting a lofty eyesore, the **Edifici Colom**, right on top of the most notorious brothel, Can Manco. A bit up from here, the once crapulous C/ del Cid leads to the **Mercat del Carme**, built over a school of thieves. The man who made the district world famous is remembered in the new **Plaça Jean Genet**, at the corner of Avinguda de les Drassanes and C/ Arc del Teatre.

Gaudí's Palau Güell

Open Mon–Sat 10.15–1 and 4.15–7; guided tours only, in groups of no more than 30, so arrive early; tours take place every 15 minutes; adm.

From C/ Arc del Teatre, C/ de Lancaster returns to C/ Nou de la Rambla, where on the right at No.3 stands the Palau Güell, Gaudí's first major project for his patron, and the first modern building to be declared a World Cultural Heritage site by UNESCO. Construction began in 1886, when the young architect was given what amounted to a blank cheque by his affluent patron. It was finished in 1888, at enormous cost, to coincide with the Universal Exhibition.

The area was an eccentric choice for the period: the Eixample, where the Modernista architects were concentrating their work, was by far the most desirable residential area. But Eusebi Güell had a fondness for the Raval, which had always been his family home, and he wanted to invest in the rundown and insalubrious district. A secret passage was built to connect this house with the older Güell residences on the Ramblas. For all the effort and expense, the family actually spent little time here, preferring their mansion by the Park Güell. During the Civil War, the Palau was taken over for use as a *cheka*, a Communist Party prison for members of the POUM, who had supported the Anarchists in the battle for Barcelona's streets in 1937 and were suspected of Trotskyite leanings. According to rumour, one prisoner here was Trotsky's secretary, Andreu Nin, son of Spanish composer Joaquim Nin and brother of Anaïs, who disappeared in Barcelona and was never heard from again. Forty years later, Antonioni used the heavy, brooding 'exquisitely incoherent' atmosphere of the palace as a setting in his film *The Passenger* (1977).

The façade is restrained for Gaudí, with the exception of the swirling ironwork incorporating the Catalan coat of arms splayed across the tympanum of the two main arches. The household's coaches passed into an interior courtyard vaulted with Gaudí's signature bare-brick parabolic arches; wooden floors muffled the clattering, and the pretty ceramic-tiled ceiling was designed to be easy to clean. The coachmen would then head down the steep ramp to the subterranean stables while the Güells and their guests glided up the sombre marble-columned staircase, topped with a patriotic red and yellow stained-glass window. The series of vestibules leading into the central hall are ingeniously designed to allow as much natural light as possible. Columned galleries overhang the street, expanding the interior space, all overhung by ornately carved coffered ceilings. Stained glass depicts Shakespearean characters—a nod to another of Güell's passions. The visitors' gallery has a particularly elaborate ceiling; among the dense, Moorish designs are secret spyholes which enabled the Güells to surreptitiously overhear their guests' conversations. A delicately decorated ladies' powder room is off to one side, where one hopes, for the guests' sake, most of the real gossip was passed on.

At the heart of the house is the lofty salon, overlooked by galleries and culminating in a magical three-storey-high parabolic cupola, a honeycombed beehive pierced with silvery shafts representing a constellation topped by the moon; this was Güell's dome of Montsalvat, the castle where the Grail was kept in Wagner's *Parsifal*. The salon has perfect acoustics and was used for concerts, dances and gatherings. The wide upper stairway formed a convenient musician's gallery, while the incongruous dour paintings of martyrs and saints wrapped around the corners attest to Güell's morose piety and complete lack of interest in painting, traits shared by Gaudí. The richest materials were reserved for the family chapel: 16ft panels of rare hardwoods and ivory sheathed in white tortoiseshell fold back to reveal an alcove which once held a sculpted altarpiece of tortoiseshell and wood, destroyed during the Civil War, and a small organ with a red marble panel to protect the ladies' modesty and hide their legs.

Many of the furnishings survived the war (by being elsewhere), including a huge Japanese-style fireplace guarded by scaly wooden serpents, and the enormous dining table, recently purchased from Güell's heirs, with sumptuous leather embossed chairs. The upper floors, which contained the family's apartments and the servants' quarters and kitchen, are still under restoration, but a steep narrow staircase leads out on to an amazing rippling roof, the best feature of the house. One of Gaudí's missions as an architect was to make roofs as interesting as the rest of the building, and here, in a space few people would actually see, he let his imagination and invention run wild to create a forest of 20 chimney sculptures, each organic and different and covered in *trencadís*. Eight were so damaged that they were rebuilt in 1988–92 by modern artists, in the manner of Gaudí. In the centre, the beehive dome of the salon is contained in a spire with a row of parabolic windows, topped by a lightning rod and an eerie bat.

Catalan Bats

They're not as obvious as the dragons, but they're there, like a B-minor chord in the Catalan bestiary. If you've ever been to Mallorca, you will recall that Palma's symbol is the bat, installed there directly after its capture in 1229 by Jaume the Conqueror. Whether or not Jaume was fluent in Arabic is unknown, but his Templar allies and counsellors were: 'bat' in Arabic has the same root as the word associated with ruins and 'to overthrow'. But the bat was not a mere message of a *fait accompli* to his new Moorish subjects, for it had a second meaning in Arabic as well—'seeing well only at night'. Idries Shah once explained:

> *Like the bat, the Sufi is asleep to 'things of the day'—the familiar struggle for existence which the ordinary man finds all-important— and vigilant while others are asleep. In other words, he keeps awake the spiritual attention dormant in others. That 'mankind sleeps in a nightmare of unfulfilment' is a commonplace of Sufi literature.*

For Güell, a peeker into esoteric corners, the bat was the perfect creature to watch over his house. You'll also see bats on Pere Falque's streetlamps along the Passeig de Gràcia, and on the Casa Oller on the same street. It's also the trademark of a Catalan wine exporter to Cuba named Facundo Bacardi Masós, who began to distil rum in 1862. The Bacardi company, however, claims that their bat is merely a bat who haunted the rafters of their first distillery. Or so they say.

Seaside Barcelona

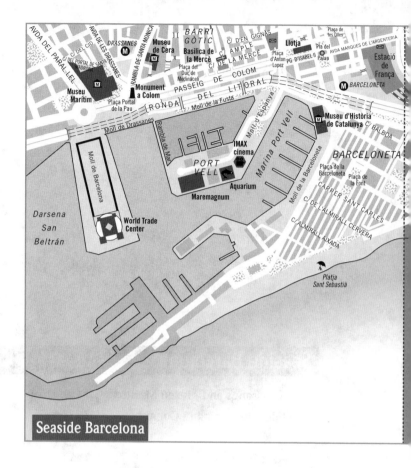

Seaside Barcelona

In the 13th and 14th centuries, Barcelona's dominance in the Mediterranean was such that her sailors boasted that 'not even a fish would dare to appear without the *quatre barres*', the flag of Catalunya. Endowed by nature with only a mediocre port (the only mediocre port between Tarragona and Perpignan), Barcelona's maritime success came by way of sheer determination and mercantile savvy. The sea was a strictly business proposition, leaving no room for any Venetian-style monuments or razzmatazz. Until 1887 sea walls, and then, later, shabby dock buildings crowded the water, which was oil-slicked and bobbing with garbage in a haze of

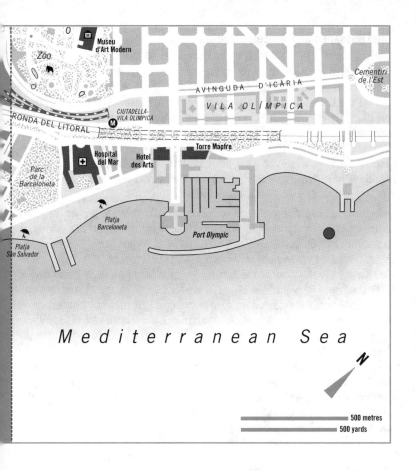

Zoo

Museu
d'Art Modern

Cementiri
de l'Est

AVINGUDA   D'ICÀRIA

VILA OLÍMPICA

CIUTADELLA-
VILA OLIMPICA

RONDA DEL LITORAL

Torre Mapfre

Hospital
del Mar

Hotel
des Arts

Parc
de la
Barceloneta

Platja
Barceloneta

Port Olympic

Platja
San Salvador

Mediterranean Sea

N

500 metres
500 yards

anchovy and diesel-stink. That was 1980. Since then, there has been
a sea change: with the same determination and savvy that made the
mess, the Ajuntament's planners have swept all the freighters and
containers away into the Zona Franca, and turned Barcelona into a
Mediterranean playground, bobbing with yachts instead of plastic
bags, lined with Blue Flag beaches instead of junk, buzzing with
clubs, bars, restaurants and shops instead of flies. On summer
weekends it can be elbow room only. For places to eat and drink in
the area, *see* pp.233–4.

The Drassanes and Museu Marítim

To begin where it all began, start in the **Drassanes** (**⓪** Drassanes), the largest and best-preserved medieval shipyards in the world. The first Arab *darsena*, or ship-yards, were replaced with bigger and better ones in 1255 by Pere II the Great, and in 1388 the Drassanes took their present form, the construction costs shared by Pere III the Ceremonious, the city and the Corts. Originally they stood smack on the water, and in their long bays 30 galleys could be built at the same time. The Spanish navy took them over in 1663 after the War of the Reapers, then in 1941 gave them back to the city, worse for wear but now beautifully restored as the **Museu Marítim** (*open daily 10–7; adm*), devoted to Catalunya's proud seafaring history.

Although the architecture steals the show—the high atmospheric vaults are long enough to melt into shadows—the exhibits below offer much to ponder. There's a display on Mallorcan cartography from the Middle Ages, when that island's Jewish community had Europe's most advanced school of map-making. There are fac-similes from the *Catalan Atlas* of Abraham i Jafuda Cresques of 1375, the *Carta de Vallseca* of 1439 that belonged to Amerigo Vespucci, and Juan de la Cosa's map of 1500, the first to show the New World. There are displays on ancient and medieval ship construction, ships' models (some in ivory, some in bottles, and instructions on how to get them in there), figureheads, seamen's chests painted with biblical warn-ings of women's wiles, and a copy of Jaume the Conqueror's famous *Llibro del Consulat del Mar*, medieval Europe's first maritime code. A full-scale replica of *La Real*, Don Juan's flagship at Lepanto, built in 1971 in honour of the 400th anniver-sary of the battle, now stars in the kid-pleasing 'Great Adventure of the Sea'—which comes with English-language headphones. You'll learn how at sea you could *smell* a galley long before you could see it (fortunately virtual reality still has its limitations). Another exhibit takes you aboard a trading ship in a storm, on an imaginary ocean liner to Argentina, and down with Narcis Monturiol in his submarine.

Moll de Barcelona and Columbus

On the far side of the Drassanes, along the Avinguda del Paral.lel, stand the last sur-viving stretch of the city's 14th-century **walls** and their gate of Santa Madrona. Lurking unexpectedly in C/ del Portal de Santa Madrona is Fernando Botero's mas-sive bronze Sumo wrestler *Gat* (1981). Another new addition, the unusual **'Smoke fountain'** by Pedro Barragán, is in the roundabout at the foot of the Paral.lel. Beyond this, the **Moll de Barcelona** is the focal point of the last stage of the waterfront redevelopment. I.M. Pei's huge semicircular **World Trade Center**, beleaguered by financial woes and indecision, partially opened in 1999, in its final state will contain offices, a convention centre, concert hall, shops and a jumbo hotel to spearhead Barcelona's ambition to become the Mediterranean's container port capital as well as its busiest cruise port. Already, half a million passengers call every year, and the city is enormously proud of the fact that it can receive nine large cruise ships simultaneously, a feat surpassed only by Miami. One hopes this inspires Barcelona to repair the tower and aerial cableway linking Barceloneta to Montjuïc strung up for the 1929 fair—the rickety old ride was as hair-raising as any in a funfair.

Barcelona's original 225-tonne seaside bagatelle, the **Monument a Colom**, a 164ft cast-iron column made of melted cannons from the castle of Montjuïc and topped with a statue of Columbus, was erected at the foot of the Ramblas for the 1888 Universal Exhibition. Despite the scaffolding currently coiled around the column (it was built so quickly and shoddily that it was rusting away), you can ascend into the crown under Columbus' feet for the big view by taking the lift up—the first one, according to Barcelona's tireless boasters, to be installed in a column (*open Oct–May Tues–Sat 10–2 and 3.30–6.30, Sun 10–7; June–Sept daily 9–9; adm*).

Columbus, Pro and Con

Barcelona's Columbus is the biggest monument to the admiral anywhere in the world, and the irony of Barcelona's honouring the one man who led to the loss of its prestige and prosperity, as Spain turned to the Atlantic and Seville took over as the country's premier port, was not lost on the citizenry from the word go. Note that he has his back to Castile, and points not to America but towards Italy (where Barcelona's merchants wish he had stayed). Actually the intention in 1888 was to catalanize Columbus, that international man of mystery. Since Catalan, along with Portuguese and Castilian, were among the languages he wrote in (not Italian), and because he always went to great lengths to cover up his origins (probably because he was illegitimate), there was a nationalist faction that claimed that he was really the Catalan Joan Colom from Girona (Gerona), which could easily be confused by a slip of the pen with Genoa (Genova). No one gives this much attention today, although in recent years Salvador de Madariaga has proposed an intriguing if entirely circumstantial theory that Columbus was from a Jewish family in Mallorca who had fled the bigotry by emigrating to Genoa, and that when Columbus was shipwrecked in Portugal in 1476 he had the *chutzpah* to completely re-invent himself. Mallorca was famous for its maps, which would explain where Columbus and his brother learned their cartography.

Barcelona does have some authenticated Columbus associations, major and very minor, all of which are celebrated in the statuary around the base of the pillar. He met Fernando and Isabel here in 1493 after his first voyage, when he received the title of Admiral of the Ocean Sea and an annual stipend that kept the wolf from the door in his later years of disappointment and hardship, when the Catholic kings reneged on all their other promises. On his second voyage he took along a Catalan priest, Bernat de Bol, who became the first bishop in the New World. Today Catalan nationalists are more likely to disclaim him altogether: a replica of the *Santa Maria* moored nearby was burned by militants in 1989, and events celebrating the anniversary in 1992 were boycotted—even the choral societies refused to sing. The biggest celebration turned out to be the statue's wedding, arranged by Catalan conceptual artist Antoni Miralda, with the Statue of Liberty. Miralda talked Birmingham into supplying the wedding ring; Paris made Liberty's wedding gown; and Valencia sewed the world's biggest pair of blue jeans for the groom. The shoes he wore are in the Museu del Calcat (*see* p.95).

Port Vell

Columbus now has a hard time being noticed at all in the flashy waterfront re-development of the Port Vell, or old port. If you aren't sailing off on a big cruise boat, you can catch a little one at the Moll de les Drassanes at Columbus' foot, a **bus nautic** to Barceloneta or a **Golondrina** 'swallow' tour, in business for over a century; their old-fashioned double-decker boats will take you out to the lighthouse and the Passeig de l'Escullera, site of Salvador Aulèstia's *Sideropoloide* (1963), a large collage of metal relics and wrecks found at the bottom of the sea. The building next to Columbus, the **Duana Nova**, or New Customshouse, is a silly neo-Renaissance wedding cake by Enric Sagnier (1902), policed by gimlet-eyed sharp-beaked griffons ready to pounce on smugglers and tear them to shreds.

A handsome wooden bridge with high undulating arches, the **Rambla de Mar**, links Columbus to the **Moll d'Espanya** and rotates to let sail boats through. The old Moll's new occupants include a huge glass and chrome shopping mall and nightlife vortex, **Maremagnum**, Piñon and Viaplana's playground with four floors of bars, restaurants and shops that make it a daytime whirl as well. There's an **IMAX cinema**, with an 88ft-high screen, an omnimax dome screen 96ft in diameter, and a 3D system for good measure, showing the usual IMAX mix of nature extravaganzas, dinosaur blockbusters and rock concerts throughout the day. Then there's an **Aquarium** that claims to be the largest in Europe (*open July–Aug daily 9.30am–11pm; June and Sept daily 9.30–9.30; Oct–May Mon–Fri 9.30–9, Sat–Sun 9.30–9.30; adm exp; audioguide available*). The star of the show is the vast central tank, encircled by a 225ft viewing tunnel equipped with a slow human conveyor belt and serenaded by gentle New Age music; the patterns of silvery fish and sharks swimming all around and over your head are remarkably soothing. From summer 2000, the aquarium is opening three new interactive centres that kids will enjoy.

On the landward side of the Moll d'Espanya is the **Moll de la Fusta**, until very recently a favourite, if slightly rundown, seaside promenade with restaurants and bars. The most famous bar was Gambrinus, topped by Mariscal's 20ft fibreglass prawn, which is currently the subject of a fierce battle for ownership as the restaurants and bars are being forced to close, apparently to make way for a new line of tourist information kiosks and an extension to the Museu Marítim. What will remain for certain is Roy Lichtenstein's brightly coloured mosaic sculpture, *Barcelona Head* (1992), a 42ft comic strip woman's head with a dragon or snake below.

The Old Seafront

Behind the Moll de la Fusta lies the old seafront, now relatively quiet, or it would be if you could wave a fairy wand and make the traffic disappear. The Passeig de Colom was widened when the sea ramparts were razed, and in 1882, to the wonder of Barcelona, it became the first street to get electric lighting. The prettiest square here, the **Plaça del Duc de Medinaceli**, was another gift of the church-burners of 1835; the land reverted to the duke, who in 1849 hired Daniel Molina of Plaça Reial fame to create a residential square. The centrepiece is the first iron monument in Barcelona, a column and fountain of 1849. The hard part was deciding whose statue should go on top, looking out to sea: the final selection was a Catalan vice-admiral, Galceran Marquet, who beat Genoa in a sea battle in 1331.

The **Capitanía General**, 14 Passeig de Colom, envelops the 17th-century convent of La Mercè, and owes its ponderous façade and incongruous little Herrera-style obelisks to Adolf Florensa, added in the 1929 campaign to spruce up the city for the International Exhibition. Inside, the Mercè's beautiful cloister, covered with ceramics, is perfectly preserved, but you'll have to write well in advance for permission to have a look. Two streets in from here is the **C/ Ample**, 'wide street'—wide enough for carriages, which in the 16th century was good enough to make it the city's most aristocratic address, where Emperor Carlos V and the kings of Hungary and Bohemia stayed, and where Barcelona's merchant princes waited for better times.

The toffs worshipped at the **Basilica de La Mercè** (*open Mon–Sat 10–1 and 6–8.30, Sun 10–1.30 and 7–8.30*). Our Lady of Mercy joined St Eulàlia as co-patroness of Barcelona when she appeared in a vision to Jaume the Conqueror, asking him to found an order devoted to the deliverance of Christians held by Barbary pirates. The first church dates from 1267, but was rebuilt to fit Counter-reformation ideals; its concave Baroque façade was transplanted from a church that was destroyed to make way for the Ajuntament's annexe. The fittings are Baroque, and there's a fine Gothic statue of the Virgin (1361) by Pere Moragues, worshipped in a side chapel added in 1888. She saved Catalunya from a plague of locusts in 1687 and, when Barcelona was hopelessly fighting the besieging Bourbons in 1714, she was made commander of the army. The Bourbons proved to be tougher than the locusts. As if to emphasize the point, her statue on the dome, destroyed in the Civil War, was recast in 1956 from melted-down bronze statues of Catalan heroes.

These days the Virgin's devotees include members of F.C. Barcelona, who sing her a hymn of thanks whenever the team wins an important match. During the third week of September, all Barcelona joins to celebrate the Festa Major de la Mercè, with music and dancing, processions of *gegants*, human towers, and the city's most spectacular and daring *correfoc*. At other times, the *plaça* by the church may well be deserted except for an early 19th-century **statue of Neptune** with four sphinxes, which finally found a home here after being shunted around half of Barcelona. Just off the square, two sweeping 18th-century bridges span C/ de la Carabassa to connect the aristocratic townhouses.

C/ Ample, now better known for bars than kings, ends at Barcelona's temple of letters, the **Correus** (1927), designed to awe visitors sending postcards from the 1929 Exhibition. Opposite, where the Ronda del Litoral highway dips underground, stood one of the glories of the 1888 fair: Domènech i Montaner's **Hotel Internacional**. Barcelona at the time had no first-class rooms to put up all its expected guests and, in a mere 53 days before the opening of the fair, Domènech and his 2,000 workers built a five-floor, steel-frame, brick-clad 1,600-room hotel, using prefabricated models and non-union workdays extended by Passeig de Colom's new electric lights. Part of the hotel extended on to a floating platform. Photos show that, as huge as it was, it didn't stint on design and had a beautiful Modernista courtyard. Domènech even kept within his budget. To the regret of many at the time and today (especially anyone who arrives in the city without a reservation) it was also the world's first disposable hotel, and was razed the next year.

Museu d'Història de Catalunya

> *Open Tues and Thurs–Sat 10–7, Wed 10–8, Sun and hols 10–2.30, closed Mon; adm.*

Back on the waterfront, round the bend from the Moll de la Fusta, stretch the old warehouses, the Magatzems Generals, rehabilitated by a Canadian team into the **Palau de Mar**, home to a row of restaurants along the marina and the Museu d'Història de Catalunya. It was designed to give an overview of Catalan history from the Palaeolithic era to the present, with an emphasis on hands-on interactive devices: millstones to grind up grain, a suit of armour with a mirror for visitors to admire their new look, a host of buttons to push, dozens of touch-screen computer terminals with more snippets, plus photos and videos and models of ships and buildings and domestic interiors. On the upper floor, a glass-topped relief lets you tramp like Gulliver across a Lilliputian Catalunya. Although it is possible to borrow a small English guidebook in the gift shop, the descriptions are almost exclusively in Catalan, which can put many exhibits, despite all the buttons and bells, out of the reach of most visitors. The rooftop café is a treat, though, with views out over the port, and the museum shop has a particularly good collection of unusual gifts.

Barceloneta

In 1718, the destruction of 61 streets and 1,262 homes in La Ribera to build the Ciutadella left many people in makeshift shelters on the beach, broke after paying for the destruction of their own homes. The misery continued until 1753, when a French military engineer with the delicious name of Prosper Verboom designed a neighbourhood for the displaced on this 25-acre triangle reclaimed from the sea. Following the most progressive planning ideas of the time, the streets of Barceloneta were laid out in a grid, with a market in the central square and long, narrow blocks of houses, permitting every room to have a window. As all houses were allowed only one upper floor, all had access to sunlight and air. Verboom's height prohibition was modified in 1837 and ignored ever since, so that most houses in Barceloneta have at least four floors, turning the straight narrow streets into mini canyons, perfect for running a maze-athon. In central Plaça de la Font, by the **market** (rebuilt in 1884), a pair of two-storey houses remain at Nos.30 and 32. On Plaça de la Barceloneta, the little 18th-century Baroque church of **Sant Miquel** (*open mornings*) is dedicated to Barceloneta's patron saint; it once sheltered the remains of the Marquis de la Mina, the chief promoter of the planned neighbourhood, but his mausoleum disappeared at the start of the Civil War.

Traditionally inhabited by families of sailors, longshoremen and fishermen, Barceloneta is still vibrant and densely populated—and not very happy that many of its seafood restaurants have moved to the Vila Olímpica. If you're around in late September after the big Festa de la Mercè, don't miss Barceloneta's smaller but exuberant *festa* starring a bizarre cartoonish general called Bum Bum (a take-off of Prosper Verboom) who leads the neighbourhood kids around the *barri* firing off cannon; in the evenings everyone ends up on the beach, or out in boats, for dancing and fireworks.

At other times you can seek out the public art: the crane-like **Balances** (1992) on 16 C/ de l'Almirall Cervera, a work by Jannis Kounellis, celebrating the port workers, or Mario Merz's **Crescendo Appare** (1992) along the Moll de la

Barceloneta, where the numbers of the Fibonacci series are embedded under glass in the pavement (while you're counting away, look up at 43 Passeig Joan de Borbó to see the **Casa de la Marina** with its distinctive wooden blinds [1953] by Coderch and Valls, one of the first buds of modern, postwar Spanish architecture). In Plaça de Mar, towards the derelict-looking tower of the aerial cableway, is the most mysterious of the city's public sculptures, *A Room Where it Always Rains* (1992) by Juan Muñoz, in which five melancholy bronze figures, human on top and beach ball below the belt, occupy a room made of bronze bamboo with a wet-looking marble floor.

The string of beaches which make up **Platja Barceloneta** get packed in summer, after being seriously cleaned up in the Olympic frenzy. They are lined with palms and decked with Rebecca Horn's lofty *Homage to Barceloneta* (1992), a swaying, stacked iron column which echoes the narrow old buildings of the *barri*. Just by the sculpture, the last of the *chiringuitos*, a creaky, wooden snack bar of the kind that had done a brisk trade on the beaches since the 19th century, held out against city pressure to close down before finally succumbing in 1993.

Vila Olímpica and Nova Icaria

Until the late 1980s, the seafront between Barceloneta and the Besos River was occupied by decrepit textile factories, warehouses, dumps, shabby housing and train yards—the dreary sprawl of Poblenou, one of several cradles of Barcelona's industrial revolution. Even if you could get to a beach, the water stank. Poblenou had a reputation as savoury as toe jam.

Poblenou was originally called Icaria, not after the obscure but excellent Greek island but after a dream that soared like the Icarus of myth. The dreamer was Etienne Cabet, who, exiled from France for his anti-monarchist diatribes, went to London. There he became a follower of Robert Owen and cooked up his own socialist workers' utopia, described in the form of a Platonic dialogue with Owen in his *Voyage en Icarie* (1842). In Cabet's Icaria, only law would rule; there would be no élite, no democracy, but a perfectly egalitarian society run by state *apparatchik* control freaks, a whole century before Stalin came up with the same great idea. Cabet's vision was promoted in Barcelona by editor, pacifist and submariner Narcis Monturiol, who headed a group of a few hundred Icarian Catalans, including Josep Anselm Clavé, founder of the Orfeó Català.

In 1848, Cabet, with 66 French and three Catalans, set sail over the Atlantic in search of Icaria, buying the land for their utopia sight unseen from a New Orleans property shark. It was a snake-infested wasteland, and the whole thing bellyflopped like Icarus himself. The survivors then purchased an old Mormon settlement in Nauvoo, Illinois, then petered out into splinter groups that limped on until the last

Icaria, in Cloverdale, California, closed shop in 1895. In Barcelona, however, Monturiol's enthusiasm had spread to the working classes, who called their neighbourhood Icaria and dreamed of better days in the sun. Not long after the collapse of Cloverdale, the Ajuntament discreetly changed the name to Poblenou.

The need to house 15,000 athletes for the Olympics propelled the Ajuntament in 1986 to undertake Nova Icaria Ltd., Barcelona's biggest urban-renewal project of the century. Coastal train tracks were laboriously relocated, and 500 acres of Poblenou were expropriated and flattened to create the **Parc de Mar**, opening up 5km of new public beaches, and the **Vila Olímpica**, a district as rigidly planned as Barceloneta, but in many ways its antithesis. The master plan was entrusted to old hands Martorell, Bohigas, Mackay and Puigdomènec, who laid out the streets and plotted the housing that would become some 2,000 apartments after the games, along with a church, sports centre, hotel, office buildings and service buildings linked to the remodelled Hospital del Mar, which served as the Olympic hospital. Each building was confidently commissioned from a past winner of the FAD Arquitectura prize, and each ducked under the occasion, while the opportunity to make a focal point, or even something vaguely interesting, out of the deluxe **Hotel des Arts** and the **Torre Mapfre**, Spain's tallest skyscrapers, was declined, leaving two boring boxes by the beach.

Bohigas stated that Nova Icaria Ltd. would be 'a homage to the utopian socialism of the 19th century' and promised that some housing would be subsidized and affordable. But that was just a promise: the wealthy snapped them up, and the few businesses that have moved into the American-style commercial areas are not exactly neighbourhood shops. What completes the chill suburban air of the Vila Olímpica is the feeling that this is the one area of Barcelona clearly more friendly to cars than people, marked by wide streets, prominent car parks (even along the marina), forbidding 'gate buildings', and big desolate spaces between the traffic, decorated with outsize fountains and sculptures. One of these, in Parc de les Cascades, is the ironic **David and Goliath** (1992), with spindly figures with kite faces, by Antoni Llena. Another, in Parc de Carles I, is the big **Culo de Úrculo** (Úrculo's arse), named after its Basque sculptor, mooning all passers-by. The metal **Pergolas** by Enric Miralles along Avinguda d'Icària resembles dead trees crossed with TV antennae. Needless to say, it's all fantastically popular, especially the **Port Olympic**, a confluence of shops, restaurants, beachside cafés and clubs, topped with the enormous headless **Copper Fish** by Frank Gehry, a glistening hunk of postmodernist bait that lures in the crowds from the beaches and promenades, where kids swish by on rollerblades and skate boards.

For the sake of contrast, continue to the end of Avinguda d'Icària, to the **Cementiri de l'Est**, the city's first monumental cemetery, founded in 1773 when all the old graveyards in the choked walled town were turned into squares and building sites. It, too, is choked, with a surreal accretion of monuments and memorials of the fathers of Barcelona industry, a preview of the lavish postmortem paraphernalia up in Montjuïc's Cementeri de Sud-Ouest, founded when this boneyard was filled up. Madrid is proud of its sculpture of Satan in the Retiro park, but here Barcelona has something just as fey in its *Kiss of Death*.

Poblenou

Beyond the Cementiri de l'Est is what remains of **Poblenou**, which lost its last factory in 1992 and has since been seeking alternative uses for the buildings left behind, as art studios, clubs and so on, although the trend seems to be to knock them down to build flats. With the beach on one side, the Vila Olímpica on the other, and the new development planned up the coast, Poblenou is positioned to pull itself up a notch or two on the social ladder. It already has its own pleasant and leafy **Rambla del Poble Nou** as a central axis. Near here, the former textile plant **Càtex**, 275 C/ de Pallars, is an unusually pretty one, with a French mansard roof. The famous Anarchist commander of the CNT, Buenaventura Durriti, worked here; it's now a civic centre, with a swimming pool and restaurant.

Meanwhile, the bodacious success of the Vila Olímpica has spurred the Ajuntament to consider the next available space along the seafront, christened **Diagonal-Mar** after the big road that has been extended to meet the sea. Plans are to make it the focus of the Culture Forum 2004, to move the zoo here from the Parc de la Ciutadella, and heaven only knows what else.

The Eixample

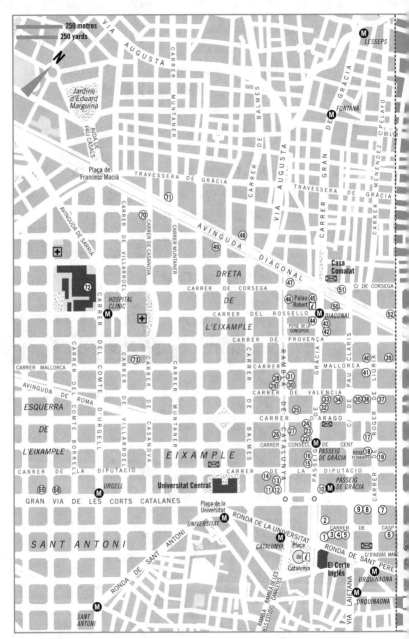

250 metres
250 yards

N

Jardins
d'Eduard
Marguina

AVDA DE
PAU CASALS

Plaça de
Francesc Macià

VIA AUGUSTA

CARRER MUNTANER

CARRER DE BALMES

CARRER DE SARRIA

AVINGUDA DE SARRIA

TRAVESSERA DE GRÀCIA

VIA AUGUSTA

CARRER GRAN DE GRÀCIA

CARRER MENENDEZ I PELAYO

C/ DE L'OR

M LESSEPS

FONTANA

TRAVESSERA DE GRÀCIA

CARRER DE GRÀCIA

71

70

CARRER DE VILLARROEL

CARRER DE CASANOVA

CARRER MUNTANER

AVINGUDA DIAGONAL

48

49

72

HOSPITAL
CLINIC

M

CARRER DEL COMTE D'URGELL

CARRER DE VILLARROEL

CARRER DE CASANOVA

CARRER MUNTANER

CARRER DE BALMES

DRETA

DE

L'EIXAMPLE

CARRER DE CORSEGA

CARRER DEL ROSSELLO

CARRER DE PROVENÇA

RAMBLA DE CATALUNYA

CARRER DE GRÀCIA

CARRER DE PAU CLARIS

CARRER DE ROGER DE LLURIA

Casa
Comalat

47

46 Palau 45
Robert

51

C/ DE CORSEGA

50

M DIAGONAL

52

PSTGE DE LA
CONCEPCIO

44

43

42

40

39

41

73

CARRER MALLORCA

AVINGUDA DE ROMA

ESQUERRA

DE

L'EIXAMPLE

CARRER MALLORCA

CARRER DE VALENCIA

28 31
29 30

33 34

35 36 37

32

25

CARRER D'ARAGO

24

CARRER CONSELL DE CENT

26 27 23

22

17

PSTGE PERMANYER 18
19

EIXAMPLE

CARRER DE LA DIPUTACIO

URGELL

Universitat Central

16
15

CARRER DE LA DIPUTACIO

PASSEIG
DE GRÀCIA

14 13

11 12

10

PASSEIG DE GRÀCIA

69 68

GRAN VIA DE LES CORTS CATALANES

Plaça de la
Universitat

UNIVERSITAT

M

RONDA DE LA UNIVERSITAT

9 8

7

2

CARRER DE CASP

1 3 4 5

6

SANT ANTONI

RONDA DE SANT ANTONI

CATALUNYA

Plaça
de i
Catalunya

M Plaça
CATALUNYA

RONDA DE SANT PERE

El Corte
Inglés

C/ D'AUSIAS MARC

M URQUINAONA

URQUINAONA

M SANT
ANTONI

RAMBLA DELS ESTUDIS

RAMBLA DE LES CANALETES

VIA LAIETANA

The Eixample

GRÀCIA

C/ L'ALEGRE DE DALT

CARRER DE L'ENCARNACIO

Ⓜ ALFONS X

GUINARDO Ⓜ

CARRER DE LEPANT

Ⓜ JOANIC
TRAVESSERA DE GRÀCIA

Hospital de la
Santa Creu
i Santa Pau
㊉
57

SAGRADA

HOSPITAL DE
SANT PAU Ⓜ

FAMÍLIA

AVINGUDA DE GAUDÍ

㊉

CARRER DE CORSEGA

CARRER DE CORSEGA

CARRER DE CORSEGA

PASSEIG DE SANT JOAN

CARRER DE DOS DE MAIG

52

VERDAGUER
Ⓜ

AVINGUDA DEL ROSSELLO

SAGRADA FAMÍLIA

39

54

CARRER DE PROVENÇA

Plaça de la
Sagrada
Família

56 Ⓜ Plaça
de Gaudí

ENCANTS
Ⓜ

C/ MALLORCA

Plaça
Verdaguer

AVINGUDA DIAGONAL

CARRER MALLORCA

CARRER DE GIRONA

53

C/ DE VALENCIA

55

CARRER DE VALENCIA

38

C/ D'ARAGO

CARRER D'ARAGO

C/ CONSELL DE CENT

PASSEIG DE SANT JOAN

CARRER DE FLOR DE CENT

CARRER CONSELL DE CENT

20 21
Ⓜ GIRONA

MONUMENTAL
Ⓜ

58

CARRER DE LA DIPUTACIO

CARRER DE LEPANT

61

GRAN VIA 62 Ⓜ DE LES CORTS CATALANES

Plaça de les
Glòries Catalanes

Ⓜ
GLORIES

TETUAN ✉

6

CARRER DE GIRONA

DE CASP

PASSEIG DE SANT JOAN

CARRER DE ROGER

CARRER DE CASP

60

67 64
66 65
63

CARRER D'AUSIÀS MARC

59

C/ D'ALI BEI

CARRER D'AUSIÀS MARC

RONDA DE SANT PERE

C/ D'ALI BEI

CARRER DE

Estació
d'Autobusos del Nord

AVINGUDA DE LA MERIDIANA

ARC DE TRIOMF Ⓜ

AVINGUDA DE VILANOVA

Ⓜ
MARINA

SANT MARTI

153

> *Barcelona, bourgeois city, dampener of every spirit. Oh, bourgeois*
> *moreton dancers and blankets. Nothing has substance. Oh!*
> *Everything is middling. Middling wealth; middling social rank.*
> *Symbol of everything middling...*

Joan Maragall

Maragall, Barcelona's leading poet at the start of the 20th century, was a bourgeois resident of the Eixample, and as the translator of the likes of Nietzsche and Goethe into Catalan he was liable to downplay his unheroic peers who took so much pride in commerce and common sense. Wonder, however, is the sense one feels today in their old stomping ground, wonder and the realization that it really is impossible to see the world as their eyes saw it. The same wonder surrounds Knossos or Machu Picchu or Milton Keynes, or any historical and geographical one-off. Like them, the Modernista masterpieces of the Eixample speak of a season that can never be recaptured; they speak of a rare combination of a blank slate, talent, skill, quirkiness, imagination and money, with Anarchist bombs providing a restless *basso continuo* in the background and Gaudí off in his corner trying to save their souls with the Sagrada Família. And perhaps most intangibly of all, they speak Catalan.

History

The facts do their usual best to elucidate. By the early 19th century, Barcelona was going crazy, bursting in its walled straitjacket. The city fathers endlessly petitioned the government in Madrid to remove the walls, and Madrid refused, fearing among other things that a bigger and perhaps even badder Barcelona would extend the firing range of its cannons on Montjuïc and in the Ciutadella. At last, in August 1854, during one of Spain's brief interludes of liberalism, permission was granted. As soon as word reached Barcelona, a wild celebration filled the streets as every man, woman and child started hacking away at walls, even with their bare hands. The Bourbon wall was made of tougher stuff than the Berlin wall: it took 34 years to dismantle; but it was so despised that not a single block of it was left in place to remind anyone that it had ever existed. You will find stretches of Barcelona's Roman and medieval walls, but Bourbon, never.

Now that the lid was off, the city in 1859 sponsored a competition for the plan of the new 'widening', or Eixample. The finalists were both Catalans. The Ajunta-ment chose the plan of municipal architect Antoni Rovira i Trias, who proposed exciting prospects and boulevards fanning out of the Old City, respectful of its axes and origins, an organic translation between old and new (you can see it engraved by his statue, *see* p.198). To Barcelona's outrage and dismay, Madrid intervened and imposed the losing scheme (to this day no one really knows why) by a Socialist engineer named Ildefons Cerdà, who designed a plan that has nothing whatsoever to do with the Old City, a modular grid of uniform wide streets, with distinct bevelled or chamfered corners (*xamfrans*) at the intersections to allow the new steam trams to turn more easily and lend a touch of grandeur to each intersection. But unlike most grids, especially American ones, Cerdà's intention wasn't to create lots to buy and sell as easily as possible. His visions were utopian: his pure abstract plan would eliminate social classes—there was no reason why one block should be better than another—and there would be gardens in the centre of each block, with light, air, windows and good drainage for all. Markets, parks, hospitals and social services would be distributed at equidistant points.

It's hard not to feel sorry for Cerdà, who spent his life and entire fortune on his vision but remains unforgiven to this day (not only has he never got a statue, but the only thing named after him in Barcelona is a ghastly traffic intersection). The fact is that few city plans have been more hated or had their intentions dragged so disdainfully in the mud. Barcelona quintupled in size over the next 50 years on the lines of the Pla Cerdà, but little more than the *xamfrans* survived its designer's dreams, and the speculators would have dumped even those as wasteful had Madrid not kept an eye on the map. The other elements of Cerdà's plan—the height and density restrictions, the parks and social services—soon went by the wayside; buildings and car parks filled in the blocks instead of gardens.

Nor did Cerdà's ideas on equality make it off the blueprints. Just as Paris has its Right and Left Banks, so Barcelona has its Right Eixample (Dreta de l'Eixample) and less desirable Left Eixample (Esquerra de l'Eixample), divided by C/ de Balmes, where the tram ran until the 1920s. To further compensate for the enforced equality of the Pla Cerdà, Modernista architects created their masterpieces for their wealthy clients. If the Barri Gòtic is Europe's largest medieval neighbourhood, the Dreta de l'Eixample (or to be more precise, the Quadrant d'Or between the Barri Gòtic, Diagonal, C/ Roger de Flor and C/ Muntaner) holds the greatest trove of 19th-century architecture, with over 150 listed Modernista buildings.

The Eixample was neglected and disfigured under Franco, but over the past decade the Ajuntament has sponsored a massive programme to restore, polish and preserve this unique legacy; in some cases, even Cerdà's gardens have been planted in the heart of the blocks. You can see the highlights of the Eixample in half a day by walking straight up the Passeig de Gràcia to the Diagonal then taking the metro over to the Sagrada Família. To see more requires perseverance: the distances are daunting and, even if the Modernistas get under your skin, you'll keel over if you try to see everything at once. One way to explore the Quadrant d'Or is by bicycle, especially on Sundays when the traffic is less intense. For suggestions of sustenance along the way, *see* pp.234–5.

Passeig de Gràcia and Around

The greatest concentration of Modernista masterpieces is along the Eixample's most elegant boulevard, the Passeig de Gràcia. In the late 18th century, when the rest of the Eixample was covered in drying calico, the old road to Gràcia was the 'Elysian fields' of dance halls, makeshift theatres, beer gardens and amusements; in the next century it would have a giant roller coaster. The first trees were planted in 1827, and by 1872 it had its first horse-drawn trams. A decade later, the Passeig de Gràcia was the centre of fashion, Barcelona's Millionaire's Row; before the advent of celebrity-gawking magazines like *Hello!*, this is where people came to stare at the nabobs, who civic-mindedly built showcase houses to receive their homage. In 1905, the municipal architect Pere Falqués added the final touch, beautiful iron-work streetlamps topped with bats that spring halfway over the street.

Now that the élite has headed for the hills, their houses mostly contain shops and offices. But the *passeig* still has an elegant, leafy air and a sea-green pavement of hexagonal blocks, decorated with the same octopi, starfish and nautilus shell motifs that Gaudí designed for the courtyard of the Casa Batlló. The very first building, on the corner of Plaça de Catalunya, the **Casa Pascual i Pons [1]** (Nos.2–4), offers a preview of coming attractions: built in 1891 by lukewarm Modernista Enric Sagnier, it has a pair of fat towers with pointy roofs in the corners. Cerdà's *xam-frans* forced architects to come up with new solutions to corners and angles, and towers in all shapes and sizes were a favourite. A case in point is just across C/ de Casp: the fancy French Gothic **Cases Rocamora [2]** (1917), by Joaquim and Bonaventura Bassegoda, is actually three buildings wrapped in a single façade, topped with a fairy-tale belvedere turret over the *xamfrà*.

At this point, a brief detour to the right down C/ de Casp will take you to the **Teatre Tivoli [3]** (1917), the heir of an 18th-century wooden playhouse, with a lavish interior of gilt plaster, and the **Casa Llorenç Camprubí [4]** (1901), at No.22, Adolf Ruiz i Casamijana's Modernista excursion into the neo-Gothic, decorated with floral motifs, fantastic animals and a charming cornice. An interesting Art Deco reaction to the same, the **Casal de Sant Jordi [5]** (1929), is on the *xamfrà* with C/ Pau Claris, guarded by a statue of St George, in place even before the building became the ministry of justice of Catalunya. The architect, Francesc Folguera i Grassi, was the first to reverse the floors, putting the owner's fancy apartment on the more private top floor instead of on the first 'noble' floor, where they had always been since the Middle Ages: it was about that time when a new nuisance was first making itself known—the noise of automobile traffic.

At 48 C/ de Casp is Gaudí's first apartment building, **Casa Calvet [6]** (1898–1900), a sturdy and for him surprisingly symmetrical stone and iron glance back to the Baroque. But even here, in his most conservative building, details show his hand—the ironwork on the façade and in the vestibule, the two crosses on the cornice, the lavish first-floor bay window (or *tribuna*, a common feature in Eixample houses, providing both a ringside seat over the street and the showcase for family display) and the plate under the knocker, whimsically shaped like a bedbug. Senyor Calvet had a passion for mushrooms, which prompted Gaudí's interest in funghi; later, especially after the Park Güell, there would be rumours that the architect was 'touched by the mushroom'. What is true is that after this building he rarely drew a straight line again. The Casa Calvet won the Ajuntament's coveted prize as the best building of 1900—the only award Gaudí ever won. But he always felt unappreciated by Barcelona, which never offered him a public commission after his streetlamps in Plaça Reial. Next door at No.46 is the sober **Casa Salvado** (1904) by Juli Batllevell; knowing that he couldn't compete with his illustrious neighbour, he built an innocuous building that would slip by unremarked.

A block north of here on C/ de Roger de Llúria runs the Gran Vía de les Corts Catalanes, one of Cerdà's three big boulevards, where the monumental **Hotel Ritz [7]** (1919) holds forth, the balliwick of the rich and famous, converted into a workers' cantina during the Civil War; the fountain in front, the **Font de Diana** (1913), shows the goddess of the hunt sitting uncomfortably over squirting conch shells. Heading back along the Gran Vía, you'll pass at No.658 the **Casa Oller [8]** (1900) by Pau Salvat, with ornate Modernista details; note the peculiar capitals by the door, carved with an owl, bat and lizards, the floral ironwork around the *tribuna* and an equally lavish vestibule. No.654, **Casa Camil Mulleras [9]** by Enric Sagnier (1904), is more subtle but deserves a look, too, especially its vestibule.

Back on the Passeig de Gràcia, at No.18, the swanky streamlined façade of stone and glass blocks rounding the corner of the Gran Vía de les Corts Catalanes and Passeig de Gràcia belongs to the **Joieria Roca [10]** (1934) by Josep Lluís Sert, although this minor masterpiece of International Modernism was greeted with tremendous hostility from the bourgeoisie as an alien intruder in their Eixample. A more recent intruder is Josep Granyer's bronze *Meditació* (1972), a bull sitting in the same pose as Rodin's *Thinker*—one of Barcelona's first witty public sculptures, and proof that the butterfly was coming out of the cocoon even before Franco died. Nearby, at 595 Gran Vía, you can't miss the wonderfully flatulent **Cine Coliseum [11]**, a big fat Beaux Arts cinema palace of 1923, famous for showing the first talkie in Spain in 1929 (Ernst Lubitsch's *Love Parade*). The eclectic **Casa Pia Batlló [12]** (1891–6), up at 17 Rambla de Catalunya, by Josep Vilaseca, has handsome wrought-iron decoration. His solution of framing a façade on a *xamfrà* with polygonal *tribunas* would be much copied throughout the Eixample. Next door at

No.19, the Viennese Seccessionist-style **Casa Heribert Pons [13]** (1909; now the Generalitat's Department of Finance) is an unusual building for Barcelona. It has balconies decorated with allegories of the arts by Eusebi Arnau, who also sculpted the goddess Diana in the ornate vestibule. Round the corner here, at 246 C/ de Diputació, the lavish, recently restored **Casa Casimir Clapés [14]** (1907), by Joaquim and Bonaventura Bassegoda, was built for a textile magnate, who reminds passers-by of the fact with reliefs on the façade. If you had days to wander the Eixample, you'd find hundreds of decorative clues about the owner of each building's profession or fancies.

Returning to the Passeig de Gràcia, you can see the kind of commercial building the bourgeois preferred, the **Unión y el Fénix Español [15]**, at 21 Passeig de Gràcia, architecture with enough heft to lift even a mundane business like insurance into the realm of heroes and gods. At No.27, the **Casa Malagrida [16]** (1905; now a bank), by Joaquim Codina, is a charming palace topped by a French dome and elaborate dragon weathervane, built for an *indiano* who made his loot in the textile trade in Argentina; note the eagle (Spain) and condor (Argentina) by the door and the original iron lamps in the vestibule.

The oldest buildings in the Eixample are just to the right, down C/ del Consell de Cent, at C/ de Roger de Llúria: the simple neoclassical **Casas Cerdà [17]** (1862–4), built by Antoni Valls on land owned by Josep Cerdà (no relation to the planner). Originally occupying the four *xamfrans* of the intersection, two were demolished and one disfigured during the Franco years, leaving only the one at 340 Consell de Cent. Turning right at the corner on to Roger de Llúria, you'll come to the entrance to the **Passatge de Permanyer [18]**, a lane of charming terraced houses from 1864, built in defiance of Cerdà's plan to have only gardens in the blocks. Now it's some of the priciest real estate in Barcelona. Opposite, a passage at 56 Roger de Llúria leads to Josep Oriol Mestres' neo-Romanesque **Torre de les Aigües [19]** (1879), a water tower built to supply the first houses on the Eixample. Restored in 1987, it now provides a focal point for a delightful garden (*open 10–6*), of the kind Cerdà intended for each block. Two blocks farther along the Consell de Cent, at the corner of C/ de Girona (No.73), is the lovely Modernista bakery **Forn Sarret [20]** (1906), its façade laced with sinuous woodwork; another, the **Forn de la Concepció [21]**, with striking paintings, is at No.74.

The Fairest of Discords

The most famous stretch of the Passeig de Gràcia, between C/ del Consell de Cent and C/ d'Aragó, is known as the **Mansana de la Discòrdia**—a pun on *mansana*, which means both 'apple' and 'block' (it actually works better in Castilian than Catalan, in which the real word is *poma*). Here any passer-by can play the role of the Trojan Paris and award the prize to the fairest of the three wildly contrasting Modernista beauties, commissioned by the city's smartest families.

Casa Lleó Morera [22]

The first, the Casa Lleó Morera, was built in 1864, making it one of the first houses in the Eixample. Between 1902 and 1906, the owner let Domènech i Montaner have his way with it, and the result is his most lavish residential project, the corner crowned with an ethereal ceramic cupola, the whole frosted with decoration inside and out by Domènech's team of master decorators, led by sculptor Eusebi Arnau. For Barcelona's élite, wealth wasn't the only thing to flaunt on a façade: the family's interests, social status, business connections and hobbies were advertised as well. As the ground floor of the Casa Lleó Morera was destined to house a photographer's studio, Arnau covered it with nymphs and reliefs relating to electricity and cameras, all sacrificed in 1943 by Loewe of Madrid, in the interests of larger shop windows; the original cupola and interior furnishings were stripped as well (after decades of criticism, Loewe remodelled the windows and door in 1992, so at least the contrast isn't quite as glaring as it was).

On the second floor, however, the nymphs survived the ruthless leather-goods-mongers, one holding a gramophone as a symbol of bourgeois leisure, one holding an electric bulb, and another a camera. A pink column gleams from the round bay window on the right; the part visible from the street is made of Carrara marble, while the base is made of cheap Catalan stone. The lions and the mulberry tree adorning the balcony are a play on the family surname—Lleó i Morera. As much as they liked to show off in front, the smart families wanted to keep from the gaze of those living behind their home (inevitable in the grid formation of the Eixample); a gorgeous stained-glass bay window of happy roosters in the country by Joan Rigalt provides both a glamorous screen and a voluptuous rush of colour, while the walls are covered in delightful ceramic mosaic portraits of the family pic-nicking in the countryside (small-scale versions of the type that Domènech would use in the Palau de la Música) and intricate floral wood inlays by Gaspar Homar; the furnishings he designed for the house are among the highlights of the Museu d'Art Modern. Next, at No.37, is Enric Sagnier's understated Louis XVI-style **Casa Mulleras**, the last building to be remodelled in the block (1910), and discordant in its way, as an example of the post-Modernista reaction to its neighbours.

Casa Amatller [23]

Two doors down at No.41 is the Casa Amatller, called 'the apotheosis of decorative arts' when it was revealed to the world (*tickets for the Ruta del Modernisme, see p.214, are on sale in the lobby, Mon–Sat 10–7 and Sun 10–2, and staff give free commentaries on the three façades; check for times of tours in English*). In 1898 Antoni Amatller i Costa, the Willy Wonka of Catalan chocolate, started the home redecorating trend on the Mansana when he hired Puig i Cadafalch to give his existing house a neo-Gothic makeover. Puig's neo-Gothic, however, is like no one else's: the façade, decorated with ceramic plaques and discreet geometric *sgraffito*, culminates in a remarkable stepped gable richly aglitter with blue, pink and cream tiles, its shape a reference to Flanders, once an unwilling colony of Spain (like Catalunya), but also the place where chocolate prices were set, so a frequent port of call for Senyor Amatller.

The whole façade is an allegory of Amatller's life and passions, one of which was Catalan nationalism, expressed by the delightful Eusebi Arnau in sculptures that in their playfulness and vigour hark back to the gargoyles in the Generalitat. Between the two doorways, we see St George battling the dragon, watched by a swooning princess; soulful figures represent painting, sculpture, architecture and music; monkeys hammer away at iron while rabbits stow the finished product, in a vignette of happy industrious workers. A bespectacled donkey engrossed in a book while his friend twiddles with a camera are references to Amatller's love of reading and his new photographic interests; the frogs blowing glass and pigs playing potter by the third window hint at Amatller's collection of Greek vases.

Perhaps Amatller spent too much time on his hobbies, because his wife ran off with an opera singer before the façade was finished; as a consequence, the *tribuna*, which in the best houses was used to show off the latest fashions to the hoi polloi in the street, was built to one side, near the bedroom of young Miss Amatller, the new lady of the house. The window decoration culminates in an almond tree, a play on the family name, with a curling letter 'A' surrounded by almond leaves. The same motif is found on the grand staircase, along with a stern eagle, and a lovely stained-glass skylight. The original elevator still wheezes its way between floors; near it, three little sculptures in the vaulted ceiling demonstrate how to make chocolate: the first creature crushes the beans, the second stirs it all up—and the greedy little third has made himself sick. The main floor retains most of its rich decoration, more sculptures by Eusebi Arnau and woodwork by Gaspar Homar, and now houses the **Institut Amatller d'Art Hispànic** (*open for tours Thurs at 11 and 12, by appointment only, © 93 216 01 75; library open Mon–Fri 10–1.30, closed July and Aug*), founded by Teresa Amatller in 1942. It houses a library and a rich collection of Roman glass; Gothic paintings by the likes of Serra, Bernat Martorell, Huguet and Bermejo; and modern works by Ramón Casas and Santiago Rusinyol in a hall designed by Gaspar Homar. The **Joieria Bagués** on the ground floor has a collection of stunning Modernista jewellery by Lluís Masriera; you can see this with a Ruta del Modernisme ticket (*see* p.214).

Casa Batlló [24]

Next door, in stark contrast to the sharp right angles, is the extraordinary Casa Batlló. This was also an older building, belonging to textile tycoon Josep Batlló, who became bored with its banality next to its neighbour. He commissioned Gaudí to give it a facelift in 1904. From the start the architect promised something completely different: 'The corners will vanish, and the material will reveal itself in the wealth of its astral curves...and it will be like a vision of Paradise.' It is also Barcelona's biggest allegory of St George and the dragon, covered with a magnificent rippling blue skin of ceramic plaques and *trencadis*—Gaudí stood in the middle of the Passeig de Gràcia and 'painted' the façade, directing workmen in the arrangement of the colours, which change according to the light that falls on it; at night it shimmers and glitters magically by streetlight. Gaudí's great collaborator Josep Maria Jujol topped it with an equally sublime coloured roof—the dragon's scaly back (the arched window is actually a peephole that allowed Gaudí to check on the progress of the Sagrada Família). The characteristic Gaudí pinnacle with its bulb dome and cross is St George's lance, piercing the dragon and placed to one side to complement the symmetry of the Casa Amatller; the colourful *trencadi-*covered chimneys, invisible from ground level, look like the dragon's multi-spiked tail. The first floor is the dragon's lair; the first balcony depicts the rose which grew from its blood, while the other balconies hint at the skulls and tibia of the dragon's victims. Other observers have seen other visions in the façade—a representation of the sea, with soft aquatic blues and greens and bubbling windows hollowed out by the waves, or an allegory of the Venice Carnival, with a pert Harlequin, balconies forming masks, and a dappled, confetti-strewn façade.

The first-floor apartment, completely redesigned for Battló down to the furniture, is just as stunning: there isn't a straight line in the whole place, and it contains what must be the most sensuous staircase in the world, based on the curve of the dragon's tail. The only way to see the apartment, however, is by renting it for a few hours. Otherwise, you can step into the vestibule from Monday to Friday to see the magnificent blue ceramic light-well, which imperceptibly avoids the effect of light glaring down into a pit by means of colour, using dark tiles at the top that gradually lighten as they descend until reaching white at the bottom. The back of the house is pretty as well, visible from an alley off C/ d'Aragó.

Squeezed between fancy façades at No.39 is the inconspicuous Regia perfume shop, with a **Museu del Perfum** (*open Tues–Fri 10.30–1.30 and 4.30–7.30, Sat 11–1.30; closed Sun and Mon; adm free*) tucked in the back, devoted to the history of the perfume bottle (sadly, you can look but can't sniff). The display begins with tiny Corinthian alabastrons from the 7th century BC and Roman glass phials, still bearing an iridescent shimmer. It culminates in the newest 21st-century scents.

Some of the prettiest are the atomizers from the early 20th century, with long tasselled pumps to spray perfume in great, film-star clouds; the fanciest split like golden eggs to reveal dozens of tiny phials. There are a couple of exclusive flask designs from Dalí (for Schiaparelli) and Lalique (for Coty Cyclamen), and some shockingly un-PC titles—it's unlikely The Little Woman would be a big seller now. The collection, built up over 40 years and now one of the biggest in the world, has bottles from all over the world, including Thailand, China and the old USSR (Red Moscow, decorated with a red star and a silhouette of the Kremlin at night).

Fundació Antoni Tàpies and Around

Round the corner from the Mansana de la Discòrdia at 255 C/ d'Aragó, the **Fundació Antoni Tàpies [25]** (*open Tues–Sun 11–8, closed Mon exc on holidays; adm*) occupies the headquarters built by Domènech i Montaner for his brother's publishing company, Editorial Montaner i Simón (1880–5). As the first expression of Domènech's theories, the building is a prototype of Modernisme, as well as an early example of the architect's love for good bare Catalan brick and iron. It was Barcelona's first domestic building with an iron frame, and the elaborate brick patterns are a reference to the Moorish-influenced *mudéjar* work of early Christian Spain. Tàpies himself loved everyday materials, which he used for the *Núvol i Cadira* (Cloud and Chair) hovering over the building like a giant steel wool pad.

Born in 1923 to a bourgeois family in Barcelona and educated at law school at the insistence of his father, Antoni Tàpies was a sickly child who relished the days spent in his sick bed, sketching and gathering a fund of images which would insinuate themselves into his later works. He turned seriously to art during the Second World War, painting in a Surrealist vein before turning to abstract works. He joined the Dau al Set group (*see* p.53) and, after its dissolution in 1953, came into his own as one of the most influential Spanish artists of the latter half of the 20th century. His 'material paintings' employ a wide range of mixed media. Like Miró, with whom he was close, he sought the extraordinary within the ordinary, while colouring much of his work with a pervasive self-referential and sometimes oblique film: graffitied walls recall those of the old Barcelona of his enclosed childhood; the recurring motifs of mirrors and wardrobes echo the images thrown back at the young invalid. These pieces, often bleak and yet hauntingly spiritual (he was drawn to Buddhism and Oriental philosophy from an early age), were created from scraps of paper and rags, found objects, sprinkled with text and letters (often his initials) and sprayed with handfuls of earth, clay and grit. In 1984 he set up this foundation for the study of contemporary and non-Western art; it displays a selection of Tàpies' art upstairs and changing exhibitions of other people's below.

There are some pretty buildings just round the corner: at 47 Rambla de Catalunya, the **Casa Miquel A. Fargas [26]** (1904), Enric Sagnier's finest Modernista work, with a splendid undulating stack of *tribunas* running up the façade and a vestibule with a beautiful mirror—and more flourishes visible in the ground-floor art gallery. At No.54, **Casa Dolors Calm [27]** was given a facelift in 1903 by Josep Vilaseca, who added the huge gallery of wood and glass (something more commonly seen on the backs of Eixample houses), no two floors alike; in the 1920s it became the prestigious Galeria Joan Prats. Modernista pharmacies are the lilies of the Eixample; the **Farmacia Bolós [28]** at No.77 is one, with a delicate stained-glass orange tree in the entrance, and a big collection of ceramic apothecary pots. Round the corner, at 241 C/ de València, the **Casa Domènech i Estapà [29]** (1909) was built by the architect of the same name, who gave it an original colourful façade using affordable stone and brick, its cornice crowned by an original doodad. No.78, the **Casa Juncosa [30]** (1909), by Salvador Viñals Sabaté, is a Modernista baroque work, with a nod to Gaudí's Casa Calvet. **Casa Josep i Ramon Queraltó [31]** (1906), on a *xamfrà* at No.88, is a Modernista work that gives an idea of what even a lesser-known architect, Josep Plantada i Artigas, could produce, although later owners have spoiled the façade.

Fundació Francesco Godia and the Museu Egipci

Back on the Passeig de Gràcia, the **Casa Olano [32]** (1885), at No.60, was used as headquarters for the Basque government at the end of the Civil War; its nickname, 'the House of the Pirate', comes from its figure of Juan Sebastian Elcano, who brought Magellan's last surviving ship back to port and became the first man to sail round the world. On the *xamfrà* at No.66, the **Casa Vídua Marfà [33]** is a quaint neo-Gothic work with trilobe arches and svelte columns designed by Manual Comas Thos in 1905; have a look inside the vestibule to see the beautiful triangular skylight of coloured glass.

The newest museum in Barcelona, the **Fundació Francesco Godia [34]** (*open Wed–Mon 10–8, closed Tues; adm*), is to the right at 284 C/ de Valencia, on the first floor of an apartment building. Paco Godia (1921–90) was a Formula 1 racing car driver, businessman and art maven. Beyond the video attesting to his prowess at the wheel and a room of trophies, there awaits an important collection of medieval art, including the costly and elegant 14th-century *Virgen de la Llet*, attributed to Llorenç Saragossa, court painter to Pere the Ceremonious. There's a collection of wooden polychrome Virgins dating from the 12th century on up, many of the earliest with uneven staring eyes. There's a brilliantly red-robed *Magdelene* by Jaume Huguet, a *Flagellation* and *Ecce Homo* by Martin Bernat, a 15th-century Flemish high relief of *Christ Bearing the Cross*, large wooden figures from a Calvary group (1300), and a choice set of medieval ceramics from the main centres of Spain. Farther along are paintings by the Master of Tamára, showing St Michael beating down the devils, and Martin de Soria's *Nativity, Epiphany,*

Ascencion (Christ leaving only footprints behind) and *Pentecost*. Godia also liked early 20th-century art: there are works by Sunyer, Manolo Hugué, Tàpies (*Portrait of Teresa*), Ramón Casas (the bright, sunny and carefree *At the Races*, 1905), Rusinyol (*Quarry on Montjuïc*), Picasso (a funny *Portrait of Pere Romeu*), José Gutiérrez Solana (his brooding and disturbing *Bullfight at Ronda*, 1927) and Joaquín Sorolla of Valencia (one of his typically luminous sea scenes, *Oxen and Boat*, 1908).

Next door, the **Museu Egipci**, or Fundació Clos (*open Mon–Sat 10–8, Sun 10–2; adm*), with enthusiast millionaire Jordi Clos' excellent private collection of Egyptian art, has just reopened here in bigger and better quarters. It offers reconstructions of tombs and a choice collection of masks, ceramics, jewellery and statuettes. There's a baby crocodile mummy that looks like a pencil, and other swaddled animals complete with X-rays. It has a nice outdoor terrace café, too.

This area is especially dense with Modernista shops and buildings. Farther down C/ de València, at No.302, the French-style **Casa Elizalde [35]** was built in 1888 and nearly knocked down illegally in 1974, when the owner thought no one was looking. Rescued at the last minute, it is now in the safe hands of the Ajuntament, which uses it as a civic centre. From its inner courtyard there's a fine view of the secret back façades of the Eixample houses. A bit farther up at the corner of C/ de Roger de Llúria, **Queviures Murria [36]** is a beautiful Modernista grocer's from 1900, still bearing tile advertisements designed by Ramón Casas and others for old Catalan liqueurs, including the most famous, Anís del Mono, with the little monkey who would later appear in paintings by Picasso, Gris and Braque. It was good stuff: Jean Charcot, the French explorer, took 125 bottles of Anís del Mono with him in 1903 to keep warm in the Antarctic. Here too, at 80 C/ de Roger de Llúria, is Juli Fossas Martinez's finest Modernista building, the **Casa Josefa Villanueva [37]** (1909), in which the central *tribunas*, inspired by the Casa Battló, culminate in a mini temple topped with a bulb and spire—there were originally two of these but one was demolished. Another block down, at the corner of C/ de València and C/ del Bruc, is the recently restored **Mercat de la Concepció [38]**, completed for the 1888 Universal Exhibition by Ruis i Taulet, who, in spite of whatever regret he felt for losing the Eixample design to Cerdà, came through with a handsome iron market building with a colourful tile roof, famous for its 24-hour flower stalls.

More by Montaner

If, in the Mansana de la Discòrdia, you gave the apple to Lluís Domènech i Montaner, be sure to follow C/ de Roger de Llúria up to C/ de Mallorca. To the right, at No.291, the design showroom of B.D. Ediciones de Diseño, stocking reproductions of Gaudí's furniture, and works by Ricard Bofill, Mariscal, etc., occupies the well-preserved offices of **Casa Thomas [39]** (1898). This was built by

Domènech for his cousins, who were famous printers and engravers, and has the earliest examples of his decorative ceramic appliqués, strange hybrid creatures, half carnation, half lizard. In 1912, Domènech's son-in-law, Francesc Guardia i Vidal, added the three neo-Gothic floors on top as a home for the family. The vestibule at 293 C/ de Mallorca is well worth a look. At 278 C/ de Mallorca, the **Palau Montaner [40]** (*open to visitors Sat 10–1, ring Ⓣ 93 487 22 33 to be sure*), home of Domènech's publisher brother, was begun in 1889 by Josep Domènech i Estapà, in a sober eclectic style, but was finished by Lluís, who gathered together his favourite collaborators to give it pizzazz, frosting the top floor with mosaics by Gaspar Homar, while showering decoration on the grand stair, with a lovely sky-light by Joan Rigalt and sculptures by Eusebi Arnau—if you're wondering where the usual dragons are lurking, they're at the bottom. The building is now the seat of the Delegació del Govern a Catalunya—Madrid's representatives in the auton-omous region. Across the street, at No.283, the neo-Pompeiian **Palau Cascades [41]**, with a rare façade inset on a *xamfrà* to allow for some palm trees in front, was designed in 1883 by Antoni Serra i Pujals. It now houses the local lawyers' college.

La Pedrera (Casa Milà) [42]

Casa Batlló created such a sensation that some even richer people, Pere Milà, a member of the Spanish Cortes, and his wife from Reus, Gaudí's home town, imme-diately hired Gaudí to outdo himself a few blocks up the Passeig de Gràcia. Here he was given a virgin *xamfrà*, and the result, the Casa Milà (1905–10), was just what the couple ordered: the most extraordinary, singular apartment building ever built, nicknamed La Pedrera, 'the stone quarry'. As much sculpture as building, the five-storey stone façade (hammered to give it the desired rough texture and supported by an extremely complex steel armature) undulates around the bevelled corners of the block like a cliff sculpted by waves of wind, pierced by windows that look as if they have been eroded into the stone, underlined by Jujol's fantastical balconies of forged iron seaweed spilling over the edges; no two are alike. The honey-coloured sea cliff culminates in a roof of cresting white sea foam—or icing. Cartoons in con-temporary newspapers compared the building to a gooey cake. The Milàs, who had been shown only a few vague freehand sketches by Gaudí before the tarpaulins went up around the work, were just as surprised as anyone when it was unveiled.

The interior courtyard is nearly as striking as the façade, with its two irregular cir-cular patios open to the sky, enclosed in winding ramps; Gaudí originally wanted residents to be able to drive to their doors, but settled for Europe's first under-ground car park, converted in 1994 into a concert hall. The original sea colours of the patios have been beautifully restored, and there are painted scenes from the *Metamorphoses* of Ovid, the founding of Rome, and the seven deadly sins. Up on the fourth floor, you can visit a re-created Modernista apartment, **El Pis de la**

Pedrera (*open daily 10–8; adm free; guided visits Mon–Fri at 6pm, Sat–Sun at 11am; July–Sept has La Pedrera by Night, with drinks and music 9pm–midnight, © 93 484 59 95*), chock full of the then latest modern gadgets—electric lights, time-saving domestic appliances and telephones. Because Gaudí dispensed with interior load-bearing walls, no two apartments are alike. The first people to move in complained snootily that none of their furniture fitted in the swirling rooms; Santiago Rusinyol joked that residents would have to have snakes for pets, instead of cats and dogs. The quiet attention to detail is extraordinary: door handles, for instance, are designed to be opened with the left hand, as the right would turn the key.

At the top of the Casa Milà, a remarkable attic, a great wavy tunnel of catenary parabolic arches, gives the impression of being inside the ribcage of a dragon—what the princess would have seen had not George arrived on time. Washing was once hung out here to dry, and later 13 apartments were squeezed between the ribs, but in the 1986 restoration all were painstakingly deconstructed to create the **Espai Gaudí** (*same ticket as El Pis de la Pedrera*). This provides a thorough overview of the man's work through models, photos, drawings and videos. The total effect is dizzying, but this is the best place to get a look at Bellesguard, Casa Vicens and his other inaccessible buildings, as well as the ones outside Barcelona. Steps lead up to the **roof**; Gaudí's installations have been called the precursors of Surrealism, Expressionism and Cubism, and you can wander around this one, a beautiful if troubling garden of chimneys and ventilators shaped like bouquets of visored knights in reddish stone (baptised the *espantabruixes*, or 'witch-scarers'), who keep company with four fat globs of Cheeze Whiz holding the stair exits, coated in white *trencadís*. The views take in much of Barcelona. Gaudí, who believed in aesthetics first and safety second, only reluctantly installed the guard rails, fearing they would spoil the effect.

Perhaps the most extraordinary thing about the roof is what it is missing. Gaudí saw La Pedrera as a pedestal for a 40ft-high statue of the Virgin Mary and a pair of angels, an idea the Milà prudently vetoed after the 1909 *Setmana Trágica* left Barcelona smouldering with another bout of church-burnings. Gaudí was furious, left an assistant to finish the job, vowed he would never work for the bourgeoisie again, and devoted the rest of his life to trying to expiate the church-torching sins of his fellow Catalans by building the Sagrada Família.

Around La Pedrera

Next to La Pedrera, at 96 Passeig de Gràcia, is the Modernista **Casa Ramón Casas [43]**, built in 1899 for the wealthy painter by Antoni Rovira i Rabassa; his friend Santiago Rusinyol had an apartment on the third floor. In 1940, Jacinto Amat made the ground floor into a shop, **Vinçon**, specializing in German porcelains; under his son Fernando, that 'incombustible investigator of the world of the designed and the designable', as the *Barcelona Design Guide* calls him, Vinçon has became the élite showcase of contemporary furnishings in Barcelona. Much of it is displayed in what was Casas' flat on the main floor, with the magnificent Modernista fireplace and woodwork by Josep Pascó i Mensas; the garden has a striking view of La Pedrera. Across the street, the **Passatge de la Concepció [44]** is another charming little lane cutting through a block. Up a block, the neo-Renaissance **Palau Robert [45]** (1903, by Frenchman Henri Grandpierre), at 107 Passeig de Gràcia, is the Generalitat's main tourist information office for Catalunya.

A block over at 122 Rambla de Catalunya, **Casa Costa [46]** (1904), topped by three distinct round windows, is one of Josep Domènech i Estapà's more original and Modernista works. At 126 Rambla de Catalunya, Puig i Cadafalch's **Can Serra [47]** (1903–8) was designed as a single family home, this time in a Renaissance Plateresque style, with sculptures by Eusebi Arnau. A religious community bought it and wanted to tear it down, and in 1981, after a 15-year battle, the compromise was to bulldoze the back of the building to make way for a sleek modern annexe that looms behind its ladylike profile, which is now used as the seat of the Diputació de Barcelona. Where the Rambla de Catalunya meets the Diagonal, slicing its way down the waffle grid, don't miss the ***Coqueta*** (1972) by Josep Granyer, the companion piece to his Thinker Bull—this a languorous, coquettish giraffe posing like an Ingres nude.

Along Avinguda Diagonal

Another local landmark, **Casa Lluís Pérez Samanillo [48]**, 502 Avinguda Diagonal, was designed by Joan Josep Hervás i Arizmendi, who married a Loire château to Modernisme to create this winner of the city prize for the best building of 1910; members of an equestrian club now hobnob here. Another block up is the striking **Casa Sayrach [49]**, 423–5 Diagonal, one of the last Modernista houses, but a gem, designed in 1915 by Manuel Sayrach, who was better known as a poet and dramatist. The double façade of sculpted windows is crowned with a sinuous cornice reminiscent of La Pedrera and a gooey-looking conical cupola; the vestibule is an orgy of undulating decoration.

Museu de la Música [50]

> *Open winter Tues and Thurs–Sun 10–2, Wed 10–8; summer Tues–Sun 10–2; closed Mon; adm.*

Two of Puig i Cadafalch's principal works are down the other end of Avinguda Diagonal. Palau Baró de Quadras (1904), at 373 Diagonal, is his most flamboyant Gothic palace, its projecting first-floor windows covered with a Flemish Plateresque menagerie of grinning fabulous creatures, plus George and the dragon designed by the indefatigable Eusebi Arnau. The pale green back façade, at 279 C/ del Rosselló, is decorated with leafy *sgraffito*. Since 1980, the palace has housed the Museu de la Música. The lovely vestibule, lit with twisting neo-Gothic wrought-iron lamp-posts, has a carved fountain with frogs squatting among the lilies, while the stairway, tiled in vivid blue and yellow, curves grandly up to the upper floors thanks to clever architectural foreshortening that makes it seem larger than it really is. Some of the rooms have retained their original fittings—softly glowing stained-glass windows, and a slightly hysterical fireplace—making a fine setting for a fascinating collection of antique and exotic instruments from the 16th century on: exquisitely inlaid Moroccan lutes, Galician bagpipes, 18th-century painted chests containing trapezoidal psalteries, Russian balalaikas and a piano that doubles as a writing desk. Mementoes of cellist Pau Casals, one of Adophe Sax's original saxophones and a particularly fine collection of Spanish guitars finish off the collection.

Opposite, at 442 Avinguda Diagonal, is the **Casa Comalat [51]** (1911), designed by one of Gaudí's followers, Salvador Valer, who, owing to the plot, had to give it two façades. The one on the Diagonal has a splendid molten Baroque crown covered with blue and yellow ceramics, and a magnificent entrance hall of tile and stained glass. Façade number two at 316 C/ de Còrsega was inspired by the Casa Batlló, wonderfully colourful and undulating, with bone-shaped arches at ground level and window galleries above which Persian blinds form an integral part of the design, all crowned by a wavy cornice with a round peephole.

Farther down, at 416–20 Avinguda Diagonal, towers Puig i Cadafalch's massive neo-Gothic apartment block, the Casa Terrades, better known as the **Casa de les Punxes [52]** (1906), or 'House of Spikes', bristling with the pointiest witch's hat roofs ever, and spires that make it a pigeon-hater's dream house. What makes it doubly effective is the fact that it's the only completely free-standing house in the Eixample. Note too the lavish ironwork, sun dial and ceramic panels. As you'd expect on a house by Puig, there's a figure of St George but also an inscription: 'Patron of Catalunya, restore our freedom.' It may have survived the Franco years, but Puig's career as an architect did not: after the Civil War he was forbidden to build.

Around Plaça Verdaguer

Plaça Verdaguer (Ⓜ Verdaguer) has as its centrepiece a **monument to Mossèn Jacint Verdaguer**, erected by the city in 1924 to the famous priest poet, hero of the Catalan *Renaixença*, and decorated with reliefs from his epic *L'Atlàntida*. One of the most interesting houses around here is the sensuous white **Casa Llopis i Bofill [53]**, at 113 C/ de Bailèn, the best-known work of one of Domènech's collaborators, Antoni M. Gallissà, who was inspired by the Alhambra. The fine floral *sgraffito*, brick and tile work is by Jujol. Just up from the square, at 108 Passeig de Sant Joan, is Puig i Cadafalch's **Palau Macaya [54]** (1901), a Modernista update of the Gothic palaces on C/ Montcada, with a Moorish touch and gold *sgraffito* on the façade and in the lovely courtyard. Eusebi Arnau sculpted the capitals of the columns; on one he added a bicycle. The rooms, unfortunately stripped of their original decoration, house the **Centre Cultural de la Fundació la Caixa**, run by Spain's largest savings bank (℡ 93 458 89 07; *open Tues–Sat 11–8, Sun 11–3, closed Mon and Aug; adm free*). The banks don't just do it out of the goodness of their heart: it's the law in Spain that they invest some of their profits in art. Over the years La Caixa has accumulated one of the most impressive collections of contemporary art in Spain, and displays some of it here, as well as mounting highly rated exhibitions. East down the Diagonal, towards the Sagrada Família, at No.332 you'll find the striking **Casa Planells [55]** (1924), a late Modernista work by Josep Maria Jujol with undulating lines similar to La Pedrera, but with a Central European flavour.

The Sagrada Família [56]

> *Entrance is by way of C/ de Sardenya; open Apr–Aug daily 9–8, March and Sept–Oct daily 9–7, Nov–Feb daily 9–6; adm.*

George Orwell, writing of the church burnings during the Civil War in his *Homage to Catalonia*, wondered ruefully why there was one that the arsonists spared, 'the ugliest building in the world', with spires 'shaped like hock bottles' looming high over the Dreta de l'Eixample. These 350ft bottles, of course, belong to Gaudí's great unfinished Sagrada Família. Slightly smaller than St Peter's in Rome, occupying an entire block of the Cerdà plan with its own metro station, the Expiatory Temple of the Holy Family is surely the most compelling, controversial and unfinished building site in the world, today the symbol of Barcelona and of the scale of its extraordinary ambition.

The church was begun on a cheap, then out-of-the-way plot in 1882, the brainchild of a bookdealer named Josep Bocabella Verdaguer, follower of reactionary Pope Pius IX and founder of a society dedicated to St Joseph (they called themselves the 'Josephines') devoted to expiating the sins of Modernisme, which seemed be to threatening Spain with catastrophe. He originally hired another architect, Francesc del Villar (one of Gaudí's professors), who planned a typical neo-Gothic church and got as far as the crypt when disagreements led to his replacement by Gaudí in 1883—in many ways a fateful choice, as the architect was only 31 and had hardly built anything, but he was pious, and that was enough for Bocabella. Gaudí finished the crypt and worked on the project off and on for the next 43 years. With each plan, it grew grander and grander, which was just fine with the Josephines, who believed in Eternity and let Gaudí do exactly as he pleased: nothing was too great for the Holy Family. At first there was plenty of money, and the building survived the *Setmana Trágica* arson in 1909, probably because it employed some 300 workers. But the *Setmana Trágica* gave Gaudí a new purpose: the temple would also expiate the sins of Catalunya.

By then it had become Gaudí's full-fledged obsession, and in 1912, after the death of his collaborator Francesc Berenguer (*see* p.51), he accepted no other commissions. When interest and money ran low, he sold everything he owned for the project, including his house, and in 1925 moved into a hut on the construction site, increasingly unwashed and unkempt, living on a diet of bread, water, fruit and vegetables, soliciting funds, even going door to door for a handful of pesetas. People crossed the street at the sight of the mad old genius with the piercing blue gaze. Fashion had moved on, away from Modernisme and Josephine piety. The critic Josep Pla wrote that the Sagrada Família reminded him of 'a pile of enormous chicken guts'. But Gaudí didn't read the papers, or care what anyone thought.

Gaudí intended the Sagrada Família to be 'an immense palace of Christian memory' and hoped that every possible aspect of Catholic doctrine was expressed in some nook or cranny of the temple. He planned three façades, dedicated to the Birth, Passion and, the main one, Glory; each façade would have four towers, symbolizing the 12 Apostles. Four higher towers rising over the crossing would be dedicated to the Evangelists, and in the centre a truly colossal 575ft tower would symbolize the Saviour, with a large tower to the Virgin on the side. Although basically Gothic in plan, the architect promised that it would go beyond Gothic, using the system of inclined columns and parabolic arches that he experimented with at the Crypt Güell (*see* p.222). There would be no buttresses, or 'crutches' as he called them. He fussed over every detail and, when a bishop asked him why he worried so much about the tops of his towers, Gaudí replied: 'Your Grace, the angels will see them.'

Gaudí started on the **Birth Façade** and oversaw the sculpture, which he based on photographs of everyday people, using a 33-year-old worker for Christ on the Cross, and a six-toed barman for a Roman soldier. He made plaster casts of plants, flowers, people and a live donkey (which survived the ordeal); if you look closely you may even see a figure of a bomb-tossing Anarchist. The new sculpture here is by the Japanese sculptor Etsuro Sotoo, who was so overwhelmed when he saw the Sagrada Família that he immediately converted to Catholicism. Gaudí finished one 394ft tower with its bright ceramic finial, then absent-mindedly wandered in front of a streetcar in 1926. Everyone thought he was a tramp: four taxis refused to take him to the hospital and finally an ambulance took him to a public ward in the medieval Antic Hospital de la Santa Creu, where he died three days later. By 1935, his followers had completed the other three towers of the Birth Façade according to his models. Orwell was wrong when he wrote that the Anarchists never damaged the Sagrada Família: they hated everything it represented, and in 1936 they broke into the workshops and set fire to every plan and model they found in the hope of preventing any further work. To add insult to injury, they broke open the tombs of Bocabella and Gaudí in the crypt.

According to the philosopher Ferrater i Mora, four elements define the Catalan character: *seny* (wisdom, good sense), measure, irony and *continuitat,* which means not only a single-minded continuity of tradition but the urge to finish a job begun. In the case of the Sagrada Família, this fourth element is proving more powerful than the other three combined. In 1954, the Josephines (who are answerable to neither city nor Church) raised enough money to continue the project in the manner of Gaudí, instructing architects to guess the master's intent from the photos of a few surviving drawings. Their work has offended purists and most architects, who believe the temple should have been left alone as a memorial to the

Projection of the finished appearance of the Sagrada Família, by Joan Rubió i Bellver, 1915.

man's unique genius; they also point out that Gaudí never even followed his own models but was ever improvising as he went along, which gave his work its unique dynamism and energy. The Josephines, however, insist that Gaudí wished the Sagrada Família to be like the cathedrals of the Middle Ages, built over the generations—he himself estimated it would take 200 years to complete, but 'my client is not in a hurry'. Gaudí worked for God. His attitude was that every day of work atones for a few more sins: finishing it was almost irrelevant.

Since 1987, architect Jordi Bonet (whose father worked with Gaudí) and sculptor Josep Maria Subirachs have been in charge of the project. Subirachs is an avowed atheist born exactly nine months after Gaudí died. He took the job on the condition that he lived on the site and had complete artistic freedom. Sufficiently thick-skinned to survive a major demonstration in 1990 of artists, architects and religious conservatives demanding that he stop, he completed the **Passion Façade** in 1998, three years ahead of schedule, using synthetic stone of reinforced concrete with resin-bonded finishes. He decorated this with robotic sculptures, including centurions derived from the 'witch-scarers' on La Pedrera, a controversial naked Christ on the Cross, a figure of Gaudí and a magic square based on the number 33. Whereas the Birth Façade has Gaudí's unmistakable textured style, resembling some primordial growth—a 'terrifying, edible beauty', as Salvador Dalí described it—Subirachs' is mechanical, sinister and kitsch, as purposefully brutal as its subject matter. The sculptor himself has stated it 'has nothing to do with Gaudí'. He is currently putting on the finishing touches: a great bronze door carved with 8,000 letters from a page of the Gospel, four huge travertine statues of the apostles, and a 25ft metal Christ, to be placed on a bridge between the two central towers.

As interest in Gaudí grows and money pours in, the pace of building has accelerated. Whatever reservations the city once had about the project have gone by the wayside, as it figures any costs will easily be met by the Sagrada Família's value as a tourist attraction—it is already the most visited site in Catalunya, with some 1.2 million annual visitors, whose tickets are the main source of the 900 million peseta yearly budget. And whatever aesthetic reservations one might have, it's impossible not to admire the devil-may-care momentum the project has gathered. At the end of 1999, the nave, which Gaudí intended to resemble 'a forest of stone', was completed, with its 147ft flat brick vaults (a lift is being installed to allow visitors to explore 'the mysterious labyrinths' promised by Subirachs). On top of this stands the awesome crane ready to construct the tower dome and four towers of the Evangelists, to be supported by vaults on the immense columns of basalt and porphyry, the strongest of stones, that are already in place. The Polytechnic University of Catalunya, the University of Deakin in Australia, and the University of Wellington in New Zealand are already drafting the transept on their computers, calculating the thrusts and how to build as Gaudí wanted, without buttresses. Bonet is concentrating on the apse, which within 10 years should be completed and roofed, and alone will be big enough to swallow the church of Santa Maria del Mar whole. The six towers over the crossing will be the grand finale, which the Josephines hope to complete by the centenary of Gaudí's death, in 2026. But the main Glory Façade poses a problem. Gaudí intended it to nudge into C/ de Mallorca, with a wide stair cascading into the next *xamfrà*, but in 1979 an apartment building was built in the way.

In the **crypt** you can visit Gaudí's tomb and the museum, a dusty collection of photos, diagrams, plaster models, bits of sculpture (air pollution has already devoured many on the Birth Façade) and Gaudí's astonishing catenary model, made of chains and small sacks weighted in proportion to the arches and the load they would have to bear, which he used to build the Crypt Güell. For a small fee you can take the lift (*open 10–5.45*) up the **Passion Towers**, for a vertiginous dreamlike ramble high over the city, with the option of a terrifying descent down the tightly spiralled staircase of the towers. Also, have a look at the **Escolas de la Sagrada Família**, a low building with a sinuous roof tucked in the corner, designed, built and paid for in 1909 by Gaudí, burned in the Civil War and not very carefully rebuilt—although you get the general idea.

Hospital de la Santa Creu i Sant Pau [57]

Avinguda Gaudí, lined with cafés, and streetlamps by Pere Falqués, leads from the Sagrada Família to a neighbourhood known as Camp de l'Arpa, or 'Field of the Dolmen', recalling a long-lost megalith. At the end stands another, completed and useful, gargantuan Modernista work: Lluís Domènech i Montaner's Hospital de la Santa Creu i Sant Pau (1902–30), covering nine whole blocks of the Eixample. Recently it has been placed on UNESCO's list of World Heritage sites—and as hospitals go, it is certainly a one-off. The genesis came from banker Pau Gil i Serra, who left four million pesetas for a hospital dedicated to his patron saint Paul. The competition for the design was won by Domènech i Estapà—but the doctors on the board of trustees vetoed it because of hygiene considerations, and Domènech i Montaner landed the job in 1901.

Disliking the labyrinthine institutional atmosphere of most hospitals, Domènech believed that beautiful surroundings were therapeutic. He conceived the hospital as a garden city of 26 pavilions on a human scale, connected by underground service tunnels, all built along a diagonal axis. The project was only a quarter built in 1911, when the money dried up, and it was decided to merge with the medieval Antic Hospital de la Santa Creu. This released funds to finish the project, which Domènech increasingly shared with his son, who took over when his father died in

1923, and finished in 1930. It's a still, uncanny place for aimless wandering, turning into an alternative universe at twilight, each brick pavilion different, topped with fantastically tiled roofs and encrusted with mosaics, lavishly decorated with sculptures by Eusebi Arnau and Pau Gargallo and their workshops. Inside, rich stained glass and elaborately wrought lamps throw strange shadows. The large **administration building** (1910) at the top of Avinguda Gaudí has the most ornate interior and is open to the public; go up the sweeping stair for the lovely view. If you fall ill in Barcelona, this is the place to go. Although plans are afoot to move some of the facilities to more modern surroundings, the UNESCO designation should prevent the hospital from rotting away—the fate of some of its outer pavilions.

Plaça de les Glòries Catalanes

Cerdà's vision of the Plaça de les Glòries Catalanes (**Ⓜ** Glories)—where the Diagonal, Meridiana and Gran Vía de les Corts Catalanes meet like the Union Jack—as the throbbing centre of Barcelona has been sabatoged by its conversion into a giant elevated roundabout for happy cars to spin round on, in the presence of Spain's largest shopping mall. In its shadow, on C/ del Dos de Maig, **Els Encants [58]** flea market remains studiously the same, with plenty of desirable junk, secondhand clothes and sneaky pickpockets (*best in the morning; open Mon, Wed, Fri and Sat*). Meanwhile, the Meridiana axis has been planted with trophy buildings in the hopes of igniting some fashion action in a generally grey area: here at 150 C/ de Lepant is the brand-new **Auditori [59]**, by Rafael Moneo, who gave Barcelona the antithesis of its Palau de la Música Catalana: a visually null building with an acoustically flawless auditorium hall clad in Canadian maple. Ricardo Bofill, who has not a squirt of Moneo's discretion, contributed an up-to-date version of the Parthenon for the **Teatre Nacional de Catalunya (TNC) [60]**, on the other side of C/ de Padilla.

Predating all this, at 749 Gran Vía de les Corts Catalanes, is the **Plaça de Toros Monumental [61]** (**Ⓜ** Monumental), the only Modernista ring in Spain, designed in 1916 by Ignasi Mas Morell and Domènec Sugrañes Gras. Made of brick, covered with blue and white *azulejos* and *trencadís*, pierced with parabolic arches and punctuated with towers supporting huge yellow, white and blue ceramic dinosaur eggs, this is Barcelona's largest and only active bullring. It's home of the **Museu Taurí** (*open April–Sept daily 10.30–2 and 4–7; adm*), with a collection of famous bulls' heads and memorabilia of the great bullfighter Manolete, who was gored in Lléida in 1947. Popular enough in 19th-century Barcelona to cause riots over spiritless bulls, bullfighting is now frowned on by most Catalans; the *corridas* that take place from April to September on Sunday afternoons rarely attract a big crowd. Barcelona's smaller bullring, Les Arenes, has closed, and even the Monumental is used more regularly for concerts and fairs than for flapping red cloaks at irate bulls.

Plaça de Tetuán

Visit Plaça de Tetuán (🚇 Tetuán) to see Josep Llimona's remarkable Modernista **Monument to Dr Bartolomeu Robert [62]**. Dr Robert became the first Catalanist mayor of Barcelona in 1899, and gave his sanction to the Tancament de Caixes, or bank strike, that year: Madrid had raised taxes on bank profits to cover its losses in the 1898 war and, rather than pay, Barcelona's banks and businesses shut down. Madrid gave them a shock by then declaring war on Catalunya; Robert resigned and no shots were fired, but his nose-thumbing at the central government canonized him as a Catalan hero. When he died in 1902, the capitalists pooled their resources to give him Barcelona's most extraordinary monument. Gaudí, a friend of Llimona, in all likelihood designed the pedestal in the style of La Pedrera, but with stone breasts and bronze nipple taps; on top is Llimona's pile of 18 Rodinesque allegorical figures, crowned by a head of the mayor, while an allegory of Catalunya whispers sweet nothings in his ear. Originally the monument stood in front of the university, until the Franco government packed it neatly away, allowing its resurrection here in 1979.

There's a clutch of good Modernista houses near here in C/ d'Ausiàs Marc. A key work of the first decade of the 20th century, **Casa Antònia Burés [63]** (1903–6), at No.42, by Juli Batllevell, has curving stone balconies and two *tribunas* supported by stone pine trees—the master builder Enric Pi (pine) used this as his signature. The monumental **Casa Roger [64]** (1888), on the *xamfrà* at Nos.33–9, was Enric Sagnier's first work in the Eixample, and he gave the bourgeoisie their money's worth in a kind of copybook of Gothic and Baroque styles, with a touch of Greek on top. Have a look in the lavish vestibule at No.37. Opposite, at No.30, the handsome stone **Casa Francesc Burés [65]** (1905) is often attributed to Gaudí's assistant Francesc Berenguer; step into the vestibule to see the spectacular stair. Elegant and curvaceous Modernista stonework and reliefs by Roque Cot Cot (apparently *not* a stage name) characterize No.22, the **Casa Antònia Puget [66]** (1906), with another sumptuous vestibule, guarded by St Anthony of Padua. Next door at Nos.16–20, the two **Casas Felip** (1901–13) were built for the same family over an extended period by Telm Fernàndez; the later half, with its *tribunas* and stone balconies, is evidence of the Felip family's rise in the world. Pop in at No.20 to see another beautiful vestibule. Opposite at No.31, the **Farmàcia Nordbeck [67]** is a Modernista gem of 1905, in which the sinuous designs and stained glass lend a fitting magical air to the place one visits for secret potions to get rid of warts.

Esquerra de l'Eixample

There are a few sights on the Left Eixample, including **Casa Golferichs [68]**, 491 Gran Vía de les Corts Catalanes (🚇 Rocafort; *usually open Tues–Fri 5–9, Sat 10–2* *and 5–9*). It's a Modernista Moorish medieval family townhouse with a rare garden by the side. It was designed in 1901 by Gaudí collaborator Joan Rubió i Bellver while still in his 20s, but already demonstrating his trademark expressive brick- and stonework, often in angular volumes (as in the wide eaves) and attention to detail. Almost knocked down in the 1980s, the house in now owned by the city. The interior was inspired by Gaudí's bishop's palace in Astorga, and some of the original decoration is intact.

Casa de Lactància [69] (1913, also known as Residència Francesc Layret), 475 Gran Vía de les Corts Catalanes (Ⓜ Rocafort), is a late-Gothic Modernista public welfare building by Pere Falqués and Antoni de Falguerra. It's crowned with an intricate parapet and relief showing an allegory of Barcelona helping the unfortunate by Eusebi Arnau. It's now a retirement home; ask to step inside to see the enchanting covered courtyard and upper gallery, delicately decorated with stained glass, wrought iron, mosaics and ceramics to form one of Barcelona's prettiest interiors.

Casa Company [70], 203 C/ de Casanova, near the Diagonal (bus No.58 or 64), is a relatively simple family house built in 1911 by Puig i Cadafalch in his 'white period', when he began to turn away from his historical fantasies. The exterior decoration is limited to iron grilles, painted festoons over the windows, and a Virgin under the deep eaves. The interior was converted into a doctor's office in 1940 and has kept much of its fine decoration. It now houses a small museum of Catalan sport (*open Mon–Thurs 10–2 and 4–7*). In the same area is Bonaventura Bassegoda's charming **Casa Parets de Plet [71]** (1910), at 231 C/ de Muntaner, with its glassy columns of *tribunas* and wrought iron.

Universitat Industrial [72], 173–221 C/ del Comte d'Urgell (Ⓜ Hospital Clinic), was built in 1895 on the site of the former Battló ceramics factory, preserving a remarkable octagonal chimney from 1860 built by Rafael Gustavino, heir of Catalunya's great building dynasty (before the family emigrated to New York and built the great hall on Ellis Island). The university's Escola del Treball was designed in 1927–31 by Joan Rubió i Bellvé and includes a superb entrance hall of huge parabolic arches decorated with *sgraffito*, covered with a stepped roof lined with windows. The church, also made of huge parabolas, is one of the the most exciting 20th-century church interiors in Barcelona. Near here, the **Mercat del Ninot [73]** (1933), at 133 C/ de Mallorca, has a monumental iron roof with semicircular arches looping over a wide single nave—an update of the Saló de Tinell in the Museu d'Història de la Ciutat.

Montjuïc

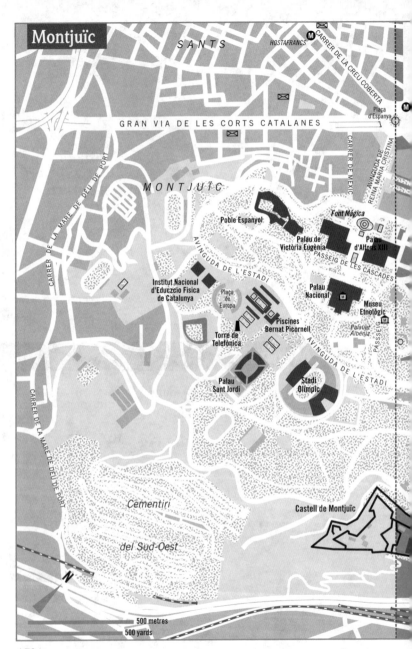

Montjuïc

SANTS

HOSTAFRANCS Ⓜ CARRER DE LA CREU COBERTA

CARRER DE LA MARE DE DÉU DE PORT

GRAN VIA DE LES CORTS CATALANES

Plaça d'Espanya Ⓜ

CARRER DE MÈXIC

AVINGUDA DE REINA MARIA CRISTINA

MONTJUÏC

Poble Espanyol

Font Màgica

Palau de Victòria Eugènia

Palau d'Alfons XIII

PASSEIG DE LES CASCADES

AVINGUDA DE L'ESTADI

Institut Nacional d'Educació Física de Catalunya

Plaça de Europa

Palau Nacional

Museu Etnològic

Palauet Albéniz

PASSEIG

Piscines Bernat Picornell

Torre de Telefònica

AVINGUDA DE L'ESTADI

Palau Sant Jordi

Stadi Olímpic

CARRER DE LA MARE DE DÉU DE PORT

Cementiri

del Sud-Oest

Castell de Montjuïc

N

500 metres
500 yards

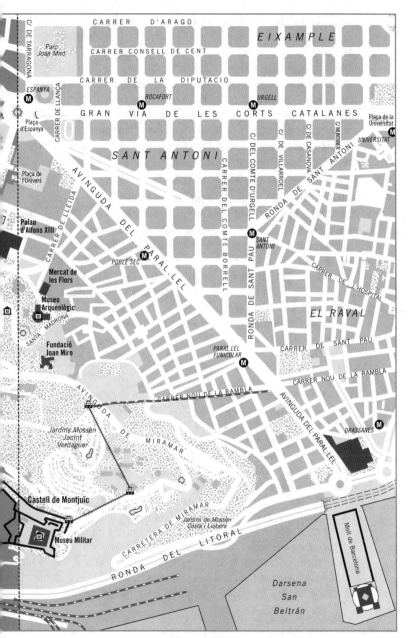

CARRER D'ARAGO

EIXAMPLE

C/ DE TARRAGONA

Parc Joan Miró

CARRER CONSELL DE CENT

CARRER DE LA DIPUTACIO

ESPANYA
Ⓜ

CARRER DE LLANÇA

ROCAFORT
Ⓜ

URGELL
Ⓜ

Plaça d'Espanya

GRAN VIA DE LES CORTS CATALANES

Plaça de la Universitat
Ⓜ

SANT ANTONI

Plaça de l'Univers

CARRER DEL COMTE D'URGELL

C/ DE VILLARROEL

C/ DE CASANOVA

C/ MUNTANER

UNIVERSITAT

AVINGUDA DEL PARAL·LEL

CARRER DE LLEIDA

RONDA DE SANT ANTONI

Palau d'Alfons XIII

CARRER DEL COMTE BORRELL

POBLE SEC

SANT ANTONI
Ⓜ

CARRER DE L'HOSPITAL

Mercat de les Flors

RONDA DE SANT PAU

EL RAVAL

Museu Arqueològic
Ⓜ
Ⓜ

SANTA MADRONA

Fundació Joan Miro

CARRER DE SANT PAU

PARAL·LEL FUNICULAR
Ⓜ

AVINGUDA DE

CARRER NOU DE LA RAMBLA

CARRER NOU DE LA RAMBLA

AVINGUDA DEL PARAL·LEL

Jardins Mossèn Jacint Verdaguer

MIRAMAR

DRASSANES
Ⓜ

Castell de Montjuïc

Museu Militar
Ⓜ

CARRETERA DE MIRAMAR

Jardins de Mossèn Costa i Llobera

Moll de Barcelona

RONDA DEL LITORAL

Darsena San Beltrán

The southern end of Barcelona (which looks like the western end on nearly every map) is closed off by the 705ft slope of Montjuïc, Barcelona's grandstand and showcase. Its peculiar name is derived either from 'Mons Jovis'—the mountain of Jove—or from the 'mountain of Jews' for the large Jewish cemetery discovered by the castle. Barcelona lost its count-kings before they had a chance to lay out any palatial gardens or hunting preserves for themselves—the source of the great parks of Madrid and other European capitals. But in compensation there was always Montjuïc, and for centuries its shady groves and fresh streams provided a place to breathe and stretch legs for a city suffocating inside its walls.

In 1914, the entire northern slope was beautifully landscaped by Jean-Claude Forestier and local architect Nicolas Rubió i Tuduri, who went on to become the Johnny Appleseed of Barcelona's parks. The driving force, of course, was a show, although unlike in 1888 politics and economics kept intruding: it wasn't until 1929 that the International Exhibition was under way. It bequeathed a permanent fair to the city and provided homes for the city's collections of medieval art and archaeology. Then, in 1992, the Exhibition's stadium was dusted off to become the centrepiece of the Olympic ring on top of Montjuïc.

Getting Around

Montjuïc is still lovely for walking, but watch out for learner drivers— every motorist in Barcelona has their first lesson on Montjuïc. In summer, a free bus runs from Plaça d'Espanya to the Poble Espanyol, and every half-hour **bus 61** from Espanya metro station takes in most of the park, making a loop from the Palau Nacional past the Poble Espanyol, the Olympic stadium and the Fundació Miró to Plaça Dante, where the **telefèric de Montjuïc** continues up to the castle. Then there's the **funicular** from the Paral.lel metro station, a good bet if you like to walk down hill rather than up; for times, *see* p.11. The aerial cable car from Barceloneta to Miramar is out of action, but a **tourist train** plies its way between Plaça d'Espanya and Miramar (*April–Sept daily 10am–11pm*). Sustenance on Montjuïc is limited: mediocre snack bars in the Poble Espanyol, café food at the Palau Nacional or the Fundació Miró, or drinks at Miramar (*closed Wed*) with a view over the Mediterranean.

Plaça d'Espanya and Around

Plaça d'Espanya is the big doughnut-shaped gateway to Montjuïc, with its six radiating streets and a Baroque **fountain** in the centre, commissioned at the last minute in 1928. No one would ever guess this is by Gaudí's great collaborator Josep Maria Jujol. His concern here was to create something that fitted in with the style of the Exhibition, and he succeeded so well that no one looks at it twice. One edge of the circular *plaça* is occupied by the city's smaller, older bullring, the Moorish-style **Les Arenes**, no longer in use but famous for having hosted Spain's first Beatles concert in 1966—a landmark event in Franco's regime, which was no friend of miniskirts, pop music and long hair. Next to it, at 20 C/ de Llança (near the Gran Vía de les Corts Catalanes), is a remarkable block of flats, the **Casa de la Papallona** (1912) by Josep Graner, who built five workmanlike floors then, overcome by a fit of whimsy, stuck an enormous yellow, blue, green and white *trencadí*-covered butterfly on top. This sets the mood for the **Parc Joan Miró** (or Parc de l'Escorxador) behind the bullring. One of the Ajuntament's first park projects in the early 1980s, laid out on the site of a slaughterhouse, it features Miró's last major work and one that has become a symbol of Barcelona, the ***Dona i Ocell*** (Woman and Bird), a 70ft-high bowling pin or phallus with a horned cylindrical head, covered with *trencadis* in homage to Gaudí. Miró intended to plant a whole forest of these, but death intervened, and rows of dwarf palms have taken their place.

Also off Plaça d'Espanya, but off the other end of the Gran Vía, in C/ de Mèxic, is Puig's **Fábrica Casarramona** (1911), a striking Modernista cotton-thread mill, with lots of exposed brick and iron; the two towers disguise water tanks. Used after the Civil War as a police barracks, the building has been restored by the Fundació La Caixa to display its ever expanding art collection.

The 1929 International Exhibition

Buildings originally dedicated to work and communications form two semicircular behemoths cupped around Plaça d'Espanya at the entrance to the fair, where the first buildings that greet the eye are two St Mark's campaniles, standing there like Venetian souvenir salt and pepper shakers. This sort of thing is miles from the first plans of 1907, to hold an exhibition celebrating electricity in 1914, that would incidently show off Montjuïc's new landscaping. When the *Setmana Trágica* and politics got in the way, the idea evolved into a fair of Spanish arts, crafts and electricity, planned for 1917, with an overall design by Puig i Cadafalch. If the 1888 Universal Exhibition heralded the first buds of Modernisme, Puig dreamed of showcasing the style in its maturity. Quashed by the World War and Barcelona's own political crisis, the fair idea was revived in 1923 by Primo de Rivera, who saw it as a vehicle to heap glory on Spain, its industry (with a passing nod to fairy electricity), agriculture, arts, sport and its benign dictator. This became the International Exhibition of 1929. Primo also hijacked the architecture, favouring an eclectic bourgeois Tuscan Noucentisme, as some called it, with a dollop of Salt Lake City Mormonism thrown in for fun. The project not only changed Barcelona's physical appearance but its blood, as a wave of workers from across Spain poured in to build the palaces and pavilions, new metro lines, hotels and post offices.

Beyond the towers, the pompous palaces line up for inspection, now hosting orthodontist-appliance fairs and the like. On the left, Plaça de l'Univers is enlivened by the **Foundry Worker**, a sculpture donated to Barcelona by its creator, Josep Llimona, in 1930 in honour of Labour Day. In between the fair buildings sparkles one of the star attractions of 1929, the **Font Mágica**, created by engineer Carlos Buigas; on certain nights it still performs its irresistible aquatic ballet of colour and light to the rhythms of Tchaikovsky and Abba, while blue searchlights radiate a peacock's tail of beams from the Palau Nacional in unforgettable cheesy splendour (*4 May–4 Oct Thurs–Sun and evenings before holidays, with shows beginning every half-hour from 9.30pm–11.30pm, ending at midnight; 4 Oct–4 May Fri–Sat 7pm–8.30pm, with shows every half-hour*).

To the right of the magic fountain is the cool, elegant **Pavelló Barcelona** (*open Nov–Mar daily 10–6.30, April–Oct daily 10–8; adm*), designed by Bauhaus architect Mies van der Rohe for Germany's exhibit. Mies, a stickler for fine materials and craftsmanship (unlike most of his disciples), once said, 'I would rather be good than original,' but here he was both, although his sleek horizontal work of travertine, onyx, glass and chrome, sited over a pair of reflecting pools, slipped right past the attention of the average fairgoer. But Barcelona's more perceptive architects were intrigued, among them Rubió i Tudurí: 'It just encloses space,' he marvelled. The original was demolished after the fair, and the present replica was reconstructed by the Ajuntament in 1986; inside, among exhibits devoted to the architect's career and legacy, the prize exhibit is Mies' perhaps all too familiar *Barcelona Chair*, denizen of a million waiting rooms.

Up from the fountains are the twin Baroque-Moderne **Palau de Victòria Eugènia** and **Palau d'Alfons XIII**, built according to Puig i Cadafalch's plans after he was dismissed from both the project (and politics) in 1923.

The Palau Nacional: Museu Nacional d'Art de Catalunya (MNAC)

Open Tues–Wed and Fri–Sat 10–7, Thurs 10–9, Sun and hols 10–2.30, closed Mon; adm.

From the fountains, a sun-baked never-ending stair and outdoor escalators—which crank up on approach (and they do usually work)—ascend to the shamelessly bombastic Palau Nacional, a five-headed beast that survived the Exhibition when it found a new role as the Museu Nacional d'Art de Catalunya.

Murals

The museum contains the world's foremost collection of Romanesque murals, rescued in the 1920s from deteriorating chapels in the Pyrenees and from the wealthy Americans who were buying up whole cloisters on the French side of the border. Barcelona's Ajuntament intervened, bought them and brought them here—all using the new Italian technique for removing them with wax. Catalan art would remain in Catalunya, thank you very much.

This unique collection demonstrates just how wealthy Catalunya was in the 11th and 12th century, when, according to the chronicles, over 90 per cent of business was transacted in gold. Catalunya attracted artists of quality, who learned their iconography from Byzantine murals and mosaics, and the illuminations in Catalan Bibles, then translated them into strikingly bold, expressive figures, sharply outlined and filled in with flat colour, predominantly rich reds, dark greens and golds. They stare out hypnotically from the old walls, some nearly 1,000 years old, with riveting dark eyes, red circles on their cheeks, stylized stringy hair and weird elongated hands that look like flippers—all the better to stand out in their original settings, in the flickering candlelight of small, almost windowless stone churches.

Gae Aulenti's arrangement of the museum in 1992 is only slightly less controversial than her Musée d'Orsay in Paris: Barcelonans grumble that it doesn't respect the architecture (as if it deserved any respect) and has a temporary look about it. But the contents of these reconstructed apses and churches have enough power to mesmerize away all misgivings. One of the first, the 12th-century Sant Joan de Boí, shows jugglers along with the *Stoning of St Stephen*, in which the hand of God descends from heaven to zap sainthood on Stephen with a laser beam. The more graceful paintings of the Pedret circle are attributed to an itinerant painter from Lombardy, whose frescoes from the Mozarabic Sant Quirze de Pedret show a familiarity with the art of Ravenna, notably in the Byzantine dress of the *Seven Foolish Virgins*. On the other hand, the artist of the strange and childlike 11th-century Sant Miquel de Marmellar could hardly draw a face, although like several other artists he struggled to depict seraphim just as the Bible described them, with six wings and 1,000 eyes. In the apse of Sant Climent de Taüll (1123), the famous *Christ in Majesty* gazes from his mandala, in one of the most commanding, direct images in medieval art, painted by an artist with a precocious sense of foreshortening and expressive line; the angels and other wide-eyed figures contribute to the powerful atmosphere of watchfulness. Santa María de Taüll, in which the Virgin holds pride of place, has the *Magi* and *Nativity* on the side walls, a striking *Last Judgement* with nasty scenes of hell, peacocks, and a David beheading a Goliath with a sausage body that makes you wonder if there isn't something to all those speculations about medieval Europeans hallucinating on mouldy bread. The columns have graffiti scratched by bored monks; one has a maze.

Beyond is a wide variety of sculpted capitals, including some from Barcelona's Sant Pere de les Puelles. There's a room full of wooden polychrome Virgins, and a harrowing *Deposition* from Santa María de Taüll, in which the Christ has movable arms and dead staring eyes. The striking painted crucifix known as the *Majestat Batlló* portrays Christ, not in the exquisite agony favoured in the rest of Spain but dressed like a king, open-eyed and serene, in the beautiful blue tunic of a sultan, symbolizing the triumph over death. Next come frescoes from Sorpe, with more unusual imagery: a servant girl peeking in on the *Annunciation* scene, and Satan as a giant bug. Of the many superb altar frontals, either painted or in low relief, the one that sticks in the mind is 12th-century *Durro Altar Frontal*, with martyrdoms that reveal a precocious knack for comic surrealism—the saints seem to be thinking of what's for dinner while being sawn in two, or having nails pounded in their heads, or being stewed in a pot. After 1200 there is an increase in narration and naturalism: the *Altar Frontal d'Avià* is a good example. At the end of the Romanesque section are murals of a knife-winged griffon from the palatine room of San Pedro de Arlanzer near Burgos, and the ceiling of the chapterhouse of Sigena in Aragón (1200), damaged by fire in 1936 but still beautiful, its Old and New Testament figures inspired by English miniatures and Norman Sicilian mosaics.

Catalan Gothic and Other Paintings

Enter the Gothic section and the atmosphere changes at once from the robust and expressive to the more decorative, courtly and elegant style of chivalry, knights, ladies and dragons. Unlike the Romanesque, this is primarily urban art, and appropriately enough begins with the 13th-century murals from the Palau Caldes (now the Museu Picasso) of *Jaume I's Siege of Mallorca*, with curious Arabic motifs in the upper section. Fine works follow by the Second Master of Bierge, including his vivid *Life of St Dominic*, with a great scene of a young scholar falling about with his books. There are gracious Gothic Virgins, in wood, stone, ivory and alabaster, smiling now instead of staring. Pere Llobet contributes his solid, heavy figures in painted and gilded stone, and other works are by the more refined Jaume Cascalls (active 1345–79), whose Virgins, St Antony Abat and head of the Dead Christ in painted alabaster are delicately expressive.

One room has 14th-century golden Florentine and Sienese paintings that came to Catalunya by way of Avignon and strongly influenced local painters, especially brothers Pere and Jaume Serra, as can be seen in their altarpiece here. The anonymous chivalric *Portraits of the Kings of Aragón* (1425) are typical of the International Gothic style, as is Joan Mates' *St Sebastian* (here a knight with a beard) and Lluís Borrassà's *Retable de Gaurdiola* (1404). Joan Antigó, a master of tender expressions, contributes a beautiful *Annunciating Angel*. The Mestre d'Ail's altarpiece of *SS Catherine and Barbara* shows Catherine stepping on the king as if he were a worm. Jaume Ferrer II (active 1430–57) painted a coolly intellectual *St Jerome*, who sits pen in one hand, church in the other, his little lion like a puppy begging for scraps at the table. Then there's the masterful *Virgin of the Councillors* (1445), the only certain surviving painting by Valencian Lluís Dalmau, who went to Bruges and then painted this for the Ajuntament's chapel. Inspired by Van Eyck (this is the first Spanish painting that shows the Flemish influences that would dominate in the 16th century), Dalmau realistically depicts the five pious city councillors who paid for the painting, keeping company with SS Eulàlia and Andrew and a choir of angels in an elaborate but naturalistic Gothic setting.

The influential International Gothic painter and miniaturist Bernat Martorell is represented only by a *Retable de St Vincenç*, while his great follower Jaume Huguet nearly fills up a big room on his own with his *Retable de Santa Maria del Pi* and the *Consecration of St Augustine* series: one amusing scene shows the saint talking to a band of heretics, one of whom is literally bowled over. Another series by Huguet, on the *Life of St Vincent*, was removed from the church of Sant Vincenç in Sarrià; note the curious scene of an exorcism in front of his tomb. Best of all is the central panel of the triptych of *St George and the Princess*, both looking very serious.

By the mid-15th century, Flemish realism arrived, visible in the brutality of the *Beheading of St Cugat* by Anye Bru, a painter who spent much of his career in Catalunya, and in Bartolomé Bermejo's memorable *Resurrection from Limbo*, in which a nude Christ wrapped in clingfilm twists before a brooding background and Satan sulks peevishly in the corner. The Mestre de la Seu d'Urgell contributes a pretty blue landscape from an organ cabinet, while Roderic d'Osono's *St Peter Enthroned* perfectly captures the saint's peasant stubbornness. Then there's the late 15th-century altarpiece by the Mestre de la Porcinuncula with a delicate Virgin, angels and St Francis offering Jesus a dish of apples.

The museum runs out of Catalans at this point, with the exception of a series of paintings on the *Life of St Francis* by 18th-century Antoni Viladomat. There is, however, a good assortment of paintings by other artists, donated by politician Francesc Cambó: a triptych of the *Baptism of Christ* by the Master of Frankfurt, showing a keen interest in nature; a golden linear *St Gregory Pope* by Pedro Berruguente; the humanist *Seven Liberal Arts and Seven Cardinal Virtues* by Giovanni de Ser Giovanni; a gracious *Portrait of a Lady* by Sebastiano del Piombo; Giandomenico Tiepolo's *Venetian Carnival*; Goya's lush and luminous *Amor and Psyche*; El Greco's *SS Peter and Paul*; Velázquez's *Saint Paul*; Zurbarán's *Immaculate Conception*; and other works by Quentin Metysys, Quentin de la Tour and Lucas Cranach. When, at some point, the Museu d'Art Modern is relocated here, the museum will offer a complete feast of old and new Catalan art.

The Poble Espanyol

Open Tues–Thurs 9am–2am, Fri–Sat 9am–4am, Mon 9am–8pm, Sun 9am–midnight; adm 950 pts, under-14s 525 pts, free adm with a reservation at a nightclub or big restaurant, 50 per cent reduction with the Bus Turístic ticket, see p.11.

A short walk just west of the Palau Nacional, you'll find the **Botanical Gardens of Montjuïc** (*open winter Mon–Sat 10–3, summer Mon–Sat 10–5*) and the **Mirador del Llobregat**, one of several Montjuïc belvederes, this one with Josep Llimona's statue of a weary *St George*, very *après* dragon. One of the favourite sections of the 1929 fair was the section devoted to Spanish handicrafts, the walled **Poble Espanyol**. Conceived as an anthology of Spanish architecture with the slogan 'Get to Know Spain in an Hour', here the replicas of famous buildings were cunningly arranged with Disneyland deftness, a bit of Andalucía here, a bit of Basque there. A few contain craft workshops, while others contain souvenir shops, cafés and restaurants—some have showings of the film *Barcelona Experience* (*hourly 10.30–8*). In 1990, when the whole tourist schtick of fake old Spain was nodding off in its polyester polkadot flounces, it was head-butted awake by fashion and something from beyond fake, the **Torres d'Avila**, the most costly, magical, monstrous, slick, tongue-in-cheek designer bar in Barcelona, concocted by Javier Mariscal and Alfredo Arribas. It's still there (*see* p.67), along with other forms of nightlife, bars and flamenco shows.

Museu Etnològic

Open Wed and Fri–Sun 10–2, Tues and Thurs 10–7, closed Mon; adm.

Montjuïc's other attractions lie east of the Palau Nacional, but signposting is at best vague. Just behind the palace, in Passeig de Santa Madrona, are the formal gardens of the **Palauet Albéniz** (1928), named after the Catalan composer. It is the official Barcelona residence of the King and Queen of Spain, whose guests are greeted by a dome painted by Dalí (*adm only by written request*). Just downhill from here, the little **Museu Etnològic** was specially built in 1972 and has a large collection from Morocco, Japan, Australia, Africa and Latin America—Amazonian shrunken heads, hot-pink skeleton dolls from Mexico, a Peruvían head-deformer and more, although only a fraction is on show at any given time, in displays that strive to put the items in context.

Below the museum, steps lead down to the oldest gardens of Montjuïc, **La Roselada**, with its Font del Gat, or 'cat fountain', a mountain spring that inspired no end of romantic verses in the 19th century. Farther down, a tall garden wall marks the entrance to the **Teatre Grec**, carved into an old quarry in 1929, and the venue for the summer Greek theatre festival. Plans are to make it part of a Ciutat de Teatre project, which will also include the large recently refurbished theatre in a wholesale flower market, the **Mercat de les Flors**, in nearby Plaça Margherida Xirgu. It's an Ajuntament-sponsored project that will, among other things, provide a home for the Teatre Lliure, Barcelona's most prestigious company.

Museu Arqueològic

Open Tues–Sat 9.30–7, Sun 10–2.30, closed Mon; adm free Sun.

Appropriately, just across Passeig de Santa Madrona from the Greek theatre is the Museu Arqueològic in the 1929 Palau de les Arts Gràfiques, a fine example of Brunelleschian Noucentisme if there ever was one. The contents are a 'prequel' to the Palau Nacional, covering Palaeolithic to Visigothic Catalunya. There are copies of the region's remarkable cave paintings of hunting and battle scenes, in black silhouette; items of the *coves* culture (c. 1000–800 BC) of the Balearics, with models of megalithic *taulas*, *taliots* and *navetas*; finds from Empúries, an ancient Greek colony north of Barcelona (including a very Picasso-like bronze mirror, showing the *Judgement of Paris*); and primitive fertility sculpture and other fascinating finds from Carthaginian Ibiza, including the beautiful *Dama de Ibiza*.

The Iberian collection is excellent, with vases and votives from the 3rd and 2nd centuries BC, stones carved with mysterious writing, a skull with a huge nail driven into it (evidence of posthumous rites, says the reassuring explanation) and silver dishes with growling dog faces. A life-sized 3rd-century BC statue of the healing god Asklepius with snake, made of Parian marble, is the central figure in a room of Roman sculpture; there are fine mosaics (the *Three Graces* was found under Miró's birthplace in the Passatge del Crèdit) of chariot races, of Bellerophon killing the Chimaera, and fish, the latter an exquisite work made of the tiniest of *tesserae*. There's also an ivory gladiator in a whacky mask, rare remains of a 2nd-century BC *ballista*, and a reproduction of a room in Pompeii, filled with fine glass, including some proto-Art Nouveau vases. The Visigoths left mosaic belt buckles, gold crosses studded with big gems, and one of their curious crowns with dangling letters, this one dedicated to IVSTERVFINE (SS Justa and Rufina), the patron saints of Sevilla.

Anella Olímpica

Above the Palau Nacional, along Avinguda de l'Estadi, the **Anella Olímpica**, or Olympic ring, holds the principal venues of the 1992 games, including the **Stadi Olímpic**, a relic of the 1929 fair. Barcelona made a bid to host the 1936 games here, but lost out to Hitler's Berlin; in defiance it decided to hold a non-fascist 'People's Olympics', only the party was spoiled by another fascist named Franco, whose revolt began the Civil War the day before the games were to open. Major surgery was required to bring the stadium up to modern Olympic standards. The interior was rebuilt to hold 70,000, while preserving the original façade and its bronzes by Pau Gargallo, a feat accomplished by lowering the field by 36ft. The stadium is now the home of F.C. Espanyol, Barcelona's 'other' football team, who count among their supporters the many fed up with the steamrolling prima donnas over in Camp Nou. When Espanyol isn't taking its licks, the gate is open for a look around and a visit to the **Galeria Olímpica** (*open April–Sept Tues–Sat 10–2 and 4–8, Sun 10–2; Oct–Mar Tues–Sat 10–1 and 4–6, Sun 10–2, closed Mon; adm*), with videos of the exuberant opening and closing ceremonies of the games. The best-kept secret of the games was when Barcelona beat Hollywood at its own game by igniting the Olympic cauldron with a flaming arrow (and in case you're wondering, you bet there was a back-up fire ready in case he missed).

The adjacent covered sports arena, the **Palau Sant Jordi**, by Japanese architect Arata Isozaki, was the architectural marvel of the games. Even the building of it was spectacular: the enormous space-frame roof was constructed on the ground and then hoisted into place using hydraulic jacks; even now it seems to hover, undulating over the surrounding portico. The Barcelonans say it resembles a sleeping dragon. On the esplanade in front are concrete pillars linked by strings of stainless steel, added by Isozaki's wife, Aiko Mijawaki.

The elegant 394ft white needle in a loop, death to any passing Zeppelin, is the **Torre de Telefònica** (1991), designed by Santiago Calatrava, to engage in lofty chitchat with the city's other designer tower, Norman Foster's up on the Collserola. The mast was aligned with the earth's axis so it can also be used as a sundial after the collapse of electronic civilization. The curving base clad in *trencadis* is a nod to Gaudí. Opposite are the **Piscines Bernat Picornell** from 1929, converted for the Olympics and the finest in Barcelona (*bring your passport and some money if you want to swim*). The adjacent Plaça de Europa is built over a massive water tank, and tucked below this is Ricardo Bofill's **Institut Nacional d'Educzio Fisica de Catalunya**, with a predictable threadbare neoclassical façade.

Fundació Joan Miró

He was probably the most Surrealistic of us all.

André Breton

On the other side of the Stadi Olímpic, the Avinguda de l'Estadi continues to the luminous white Fundació Joan Miró (*open Tues–Wed and Fri–Sat 11–7 [July–Sept 10–8], Thurs 10–9.30, Sun and hols 10–2.30, closed Mon except hols; adm*). Miró wanted his native Barcelona to have his own collection of art, and in 1972 asked his friend Josep Lluís Sert to design its home. The building, bathed in natural light, is a bookend to Sert's earlier Maeght Foundation in St-Paul-de-Vence, and in 1986 it was enlarged in the same style by Sert's collaborator, Jaume Freixa, to contain the growing collection. The core, of course, is an excellent sampling of the artist's own paintings, sculptures, textile works and drawings made between 1917 and the 1970s. Not all are bright and colourful—most strikingly the lithographs of the *Barcelona Series* inspired by the horrors of the Civil War.

Miró (1893–1983) moved to Paris in 1919 where he joined Breton's Surrealist movement, only to go a step beyond the other Surrealists by evolving his own playful, personal language to express the dream reality of the creative unconscious. He spent most summers at the family farm at Montroig near Tarragona and, when money was short, ruefully returned to his old studio at 4 Passatge del Crèdit (*see* p.98). His early pre-Paris paintings reveal a fascination with Cézanne and the Cubists, geometric landscapes, still lifes and portraits, which glow eerily in bright, mad colours. Central to all his works, in all media, is the tension between abstraction and representation; he claimed that this duality came from the *seny i rauxa* (common sense and uncontrolled passion) at the heart of the Catalan identity of which he was always intensely proud. He was both poet and artisan, a fastidious craftsman and a deliriously spontaneous creator.

The turning point from perceptual to conceptual came in the early 1920s when he painted a series of objects, as in *Still Life I* and *Still Life II*, in a typically single-minded search for the extraordinary in the commonplace. By 1930, he was, on Matisse's advice, experimenting with automatic painting, allowing his hand to guide him unconsciously, drawing great motifs in black paint and filling in the colour later. This was also the period in which he began a series of 12 tiny oil paintings on wood panels, such as the precise and exquisite *Flame in Space and Nude Woman* (1932), which blazes with sharp, jewel-like colours. He was invited to contribute a painting to the Spanish Pavilion in the 1937 World's Fair in Paris, along with Picasso's *Guernica* and Alexander Calder's *Mercury Fountain*. Miró's passionate *The Reaper (Catalan Peasant in Revolt)* disappeared almost immediately after the exhibition, but Calder's lissom sculpture-fountain, dedicated to the mercury-mining towns of Almaden, has been remounted here, endlessly spilling spellbinding silvery globules from scoop to scoop. The red circle spiralling slowly above the fountain could almost have been lifted from Miró's own peculiar sign language, honed throughout his life; the circle, for example, repeatedly appears with a tall, inclined crescent shape, clearly phallic, which represented what Miró described as 'le bonheur conjugal', and added as explanation, 'Lovers are forms that struggle, that devour each other.' Another favourite in his vocabulary is the asterisk, recalling the merrily perverse and pervasive Catalan fascination with arseholes, either of *cagoners* (*see* p.62) or Barça football fans, the *culés*.

Most of the works in the foundation are the output of Miró's last two decades. Among the most startling is the brilliant white *Solarbird* (1968), a sensuous, undulating sculpture in flight against a deep blue wall, and the funniest is a bronze, *The Ladder of the Evading Eye* (1971), with a staring eyeball poised at the top of a wobbling ladder. Some of his mature works, particularly those done after a visit to Japan, are marked by a desire to isolate the language of signs and refine the colours in order to create a state of mind which would 'go beyond painting'; one of the loveliest is *The Day* (1974), a dark inky swoop culminating in a vermilion circle. The puckish playfulness is still there: the collection opens with an enormous, mischievous tapestry, and an outdoor gallery is dotted with a menagerie of fantastical sculpted creatures. Besides a home to Miró's own works, the Fundació was conceived as a forum for experimentation and study and holds wide-ranging special exhibitions of contemporary art as well as a permanent collection of works made by artists in homage to Miró, including Chillida's luminous, exquisitely balanced *Homage to Miró* (1985).

Castell de Montjuïc and Around

To the east, beyond the Fundació Miró, are the **Jardins Mossèn Jacint Verdaguer**, named after the great Catalan poet. Near the pond, a sculpture by Ramon Sabi incorporates some of his most famous lines, and another sculpture in honour of the Catalan national dance, the ***Sardana***, stands opposite the old entrance to the fun park (a burned-out shell, earmarked to be replaced in 2004 for the Forum of Cultures with a new bucolic 'macropark' with a lake in the centre). The gardens are especially pretty in spring, when water trickles lazily down the stepped terraces and the flowers burst into colour.

One of the more outlandish state myths ever concocted has it that Hercules came to the highest point of Montjuïc after making the Pyrenees as a tomb for his lover Pirene; he was impressed enough with the view of the plain below to vow that he would one day return to found a great city there. During his later labours, he was in command of a Greek fleet that ran into the mistral; eight ships found a safe anchor in Marseille, but the ninth went missing. After a search, Hercules discovered it safe and sound here and, remembering his vow, founded a city and named after the ninth boat, *barca nona*.

For centuries, fires would burn on the brow of Montjuïc to guide Barcelona's fishing fleet home. In the Reapers' War in 1640, the beacon tower was converted into a castle in 30 days, against the Castilian army of Felipe IV, before Barcelona was starved into submission. The rest of its history is singularly unhappy. After the siege of Barcelona in 1714, Bourbon troops blew up the old castle and in 1759 replaced it with another that would specialize in interning and torturing Catalan political prisoners. In 1842, General Espartero, faced with unrest over the repeal of rent control legislation, lobbed over 1,000 shells from the castle on to the city, destroying 400 buildings. In 1896, after the Corpus Christi bombing, Anarchists, and anyone in Barcelona who looked like one, were herded up here to be tortured so badly that several died; five were executed after trumped-up charges, and 61 were sent to die in a penal colony. In 1909, the Anarchist founder of Barcelona's secular Modern Schools, Francesc Ferrer, was executed here after a sham trial following the *Setmana Trágica*—even though Ferrer wasn't even in Barcelona at the time—raising a storm of protest throughout Europe and giving the Anarchists their finest martyr. A decade later in the infamous La Canadiense electrical strike (the worst and bloodiest in the city's history, putting the lights out in Barcelona, causing severe food shortages, and shutting down 70 per cent of its industry), 3,000 workers were imprisoned in the castle.

In 1960 the military ceded the castle to the city, which has used this haunted ground for its **Museu Militar** (*open Tues–Sun 9.30–8, closed Mon; adm*), with an intriguing 23,000-piece collection of models, maps, weapons, lead soldiers (a Spanish speciality) and armour from around the world accumulated by that insatiable hoarder Frederic Marés. It also has the city's one and only surviving statue of Franco, and the medieval tombstones from the Jewish cemetery discovered nearby. Marés' statue of the Bruc drummer boy in the gardens commemorates a young hero of the war against Napoleon. After the uprising of the Dos de Mayo in 1808 in Madrid, the Catalans rebelled against the French, in spite of Napoleonic sweet talk about Catalan self-determination. Four thousand French troops were met at the Bruc pass by Montserrat by a third as many Catalan *guerrillas*, who defeated the French because the sound of the boy's incessant drumming from various points ricocheted off the rocks and led the French to believe they were surrounded by a mighty arm. When the Catalans, for all their troubles, got the reactionary absolutist Fernando VII, some had second thoughts: 'If only he'd played with his balls instead of playing the drum' became a saying. He looks over the spot where Falangist prisoners and suspected fifth columnists were brutally rounded up and shot during the Civil War.

Below, near the aerial cable-car station at **Miramar**, you can enjoy an especially fine view of the city over a drink. Next to the bar, incongruously overlooking the bustling docks, is the superb if rather neglected succulent section of the **Jardins de Mossèn Costa i Llobera**, a Manhattan of towering cacti interspersed with exotic specimens that look as if they have dropped in from another planet.

To the west, enjoying the city's finest view over the Mediterranean, are some of the finest Modernista contributions to the whole stylistic hodgepodge of Montjuïc: the big bourgeois tombs in the **Cementiri del Sud-Oest**, founded in 1883. The burghers of Barcelona wanted to face eternity in comfort and often employed the architects of their homes in the Eixample to design their last homes here: the classic is Puig i Cadafalch's Gothic Dutch tomb for the Amatllers, with sculptures by Eusebi Arnau. Jammed together they make a fantastical city of the dead, an extravaganza piled on hairpinning lanes along carefully arranged posthumous class lines. The only place that can match it is the Staglieno Cemetery in Barcelona's archrival Genoa. Above the cemetery on C/ de la Mare de Déu de Port, the **Fossar de la Pedrera** is the old stone quarry where Republicans were shot and buried in a communal grave after the Civil War, marked by a memorial of 1985 and stone columns listing the known dead (Hugh Thomas, in his *Spanish Civil War*, estimates that 10,000 were shot in Barcelona in the first month, and 20,000 over the next two decades). The most famous victim was the Catalan president Lluís Companys, who was captured by the Gestapo in Belgium in October 1940 and handed over to Franco, who had him secretly taken here and shot. Companys' last request was to take off his shoes so he could feel his homeland under his feet as he died.

Around the Edge

On the map, the ragged edges of the Eixample's grid mark its contact with older, once independent towns. **Gràcia**, the most interesting of the former towns, is full of character and a great place for a meander, but thanks to the Ajuntament even the dustiest and most woebegone industrial wasteland now has some landmark park or building to tempt you on to the metro for a look. The Collserola foothill to the north, the Zona Alta, once held the summer retreats of the noble and rich, but the trams attracted moneyed Barcelona in the early 20th century, leaving some fine works by Gaudí, especially the sublime **Park Güell**. And above the rich suburbs rises the city's mountain girdle, with fun **Tibidabo** and the utterly delightful **Collserola Park**, with views down on the city that bring home Barcelona's uniquely privileged position. We follow this peripheral area more or less anticlockwise.

For places to eat and drink in these areas, *see* pp.236–7.

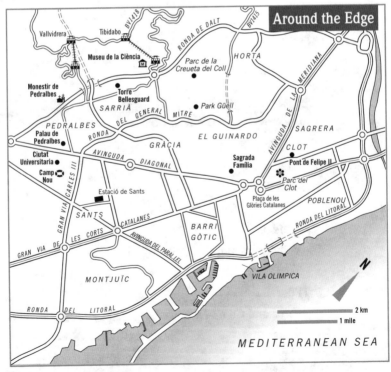

Sagrera, Clot and El Guinardo

Inland from Poblenou, **Sagrera** is a hard-scrabble old industrial neighbourhood, but a compelling one to visit for the **Pont de Felipe II** (perhaps better known as the Pont de Calatrava), one of the most beautiful contemporary bridges in Europe, incongruously suspended over train tracks along dusty rundown C/ de Felipe II (**Ⓜ** Bac de Roda). Designed by Santiago Calatrava in 1987, it is made of two racing parabolic arches that resemble a sculpture more than a work of engineering; plans are to create a park below and possibly a station for a new high-speed train on a European gauge, linking Barcelona to Madrid and France.

The rather unfortunately named neighbourhood of **El Clot**, also on the wrong side of Plaça de les Glòries Catalanes, has one of the cosiest of the city's new parks, the **Parc del Clot** (**Ⓜ** Clot), designed in 1986 by Daniel Frezies and Vicente Miranda. It incorporates an old RENFE viaduct over an artificial lake, and old walls amid gardens planted with palms; a cloister-pergola contains Bryan Hunt's *Rites of Spring,* a frozen bronze cascade. Nearby in Plaça de Font i Sagué, the pretty brick and glass **Mercat del Clot** (1889) is by Pere Falqués.

Things begin to get steep at **El Guinardó**, above the Hospital de la Santa Creu i Sant Pau. The wooded park cascading down the hill, **Parc del Guinardó** (**Ⓜ** Guinardó), was opened in 1910, making it one of the oldest in Barcelona; like most of the others of the era it was redone by the great Montjuïc gardening team of Forestier and Rubió i Tuduri. The newer and smaller **Parc de les Aigües** (**Ⓜ** Alfons X), by the entrance of La Rovira tunnel, has yet another of Barcelona's submarines, this one stuck firmly in the ground like a subterrine, and the **Casa de les Altures**, a charming neo-Moorish folly of 1890.

Gràcia

Gràcia, the most distinctive of all the towns absorbed by the growing city, was a vortex for liberal and progressive ideas throughout the 19th century: workers, Anarchists, feminists, vegetarians, Protestants and ardent Republicans flourished here, formed societies and movements, and published an astounding number of progressive periodicals (even one in Esperanto). On three occasions its convictions erupted into open revolt that had to be put down by the Spanish army. It was annexed to Barcelona in 1898, not altogether willingly, and in the 1960s it once again became a centre of alternative ideas, a citadel of left-wing liberalism (as much as such things were allowed under Franco). Today Gràcia has a laid-back neighbourhood atmosphere, of narrow streets wandering between compact squares that offer a nice contrast to the Barcelona of big art and monuments. In late August it hosts a lavish *festa major*, each street striving to be the brightest or most outlandish, hosting tumultuous parties, dancing and music to the delight of the thousands who pour in from Barcelona, and to the sniffy protests of some locals who would prefer it remained a private party. Cries for Gràcia's independence from Barcelona, frequent in the 1960s, are still occasionally raised, but not too seriously.

Gràcia begins just north of the Diagonal (**Ⓜ** Diagonal, or take bus No.22 or 24 from Plaça de Catalunya), with the Passeig de Gràcia leading up to its front door. At 2–4 Passeig de Gràcia, the street narrows when it meets the massive **Casa Fuster** (1908–11), the last residential project of Domènech i Montaner, done with the assistance of his son Pere. It repeats the form of his previous buildings, but with a minimum of decoration (except under the tower and balconies)—one gets the feeling that his heart was more in his hospital project. There are other Modernista buildings here, notably the **Casa Cama** (1905), at 15 C/ Gran de Gràcia (the continuation of the Passeig de Gràcia), with its beautiful wrought-iron and leaded *tribuna* and vestibule, designed by Gràcia's unofficial architect, Francesc Berenguer Mestres (1866–1914). Berenguer never received his diploma, but left architecture school at 21 to marry and to work for Gaudí (a fellow citizen of Reus), becoming his most diligent assistant, his draughtsman and foreman—all in all, the one who really got things done and translated inspiration into bricks and mortar. He was also a Modernista architect of distinction in his own right, although a complete account of his contributions to Gaudí's masterpieces may never be known. With seven children to support, he designed private and public buildings, especially in Gràcia, although because he had no diploma most of his work was signed in the records by others. There are seven of his apartment buildings on this street alone, Nos.13, 15, 50, 61, 77 (one of his best), 196 and 237. When he died at the age of 48, Gaudí mourned that he had lost 'his own right arm' and he didn't seem to be exaggerating: he spent his last 12 years on the Sagrada Família and built relatively little of that, compared to his earlier career.

A right turn on to C/ de Goya will talk you to the spiritual heart of Gràcia, **Plaça Rius i Taulet**, named after Barcelona's go-getting mayor of 1888, and dominated by the 125ft **Torre del Rellotge**, adorned with symbols of the zodiac. Designed by Antoni Rovira i Trias in 1864, it was almost destroyed six years later when it rang the alarm after military recruits revolted against conscription: the besieging Spanish army shot out one of its bells. The tower has been a symbol of liberty ever since, and gave its name to a famous progressive Catalan weekly, *La Campana de Gràcia*. The square is flanked by the Gràcia's **town hall**, embellished with florid lamps and the town's coat of arms, built in 1905 by Francesc Berenguer. Farther down C/ de Siracusa is the **Plaça del Poble Romaní**, dedicated to Romany language and culture, in the heart of Gràcia's long-established Catalan-speaking Romany community. Then at the end of the street there's **Plaça John Lennon**, a blank, new square constructed in 1993 with a record-shaped plaque inscribed 'Give peace a chance'. The **Plaça del Sol** is the centre of Gràcia's nightlife and a

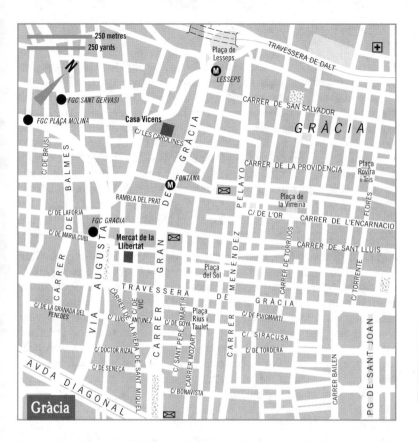

Gràcia

favourite spot for the neighbourhood dogs, despite being soullessly revamped in 1987 for the imperatives of an underground car park. It is surrounded with lively bars, restaurants and cafés, with chairs and tables spilling into the square on warm summer nights.

The oldest part of Gràcia is sandwiched between C/ Gran de Gràcia and Vía Augusta, with the lively little iron **Mercat de la Llibertat** (1893) at the centre. Originally designed as an open-air market, it was capped with a Modernista wrought-iron roof in 1893 by the tireless Berenguer, and adorned with the town coat of arms, which doubles up as drinking fountains. The **Rambla del Prat**, two blocks farther up, is Gràcia's showcase for Modernista architecture; some buildings have been renovated, others not, but many retain their fanciful façades, painted ceilings, wood-panelled staircases and elaborate ironwork. At No.18, four masks gaze out from the old **Bosque cinema**, included portraits of a youthful Picasso and the sculptor Pau Gargallo, who added them when the old Teatre del Bosc was renovated in 1917.

Back on the other side of the C/ Gran de Gràcia are more charming squares. The first is the old-fashioned **Plaça de la Virreina**, built at the end of the 19th century on land donated by the wealthy widow of the Viceroy of Peru. The serene parish church of St Joan, which looks as though nothing has ever disturbed it, was severely damaged during *Setmana Trágica* of 1909 and was restored by Berenguer, who obviously never slept. He was also responsible for many of the homes around here, including the handsome **Casa Rubina** on 44 C/ de l'Or, embellished with curving, whimsical iron balconies, shimmering mosaics and stark brickwork. Another of the neighbourhood's characters is remembered in **Plaça Rovira i Trias**, which is named after the architect (1826–89) whose winning plan for the Eixample was overturned by the politicians in Madrid. A contemplative bronze statue of him sits on a park bench; an engraving of his rejected plan lies at his feet.

Not far from the metro station Fontana is Gaudí's very first house, the **Casa Vicens** (1883–5), 18–24 C/ de les Carolines. A clean break from academicism, 'a nightmarish farrago of Moorish and Gothic elements' according to the *Dictionary of Architecture*, it was also one of the first colourful buildings in Barcelona, covered with brickwork and checkerboard patterns of green and white tiles (the owner was a tile merchant, but even so the house nearly bankrupted him). The delightful iron gate and fence of date-palm fronds, one of Gaudí's most distinctive early works, has been attributed by some to a very young Berenguer. A series of frothy wrought-iron balconies, full of dragons and bats, culminates in whimsical turrets, guarded by a cherubic statue of a pensive child. The interior is equally resplendent but inaccessible, although the elegant circular glass smoking room with its Moorish ceiling can be obliquely admired from outside. From the beginning Gaudí concerned himself greatly with the siting of his buildings; originally the exotic garden was much larger and the house much smaller (it was doubled in size in 1925). There's a story that, when a good friend of Gaudí's mother came to Barcelona and was taken on a tour to see this and his other buildings, she wasn't surprised. Antoni's been doing that stuff since he was a kid, she said.

Uphill again, near the Lesseps metro, is a rather ugly tangle of main roads surmounted by a small park, where Gràcia's old men while away the summer evenings with a game of *boules*, overlooked by the church of Els Josepets. This old heart of Gràcia now looks forlorn among the fierce spikes of the surrounding development. At 30 Plaça de Lesseps, the **Casa Ramos** (1906) is a pretty blue and white tiled Modernista building by Jaume Torres, formed of three houses linked by a single façade, delicately traced with a simple floral motif.

Park Güell

Toto, I don't think we're in Kansas any more.

The Wizard of Oz

One of the 20th century's greatest evocations of the infinite variety and magic of life, Gaudí's Park Güell occupies one of Barcelona's great balconies, 'Bald Mountain', Mont Pelat (from Ⓜ Lesseps, walk 400 yards up the Travessera de Dalt, then turn left up steep C/ Llarrard, or take bus No.24 from Plaça de Catalunya; *open daily Nov–Feb 10–6, Mar and Oct 10–7, April and Sept 10–8, May–Aug 10–9*). The park, at once Surrealist—it was a major source of inspiration for Miró and Dalí—and Abstract *avant la lettre*, owes its existence to Eusebi Güell, who bought two farms here in 1902 to lay out an exclusive English garden suburb (hence the English 'K' in Park), carefully kept away from the public tram lines to maintain its island like exclusivity (when Gaudí died after being struck by a tram, the joke went around that they were getting their revenge). To attract buyers Güell gave his pet architect free rein to design some amenities: a grand entrance to the estate, a pair of lodges, a central market area for residents, and terraced drives. It was a complete flop, but Güell was too rich to care. He left his fancy palace in El Raval to live in the park's Can Muntaner, and allowed charities to stage fund-raising parties here. After his death in 1918, his family donated the park to the city. In 1984 it was listed as a UNESCO World Heritage Site, and in 1995 it underwent a 1,500 million peseta restoration.

In the midst of the dull, not-so-hoity-toity *urbanización* that actually was built on Bald Mountain, the Park Güell glows like an enchanted mirage. As in most of Gaudí's work, there are layers of symbolism in every aspect of the park's decoration—some of it personal, some of it from Güell, all of it as inventive and playful as the architecture itself. There's the usual Catalanism, but also, according to Josep M. Carandell (*see* **Topics**, p.58), much more: Masonry, Rosicrucianism, alchemy and all the mishmash of religions and mysteries that fascinated the *fin de siècle* elite. Carandell suspects that the park never achieved its purported aims as a suburb because potential tenants were screened and none measured up to the spirit of the secret philanthropic Catholic Masonic work of its creators. The truth may be that Güell, Gaudí and Trias (the lawyer who bought the third and last house in the park of the 40 that were planned) didn't really want any neighbours in their temple to begin with. And, incidentally, their three houses form a Masonic right angle.

The stone wall surrounding the park is topped by a red and white band of *trencadis* and medallions shaped like cigar bands as a reference to Güell's tobacco interests. To the left of the entrance, the words *alaba/por* are an anagram of *labor* and *paa*, which in 19th-century Masonry meant a boardinghouse, hinting that Güell and

Gaudí saw the park as a kind of outdoor lodge of labour. On either side of the gate (a copy of the palm-frond grille from the Casa Vicens, added post-Gaudí) are two fairy-tale **pavilions** as bright as candy, possibly inspired by a staging in 1900 of a Catalan translation of Engelbert Humperdinck's opera *Hansel and Gretel*. Both are crowned by superb sloping roofs of swirling coloured mosaics, cupolas, mushroom forms (a magic *Amanita muscaria* on the wicked witch's house) and Gaudí's signature steeple with its double cross (on the good children's house).

The grand stair swoops around the most jovial **salamander** imaginable, clinging to the fountain and covered with brightly coloured *trencadis* that symbolize fire. Güell studied in Nîmes, a city that was Catalan in the early Middle Ages and has a Place de la Salamandre in honour of François I, who dallied in alchemy and made the creature his personal symbol, as one who burns but is not consumed. The symbol of Nîmes is a crocodile and a palm tree, and there was a statue of one with two palm trees in that city's Parc de la Fontaine, a favourite haunt of the young Güell. Originally there were two palms planted by Gaudí's salamander, too. Above the salamander is a tripod with a stone representing an omphalos, the navel of the universe: a reference to the Pythia and omphalos at Delphi as the seat of wisdom. The bench above is shaped like a Greek tragic mask.

The Parc de la Fontaine has a Roman temple, and so does the Park Güell. On top of the stair opens the remarkable cavernous **Sala Hipóstila**, planned by Gaudí as a covered market. Known as the Hall of a Hundred Columns (actually there are only 86, a number that reoccurs in other measurements in the park), its thick forest of Doric columns are hollow inside, allowing rain water to run down into a vast cistern below, designed to store water for emergencies or irrigation. The shallow vaults of the ceiling look as if they were soft as marshmallow, covered with white *trencadis* and beautiful plafonds, representing four large suns (the four seasons), the phases of the moon, and spiralling shapes, designed by Gaudí and brilliantly executed by Josep Maria Jujol, who used reject ceramics from Gaudí's other projects supplemented by whatever broken glass or plates the park's workmen found in the streets. If you look closely at the plafonds (perhaps best in the evening, when the new lighting system at the base of the columns illuminates the ceiling), you can see that Jujol didn't limit himself to ceramics, stone and glass—there are wine goblets, bottles and even porcelain dolls stuck up there too.

The scalloped roof of the hall is rimmed with a snaking ceramic collage that also serves as the back of the **serpentine bench**, a masterpiece of three-dimensional art, a Surrealist, Cubist collage that predates Surrealism, Cubism and collages. To form the mould of the seat, Gaudí got a naked man to sit in wet plaster, while the *trencadi* design was the work of Jujol, who was so inspired that he broke up his own cupid-painted dinner ware for the project. The seemingly random patterns of colour, and simple and abstract designs, offer new delights with each turn and change of light; during the restoration it was discovered with some consternation that they had to match 21 different tones of off-white. Among the figures are stylized crabs and symbols of the zodiac, and Catalan or Latin graffiti, inscribed in the clay before firing by Jujol and so well hidden that the words weren't discovered until the 1950s. No one knows what's going on here; some believe the words form a mysterious dialogue, perhaps with the Virgin Mary, who trampled the serpent, symbolized by the bench. But the snake was also the symbol of health, linked to the Greek healer god Asclepius. The platform by the bench was known as the Greek Theatre, and there were plans to stage *Oedipus Rex* (a play about epidemics, one of Güell's great interests; he wrote a book on vaccine theory) with temporary seating overlooking the city, but the *Setmana Trágica* got in the way.

Then there are Gaudí's extraordinary **porticoes** and **viaducts**, 3km of them, as serpentine as the beach, sloping in and out of the hillside, all made of stone found on the site and fitted together to form magical sinuous passageways with walls shaped like curling waves and fanciful stone tree-planters with aloes growing on top. They drove Dalí crazy. None of the viaducts are alike; one has a column that resembles Carmen Miranda holding a pile of rocks on her head instead of fruit salad, called the Bugadera—but Carandell suspects she is really 'Sister Mason'. Just off the path leading to the nub of the hill is a six-lobed truncated stone tower called the **Chapel**, shaped like a Rosicrucian rose, but hermetically sealed; if there's an underground entrance, no one ever has found it. There are three stone crosses on the chapel, esoterically pointed on top like arrows; look towards the east and the three merge to form a single arrow.

Gaudí lived for 20 years with his elderly father and niece in the Torre Rosa, designed by Francesc Berenguer as a house to show potential buyers, although as there were none (or so they said) Gaudí bought it. It's a rosy-pink cottage with green shutters and creamy swirls around the windows and doors, with a morel-shaped chimney covered with *trencadís* and a little garden filled with flowers which Gaudí wrought from bits of cast-off fencing. Now the **Casa-Museu Gaudí** (*open Mar–Sept daily 10–7, Nov–Feb daily 10–6; adm*), it contains plans and examples of the wonderful organic furniture that Gaudí designed for the Palau Güell, the Casa Calvet and Casa Batlló: plush gold-embossed curving seats for people with very small behinds, chairs based on bone structures, immense wooden cabinets which seem to ripple along the walls, and dripping stained-glass chandeliers. Upstairs is Gaudí's bedroom, incongruously simple, with a narrow bed and a framed copy of his prayer book and death mask. A reverential cabinet holds a touchingly sparse collection of his effects, including a napkin 'used by Gaudí with his initials'.

Around Park Güell

Up from the Park Güell, bus No.25 (or Ⓜ Penitents) continues to a newer urban space, the **Parc de la Creueta del Coll**, created in 1981–7 by Bohigas, Martorell and Mackay from an abandoned quarry, with a popular palm-rimmed swimming pool and beach as its centrepiece. The *de rigueur* public art is here as well: Ellsworth Kelly's vertical piece shoots up into the sky, and Eduard Chillada's giant gentle claw, the *Elogi de l'Aigua* ('water eulogy'), is once again suspended over the water after dramatically collapsing in 1998 and injuring three people; park-goers remain wary of it.

Horta: The Labyrinth and Velódrom

When Barcelona boomed in the 1960s, it was at the expense of the old aristocratic estates that skirted the Collserola foothills. One, however, escaped the bulldozers: the beautiful and atmospheric **Parc del Laberint d'Horta**, on Passeig del Vall de Hebrón, on the far northwestern edge of Barcelona (10-minute walk from Ⓜ Montbau; *open Tues–Sun Nov–Feb 10–6, Mar and Oct 10–7, April and Sept 10–8, May–Aug 10–9; only 750 people admitted at a time; adm, free Wed and Sun*). Originally occupying 133 acres (now reduced to 17), the park was the brain-child of the Marques de Alfarràs, a true son of the Enlightenment. He designed the master plan in 1791 on the theme of Love and Disappointment and hired Italian architect Domenico Bagutti to lay out the gardens, lake, waterfall, canals, pavilions, statuary and a not-so-easy cypress **maze**, its centre marked by a statue of Eros. The park became famous for its cultural evenings and theatrical performances. In 1802, Carlos IV, one of several kings who came to visit, remarked that 'it was too much for one man', but the *marques*, quick on his toes, replied that 'it was too little to offer to a monarch'. His descendants added a romantic garden to the scheme and held on to the park until 1967, when they sold it to the city. After years of neglect and vandalism, the park has recently undergone a superb restoration with EU funds. The ruined neo-Arab-Gothic country house, built next to a 12th-century watch tower, is slated to be repaired as well.

Entrance to the park is by way of a footbridge near the award-winning **Velódrom**, by Esteve Bonell (1984), set in its own park with a 'sculpture-poem' by Joan Brossa and a 1992 reconstruction of Josep Lluís Sert's **Pavilion of the Spanish Republic**, built for the 1937 Paris Exposition Universal as a cry of defiance in the midst of the Civil War: the original housed Picasso's *Guernica*, Juli González's *Montserrat*, Miró's lost *El Segador* ('The Reaper') and Calder's *Mercury Fountain* (now in the Fundació Miró, *see* p.188). In front, Claes Oldenburg's ***Matches*** (1992) are colossal colourful versions of your everyday fire-makers, only bent and useless. Other Olympic facilities are to the south of the Ronda de Dalt bypass, including the metal pergolas of the **archery pavilion**, on C/ Basses d'Horta, by the late Enric Miralles, architect of the Scottish Parliament building.

Tibidabo

For an incomparable view over Barcelona, ascend the highest peak of the Collserola range, the 1,804ft Tibidabo, just west of the city. Its name, peculiar even by Catalan standards, comes from the Gospel of St Matthew, which quotes the devil trying to tempt Christ while he fasted in the desert: '*Haec omnia tibi dabo si cadens adoraberis me*' ('All this I will give to you if you will fall down and worship me'). Purists might claim the incident really took place in the Sinai, but a Catalan would counter, 'Just what's so tempting about a rocky desert?' Whereas the view from here, encompassing Barcelona, Montserrat, the Pyrenees and even Mallorca, is a pretty seductive offer, or at least it was before it was shrouded in veils of smog.

The FGC Avinguda del Tibidabo will get you as far as Plaça de John F. Kennedy; the landmark here is the brightly coloured, dainty mosaic filigree Modernista tower and cupola of **La Rotonda** (1918), designed by Adolf Ruiz i Casamitjana for a hotel, now converted into a clinic. The Tramvia Blau (*for schedules, see p.11*) leaves from here, ascending Avinguda Tibidabo to link up with the funicular, passing a second Modernista landmark on the left at No.31, the large **Casa Rovir-alta,** or 'White Friar' (1913), by Joan Rubió i Bellvé, a striking *mudéjar* fantasy in white stucco and elaborate, corbelled, angular brickwork; the lavish interior is now the Asador de Aranda restaurant, where Madonna was once famously entertained by a male stripper. Just up at No.56 is another fine work by Rubió, the **Casa Casacuberta** (1907), now a school. The two were key works in the development of this area as an exclusive 1,235-acre garden residential district by Dr Salvador Andreu, who struck it rich with his patented cough lozenges. He purchased the land in 1899 for 500 pesetas, made it a priority to install a tram—unlike Güell for his residential project—and over the next 15 years saw his investment multiply 600 times in one of the canniest property coups in Barcelonan history. Now offices and services occupy most of the fancy buildings.

If you have the kids in tow, you may want to get off halfway up to visit the **Museu de la Ciència**, at 55 C/ Teodor Roviralta (*open Tues–Sun 10–8; adm*), which can easily be combined with an evening at Tibidabo for a full day out. The handsome building was designed as an asylum by Josep Domènech i Estapà in 1894, but the inmates have been replaced by babbling children and teenagers. Even if the explanations are only in Catalan and Spanish, there's enough hands-on science exhibits to keep most entertained for at least a couple of hours. There's also a particularly manic *toca toca* ('touch touch') section for tots under five, and something you don't see every day: a giant portrait of Einstein, made entirely of flies. Outside the museum by the Ronda de Dalt there's a full-scale model of Narcis Monturiol's submarine.

There are two ways to get to the top of Tibidabo: the direct Tibibus (*July and Aug only, every half-hour from Plaça de Catalunya from 11.30am*), or by taking the Tramvia Blau to the end of the line at **Plaça Dr Andreu**, where you can stop for a cocktail at one of the panoramic bars. The best time to go is in the late afternoon on a clear day, as dusk falls and the lights begin to twinkle in the great city below. Good old Dr Andreu also founded the company that built the **Funicular del Tibidabo** (*for schedules, see p.11*), which from Plaça Dr Andreu creaks up past the Fabra Observatory and a colourful Modernista water tower to the summit and its crowning glory—the huge, spiky neo-Mormon expiatory temple of **Sagrat Cor**, built in atonement for the *Setmana Trágica* of 1909, just as its model, the Sacre Cœur in Montmartre, was built to purge the revolutionary guilt of the 1870 Paris Comune. The first enormous open-armed Christ on top was by Frederic Marés, but it was melted down for ammunition during the Civil War, and replaced by the present version by Josep Miret when the neo-Gothic upper section was completed in the 1960s. The best bit is the crypt (1911), built by Enric Sagnier, who was also responsible for the huge fairy-tale townhouse visible from Plaça Dr Andreu. A lift sweeps you up to the roof for more truly staggering views.

The **Parc d'Attracciones** (*open Tues–Fri 11–7, Sat–Sun 11–9; adm 2,400 pts to ride everything*) is the oldest in Spain and is still going strong, offering all the usual chills and thrills—bumper cars, a wicked House of Horrors, a harrowing aeroplane ride and one of the most panoramic ferris wheel rides imaginable. Admission includes the **Museu d'Autòmats del Tibidabo**, with grinning wooden fortune-tellers, mechanical bands and other carnival gizmos from the 19th century onwards. The most famous inmate is saucy Los Manyos, an impudent, winking, pigtail-tossing, coin-operated temptress. Just south, another summit of the Collserola (linked to the funfair by a little tourist train in summer) is occupied by Norman Foster's slender and dynamic 800ft **Torre de Collserola** (*open summer Sat–Sun 11–7, Wed–Fri 11–2.30 and 3.30–7; winter Sat–Sun 11–7; adm*), a high-tech telecommunications tower built for the Olympics, 'pure sculpture', as Sir Norman himself describes it. A glass lift shoots to the 10th-floor observation deck for giddily vertiginous views down on Tibidabo itself.

Bellesguard

Barcelonans with the readies have been playing country squire at the foot of the Collserola at least since 1400, when King Martí the Humane, the last Catalan king of the house of Barcelona, built his summer residence at Bellesguard. Five hundred years later, Antoni Gaudí was commissioned to build a villa by the ruins, the **Torre Bellesguard**, at 46 C/ Bellesguard (follow the road along the Ronda de Dalt west from the Museu de la Ciència). The historical connotations inspired Gaudí to create a tall, neo-Gothic castle (1900–5), with his trademark four-armed cross at the top of the pinnacle. But the turn of the 20th century also marked a turning point in Gaudí's career: the stone walls hide a wonderfully inventive interior of vaults and brickwork, a major but inaccessible work enjoyed by the lucky heirs of the owners (see the photos in the Espai Gaudí, *see* p.166). From C/ Valeta d'Arquer you can have a look at Gaudí's viaduct with slanted columns, a foretaste of the Park Güell.

Vallvidrera and the Collserola Park

It is hard to believe that bold, brassy Tibidabo forms part of one of the loveliest and most serene urban parks in Europe; behind the famous peak are over 16,000 acres of undulating forests, dotted with fountains, forgotten villages, churches and old farmhouses, all seemingly a world away from the urbane city at their feet. Take the FGC train from Plaça de Catalunya to Baixador de Vallvidrera station. From here, shallow stone steps curve through the shady woods for about 10 minutes and emerge near an old, honey-coloured farmhouse, covered with a twisting wisteria and guarded by a pair of weary yellow dogs. This is the 18th-century Vil.la Joana, now the **Museu Verdaguer** (*open Tues–Sun 10–2, closed Mon; adm free*), dedicated to the poet Jacint Verdaguer 'Mossèn Cinto' (1845–1902), whose nationalistic poems tinged with nostalgia, sentimentality and an extraordinary gift for imagery struck a chord with millions during the late 19th century, when he enjoyed the reputation of a 'Catalan Homer'. In 1877, his epic *L'Atlàntida* won first prize at the *Jocs Florals* Catalan poetry competition; his second epic, *Canigó*, about the legendary origins of Catalunya in a Pyrenean monastery, was published to great acclaim in 1885. After that he went a bit loopy and wrote almost nothing else of note—and died in these rooms, some of which have been kept, rather eerily, as they were at his death. But it is a quiet, peaceful house, with stone floors, long, cool galleries and a veranda looking out towards Montserrat.

Across from the museum is the Collserola Park's helpful **information centre** (© 93 280 35 52, no English spoken, but they do their best to accommodate visitors), which can provide maps and leaflets on the trails, botanical walks, picnic spots, springs and activities. There is good walking, cycling and horse-riding, and the centre can also provide information on the wildlife that inhabits the Mediterranean forest. An easy hike leads up to **Vallvidrera**, a pretty hilltop town, along a shady botanical walk past the **Font de la Budellera**, designed by J.P. Forestier in 1916. The spring ripples down three stone tiers to a pool, decorated with an ingenious design by Antoni Tàpies and sculpted by Pere Casanovas, which re-creates the Barcelona coat of arms. Up in sleepy Vallvidrera itself, have a drink at Can Josean (with dizzying views) or Can Trampa. There is a bus (no.211) which links the village with Tibidabo, via Norman Foster's tower, or, better still, take the funicular down to Peu del Funicular FGC station from the fairy-tale Modernista station, with its gingerbread windows and roof.

Sarrià

West of Gràcia, things get more exclusive. Sarrià (FGC Sarrià) the last independent township to be annexed to Barcelona, is slightly schizophrenic: the new part is full of smart homes with gardens and doormen (owned by families who have more than double the city average of books per home), and a liberal sprinkling of pretty green parks slotted between chic apartment buildings. Old Sarrià, on the other hand, hasn't changed much at all. The main street, C/ Major de Sarrià, connects a number of small squares with a lazy, village atmosphere. A church has stood on Plaça Sarrià for more than a millennium, although the present **Sant Vicenç** dates only from the early part of the 20th century, after its predecessor went up in flames along with the parish records. Just off the square is a lively, red-brick Modernista **market** (1911) with pretty green shutters and heaped stalls of produce. Farther up, **Plaça Sant Vicenç** is surrounded by a higgledy-piggledy collection of narrow, arcaded houses, all painted in different colours, with a statue of the saint in the centre. The local Fira de Sant Ponç (Pontius), who was patron of beekeepers and herbalists, is held here on 14 May.

C/ Major meanders steeply up to the **Passatge Sta Eulàlia**, where the city's co-patroness supposedly lived with her merchant father. A Capuchin convent stood here centuries ago, hidden by woods and farmland, but fell into ruins and was utterly destroyed along with the forests by a rapacious Englishman in the early 19th century. The knobby, dry hill has since become known as the Sarrià Desert. The imposing residence at its summit was once a simple farmhouse, but the 19th-century owners got carried away and started adding extravagantly florid bits of 16th- and 17th-century palaces, in a sort of grown-up precursor to the Lego set.

Chi chi Sarrià has some of the city's finest private schools; one of them, the **Col.legi de les Teresianes**, 41 C/ de Ganduxer (FGC Les Tres Torres; *open Sept–June Sat only 11–1 by appointment,* © *93 212 33 54*), was built by Gaudí in 1890. Although constrained by finances and the need to build quickly and functionally, he endowed the building with elaborate wrought-iron details and defined the corners with his favourite cross-crowned steeples. The interior is famous for its magical upper corridor of white, rhythmic parabolic arches.

Pedralbes

To the southwest of Sarrià is another fashionable residential area, Pedralbes, the 'white stones'. At the top of the Avinguda de Pedralbes, a cobbled lane leads up to the handsome Gothic **Monestir de Pedralbes**, where the **Col.lecció Thyssen-**

Bornemisza occupies the renovated dormitory (take bus no.22 from Plaça de Catalunya or walk from Sarrià's FGC Reina Elisenda; *open Tues–Sun 10–2, closed Mon; adm*). Although Madrid received the bulk of the baron's collection, his Catalan beauty-queen wife made sure that 72 of his paintings settled in Barcelona. These were chosen to match the setting and are mostly religious works by early Italian masters such as Lorenzo Daddi, Lorenzo Monaco and Fra Angelico, whose sublime, ephemeral *Madonna of Humility* steals the show. There are smaller works by Lotto, Titian, Tintoretto and Veronese, and a fairy-tale *Stoning of St Stephen* by Dosso Dossi. There are also later pictures by Giambattista and Giandomenico Tiepolo, Guardi and Canaletto. The collection also includes an excellent portrait by Velázquez of *Mariana de Austria* with her Habsburg face, a foxy *Santa Marina* by Zurbarán, and paintings by Rubens and Lucas Cranach (a *St George*, for Catalunya).

For a few pesetas more, your ticket can include a tour of the **convent** itself, founded for noble ladies by Elisenda, the fourth wife of Jaume II, in 1326, and still sheltering a community of 24 Poor Clares. It is a rare time capsule of 14th-century Catalan Gothic, built quickly and scarcely altered since, and still maintaining its air of a walled hamlet. The three-storey cloister with its delicate columns, garden and fountains is serene and lovely, surrounded by the Poor Clares' tiny prayer cells and the small, irregular **Capella de Sant Miquel**. This houses the finest Gothic fresco cycle in Catalunya, Ferrer Bassa's *Seven Joys of the Virgin* and the *Passion*, painted in 1346, two years before the Black Death killed the painter and a third of the population of Barcelona. Akin to the work of Simone Martini and the Lorenzettis of Siena (the *Virgin Enthroned*, encircled by angels, is archetypally Sienese), Bassa's feeling for colour, expression and technique is way in advance of other Catalan painters of the day. Elsewhere you can visit the kitchen, refectory, stables and storeroom, where an intricate series of 3D dioramas on the life of Christ by Joan Marí has been installed. The single-naved church contains stained glass by Mestre Gil and the lovely alabaster tomb of Queen Elisenda, sculpted in 1364, shortly before her death—she wasn't taking any chances.

There are some handsome Modernista houses in the environs: above the convent, take C/ Montefideo to the left to C/ de Panamà, where at No.13 the **Villa Hèlius** (1908) is decorated with *sgraffito*, fancy ironwork and colourful ceramics. Nearby at No.21 is a typical Catalan *masía*, or farmhouse, from the 17th century that was gobbled up by the city. Below the convent, the house at **8 Plaça de Pedralbes** (1915) is by Salvador Valeri and has a curvaceous party-style façade covered with colourful reliefs and mosaics.

The border of lower Pedralbes is the Avinguda Diagonal, extended here in the 1920s to reach the **Palau de Pedralbes** at No.686 (Ⓜ Palau Reial), a present to Alfonso XIII from Eusebi Güell's heirs to thank him for making their father a count.

It became headquarters of the Republican government at the end of the Civil War; from here President Azaña joined the rest of Barcelona on 29 October 1938, tearfully cheering as the last 12,673 members of the International Brigades marched down the Diagonal towards France and away from a hopeless cause. Dolores Ibárruri, La Pasionaria, was on hand to give a moving speech. 'You are history. You are legend. You are the heroic example of the solidarity and the universality of democracy...'

Franco made the palace his official residence in Barcelona, and more recently King Juan Carlos' daughter, Christina, held her wedding banquet here in 1997. These days, however, the main business of the palace is to shelter the beautiful if fragile **Museu de Cerámica** (*open Tues–Sun 10–3, closed Mon; adm, joint ticket with Museu des les Arts Decoratives*), with a collection garnered from the famous ceramic centres of the Crown of Aragón—Paterna, Teruel, Manises, Barcelona—as well as from 13th-century Arab-Catalan Mallorca. Among the most charming exhibits are the cartoonish series of tiny tiles depicting Catalan occupations and characters: among the blacksmiths, milkmaids and shopkeepers is a naughty little boy having his bottom smacked, an old lady smoking a pipe with a wicked grin and a tambourine, and, of course, the *cagoner*, squatting with a little pyramid of shit under his bare buttocks. The upper floor is devoted to modern and contemporary ceramics, a mixed bag, but with some lovely organic pieces and a handful of ceramics by Picasso and Miró.

In the opposite wing of the palace is the **Museu de les Arts Decoratives** (*same hours*), set in a series of galleries overlooking an enormous throne room. The collection contains tapestries, furniture and handicrafts from the Middle Ages to the present, and culminates with an eccentric exhibition tracing the evolution of Spanish industrial design. Here you'll find everything from a mop and bucket to a urinal and a 6ft blow-up pen, with some remarkable pieces of 20th-century furniture in between. Leafy trees shade the surrounding **park,** laid out in 1925 by Nicolas Rubió i Tuduri, deflecting the summer sun and the sound of the traffic, making a delicious retreat dotted with lily ponds and secret bowers. Tucked away in a tiny bamboo forest is a fountain by Gaudí, only discovered in 1983 under the ivy, in the shape of a dragon spewing water from curling jaws. At the entrance stand forlorn statues deemed lewd by prim 19th-century Barcelonans and moved here from Plaça de Catalunya to spare society's blushes.

Behind the park, at 15 Avinguda de Pedralbes, is a fence and gate guarded by one of Gaudí's first and most formidable ironworks, the **Pedralbes Dragon** (1884). For once this isn't St George's victim, but that of another Catalan hero—Hercules —as described by Verdaguer in his epic *L'Atlàntida*. The orange tree on the right-hand post symbolizes the golden apples of the Hesperides. Spanning 18ft, the dragon writhes across the gate, whips its scaly tail, and roars, baring long, pointy teeth. It also incidentally guarded Eusebi Güell's own orange grove and country house, to which Gaudí contributed his very first buildings for his patron, the exotic, Hindu-inspired, corbel-roofed gatehouse and stable now known as the **Pabeliones Finca Güell**, which were also the first to be decorated with his signature *trencadis* and Greek cross. Since 1978 they have been the seat of the Catedra Gaudí, a section of Barcelona's architecture school dedicated to the study of Gaudí's works (*open Mon–Fri 9–2*). These days the Pabeliones slightly jar with the surrounding clumps of bright, new buildings of the Universitat Politècnica de Catalunya, which has managed to gather as many FAD-winning architects as the Vila Olímpica. Dedicated Gaudíphiles should continue from here down C/ de Manuel Girona, where at No.55 is Gaudí's **gate to the Finca Miralles** (1901). The farm is long gone, but the swirling entrance remains all by itself in the midst of modern apartment blocks, like something that landed from another planet.

Farther up the Avinguda Diagonal, the **Parc de Cervantes** (Ⓜ Zona Universitaria) was one of the few green spaces opened up under Franco, in 1965, and has since become famous for its lovely rose gardens, with over 200 varieties, grassy lawns, shady picnic groves, and an intriguing sculpture called ***Dos Rombs*** (1977) by Andreu Alfaro, made out of aluminium bars that form a rhomboid from whatever angle you look at it.

Barça and Camp Nou

Barça of course means FC Barcelona, the city's very beloved and very wealthy football club, magnificently headquartered in Europe's largest stadium at **Camp Nou** (Ⓜ Collblanc), south of the Diagonal and the Zona Universitaria. You've probably seen their blue and burgundy jerseys, caps and banners for sale in every kiosk and souvenir stand and, if you're a supporter, getting a ticket for one of the 120,000 seats for a match was probably one of your first concerns. If you don't succeed, you can always take some consolation in the excellent **Museu del Futbol Club Barcelona**, at entrance gate 9 (*open Tues–Sat 10–6.30, Sun 10–2, closed Mon*).

The museum is the most popular in Barcelona (along with the Museu Picasso) and yet, despite the crowds, maintains a hushed and reverent silence, akin to that in any great cathedral. The collection begins with photographs, newspaper articles and cartoons of the first heroes of the field, and some of the mementoes donated by the club's early president Hans Gamper (1871–1931), including a silver cigarette case given to him by Everton FC in 1924. There are models of the early stadiums, with tiny figures squatting on the perimeter walls; passers-by nicknamed the early fans '*culés*' after the singular sight of rows of bottoms hanging over the fence. Barça has more members than any other club in the world; even the pope, visiting in 1982, signed the Book of Honour and accepted membership. This was the year that the stadium hosted the opening of the World Cup and the club commissioned

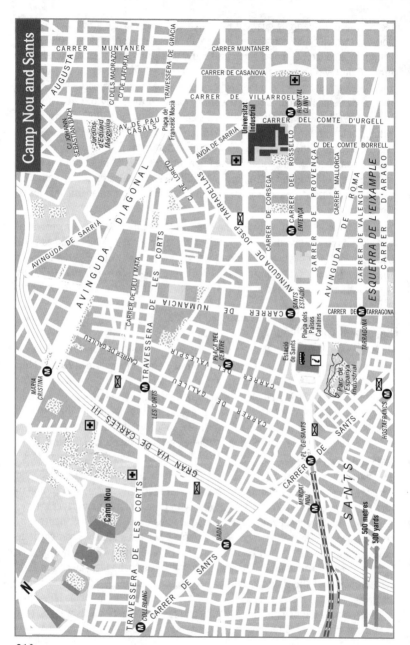

Camp Nou and Sants

CARRER MUNTANER
CARRER MUNTANER
CARRER DE CASANOVA
CARRER DE VILLARROEL
HOSPITAL CLINIC
Universitat Industrial
CARRER DEL COMTE D'URGELL
C/ DEL COMTE BORRELL
CARRER DE CORSEGA
CARRER DEL ROSSELLO
CARRER DE PROVENÇA
CARRER MALLORCA
CARRER DE ROMA
AVINGUDA DE VALENCIA
CARRER D'ARAGO
ESQUERRA DE L'EIXAMPLE
CARRER DE TARRAGONA
AUGUSTA
C/ DELS MADRAZO
C/ DE LAFORJA
TRAVESSERA DE GRACIA
Plaça de Francesc Macià
AV DE PAU CASALS
AVDA DE SARRIA
C/ JOHANN SEBASTIAN BACH
Jardins d'Eduard Marquina
C/ DE LONDRES
C/ TARRADELLAS
AVINGUDA DE SARRIÀ
DIAGONAL
AVINGUDA DE
AVINGUDA DE JOSEP TARRADELLAS
CARRER DE DEU I MATA
CARRER DE LES CORTS
TRAVESSERA DE LES CORTS
CARRER DE NUMANCIA
EMENÇA
SANTS ESTACIÓ
Plaça dels Països Catalans
TARRAGONA
MARIA CRISTINA
CARRER DE GALILEU
PLAÇA DEL CENTRE
CARRER DEL VALLESPIR
CARRER DE GALILEU
LES CORTS
CARRER DE
Estació de Sants
Parc de l'Espanya Industrial
HOSTAFRANCS
GRAN VIA DE CARLES III
Camp Nou
TRAVESSERA DE LES CORTS
BADAL
MERCAT NOU
CARRER EL DE SANTS
SANTS
COLL BLANC
CARRER DE SANTS
CARRER DE SANTS

500 metres
500 yards

Miró to design the posters. Queues form in awed silence for an obligatory photograph with the prize exhibit, the European Cup, won in the golden year of 1992, with the boots that kicked the winning goal carefully displayed alongside, and there is video footage of the game in an alcove which periodically erupts with cheers. The present stadium, which you can view from the royal gallery, was built in 1957, the money raised by loyal fans paying their fees up to five years in advance—a first act of architectural self-affirmation of Catalan will after the Civil War. In front is a traditional farmhouse from 1702, a potent symbol of national roots and now the club's office.

Down Avinguda Diagonal

If you're in Barcelona on business, more likely than not you'll find yourself in this upper section of the Diagonal. Big buildings began sprouting up here in the 1960s 'miracle' years, when Franco gave up on autarchy and Spain had the fastest growth-rate in Europe as it made up for all the years of treading water. Among the best buildings are the four **Torres d'Oficines Trade** (1966–9), at the intersection with Gran Vía de Carles III, by José Antonio Coderch and Manuel Valls, with their sensuously curving tinted walls of glass. Down from here is the 980ft 'horizontal skyscraper' of **L'Illa**, an enormity by Madrid architect Rafael Moneo, begun in 1986 and encompassing a posh shopping mall, hotel and conference halls.

Circular **Plaça de Francesc Macià** is the centre of this business district, such as it is; from here Avinguda Pau Casals leads up to the charming **Jardins d'Eduard Marguina** (or Turó Park), designed in 1934 by Rubió i Tuduri, and featuring an oval pond of water lilies and statues, including *Le Ben Plantada*, the classically beautiful and wise goddess woman rooted in the soil who was the guiding symbol of the Noucentistas. One street behind the park, C/ Johann Sebastian Bach has two apartment buildings important in the annals of Barcelona's modern architecture: No.7, built in 1961 by Coderch and Valls, with a skin of wooden slats, and No.28, one of the first (and pre-megalomaniac) works by Ricardo Bofill. The real gem in the area, a few blocks to the east, is the Expressionist-Art Deco **Clínica Barraquer** (1936), at 314 C/ Muntaner (FGC Muntaner), designed by Joaquim Lloret Homs and its owner, Joaquim Barraquer, a famous ophthalmologist. Although spoiled in the remodelling of the 1960s, when the vertical pillars on the façade were added along with two additional floors, the interior has kept much of its original charm and dynamism. Dr Barraquer was celebrated for restoring people's vision, and it's nice to think that his handsome building was the first thing his patients saw.

Sants

Sants, on the far left of the Eixample, grew up along the C/ de la Creu Coberta, the old Roman road to the rest of Spain. Like Poblenou, it was the setting for

Barcelona's giant textile mills in the 19th century, including Güell's **Vapor Vell** with its tremendous tall brick chimney, at 51 C/ de Galileu, now being converted into a public library. Sants has Barcelona's main train station (**Ⓜ** Estació Sants), where you can also see the bleak dead end of Barcelona's postmodern design, the FAD-award-winning **Plaça dels Països Catalans** (1981–2). It was originally a traffic intersection, and the architects, Helio Piñón and Albert Viaplana, were given a difficult brief: they could not build or plant anything because of train tracks directly below. Their response was to create a minimalist playground dotted with metal pole 'trees' and canopies that compose a poem that designers adore and the average Josep avoids like the plague; unfortunately it has become the template for a dozen equally new squares around Barcelona, but they don't even have train tracks for an excuse.

On the southern side of the station, the **Parc de l'Espanya Industrial** (named after the huge mill that once stood here), designed in 1986 by Luis Peña Ganchegui, is far more convivial, with a boating lake and *St George and the Dragon* (1985), by Andres Nagel, the largest of all dragon and Jordi sculptures in Barcelona, and the most popular, at least with the small fry, who use it as a slide. The park's landmark is a column of extra-galactic pin-heads in dainty metal tutus, disguised as light fixtures.

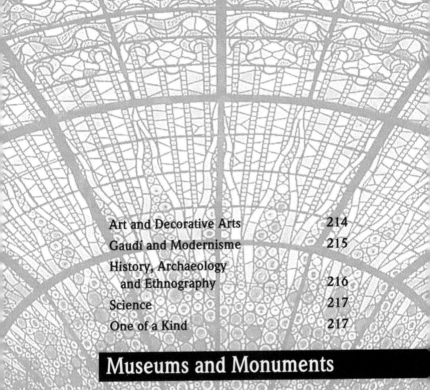

Museums and Monuments

Although Madrid, like most capitals, has sucked up all the masterpieces, Barcelona still has a stunning and often unique collection of museums and monuments, enough in fact to leave you noticeably poorer when you leave. There is, however, relief: holders of transport cards (Barcelona Card or Bus Turístic cards) often get a discount, while two schemes offer bigger reductions:

Articket: This costs the bizarre sum of 2,496 pts (or 15 euros) and offers half-price or free admission to six of Barcelona's most popular art centres: Palau Nacional, Museu d'Art Contemporani de Barcelona, Fundació Joan Miró, Centre de Culture Contemporani, Fundació Antoni Tàpies and the Centre Cultural Caixa Catalunya, in La Pedrera. It can be bought at any of the above institutions or at a tourist information office.

Ruta del Modernisme: A route marked with red roses in the pavement passes Barcelona's foremost Modernista buildings, and you can get a 50% discount on a book of tickets to the main sights (the Palau Güell, Palau de la Música, La Pedrera, Fundació Antoni Tàpies, Museu d'Art Modern, Museu de la Música, Sagrada Família and Museu de Zoologia), available through the Caixa Catalunya's Tel-Entrada service or at the Centre de la Modernisme, in the lobby of the Casa Amatller, 41 Passeig de Gràcia, © 93 488 01 39. The price (2,500 pts) includes a comprehensive booklet on the sights and countless others hidden along the trail.

Art and Decorative Arts

Centre de Cultura Contemporani (CCCB), 5 C/ Montalegre, © 93 306 41 00, *www.cccb.es* (🄼 Catalunya; *open Tues, Thurs and Fri 11–2 and 4–8, Wed and Sat 11–8, Sun 10–3; adm*). Changing exhibits of 20th-century art, architecture and urban design; *see* p.130.

Col.leció Thyssen-Bornemisza, 9 Baixada del Monestir, © 93 280 14 34 (FGC Reina Elisenda; *open Tues–Sun 10–2, closed Mon; adm*). Religious art from the 13th to 18th centuries, in the 14th-century monastery of Pedralbes; *see* p.204.

Fundació Antoni Tàpies, 255 C/ d'Aragó (🄼 Passeig de Gràcia; *open Tues–Sun 11–8, closed Mon exc on holidays; adm*). Works by Tàpies and major exhibitions of contemporary art; *see* p.162.

Fundació Francesco Godia, 284 C/ de Valencia, © 93 272 31 80, *www.fund acionfgodia.org* (🄼 Passeig de Gràcia; *open Wed–Mon 10–8, closed Tues; adm*). Medieval and modern art; *see* p.163.

Fundació Joan Miró, Plaça Neptú, Montjuïc, © 93 329 19 08, *www.bcn .fjmiro.es* (⓪ Paral.lel, then *funicular de Monjuïc; open Tues–Wed and Fri–Sat 10–7 [July–Sept 10–8], Thurs 10–9.30, Sun and hols 10–2.30; closed Mon except hols; adm*). Works by Miró and friends in a lovely setting; *see* p.188.

Museu d'Art Contemporani de Barcelona (MACBA), Plaça dels Àngels, © 93 412 08 10, *www.macba.es* (⓪ Catalunya; *open Tues–Fri 12–8, Sat 10–8, Sun 10–3, closed Mon; adm*). Richard Meier's handsome white museum picks up in the 1940s where the Museu d'Art Modern leaves off; *see* p.130.

Museu d'Art Modern, Parc de la Ciutadella, © 93 319 57 28 (⓪ Ciutadella; *open Tues–Sun 9–7, closed Mon; adm*). Catalan painting and sculpture from 1840 to 1930; *see* p.123.

Museu de les Arts Decoratives, 686 Avinguda Diagonal, © 93 280 50 24 (⓪ Palau Reial; *open Tues–Sun 10–3, closed Mon; adm*). Decorative arts from the Middle Ages to 20th-century Catalan design; *see* p.208.

Museu de Cerámica, 686 Avinguda Diagonal, © 93 280 16 21 (⓪ Palau Reial; *open Tues–Sun 10–3, closed Mon; adm*). Beautiful ceramics from medieval Spain to the present; *see* p.208.

Museu Diocesà, Pla de la Seu, © 93 315 22 13 (⓪ Jaume I; *open Tues–Sat 10–1.30 and 5–8, Sun 11–2, closed Mon; adm*). Catalan medieval art; *see* p.94.

Museu Frederic Marés, Plaça Sant Iu, © 93 310 58 00 (⓪ Jaume I; *open Tues–Sat 10–5, Sun and hols 10–2, closed Mon; adm*). Religious art, fans, forks, spectacles, hatpins and playing cards; *see* p.89.

Museu Picasso, 15 C/ Montcada, © 93 319 63 10 (⓪ Jaume I; *open Tues–Sat 10–8, Sun and hols 10–3, closed Mon; adm*). Most popular museum in Barcelona, with a wide range of very early works and some others; *see* p.113.

Museu Tèxtil i de la Indumentària, 12 C/ Montcada, © 93 319 76 03, (⓪ Jaume I; *open Tues–Sat 10–8, Sun 10–3, closed Mon; adm*). Textiles, clothes and fashion in a Gothic palace; *see* p.115.

Palau Nacional (Museu Nacional d'Art de Catalunya), Montjuïc, © 93 423 71 99, *www.gencat.es/mnac* (⓪ Espanya; *open Tues–Wed and Fri–Sat 10–7, Thurs 10–9, Sun and hols 10–2.30, closed Mon; adm*). Superb, unique collection of Romanesque and Gothic art; *see* p.182.

Gaudí and Modernisme

Casa-Museu Gaudí, Park Güell, © 93 219 38 11 (⓪ Lesseps; *open Mar–Sept daily 10–7, Nov–Feb daily 10–6; adm*). Long-time residence of the architect, with memorabilia and some of the furniture he designed; *see* p.201.

Espai Gaudí and El Pis de la Pedrera, 261 C/ Provença, ✆ 93 484 59 95, *www.caixacat.es/fundcat.html* (Ⓜ Diagonal; *open daily 10–8; adm*). Overview of Gaudí's work and a flat furnished as it was *c.* 1910; *see* p.165.

Museu del Sagrada Família, 401 C/ de Mallorca, ✆ 93 207 30 31 (Ⓜ Sagrada Família; *open April–Aug daily 9–8, March and Sept–Oct daily 9–7, Nov–Feb daily 9–6; adm*).

Palau Güell, 3–5 C/ Nou de la Rambla, ✆ 93 317 39 74 (Ⓜ Liceu; *open Mon–Sat 10.15–1 and 4.15–7; guided tours only, in groups of no more than 30, so arrive early; tours take place every 15 minutes; adm*). The plush and spooky house that Gaudí built for his princely patron; *see* p.136.

Palau de la Música Catalana, 2 C/ Sant Francesc de Paula, ✆ 93 295 72 00 (Ⓜ Urquinaona; *guided tours daily 10–3.30*). Domènech i Montaner's fantasy concert hall; *see* p.110.

History, Archaeology and Ethnography

Museu Arqueològic, 39–41 Passeig de Santa Madrona, Montjuïc, ✆ 93 424 65 77 (Ⓜ Poble Sec; *open Tues–Sat 9.30–7, Sun 10–2.30, closed Mon; adm free Sun*). Palaeolithic to Visigothic artefacts from Barcelona and Catalunya; *see* p.187.

Museu Barbier-Mueller d'Art Precolumbi, 14 C/ Montcada, ✆ 93 310 45 16 (Ⓜ Jaume I; *open Tues–Sat 10–8, Sun 10–3, closed Mon; adm*). Precolumbian art; *see* p.115.

Museu Egipci, 284 C/ de Valencia, ✆ 93 488 01 88 (Ⓜ Passeig de Gràcia; *open Mon–Sat 10–8, Sun 10–2; adm*). Ancient Egyptian ceramics, jewellery and animal mummies; *see* p.164.

Museu Etnològic, Passeig de Santa Madrona, ✆ 93 424 68 07 (Ⓜ Poble Sec; *open Wed and Fri–Sun 10–2, Tues and Thurs 10–7, closed Mon; adm*). Ethnological collection from around the world; *see* p.186.

Museu d'Història de Catalunya, 3 Plaça Pau Vila, ✆ 93 255 47 00 (Ⓜ Barceloneta; *open Tues and Thurs–Sat 10–7, Wed 10–8, Sun and hols 10–2.30, closed Mon; adm*). Inclusive history of Catalunya, including the kitchen sink; *see* p.146.

Museu d'Història de la Ciutat, Plaça del Rei, ✆ 93 315 11 11 (Ⓜ Jaume I; *open Oct–June Tues–Sat 10–2 and 4–8, Sun and hols 10–2; July–Sept Tues–Sat 10–8, Sun and hols 10–2; closed Mon; adm*). History of Barcelona and Roman excavations; *see* p.87.

Museu Marítim, Avinguda Drassanes, ✆ 93 342 99 20 (Ⓜ Drassanes; *open daily 10–7; adm*). Barcelona's great seafaring past, in its medieval shipyards; *see* p.142.

Museu Militar, Castell de Montjuïc, ✆ 93 329 86 13 (Ⓜ Paral.lel, then funicular and *telefèric de Montjuïc; open Tues–Sun 9.30–8, closed Mon; adm*). Military collections from around the world; *see* p.191.

Science

Museu de la Ciència, 55 C/ Teodor Rovirala, ✆ 93 212 60 50 (FGC Tibidabo; *open Tues–Sun 10–8, closed Mon; adm*). Popular hands-on science; *see* p.203.

Museu de Geologia, Parc de la Ciutadella, ✆ 93 319 68 95 (Ⓜ Arc de Triomf; *open Tues–Sun 10–2, closed Mon; adm*). Minerals, fossils and rocks from across Spain; *see* p.125.

Museu de Zoologia, Parc de la Ciutadella, ✆ 93 319 69 12 (Ⓜ Arc de Triomf; *open Tues–Wed and Fri–Sun 10–2, Thurs 10–6.30, closed Mon; adm*). Classic zoology exhibits; *see* p.125.

One of a Kind

Galeria Olímpica, Estadi Olímpic, Montjuïc, ✆ 93 426 06 60 (Ⓜ Paral.lel then *funicular de Montjuïc; open Apr–Sept Tues–Sat 10–2 and 4–8, Sun 10–2; Oct– Mar 10–1 and 4–6, Sun 10–2; closed Mon; adm*). Exhibits on the 1992 Olympics; *see* p.188.

Gran Teatre del Liceu, 51 Ramblas, ✆ 93 485 99 00, *www.liceubarcelona.com* (Ⓜ Liceu; *open for visits 9.45am–11am, last admission 10.15; adm*). Tours of Barcelona's spectacularly re-created opera house; *see* p.78.

Museu d'Autòmats del Tibidabo, Parc d'Atraccions del Tibidabo, ✆ 93 211 79 42 (FGC Tibidabo, then Tramvia Blau and *funicular de Tibidabo; open Tues–Fri 11–7, Sat–Sun 11–9; adm with park*). Fascinating collection of coin-operated fortune-tellers and other fairground automata; *see* p.204.

Museu del Calcat, 5 Plaça Sant Felip Neri, ✆ 93 301 45 33 (Ⓜ Jaume I; *open Tues–Sun 11–2, closed Mon; adm*). Old shoes, big shoes, little shoes; *see* p.95.

Museu de Carosses Fúnebres (Hearse Museum), 2 C/ Sancho de Ávila, ✆ 93 484 17 20 (Ⓜ Marina; *officially open daily 10–1 and 4–6, but ring for an appointment; adm free*). Located in the town council's funeral services building; when you exit the metro station, follow the signs for Servies Funeraris, an inconspicuous modern three-storey building, and ask at the desk. Down in the creepy gloom of the basement, rows of elaborate funeral coaches attended by costumed dummies and plumed horses line up in a macabre parade. The white Cinderella carriages carried children and young, unmarried women, and all have varying degrees of ornamentation, depending on the status of their passengers. Some have grand names: 'Imperial', 'Gòtica' and 'Grand Doumond' (which sounds more like a second-rate magician at a seaside resort). Photographs lining the walls attest to the glamour and pomp that attended these processions. Most extraordinary is the fact that these coaches were in use until the 1950s, when they were finally superseded by motorized transport.

Museu de Cera, 7 Passatge de la Banca, off the Rambla de Santa Monica, ✆ 93 317 26 49 (Ⓜ Drassanes; *open winter daily 10–1.30 and 4–7.30, summer daily 10–8; adm exp*). Waxworks of the famous, historical, wicked and farcical; *see* p.76.

Museu del Clavegueram (Sewer Museum), 98 Paseo de Sant Joan, ✆ 93 209 15 26 (Ⓜ Verdaguer; *officially open Tues–Sat 10–1 and 4–6, Sat–Sun 10–2, closed Mon, but call for an appointment*). Barcelona is so proud of its sewers that it says come on down! Long ramps descend past a series of exhibits outlining the history of sewers from Mesopotamian times onwards, and reveals how recent challenges—planning a new system for the Eixample or dealing with the extra detritus of the Olympic games—were resolved. The highlight is a tour around the sewers themselves to the musical accompaniment of flushing water and squeaking rats.

Museu del Còmic i la Il.lustració, 25 C/ Santa Carolina, ✆ 93 348 15 13 (Ⓜ Hospital de Sant Pau; *open Mon–Sat 10–2 and 5–8, closed Sun*). The history of Spanish and Catalan comic books.

Museu Eròtica, 96 bis Ramblas, ✆ 93 318 98 65 (Ⓜ Liceu; *open daily 10am–midnight, adm*). International erotica in all its tawdry glory; *see* p.79.

Museu del Futbol Club Barcelona, Camp Nou, Entrance Gate 9, Avinguda Arístides Maillol (Ⓜ Collblanc; *open Tues–Sat 10–6.30, Sun 10–2, closed Mon*). Barça's showcase of past glories and knicknacks; *see* p.209.

Museu de la Música, 373 Avinguda Diagonal, ✆ 93 416 11 57 (Ⓜ Diagonal; *open winter Tues and Thurs–Sun 10–2, Wed 10–8; summer Tues–Sun 10–2; closed Mon; adm*). Musical instruments in a Modernista house by Puig i Cadafalch; *see* p.167.

Museu del Perfum, 39 Passeig de Gràcia, ✆ 93 215 72 38 (Ⓜ Passeig de Gràcia; *open Tues–Fri 10.30–1.30 and 4.30–7.30, Sat 11–1.30, closed Sun and Mon; adm free*). Perfume bottles; *see* p.161.

Museu Taurí, 749 Gran Vía de les Corts Catalanes, ✆ 93 245 58 02 (Ⓜ Monumental; *open April–Sept daily 10.30–2 and 4–7; adm*). Taurine memento mori; *see* p.174.

Museu Verdaguer, Carretera de les Planes, Vallvidrera, ✆ 93 315 11 11/204 7805 (FGC Baixador de Vallvidrera; *open Tues–Sun 10–2, closed Mon; adm free*). Home of 19th-century Catalunya's greatest poet; *see* p.205.

Pavelló Barcelona, Montjuïc (Ⓜ Espanya; *open Nov–Mar daily 10–6.30; April–Oct daily 10–8; adm*). Re-creation of Mies van der Rohe's masterpiece; *see* p.182.

Poble Espanyol, Montjuïc, ✆ 93 423 69 54 (Ⓜ Espanya; *open Tues–Thurs 9am–2am, Fri–Sat 9am–4am, Mon 9am–8pm, Sun 9am–midnight; adm*). Spain's answer to Disneyland's Main Street, only Spain did it first; *see* p.186.

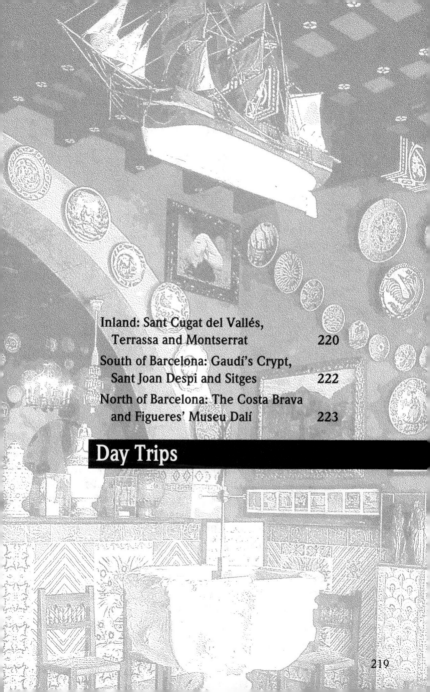

Day Trips

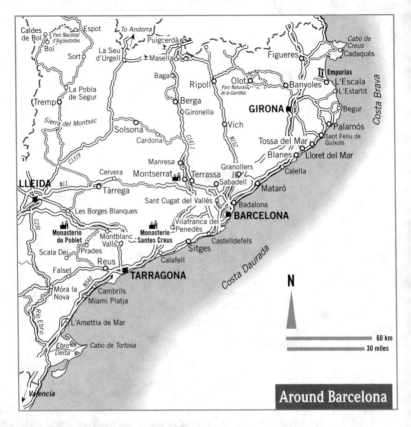

The following selection is only a sampler of possible excursions from Barcelona: for more ideas, contact the Ajuntament's tourist office (*see* p.24), which has a wealth of information on Catalunya, its mountains, beaches, wine cellars, Romanesque and Modernista architecture and the fascinating cities of Girona and Tarragona.

Inland: Sant Cugat del Vallés, Terrassa and Montserrat

Sant Cugat (30 mins) and Terrassa (1 hour) are reached on FGC trains from Plaça de Catalunya. There's a daily Juliá bus to Montserrat (departure 9am, return 7pm, © 93 490 40 00), leaving from 5 Ronda de la Universitat, or there are FGC trains from Plaça d'Espanya, with departures starting at 9am; get off at Aeri de Montserrat station to catch the teleféric to the monastery.

Northwest of Barcelona, **Sant Cugat del Vallés** grew up around the Visigothic **Monasterio de Sant Cugat** (*open Tues–Sun 9–1 and 3–6, closed Mon; adm*).

According to legend founded by Charlemagne, the Gothic church that now stands is as austere as Barcelona's Sant Pi. The late 12th-century cloister is a Romanesque masterpiece, with 144 carved capitals by the monk Arnau Cadell. Another Catalan masterpiece, the *Retable of all the Saints* by Pere Serra (1395), is in the small museum in the chapter house, portraying the Virgin and Child with an angelic sextet, surrounded by most of the saints on the calendar.

Industrial **Terrassa** is Catalunya's third-largest city. Cloth was the mainstay of the Catalans' medieval empire, and early examples from Terrassa and the rest of the world are displayed in the **Museu Textil**, 25 C/ Salmerón (*open Tues–Wed and Fri 9–6, Thurs 9–9, Sat–Sun 10–2, closed Mon; adm*), one of the most important collections of its kind. A 6th-century bishopric, Terrassa has a rare ensemble of three Visigothic-Romanesque churches painted with early murals in its **Parque de Vallparadís**; the main church, **Santa Maria**, has excellent Gothic retables by Huguet and 9th–12th-century frescoes. A smattering of Modernista factories add grace notes to the newer parts of the city: one on the Rambla d'Egara, by Lluís Muncunill, is now the **Museu de la Ciència i de la Tècnica de Catalunya** (*open Sept–June Tues–Fri 10–7, Sat–Sun 10–2.30; July–Aug Tues–Sun 10–2.30; closed Mon; adm*), dedicated to Catalunya's industrial revolution; note the beautiful Catalan brick-vaulted ceiling. Another building by Muncunill, the **Masia Freixa** (1907), with an undulating roof and Gaudiesque parabolic arches, is in the Parc Municipal de St Jordi.

Montserrat, the spiritual heart of Catalunya, looms 40km northwest of Barcelona up the River Llobregat. It's an isolated, fantastical 10km massif made of jagged pudding-stone pinnacles rising precipitously over deep gorges, domes and shallow terraces—it looks as if it were dropped from heaven just to prove all things are possible. St Peter, they say, came here to hide an image of the Virgin carved by St Luke in a cave; in another grotto, the good knight Parsifal discovered the Holy Grail—a legend used by Wagner for his opera. In 880, the statue of the Virgin was rediscovered on Montserrat, and Count Wilfred the Hairy of Barcelona built a chapel to house it. In the Middle Ages only Compostela attracted more pilgrims in Spain.

The monastery and the church can hardly compete with the fabulous surroundings, but the enthroned Virgin of Montserrat presides over the altar; the famous boys' choir, or **Escolanía**, founded in the 13th century—the oldest music school in Europe—still performs daily at 1 and 6.45pm, except in July. The **Museu de Montserrat** has two sections of gifts given to the monastery, including Old Masters and 19th-century Catalan paintings. Best of all is the mountain itself: an easy walk, **Los Degotalls**, takes in a wonderful view of the Pyrenees. A funicular ascends to **Santa Cova**, where a chapel marks the finding place of the *Moreneta;* another will lift you up to the **Hermitage of Sant Joan**, from where an hour's spectacular walk leads to the **Hermitage of Sant Jeroni**.

South of Barcelona: Gaudí's Crypt, Sant Joan Despi and Sitges

For the Colonia Güell, take the FGC train from Plaça d'Espanya to Molí Nou, followed by a 10-minute walk. For Sant Joan Despi, take the FGC from Plaça d'Espanya and get off at Cornellà, then take bus no.52; or take the train direct from Estació de Sants. Trains from Estació de Sants depart every half-hour for Sitges (50 mins).

Labour disputes in Barcelona led Eusebi Güell to close his Vapor Vell mills in Sants in 1891 and replace them with a little adventure in rural paternalism at **Santa Coloma de Cervelló**. The **Colonia Güell** was planned as a pseudo workers' cooperative, around a textile mill, with houses, store, school and other Modernista brick buildings for the workers designed by Gaudí's assistants Francesc Berenguer and Joan Rubió Bellver. In 1898 Güell asked Gaudí to design a church. Typically, he planned something grand—his sketches look like a cross between Coney Island and the Emerald City—but only the magical primordial grotto of a **crypt** was completed (© 93 640 29 36; *open Mon–Wed and Fri–Sat 10–1 and 4–6, Sun and Thurs 10–1.15; adm*). One of the most striking spaces of the 20th century, it has no right angles and no straight lines—the huge columns incline at weird expressionist angles. If you've been to the Sagrada Família, you've seen Gaudí's complex web of chains and weights that he photographed and reversed to help work out the problems of stress and loads in hyperbolic paraboloids, something architects like Frank Gehry now do with the aid of sophisticated computers. Gaudí had only the lightning of his brainstorms, plus something else modern architects don't have: Catalan bricklayers. There is no steel reinforcing anything, anywhere: the whole crypt is made of rough-hewn stone and brick, brightened with stained glass and *trencadí* collages.

Gaudí's greatest collaborator, Josep Maria Jujol, left two gems in nearby **Sant Joan Despi**. His masterpiece, the **Casa Negre** (1915–30; now the town hall), was a traditional house that Jujol transformed into a Modernista butterfly, its undulating façade covered with sinuous *sgraffito* and plaques; the interior is just as remarkable, with a beautiful blue stair rising to the attic under an octagonal vault. His remarkable two-family villa, **Torre de la Creu** (1913–16), at Passeig de Canalies, is nicknamed the 'Tower of Eggs': it's made of five cylinders topped with egg-shaped domes, decorated with mosaics by his daughter Tecla Jujol.

Wedged between the mountains and a long crescent of sand, **Sitges** is by far the most attractive resort of the Costa Daurada. In summer half of Europe's yuppies and gay community washes up here. A perfect sun-bleached Baroque church stands on a promontory over the sea, and tucked around behind it, in the oldest part of town, Santiago Rusinyol bought two fisherman's houses and merged them to create the **Cau Ferrat**, scene of his famous *festes Modernistes*, bringing together poets, writers, artists and musicians. Manuel de Falla composed his *Nights in the Gardens of Spain* and *Love, the Magician* while staying here. In 1933, the house became a museum (*all three Sitges museums open Tues–Fri 9.30–2 and 4–6 [5–9 in summer], Sat 9.30–7, Sun 9.30–3, closed Mon; combined adm available*), vertiginously packed with iron, ceramics and paintings, and there are two fine El Grecos.

Adjacent, the **Museu Maricel** occupies a summer palace created for American millionaire Charles Deering out of a ruined hospital and a few fisherman's houses. Inside, there's a lovely belvedere over the sea, and an eclectic collection of art, including murals called *Allegories of the World War* (1916–17) by Josep María Sert. In the centre of town, guided tours on the hour (usually in Catalan) will take you through a neoclassical house, the **Museu Romántic**, 1 C/ Sant Gaudenci, which conjures up 19th-century provincial elegance and piety in bizarre biblical grisaille frescoes. It also has a massive doll collection.

North of Barcelona: the Costa Brava and Figueres' Museu Dalí

SARFA buses from Barcelona, © 93 265 11 58, go to Lloret, Tossa del Mar and the other coastal villages as far as Palafrugell and Begur. All trains from Barcelona to France stop in Figueres.

The Costa Brava ('Wild Coast') officially begins at Blanes north of Barcelona and winds its serpentine way up to the French border. Mother Nature was lavish, tipsy even, as she sculpted out one scenic cove after another beneath pine-crowned cliffs, tucking lovely sandy beaches among strange boulder formations and rocky wind sculptures, where 50 years ago fishermen berthed their boats. On the other hand, few places have been more built up. **Lloret del Mar** in particular, with its wide beach, is a British-Dutch package-holiday paradise, and **Tossa del Mar** is nearly as busy, although far more pretty, with a lovely historic centre. The Costa Brava proper is farther north and almost inaccessible by public transport; **Begur** and **Palafrugell** are the main hubs for visiting the lovely coves and beaches, although doing these as a day trip from Barcelona would be a penance—it's best to stay a few days if possible, if you've booked well in advance.

Figueres, however, is a popular day trip from Barcelona for 'the spiritual centre of Europe', as its creator proclaimed: everyone else calls it the **Teatre Museu Dalí** (© 972 51 18 00; *open July–Sept daily 9–7.15, Oct–June daily 10.30–5.15; adm exp*). Salvador Dalí, born here in 1904, created this dream museum in 1974 in a crazy reconstruction of his home town's old municipal theatre. The result is the most visited museum in Spain after the Prado. Even its catalogue is intended to misinform. Inside, expect the outrageous: the former stage has a set by Dalí, accompanied by a full orchestra of mannequins; a coin-fed Cadillac waters its snail-covered occupants. Dalí himself, who died in 1989, is entombed nearby, the museum's final exhibit. You can also visit Dalí's house just outside the beautiful village of Cadaqués: the **Casa-Museu de Port Lligat** (*open mid-Mar–Nov, only 8 people at a time, book on ✆ 972 25 80 63*).

The Irrational Organization of Dalí's Life

It's a shame that the great masturbator didn't live for ever, because Dalí was one of the funniest characters Spain ever produced—his whole life was a schtick that no performance artist could ever equal. Gifted with an impeccable academic technique, he became the most famous Surrealist of them all while still in his 20s, when he painted his first 'hand-painted dream photographs', as he called them, of melting watches and human bodies fitted with sets of spilling drawers. Dalí loved the camera, and was one of the first artists to get involved with the cinema, in his 1929–30 collaborations with Luis Buñuel— *Un Chien Andalou* and *L'Age d'Or*, which caused riots when they were premiered in Paris. During the Civil War he offered to go to Barcelona and run a Department for the Irrational Organization of Daily Life (only to be told: thanks anyway, but it already exists).

If traditional Surrealists drew their inspiration from the irrational well of the unconscious, Dalí claimed his came from 'critical paranoia'—a carefully cultivated delusion, a conscious suspension of rational thought, a way of art and a way of life. Dalí, with his alert moustache-antennae tuned into the outrageous, did it with the deadpan humour of a Buster Keaton. The serious art world considered him a publicity-mongering buffoon who produced little of value after the 1930s, and who flamboyantly, facetiously and sometimes cruelly broke every taboo: he claimed to support Franco (although he lived in the USA between 1940 and 1955); he got up to all sorts of sexual shenanigans (his Russian wife Gala, formerly married to French poet Paul Eluard, liked boys; Dalí preferred to watch); he painted religious kitsch while all the while arguing that Christ was made of cheese; and he signed his name to anything his forgers produced. In his reclusive, suffering old age in Figueres he was exploited by art dealers.

Food and Drink

Catalan Cuisine

The creativity and buzz of Barcelona extends into the kitchen—even some of the most traditional recipes have daring combinations of ingredients (salt cod and honey, for instance)—making the city a natural for cosmopolitan nouvelle cuisine. As Coleman Andrews writes in his classic *Catalan Cuisine*, four sauces underpin it: *allioli* (fresh garlic pounded with olive oil and served with meat and fish); *sofregit* (onions, olive oil and tomatoes cooked for ages and melted together); *picada* (roast almonds, hazelnuts, fried bread, garlic, parsley and sometimes saffron and bitter chocolate), a secret ingredient added towards the end of cooking; and *samfaina* (like ratatouille, but cooked down to a thick paste when used as sauce).

Classic dishes to look out for are *sarsuela* (an elaborate seafood casserole), *arròs negre* (rice with fish, shellfish and cuttlefish), *canalons a la barcelonesa* (cannelloni filled with meat and topped with béchamel), *fideus a banda* (noodles with fish, served separately) and *suquet* (fish and potato soup). *Botifarra amb mongetes*—pork sausage, black or white, with beans—is a staple, as is *escudella*, a hearty pork, chicken and vegetable stew. Roast aubergines, peppers and onions (*escalivada*) is a popular side dish. An *amanida catalana* is a kind of chef's salad. In summer you'll find *esqueixada,* made of salt cod, tomatoes, onions and olives. One very simple but delicious dish that the Catalans claim as their very own is *pa amb tomàquet* (day-old bread, rubbed with ripe tomato, and sprinkled with salt and oil). If the bread is toasted it becomes a *torrade*, but *torrades*, like Italian *bruschetta*, can have just about anything on top to form the classic Catalan *tapa*. *Crema catalana*, similar to *crème brûlée*, is the classic dessert.

As for drinks, the Alt Penedès west of Barcelona produces Catalunya's finest wines and *cava* (made like champagne, but much cheaper). Also worth trying are the mighty reds from Priorat.

Restaurants

Barcelona doesn't dine quite as late as Madrid, but almost: restaurants open at around 8 or 8.30pm and stay open until midnight—some much later. The range is vast: there are places that serve the very finest Catalan cuisine and others that feed the masses with more standard fare. Alongside these native eating houses are also numerous restaurants from other regions of Spain and the world, with a reputed 600 Chinese restaurants sprinkled around town for good measure. As a general rule, book ahead for the more expensive restaurants. These also tend to close down in August, when you'd do well to ring ahead and see if anyone's at home.

The restaurants listed here are split into three categories. Prices are for a three-course meal with wine, per person.

expensive	∞∞∞	above 5,500 pts
moderate	∞∞	3,000–5,500 pts
inexpensive	∞	under 3,000 pts

Cafés, Bars and Tapas

Although there are places that specialize in coffee or cocktails or tapas, most serve all three, along with a selection of sandwiches (*bocadillos*). Tapas are not as essential to the local eating habits as in Madrid or elsewhere in Spain, but are usually regarded as warm-ups to the main event. If you're a big fan, however, there are a handful of places, usually Basque or Gallego, that specialize in the delicious titbits that can take the place of a light meal (but usually cost just as much if not more).

Coffee-drinkers will find their favourite brew everywhere, but tea-drinkers may have cause for despair and want to resort to the hotel breakfast. Traditional breakfast coffee with milk (*café amb llet*) comes in a cup big enough for dunking. If you order a plain *café*, you'll get an espresso; for a lashing of milk in it, ask for a *tallat*. If you prefer your coffee more diluted, ask for a *cafè americano*. Many cafés are linked to cake shops, the better to cater to the Catalan sweet tooth. *Granjas*, or dairy bars, are an old Catalan institution, favourite places to indulge in a late-afternoon pick-me-up of pastries (especially *ensaïmadas*, airy pastry spirals sprinkled with powdered sugar), curd cheese with honey, *crema catalana*, milk-shakes and rich hot chocolate smothered in whipped cream (*suizo*). *Orxaterias/horchaterias* are tiger milk bars, specializing in *orxata* (*horchata* in Castilian), a pale refreshing drink made of crushed tiger nuts.

All bars serve wine by the glass (*negre* for red, *blanco* for white, *rosado* for rosé) but don't expect anything special unless you go to a wine bar or old-fashioned *bodega*, with big oak barrels. The Damm company has sewn up the local beer market, with its Estrella lager and the heavier Voll-Damm. In the summer, it's somehow most refreshing when served draught (a *caña* is a small one, a *jarra* is a pint).

Las Ramblas   *see map, p.75*

Restaurants

∞ **Les Quinze Nits**, 6 Plaça Reial, ℗ 93 318 95 76 (Ⓜ Liceu) always has long queues of tourists and locals stretched halfway across the square. The stylish, simple décor, good food and reason-able prices are the main draw. The same owners run the equally popular **La Fonda**, C/ dels Escudellers, ℗ 93 302 75 15, using the same winning formula.

- **Pinocho**, Mercat de la Boqueria, ✆ 93 317 17 31 (Ⓜ Liceu) is run by a real character, who offers good home-cooked food and tapas in the hurly-burly of the market (early morning to lunchtime only).
- **Garduña**, 17 C/ de Morera, ✆ 93 302 43 23 (Ⓜ Liceu), also located in the Boqueria market, has a good set menu at 1,075 pts and charming rooms upstairs.
- **Restaurante Romesco**, 28 C/ de Sant Pau, ✆ 93 318 93 81 (Ⓜ Liceu) is a classic budget favourite just off the Ramblas, a noisy, cheerful establishment serving heaped platefuls of fried rice and beans to young foreigners.

Cafés, Bars and Tapas

Amaya, 20 Ramblas, ✆ 93 302 10 37 (Ⓜ Drassanes) serves some reliable Basque tapas near the bottom of the Ramblas.

Bar Pastis, 4 C/ de Santa Monica (Ⓜ Drassanes), near the arts centre, is a quirky and colourful Marseille-inspired institution from the 1940s.

Boadas, 1 C/ dels Tallers, ✆ 93 38 95 92 (Ⓜ Catalunya) is a famous Art Deco cocktail bar from 1933 that introduced Cuban drinks to Barcelona.

Bosc de les Fades, just outside the Museu de Cera (Ⓜ Drassanes) is a bar kitted out like a fairy-tale grotto. Take the small fry here for a soda pop.

Café de la Opera, 74 Ramblas, ✆ 93 302 41 89 (Ⓜ Liceu) is an institution and the classiest place on the Ramblas, founded in 1929 opposite the Teatre del Liceu. Art Deco opera heroines etched in the mirrors watch clients watching the passing parade from the four corners of the earth.

Café Zurich, 1 Plaça de Catalunya, ✆ 93 317 91 53 (Ⓜ Catalunya) is not the original much loved Zurich but a shinier clone installed in the same spot in the new Triangle mall, with strategically placed tables.

Granja Viader, 4 C/ d'En Xuclà (near the Església de Betlem), ✆ 93 318 34 86 (Ⓜ Liceu) has been going since 1870, serving luscious milkshakes, hot chocolate, *crema catalana*, *ensaïmades* and curd cheese with honey. *Closed Sun.*

El Corte Inglés, 24 Plaça de Catalunya, ✆ 93 306 38 00 (Ⓜ Catalunya) is on top of the big department store, a popular café with great views over the city.

Barri Gòtic

see map, pp.84–5

Restaurants

- ∞ **Agut d'Avignon**, 3 C/ Trinitat, ✆ 93 302 60 3 (Ⓜ Jaume I), just off C/ de Avinyó, is one of Barcelona's swankiest restaurants: classic Catalan cuisine prepared with the freshest seasonal ingredients and some imaginative twists of their own. Try the excellent stuffed cabbage leaves or the wild boar with strawberry sauce.

∞ **Pitarra**, 56 C/ de Avinyó, ✆ 93 301 16 47 (Ⓜ Jaume I), founded in 1890 and decorated with memorabilia devoted to the eponymous poet, serves fine, traditional Catalan cuisine; try the tuna carpaccio with marinated tomatoes. *Closed Sun.*

∞ **Ateneu**, next to the Ajuntament at 2 Plaça de Sant Miquel, ✆ 93 302 11 98, *www.ateneu.com* (Ⓜ Jaume I), with its adjoining cigar bar, serves delicious and creative seasonal Catalan cuisine in graceful, romantic surroundings, with contemporary art on the walls. It draws a mixed, animated crowd of artists, politicians and intellectuals. The lunch *menu del día* is superb value at 1,200 pts; the evening menu is 2,500 pts. *Closed Sat lunchtime, Sun and hols.*

∞ **Can Culleretes**, 5 C/ d'En Quintana, ✆ 93 317 31 22 (Ⓜ Liceu), tucked down a little sidestreet off C/ de la Boqueria, is the city's oldest restaurant. It's friendly and very popular, with photos of local celebrities lining the walls. They serve big platefuls of good-value traditional Catalan dishes and have a good and inexpensive wine list.

∞ **Agut**, 16 C/ d'En Gignàs, ✆ 93 315 17 09 (Ⓜ Jaume I) is warm and traditional. It has been serving up succulent Catalan specialities since 1924.

∞ **El Gran Café**, C/ de Avinyó, ✆ 93 318 79 86 (Ⓜ Liceu) is a grand, old, galleried Modernista restaurant with dark wooden panelling, elaborate light fittings, chandeliers and long-aproned waiters. The food is hearty Catalan and the prices extremely reasonable.

∞ **La Veronica**, 30 C/ de Avinyó, ✆ 93 412 11 22 (Ⓜ Jaume I) is sleek and new. It's where bright young things chatter over excellent pizzas and Mediterranean dishes; the décor is ultra-modern with tomato-red and white walls and a fabulous sheet of wall lights.

∞ **Pla**, 5 C/ de Bellafila, ✆ 93 412 65 52 (Ⓜ Jaume I), tucked down a sidestreet behind the Ajuntament, is delightful, small and chic. It serves excellent and very creative Catalan cuisine.

◇ **Mesón Jesús**, 4 Cecs de la Boquería, ✆ 93 317 46 98 (Ⓜ Liceu), on a street between C/ de la Boqueria and Plaça de Sant J. Oriol, is an enshrined favourite for good, cheap Catalan fare in a cosy, traditional setting.

◇ **Restaurante Pakistani**, 3 C/ d'En Carabassa, ✆ 93 302 60 25 (Ⓜ Drassanes) serves good and very cheap Pakistani food, including some vegetarian dishes.

◇ **Irati**, 17 C/ del Cardenal Casanyes (Ⓜ Liceu) is great for exquisite reasonably priced Basque tapas, pinchos and txacolis wine.

◇ **Compostela**, 30 C/ de Ferran (Ⓜ Jaume I) draws crowds for its popular Galician specialities such as pulpo and tetilla cheese, for a meal or just tapas. *Closed Tues.*

◇ **Venus**, 25 C/ de Avinyó, ✆ 93 301 15 85 (Ⓜ Jaume I) is a simple, arty café and delicatessen, with a good range of vegetarian dishes and delicious pastries.

◇ **Solkai**, 5 C/ del Palau, ✆ 93 317 90 94 (Ⓜ Jaume I) is a sleek, minimalist restaurant and café with an excellent salad buffet at lunchtimes and a selection of main courses; try the chilled soups, tomato or leek.

Cafés, Bars and Tapas

El Café de Ferran, 59 C/ de Ferran, ✆ 93 392 10 76 (Ⓜ Liceu) serves coffee and tasty pastries just off Plaça de Sant Jaume.

El Paraigua, 2 Pas de l'Ensenyança (Ⓜ Jaume I), on Plaça de Sant Miquel, is the place to tipple to classical music. The setting is a pretty Modernista umbrella shop of 1902, transferred here piece by piece from the Ramblas.

Els Quatre Gats, 3 C/ Montsió, ✆ 93 302 41 40 (Ⓜ Catalunya) is perfect for stopping for a coffee or an aperitif. It's in the replica of the famous Modernista taverna; there's a smart, expensive restaurant in the back as well.

Granja Dulcinea, 2 C/ de Petritxol, ✆ 93 302 68 24 (Ⓜ Liceu) is a classic for atmosphere and frothy, sweet dairy delights.

L'Ascensor, 3 C/ de Bellafila, ✆ 93 318 53 47 (Ⓜ Jaume I) is a classic, old-fashioned café and bar named after its antique lift—a great place to end the day. It opens at 6.30pm.

La Cerería, 3–5 Baixada de Sant Miquel, ✆ 93 301 85 10 (Ⓜ Liceu), near Plaça de Sant Miquel, serves a wonderful range of delicious cakes, pastries and chocolates in its teashop with a tiny terrace.

La Vinateria del Call, C/ de Sant Domènec del Call 9, ✆ 93 302 60 92 (Ⓜ Liceu) is the place for some of the best wines and freshest tapas in the city. Sit at one of the old wooden tables and select from the menu. The service is charming and friendly.

Meson de Café, 16 C/Llibreteria, ✆ 93 315 07 54 (Ⓜ Jaume I) is a classic and is widely reputed to serve the best cup of java in Barcelona.

Portalón, 20 C/ de Banys Nous, ✆ 93 302 11 87 (Ⓜ Liceu) is the most atmospheric old wine *bodega* in the city. *Closed Sun and Aug.*

Schilling, 23 C/ de Ferran, ✆ 93 317 67 87 (Ⓜ Liceu) is a fashionable spacious café that is both popular and hip. It's packed with locals and tourists—a good place to find a cup of tea and the usual café-bar favourites.

The Bagel Shop, 25 C/ de la Canuda, ✆ 93 302 41 61 (Ⓜ Catalunya) is run by a Canadian and not at all *tipico*, but it serves pancake stacks with maple syrup on Sunday mornings when you need them.

Xocoa, 11 C/ de Petritxol, ✆ 93 301 11 97, *www.xocoa.com* (Ⓜ Liceu), a coffee shop and pâtisserie, serves rich, melt-in-the-mouth chocolate truffle cakes.

La Ribera

see map, p.109

Restaurants

∞ **Hoffman**, 74–8 1° C/ de l'Argenteria, ✆ 93 319 58 89 (Ⓜ Jaume I), with a celebrated culinary school next door, offers creative cordon bleu dishes served with quiet aplomb in a series of cosy little plant-filled rooms on the first floor. Booking is essential. *Closed Sat, Sun, Aug and Semana Santa.*

Passadís d'en Pep, 2 Pla del Palau, ✆ 93 310 10 21 (Ⓜ Barceloneta) is gourmet heaven, although it's hard to find (down a long unmarked corridor). The prices are fairly hefty but you don't even have to look at a menu: food is simply brought to you, including some of the city's finest seafood.

Set Portes, 14 Passeig d'Isabel II, ✆ 93 319 30 33 (Ⓜ Barceloneta) is one of the city's most famous restaurants, founded in 1836 (*see* p.120) and now more popular than ever, serving delicious rice and seafood.

Brasserie Flo, 10 C/ de les Jonqueres, ✆ 93 319 31 02 (Ⓜ Urquinaona), not far from the Palau de la Música Catalana, has an elegant mix of Modernista and modern décor. The cuisine is French and Catalan with a fabulous array of deserts. (Prices are at the top end of this category.)

El Foro, 53 C/ de la Princesa, ✆ 93 310 10 20 (Ⓜ Jaume I) serves pizzas, pasta and Argentine-style grilled meats to a fashionable clientele. There's a resident DJ on Saturday nights. *Closed Sun.*

Euskal Etxea, Plaçeta de Montcada, ✆ 93 310 21 85 (Ⓜ Jaume I) serves up the best Basque food in Barcelona and also does excellent regional tapas.

Vascelum, 4 Plaça de Santa Maria, ✆ 93 319 01 67 (Ⓜ Barceloneta), facing Santa Maria del Mar, is a simple, stylish seafood restaurant with polished wooden floors and walls lined with bottles. The wine list is extensive and very good.

Salero, 60 C/ del Rec, ✆ 93 319 80 22 (Ⓜ Jaume I) is one of the most fashionable of the Born-district restaurants, a beautiful, cool white space serving an imaginative fusion of Mediterranean and Oriental cuisine at lunchtime. It's also a very relaxing place to while away an afternoon over a coffee. *Closed Sun eve and Mon.*

Senyor Parellada, 37 C/ de l'Argenteria, ✆ 93 310 50 94 (Ⓜ Jaume I) is where night owls hang out to dine on *estofats, manitas de cerdo*, fish platters and old-fashioned recipes in a magnificent 18th-century building. Booking vital. *Closed Sun and hols.*

Cal Pep, Plaça de les Olles, ✆ 93 310 79 61 (Ⓜ Barceloneta) is the place for excellent grilled fish and seafood, run by the same charismatic owner as the more expensive Passadis del Pep. There is a restaurant (⬤⬤⬤) but most people choose to line up at the bar for the excellent tapas.

Rodrigo, 67 C/ de l'Argenteria, ✆ 93 310 30 20 (Ⓜ Jaume I), near the Santa Maria del Mar, offers excellent home-cooking at very reasonable prices. Though full meals are served only at lunchtime, a wide selection of sandwiches is available at night.

Pla de la Garsa, 13 C/ dels Assaonadors, ✆ 93 315 24 13 (Ⓜ Jaume I) serves tasty tapas or inexpensive meals in cosy and very pleasant surroundings.

Sandwich and Friends, 27 Passeig del Born, ✆ 93 310 07 86 (Ⓜ Jaume I) is great for a quick lunch. There are no fewer than 75 kinds of *bocadillos* served up in a modern, colourful café-gallery with a huge Pop Art-style fresco splashed along one wall.

Cafés, Bars and Tapas

Café de l'Hivernacle, Parc de la Ciutadella, ℰ 93 310 22 91 (Ⓜ Barceloneta), near the Museu de Zoologia, is an elegant, light-filled and very relaxing café with wicker and palms.

El Xampanyet, 22 C/ Montcada, ℰ 93 319 70 03 (Ⓜ Jaume I) is a charming old *cava* and cider bar, full of bonhomie and the lingering aroma of anchovies.

Espai Barroc, 20 C/ Montcada, ℰ 93 310 06 73 (Ⓜ Jaume I) is on the ground floor of the Palau Dalmases, a place to sit and sip in surroundings of total Baroque excess. An experience.

Estrella de Plata, 9 Pla del Palau, ℰ 93 319 60 07 (Ⓜ Barceloneta) is a long-established port bar now serving gourmet (and pricey) tapas, some of which you'll find nowhere else in town.

La Floreta, 4 Plaça de les Olles, ℰ 93 268 13 84 (Ⓜ Barceloneta) is a flower shop converted into a café, with a choice of teas, juices, milkshakes, pastries and snacks.

La Vinya del Senyor, 5 Plaça de Santa Maria, ℰ 93 310 33 79 (Ⓜ Jaume I) has a fantastic selection of 250 wines by the bottle, 20 by the glass, and titbits (*platillos*) to accompany them, with tables overlooking the façade of Santa Maria del Mar.

Tèxtil Café, 12 C/ Montcada, ℰ 93 268 25 98 (Ⓜ Jaume I) is a popular café with tables clustered in the 14th-century courtyard of the Gothic palace that now houses the textile museum; they also do light lunches.

El Raval *see map, p.129*

Restaurants

∞ **Ca l'Isidre**, 12 C/ de les Flors, ℰ 93 441 11 39 (Ⓜ Paral.lel) is in the music-hall district. This warm, intimate restaurant has long been a favourite of artists as well as King Juan Carlos, and serves lovely food based on the freshest ingredients, accompanied by a magnificent wine list.

∞ **Casa Leopoldo**, 24 C/ de Sant Rafael, ℰ 93 241 30 14 (Ⓜ Liceu) is a classic, atmospheric family-run establishment founded in 1929 and serving tasty grilled fish and oxtail stew. *Closed Sun eve, Mon and Aug.*

∞ **Quo Vadis**, 7 C/ del Carme, ℰ 93 317 74 47 (Ⓜ Liceu) is stiffly elegant but offers superb traditional Catalan dishes

and an excellent wine list. *Closed Sun and Aug.*

∞ **Silenus**, 8 C/ dels Angels, ℰ 93 302 26 80 (Ⓜ Catalunya), near the Museu d'Art Contemporani, serves excellent international and Catalan food in a charming, relaxed setting with contemporary art on the walls. Long, light and pretty, with comfortable sofas, it is also a good place to relax over coffee, mornings or afternoons.

∞ **Can Lluis**, 49 C/ de la Cera, ℰ 93 441 11 87 (Ⓜ Sant Antoni) is a piquant favourite of the old music-hall crowd; try the *bacalao* (salt cod). There's an inexpensive *menu del dia. Closed Wed eve and Sun.*

Méson David, 63 C/ de les Carretes, ✆ 93 441 59 34 (Ⓜ Sant Antoni) serves authentic Gallego cuisine, with hearty portions at reasonable prices.

Cafés, Bars and Tapas

Els Tres Tombs, 2 Ronda de Sant Antoni, ✆ 93 443 41 11 (Ⓜ Sant Antoni) is a great place to sit outside and watch the world buzz by. It opens at 6am for early birds and night owls staggering home from clubs.

Fortuny, 31 C/ del Pinto Fortuny, ✆ 93 317 98 92 (Ⓜ Liceu) is a former *bodega* that is now a trendy and laid-back bar, patrolled by toy robots. *Closed Mon.*

Horchateria El Carmen, C/ del Carme (Ⓜ Liceu) is a godsend on a hot day, with ice creams and *orxata*.

Horchateria Fillol, Plaça de la Universitat (Ⓜ Universitat) serves pastries, milkshakes, *orxata* and coffees to put pep in your step and glide in your stride.

Theseo, 119 C/ del Comte Borrell, ✆ 93 453 87 96 (Ⓜ Sant Antoni) is a relaxed café, restaurant, bar and gallery.

By the Sea

see map, pp.140–41

Restaurants

∞∞ **Antigua Casa Solé**, 4 C/ Sant Carles, ✆ 93 221 51 12 (Ⓜ Barceloneta), with its pretty blue and white tiles, wealth of flowers and astonishing range of seafood, has been popular since it opened well over a century ago; Barceloneta locals recommend it despite the multilingual menus.

∞∞ **Els Pescadors**, 1 Plaça Prim, ✆ 93 225 20 18 (Ⓜ Poblenou) is a little farther out (off maps), in Poblenou. This very romantic place is set back from the seafront and has superb fish and seafood served impeccably on a heavenly terrace.

∞ **La Llotja**, Museu Marítim, Avinguda de les Drassanes, ✆ 93 302 64 02 (Ⓜ Drassanes) is located in the vast, vaulted 13th-century shipyards. The restaurant is run by a local food critic and gourmet, who serves very fine Catalan food, including a medieval dish of saffron and chicken to go with the setting.

∞ **El Salón**, 6 C/ Hostal del Sol (just behind the Correus), ✆ 93 315 21 59 (Ⓜ Barceloneta) has a lovely, slightly louche Baroque atmosphere, with guttering candles and plush red velvet sofas. The food is rich and excellent with great desserts; another plus is the excellent cocktails at the bar.

∞ **Can Ros**, 7 C/ Almirall Aixada, ✆ 93 221 45 79 (Ⓜ Barceloneta) is one of the best places for seafood in Barceloneta. While waiting for a main course of *paella* or *arròs negre*, sample some of the fresh seafood *hors-d'œuvre*, or steamed mussels and clams in tomato sauce. *Closed Wed eve.*

∞ **Cangrejo Loco**, Port Olympic, ✆ 93 221 05 33 (Ⓜ Ciutadella-Vila Olímpica) is one among the plethora of fish restaurants in the Port Olympic. The Cangrejo has excellent seafood and service, and during the summer months has outdoor tables on the upper level with fine views of the sea.

- **La Dentellière**, 26 C/ Ample, ☎ 93 319 68 21 (Ⓜ Drassanes) has

good simple food and fondues. *Closed Sun and Aug.*

Cafés, Bars and Tapas

Bodega la Plata, 28 C/ de la Mercè, ☎ 93 315 10 09 (Ⓜ Drassanes) is a very popular and characterful neighbourhood bar. It's a key stop for wine and tapas.

Cava Universal, 4 Plaça Portal de la Pau, ☎ 93 302 61 84 (Ⓜ Drassanes) is a classic bar that has been there forever, in the shadow of Columbus, with outdoor tables for watching the ebb and flow from the Ramblas to the Port Vell.

Celta la Pulpería, 16 C/ de la Mercè, ☎ 93 315 00 06 (Ⓜ Drassanes) serves great Gallego seafood tapas and is an essential stop along a Mercè bar crawl.

El Tío Che, 44 Rambla de Poblenou (off the maps), ☎ 93 309 18 72 (Ⓜ Poblenou) has served *orxata* and ices (*granizats*) since 1912. *Closed Wed in winter.*

El Vaso de Oro, 6 C/ Balboa, ☎ 93 319 30 98 (Ⓜ Barceloneta), on the edge of Barceloneta, is a stand-up-only bar that makes its own excellent beer to go with a plethora of tapas.

Taberna del Prior, 18 C/ Ample, ☎ 93 268 74 27 (Ⓜ Drassanes) has a wide range of hams suspended from the ceilings, *cava* and tapas. Try the succulent grilled cuttlefish. They also do reasonably priced sandwiches at lunchtime.

The Eixample

see map, pp. 152–3

Restaurants

∞ **Jaume de Provença**, 88 C/ de Provença, ☎ 93 430 00 29 (Ⓜ Hospital Clinic) offers Catalan cuisine at its most elaborate—a typical dish is fillet of turbot with saffron lobster. *Closed Sun eve and Mon.*

∞ **Casa Calvet**, 48 C/ de Casp, ☎ 93 413 40 12 (Ⓜ Urquinaona) is one of the city's most innovative restaurants, serving creative and imaginative Mediterranean dishes in a house designed by Gaudí.

∞ **Beltxenea**, 275 C/ Mallorca, ☎ 93 215 30 24 (Ⓜ Passeig de Gràcia/ Diagonal) is a charming, romantic restaurant with some of Barcelona's best and most ambitious Basque cuisine

served on a garden terrace. *Closed Sat lunch and Sun.*

∞ **La Targa Florio**, 190 C/ de Villarroel, ☎ 93 430 72 79 (Ⓜ Hospital Clinic) is filled with heaving crowds, lending weight to the claim that it's the finest Italian restaurant in Spain.

∞ **Reguant**, 15 C/ de Casanova, ☎ 93 424 63 48 (Ⓜ Hospital Clinic) serves the freshest seasonal local cuisine in a tranquil and romantic setting. *Closed Sun and hols.*

∞ **L'Olivé**, 171 C/ Muntaner, ☎ 93 430 90 27 (Ⓜ Hospital Clinic) is a very popular place serving traditional Catalan food, with the emphasis on fish and fresh market ingredients. Try the *fricandó*, a meat and veg stew.

∞ **Tragaluz**, 5 Passatge de la Concepció, ✆ 93 487 01 96 (Ⓜ Diagonal), with a spectacular skylight, offers stylish modern fare. Downstairs is an equally relaxed and fashionable cocktail bar. Across the street is **El Japonés**, ✆ 93 487 01 96, a bright and airy Japanese restaurant run by the same owners.

∞ **Madrid/Barcelona**, 282 C/ d'Aragó, ✆ 93 215 70 26 (Ⓜ Passeig de Gràcia) is named after the railway line that once ran alongside it. The place is a young and funky hangout which serves modern Catalan dishes.

◊ **L'Hostal de Rita**, 279 C/ d'Aragó, ✆ 93 487 23 76 (Ⓜ Passeig de Gràcia) is always busy and has long queues, but it's worth it for the hefty portions of Catalan cooking. It's run by the same folks as Les Quinze Nits in Plaça Reial.

◊ **Ca La Yaya Angela**, 5 Plaça de Tetuán, ✆ 93 246 20 93 (Ⓜ Tetuan) serves very fresh regional cooking at good prices, cheerily dished up.

◊ **L'Atelier**, 108 C/ Muntaner, ✆ 93 323 29 48 (FGC Provença) is a popular haunt with lots of choice. The *menu del día* costs around 2,000 pts.

Cafés, Bars and Tapas

Bauma, 124 C/ de Roger de Llúria, ✆ 93 459 05 66 (Ⓜ Verdaguer/ Diagonal) is a laid-back, welcoming café which attracts the local artists.

Bracafé, 2 C/ de Casp, ✆ 93 302 30 82 (Ⓜ Catalunya), named Bra as in Brazil, is good for an aromatic dose of coffee.

Café Torino, 59 Passeig de Gràcia, ✆ 93 487 75 71 (Ⓜ Passeig de Gràcia) is one of the city's most elegant cafés, with a fine selection of pastries and cakes.

Fats, 206 C/ del Rossello, near Rambla de Catalunya, ✆ 93 487 12 21 (Ⓜ Diagonal) features excellent high-calorie tapas and beer.

La Bodegueta, 98 Rambla de Catalunya, ✆ 93 215 48 94 (Ⓜ Passeig de Gràcia) is the place to join the rest of Barcelona down in the cellar for *cava* and excellent wines, with *pa amb tomàquet* and other snacks to soak it all up. There are inexpensive lunch menus, too.

Laie Llibreria Café, 85 C/ de Pau Claris, ✆ 93 302 73 10 (Ⓜ Passeig de Gràcia) is Barcelona's original and best book-shop-café, with a wonderful interior terrace.

Mas i Mas, 300 C/ de Corsega, ✆ 93 237 57 31 (Ⓜ Diagonal) is a popular and stylish café with good tapas and a lunch menu.

Mora, 409 Avinguda Diagonal, ✆ 93 416 07 26 (Ⓜ Diagonal) is Barcelona's most famous cake shop and one of the city's chicest establishments, a place to linger over a late breakfast and the papers. It also has a restaurant serving inexpensive meals. *Closed Sun.*

Velòdrom, 213 C/ Muntaner, ✆ 93 430 51 98 (Ⓜ Hospital Clinic) opened shortly after the Civil War and is a two-storey yellowing unpretentious bar preserved in aspic, only because no one has bothered to ever change anything. Heterogenous clientele and billiard tables too. *Closed Aug, Easter and Christmas.*

Restaurants

∞ **Botafumeiro**, 81 C/ Gran de Gràcia, ✆ 93 218 42 30 (Ⓜ Fontana) is a fine, lofty Galician seafood restaurant with live guitar music, and oysters at the bar.

∞ **La Troballa**, 69 C/ de la Riera de Sant Miquel (FGC Gràcia) is a tiny, quietly stylish establishment with whitewashed walls and wooden floors, serving traditional seasonal Catalan dishes such as magret of duck with apple, and rabbit pate with caramelised onions.

∞ **Flash-Flash**, 25 C/ de la Granada del Penedès, ✆ 93 237 09 90 (FGC Gràcia) serves 100 different omelettes, although their potato one remains

Barcelona's special favourite. The décor is pure retro black and white, with fabulous white leatherette banquettes. It's open till 2am.

∞ **Txistulari**, 16 C/ Doctor Rizal, ✆ 93 237 13 26 (Ⓜ Fontana) offers Basque cuisine and *pintxos* (crusty French bread with a variety of toppings) at lunchtimes and in the early evenings.

๑ **On Li Lu**, C/ Sant Pere Màrtir, ✆ 93 415 72 14 (Ⓜ Diagonal) is the place to come for a cheese fest, a pretty and friendly little restaurant with soft candlelight. They offer raclette and fondue along with more classic fare.

Cafés, Bars and Tapas

Café Sol Solet, Plaça del Sol, ✆ 93 217 44 40 (Ⓜ Fontana) has a faded boho chic, with tiled floors, marble tables and wooden panelling. The tapas include an unusual wholefood and often vegetarian mixture of salads and tortilla.

El Roble, 7 C/ Luis Antunez, ✆ 93 218 73 87 (FGC Gràcia) is a bustling neighbourhood favourite, with big boards listing all the Gallego seafood tapas on

offer, and great waiters with long aprons and a line in silly jokes.

Salambó, 51 C/ de Torrijos, ✆ 93 218 69 66 (Ⓜ Joanic) is a classy and relaxing two-storey café with an unusual selection of teas and healthy food. There are outdoor tables and billiards, too. *Open noon till 3am.*

Virreina, Plaça de la Virreina, ✆ 93 237 98 80 (Ⓜ Fontana) is a delightful little café with a terrace on a tranquil square.

All these eating places are off the area shown on our maps, unless otherwise stated.

Restaurants

∞ **Gaig**, 402 Passeig Maragall, ✆ 93 429 10 17 (Ⓜ Horta) is old and famous,

having been under the culinary care of the Gaig family for four generations.

Meals served are of a refined Catalan variety, with such delicacies as *arròs de colomí amb ceps* (pigeon in rice with wild mushrooms). The wine cellar is out of this world.

∞∞ **Asador de Aranda**, 31 Avinguda Tibidabo, ✆ 93 417 01 15 (FGC Avinguda Tibidabo) serves Castilian cusine, specializing in roast lamb, served with homemade bread in a beautiful Modernista setting. *Closed Sun eve.*

∞∞ **La Venta**, Plaça Dr Andreu, ✆ 93 212 64 55 (Tramvia Blau) serves seasonal Catalan cuisine in a pretty setting above the hurly burly. *Closed Sun.*

∞∞ **Eldorado Petit**, 51 Dolors Monserdà, ✆ 93 204 55 06 (FGC Sarrià) is another award-winning restaurant in a lovely turn-of-the-20th-century building, with an elegant bar and a menu that changes according to market availability and chef Luis Cruañas' refined muse. *Closed Sun.*

∞∞ **Vía Veneto**, 10–12 C/ Ganduxer, ✆ 93 200 72 44 (FGC La Bonanova) is one of the city's most glamorous restaurants. It has won several prizes for its exquisite and innovative Catalan dishes, such as *pequeños calabacines en flor en salsa de hígado de oca* (tiny flowering zucchini in goose liver sauce),

prepared by Josep Monje. *Closed Sat lunch and Sun.*

∞∞ **Neichel**, 16 Avinguda de Pedralbes, ✆ 93 243 84 08 (Ⓜ María Cristina) has an elegant modern dining room, the perfect stage for some of the most creative and refined cuisine in Spain, prepared by French chef Jean-Louis Neichel. The magnificent cheese and pastry chariots that round off the meal are legendary. Set menus cost 8,000 and 9,500 pts. *Closed Sat lunch, Sun and Aug.*

∞∞ **A La Menta**, 50 Passeig Manuel Girona, ✆ 93 204 15 49 (Ⓜ María Cristina) is at the lower end of this price category. You can dine well on *mariscos* or have a steak grilled at your table.

∞ **El Vell Sarrià**, 93 C/ Major de Sarrià, ✆ 93 205 45 41 (FGC Sarrià) is delightfully old-fashioned, with an outdoor terrace in summer, and a cosy dark wooden interior with low beams and lace tablecloths inside. Solid Catalan dishes are served by dignified older waiters in long aprons.

∞ **Manolete**, 132 C/ Laforja (*see* map p.197), ✆ 93 00 20 70 (FGC Muntaner) is a romantic little spot if you want to splash out a bit for lunch. It also has an excellent wine cellar.

Cafés, Bars and Tapas

Mirablau, Plaça Dr Andreu, ✆ 93 442 31 00 (Tramvia Blau) is a glassed-in bar with one of the very best views in Barcelona, open from 11am till 4.30am

Sandor, 5 Plaça Francesc Macià, ✆ 93 200 89 13 (Ⓜ Hospital Clinic) is an atmospheric and traditional café with a terrace on the square.

Vegetarian

Falafel places are springing up all over the place for a quick snack, and more and more restaurants are offering vegetarian options, but Barcelona has a surprisingly good range of very decent vegetarian establishments.

Biocenter, 25 C/ del Pinto Fortuny (*see* map p.129), ✆ 93 301 45 83 (Ⓜ Liceu) has a generous salad bar and various hot dishes to choose from. *Closed Sun.*

Corts Catalans, 603 Gran Vía de les Corts Catalanes (*see* map pp.152–3), ✆ 93 301 03 76 (Ⓜ Universitat) has a 1,100 pts daily *menú.*

Juicy Jones, 7 C/ del Cardenal Casanyes (*see* map pp.84–5) is a good place to eat at the counter, or head downstairs to the basement with its great flowery wall paintings and gingham tablecloths. The staff couldn't be nicer, 1,000 pts will get you three delicious courses, and they also serve organic wines and beers.

La Buena Tierra, 56 C/ de l'Encarnacio (*see* map p.197), ✆ 93 219 82 13, up in Gràcia, is cosy, with deliciously imaginative specialities and a pretty garden.

La Flauta Magica, 18 C/ de Banys Vells (*see* map p.109), ✆ 93 268 49 64, is one of Barcelona's nicest and most imaginative vegetarian restaurants. It also serves some organic meat dishes. The atmosphere is young and stylish, the décor a funky blend of peach and violet dimly lit with candles, and the service friendly and welcoming.

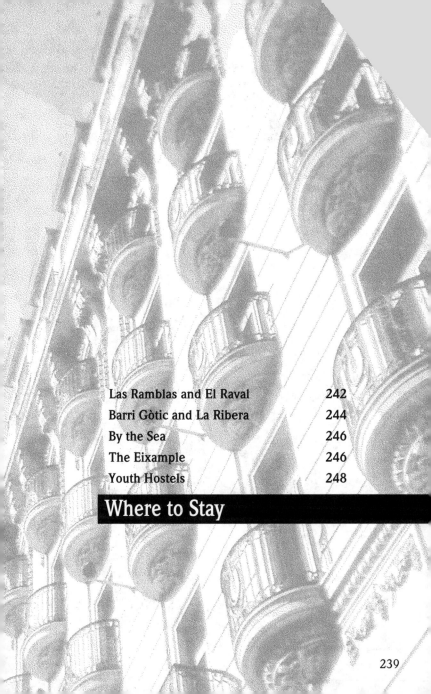

Where to Stay

City Centre Hotels

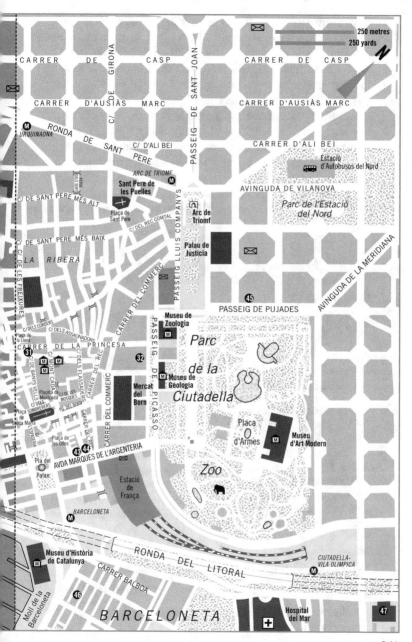

250 metres
250 yards

N

CARRER   DE   GIRONA   CASP

PASSEIG DE SANT JOAN

CARRER   DE   CASP

CARRER   D'AUSIÀS   MARC

C/ DE GIRONA

CARRER   D'AUSIÀS MARC

M URQUINAONA

RONDA   DE   SANT   PERE

C/ D'ALI BEI

CARRER   D'ALI BEI

Estació
d'Autobusos del Nord

ARC DE TRIOMF

Sant Pere de
les Puelles

C/ DE SANT PERE MÉS ALT

C/ DEL REC COMTAL

Plaça de
Sant Pere

AVINGUDA DE VILANOVA

Parc de l'Estació
del Nord

PASSEIG LLUIS COMPANYS

Arc de
Triomf

C/ DE SANT PERE MÉS BAIX

C/ DE LA   RIBERA

Palau de
Justicia

C/ DE LES FREIXURES

AVINGUDA DE LA MERIDIANA

CARRER DEL COMMERC

PASSEIG DE PUJADES

45

C/ DELS CORDERS

C/ DELS ASSAONADORS

Museu de
Zoologia

Plaça de
la Llana

CARRER   DE   LA   PRINCESA

31

Parc

C/ DE MONT CADA

M M

32

PASSEIG DE PICASSO

de

CARRER DEL REC

C/ DE BANY VELLS

C/ DELS FLASSADERS

C/ DE LES MOSQUES

Museu de
Geologia

la

M

Plaçeta de
Montcada

PS. DEL BORN

Mercat
del Born

Ciutadella

Plaça
de
Santa Maria

C/ SOMBRERERS

CARRER DEL COMMERC

Plaça de
les Olles

Plaça
d'Armes

Museu
d'Art Modern

M

43 44

AVDA MARQUES DE L'ARGENTERIA

Zoo

Pla del
Palau

Estació
de
França

M BARCELONETA

RONDA   DEL   LITORAL

Museu d'Història
de Catalunya

M

CARRER BALBOA

CIUTADELLA-
VILA OLIMPICA

M

Moll de la
Barceloneta

46

BARCELONETA

Hospital
del Mar

47

There are good places to stay all over Barcelona, with cheaper choices clustered in and around Barri Gòtic. Sentimental travellers should stay on the Ramblas, 'the world's most beautiful street', Barcelona's favourite hotel address for the past century. Be aware, though, that exterior rooms may offer colourful views of teeming evening strollers but can be noisy. Wherever you want to stay, it's essential to book accommodation in advance: some of the most popular hotels are fully booked months ahead. If do you arrive without a reservation, there are low-cost booking services in the airport, Estació de Sants and at the city's main tourist office on Plaça de Catalunya.

The hotels listed here are split into five price categories. Prices are for a double room.

luxury	∞∞∞∞∞	above 30,000 pts
expensive	∞∞∞∞	18,000–30,000 pts
moderate	∞∞∞	7,000–18,000 pts
inexpensive	∞∞	3,000–7,000 pts
cheap	∞	under 3,000 pts

Las Ramblas and El Raval

Hotels in this section are marked on the map on pp.240–1 and are numbered accordingly.

∞∞∞∞∞ **8** ★★★★**Le Meridien Barcelona**, 111 Ramblas, ✆ 93 318 62 00, ✉ 93 318 77 76, is at the top of the line, imposing, pink, hyper-plush and used to coddling finicky opera and rock stars. A favourite with businessmen, it has a 200m² presidential suite for those with a spare several thousand pesetas. The restaurant, Le Patio, serves some of the city's finest Mediterranean cuisine.

∞∞∞∞ **7** ★★★★**Rivoli Ramblas**, 128 Rambla dels Estudis, ✆ 93 302 66 43, ✉ 93 317 20 38, *rivoli@alba.mssl.es*, has a stylish new Art Deco design throughout, a cocktail-piano bar, a

gym equipped with sauna and Jacuzzi, and a delicious rooftop terrace with great views over the old centre.

∞∞∞∞ **9** ★★★**Hotel Ambassador**, 13 C/ del Pinto Fortuny, ✆ 93 412 05 30, ✉ 93 302 79 77, is a handsome hotel inaugurated during the 1992 Olympics. Along with all the usual luxurious frills, the Ambassador has a discreet rooftop terrace with garden and swimming pool.

∞∞∞∞ **3** ★★★**Duques de Bergara**, 11 C/ Bergara (behind the Triangle mall), ✆ 93 301 51 51, ✉ 93 317 31 79, has been recently and expensively modernized; the Modernista reception has been left intact, and, although the rooms have been rather blandly revamped, the terrace swimming pool is a charming retreat.

∞∞∞ **37** ★★★**Oriente**, 45 Ramblas, ✆ 93 302 25 58, @ 93 412 38 19, is a mouldering classic occupying one of the street's oldest buildings, the former monastery of the Colegio de San Bonaventura, built in 1670. The cloister now gaily serves as the hotel ballroom. Come here for faded grandeur and atmosphere, but be aware that rooms overlooking the Ramblas can be noisy.

∞∞∞ **4** ★★★**Continental**, 138 Rambla de les Canaletes, ✆ 93 301 25 70, @ 93 302 73 60, has rooms with balconies over the Ramblas, and offers good value for its location and very pleasant staff.

∞∞∞ **38** ★★★**Gaudí**, 12 C/ Nou de la Rambla, ✆ 93 317 90 32, @ 93 412 26 36, *gaudi@hotelgaudi.es*, *www. hotelgaudi.es*, despite the curly glass and wrought-iron porch, and the crazy *trencadi* fountain at the entrance, has newly renovated modern instead of Modernista rooms, but offers views of the great roof of the Palau Güell (*see* p.XXX). There is also parking and a reasonable, if undistinguished, cafeteria.

∞∞∞ **41** ★★**Cuatro Naciones**, 40 Ramblas, ✆ 93 317 36 24, @ 93 302 69 85, opened its doors at the beginning of the 19th century and for the next 100 years was Barcelona's best hotel; it's not so bad nowadays, either.

∞∞∞ **10** ★★★**Turin**, C/ del Pinto Fortuny, ✆ 93 302 48 12, @ 93 302 10 05, doesn't ooze charm, but is a slick, convenient establishment with car parking and rooms with air-conditioning.

∞∞∞ **18** ★★★**Moderno**, 11 C/ de l'Hospital, ✆ 93 301 41 54, @ 93 302 78 70, is a comfy, fussily furnished home from home, with wrought-iron balconies overlooking the street on the edge of El Raval.

∞∞∞ **2** ★★**Meson Castilla**, 5 C/ de Valldonzelia, ✆ 93 318 21 82, @ 93 412 40 20, *hmesoncastilla@ teleline.es*, is tucked down a quiet sidestreet near the Museu d'Art Contemporani. It has a delightful little interior garden with wrought-iron tables and chairs, and spacious, air-conditioned bedrooms.

∞∞∞ **19** ★★★**San Agustin**, 3 Plaça Sant Agustí, ✆ 93 318 16 58, @ 93 317 29 28, is an elegant and peachy place on a leafy little square. Try for an attic room with beamed ceilings and views of the old city.

∞∞∞ **23** ★★**Espanya**, 9–11 C/ de Sant Pau, ✆ 93 318 17 58, @ 93 317 11 34, has a beautiful ground floor decorated by Domènech i Montaner. The functionally furnished rooms are disappointing after all the Modernista grandeur, but have en suite bathrooms. It's popular with college groups.

∞∞∞ **22** ★★**Peninsular**, 34–36 C/ de Sant Pau, ✆ 93 302 31 38, @ 93 412 36 99, is another hotel nestled in the shell of a disused convent, with rooms set along curved balconies overlooking a spacious, light-filled inner courtyard filled with plants and flowers. It is good value and fills up quickly.

∞∞
(21) ****Principal**, 8 C/ Junta de Comerç, ✆ 93 318 89 70, @ 93 412 08 19, *hotel@hotelprincipal.es, www. hotelprincipal.es*, is eccentrically decorated but welcoming. Two doors up is the bright ochre and yellow façade of the **Joventut**, run by the same people.

∞∞
(40) ****Hotel de l'Arc**, 19 Ramblas, ✆ 93 301 97 98, @ 93 318 62 63, is simple and unassuming, but with reasonable facilities.

∞∞
(1) *****Hotel Inglaterra**, 14 C/ de Pelai, ✆ 93 505 11 00, @ 93 505 11 09, *hi@hotelinglaterra.com*, has very modern rooms and spanking-new comforts. There's a terrace on the sixth floor.

∞∞
(4) **Toledano**, 138 Ramblas, ✆ 93 301 08 72, @ 93 412 31 42, *toledano @idgrup.ibernet.com*, is the chintzy choice. The same people also run the slightly cheaper **Hostal Capitol** beneath it, which can be noisy. Both also offer rooms for three or four.

∞∞
(39) **Hostal Morató**, 50 C/ Nou de la Rambla, ✆ 93 442 36 69, in the heart of El Raval, has been recently refurbished. It is basic but clean and all rooms have balconies. Downstairs there is a pleasant little café.

∞∞
(16) **Las Flores**, 79 Ramblas, ✆ 93 317 16 34, up a narrow white staircase, is a spotless pension run by a kindly old couple. It has rooms with bath.

∞∞
(15) ***Hotel Internacional**, 78–80 Ramblas, ✆ 93 302 25 66, @ 93 317 61 90, is a newly refurbished, cheerful hotel overlooking the Mercat de la Boqueria, which attracts an occasionally rowdy, pleasure-seeking crowd.

∞
(17) **Tamashiro**, 93 C/ de l'Hospital, ✆ 93 329 54 87, is a plain and basic choice.

∞
(20) **La Terassa**, 11 C/ Junta de Comerç, ✆ 93 302 51 74, @ 93 301 21 88, is run by the same people as the Jardí, but is slightly less well equipped and is cheaper as a result. Breakfast is served on the pretty interior patio in summer.

Barri Gòtic and La Ribera

Hotels in this section are marked on the map on pp.240–1 and are numbered accordingly.

∞∞∞∞
(12) ******Colón**, 7 Avinguda de la Catedral, ✆ 93 301 14 04, @ 93 317 29 15, is the grandest hotel in the quarter, in a historic building with fine views of the cathedral, a garage, air-conditioning and other amenities.

∞∞∞∞
(28) ******Hotel Gótico**, 14 C/ Jaume I, ✆ 93 315 22 11, @ 93 315 21 13, rivals the Colón's comforts if not its

atmosphere, after being completely refurbished in 1999. It has surprisingly reasonable prices (at the lower end of this category) for its location and facilities.

∞∞∞∞
(26) ******Grand Hotel Barcino**, 6 C/ Jaume I, ✆ 93 302 20 12, @ 93 301 42 42, offers unbridled, if slightly soulless, luxury.

★★★Suizo, 12 Plaça del Angel, ☎ 93 310 61 08, 📠 93 310 40 81, is a relatively small hotel that offers a carefully cultivated 19th-century ambience and a beautiful bar. The nicest and quietest rooms overlook Baixada Llibreteria.

★★★Rialto, 42 C/ de Ferran, ☎ 93 318 52 12, 📠 93 318 53 12, is an exceptionally, if blandly, comfortable hotel, geared unobtrusively towards businesspeople.

★★★Park, 11 Avinguda Marques de l'Argenteria, ☎ 93 319 60 00, 📠 93 319 45 19, is an architectural landmark from the 1950s and close to the arty nightlife of the Born area.

★★★Nouvel Hotel, 20 C/ de Santa Anna, ☎ 93 301 82 74, 📠 93 301 83 70, is convenient for the shopping district and the Ramblas in a sympathetically renovated Modernista building with marble floors, huge gilt mirrors and carved wooden fittings. The staff are very friendly and the rooms are prettily decorated with ornate tiled floors and large marble bathrooms.

★★Adagio, 21 C/ de Ferran, ☎ 93 318 90 61, 📠 93 318 37 24, is newly renovated, central, simply furnished with all mod-cons, including soundproofing, and has friendly reception staff who are good sources of local knowledge. They also exhibit some (usually dire) local art in the lobby.

★Rey Don Jaime I, 11 C/ Jaume I, ☎/📠 93 310 62 08, offers good value and a touch of class in its tiny dark wood and gilt lobby.

★Triunfo, 22 Passeig de Picasso, ☎/📠 93 315 08 60, is a sweet, simple little *pensión* just between the arty nightspots of the Born and the Parc de la Ciutadella.

★Hotel Oasis, 17 Pla del Palau, ☎ 93 319 43 96, 📠 93 412 31 68, is an old budget favourite with well-equipped rooms, some with air-conditioning. It can get a bit noisy, but is well placed for the waterfront nightlife.

★★Hs Layetana, Plaça de Ramón Berenguer III el Gran, ☎ 93 319 20 12, offers a room with a view of the Roman walls, in an attractive 19th-century building. It can be a bit noisy with the traffic from nearby Vía Laietana.

★★Hostal Fontanella, 71 Vía Laietena, ☎ 93 317 59 43, is so warm and friendly that you won't notice the traffic. There are weekend toiletry kits in the rooms, and the owner is very maternal.

★★Hostal Jardí, 1 Plaça de Sant Josep Oriol, ☎ 93 301 59 00, 📠 93 318 36 64, is the most popular budget hotel in the area, with scrupulously clean rooms set around a central courtyard, although the nicest overlook the tree-filled Plaça del Pi. Book well in advance.

★★Hs Rembrandt, 23 C/ Portaferrisa, ☎ 93 318 10 11, is one of the better cheaper choices.

Levante, 2 Baixada de Sant Miquel, ☎ 93 317 95 65, is friendly and not too noisy at night.

Lourdes, 14 C/ de la Princesa, ☎ 93 319 50 31, is a clean and pleasant bargain, and nicer than the Pinar, which is in the same building.

Maldà, 5 C/ del Pi, ✆ 93 317 30 02, is small and cheerful, up two flights of stairs inside Barcelona's first shopping arcade, and, though a bit hard to find, its sunny, quiet rooms (none are en suite) are very good value.

★Roma Reial, Plaça Reial, ✆ 93 302 03 66, ✆ 93 301 18 39, bright and refurbished, is one of the better budget options on the square, which mainly attracts young backpackers.

Pension Ambos Mundos, 10 Plaça Reial, ✆ 93 318 79 70, ✆ 93 412 23 63, is run by very friendly South Americans. All the prettily tiled rooms have en suite bathrooms.

By the Sea

Hotels in this section are marked on the map on pp.240–1 and are numbered accordingly.

★★★★★Arts Barcelona, 19–21 C/ Marina, ✆ 93 221 10 00, ✆ 93 221 10 70, occupies one of the two Olympic towers of the Port Olympic in a class by itself, offering stunning views of the sea and city and with a fantastic seaside pool. Look for reduced weekend rates and other price packages.

★★★Metropol, 31 C/ Ample, ✆ 93 310 51 00, ✆ 93 319 12 76, is a 19th-century hotel that was grandly refurbished for the Olympics. Plush and well-equipped, the only downside is the piped Muzak.

Marina Folch, C/ del Mar, ✆ 93 310 37 09, ✆ 93 310 53 27, is tucked in the web of streets that make up Barceloneta. There are only 10 rooms in this charming hotel, so be sure to book in advance.

The Eixample

Hotels in this section are marked on the map on the opposite page, and numbered accordingly.

★★★★★Husa Palace, 668 Gran Vía des les Corts Catalanes, ✆ 93 318 52 00, ✆ 93 318 01 48, was known as the Ritz until 1995, but despite the change of owners and names it remains Barcelona's classic grand hotel, as it has been since 1919, offering luxury in every sense of the word.

★★★★★Claris, 150 C/ de Pau Claris, ✆ 93 487 62 62, ✆ 93 215 79 70, gives luxury a twist, blending refined modern design with a connoisseur's collection of ancient art treasures.

★★★★Condes de Barcelona, 73 Passeig de Gràcia, ✆ 93 484 22 00, ✆ 93 488 06 14, elegantly designed from twin façades forming an old Modernista palace, is as stylish inside as out, and has huge marble bathrooms that you could get lost in.

★★★★Hotel Majestic, 68 Passeig de Gràcia, ✆ 93 488 17 17, ✆ 93 488 18 80, is made up of three sumptuous buildings recently knocked into one and dragged back from the 1970s to become one of the city's chicest establishments. It has

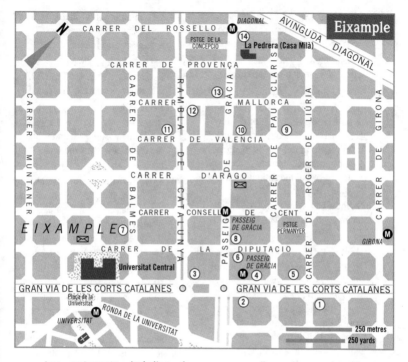

CARRER DEL ROSSELLO

PSTGE DE LA CONCEPCIO

La Pedrera (Casa Milà)

CARRER DE PROVENÇA

CARRER RAMBLA DE CATALUNYA

GRACIA

CARRER MALLORCA

CARRER DE VALENCIA

CARRER D'ARAGO

CARRER CONSELL DE CENT

PASSEIG DE GRACIA

PSTGE PERMANYER

EIXAMPLE

CARRER DE LA DIPUTACIO

PASSEIG DE GRACIA

Universitat Central

GRAN VIA DE LES CORTS CATALANES   GRAN VIA DE LES CORTS CATALANES

Plaça de la Universitat

RONDA DE LA UNIVERSITAT

UNIVERSITAT

GIRONA

250 metres
250 yards

two restaurants, including the Drolma, which offers just 10 tables for true gourmets.

****Gran Hotel Havana, 647 Gran Vía de les Corts Catalanes, ℗ 93 412 11 15, ℗ 93 412 26 11, is in a Modernista building with Avant Garde décor inside much sought after for fashion shoots. It's at the lower end of this price category.

****Regente, 76 Rambla de Catalunya, ℗ 93 487 59 89, ℗ 93 487 32 27, behind a Modernista façade, has an air of stolid stateliness and lots of oak and gilt. Rooms are traditionally stylish, with fabulous views from the upper floors, and the service is impeccable. There is an attractive, if small, rooftop pool with more astounding views and a bar.

****Avenida Palace, 605 Gran Vía de les Corts Catalanes, ℗ 93 301 96 00, ℗ 93 318 12 34, is a favourite older hotel. Rooms from the fourth floor upwards have retained some of their older furnishings and offer the best views. It's at the lower end of this price category.

****Derby, 28 C/ Loreto (*see* map, p.210), ℗ 93 322 32 15, ℗ 93 410 08 62, is on a convenient street just off Avinguda Diagonal in the heart of the business district. The smooth service and very comfortable rooms are aimed at business travellers, which means that weekend discounts are sometimes possible.

☙☙☙☙
(6) ★★★★**Sant Moritz**, 264 C/ de la Diputacio, ✆ 93 412 15 00, ✉ 93 412 12 36, is a very polished establishment with an award-winning restaurant, the San Galen.

☙☙☙
(2) ★★★**Gran Via**, 642 Gran Vía de les Corts Catalanes, ✆ 93 318 19 00, ✉ 93 318 99 97, is one of the few hotels here that has resisted the urge to remodel, preserving a touch of 19th-century grace from its courtyard to its lounge and the antique furnishings in the rooms. They have recently had a bit of a tweak, but nothing serious has marred the air of a past golden age.

☙☙
(7) **Hostal Eden**, 55 C/ de Balmes, 1st and 2nd Floors, ✆/✉ 93 452 66 20, *hostaleden@teleline.es*, *www.barcelona-on-line.es/hostaleden*, is one of the area's pleasant budget surprises, up a staircase in an old Eixample building, with 25 spotless, whitewashed and endearingly eccentric rooms—some have whirlpools set behind beautiful sliding wooden doors, and some have patios. There is coin-operated Internet access.

☙☙
(5) ★★**Hs Palacios**, 629 bis Gran Vía de les Corts Catalanes, ✆ 93 301 30 79, is centrally located and a bargain.

☙☙
(8) ★★**Hs Oliva**, 32 Passeig de Gràcia, ✆ 93 488 01 62, has large, airy rooms and great views, and is one of the cheapest in the street that Gaudí made famous.

☙☙
(12) ★★**Hs Windsor**, 84 Rambla de Catalunya, ✆ 93 215 11 98, is a bit dearer than the above but also a bit nicer, with some of the best views on the street. Book early in the summer and try to get a room with a balcony overlooking the Rambla.

☙☙
(14) **Paseo de Gracia**, 102 Passeig de Gràcia, ✆ 93 215 58 24, ✉ 93 215 37 24, is also reasonable for this chi chi district. Try to get a room on the eighth floor, where some have retained the old Modernista fittings and there are splendid views.

Youth Hostels

Ring ahead for these to make sure there's room.

Numbered hostels in this section are marked on the map on pp.240–1.

Hostel de Joves [45], 29 Passeig de
(45) Pujades, ✆ 93 300 31 04, is probably the nicest of the official IYHF hostels.

Albergue Pere Tarrés, 149–51 C/ Numancia (*see* map, p.210), ✆ 93 410 23 09 (Ⓜ Les Corts), is closest if you arrive at Estació de Sants. It also has a pretty roof terrace. IYHF cards are required.

Albergue Mare de Déu de Montserrat, 41–51 Passeig de la Mare de Déu del Coll (off maps), ✆ 93 210 51 51 (Ⓜ Vallcarca), is way out in the wilds. You will need a IYHF card.

Albergue Kabul, 17 Plaça Reial, ✆ 93
(36) 318 51 90, ✉ 93 301 40 34, is a more centrally located, privately run youth hostel, with rooms that house from two to 12 people.

Entertainment and Nightlife

Cinema, Dance and Theatre

There is always something to do in Barcelona, especially from June to August, when the city's **Grec festival** brings in concerts, theatre and dance at Montjuïc's Teatre Grec, the Plaça del Rei and other venues. The **information centre** for the Grec and other cultural events is the Palau de la Virreina on the Ramblas, ✆ 93 301 77 75.

News-stands sell the weekly *Guia del Ocio* (125 pts) with detailed listings of events; its 'Cine' section has a list of **films** shown in their original language (VO) and of the excellent, unusual fare shown by the Filmoteca de la Generalitat, located in the Cine Aquitania, 33 Avinguda de Sarrià, ✆ 93 410 75 90 (Ⓜ Hospital Clinic).

Dance fans can take in performances at the Generalitat's L'Espai de Danza i Música, 63 Travessera de Gràcia, ✆ 93 414 31 33 (Ⓜ Diagonal).

If you understand Spanish and/or Catalan, Barcelona offers some of the most innovative **theatre** anywhere, with over 20 active theatres: you can buy tickets over the phone with Tel-Entrada (✆ 902 10 12 12) or through the Internet (*www.telentrada.com*). Language in many cases is secondary to the multimedia performances by the city's most innovative companies: La Cubana, Els Comediants, La Fura dels Baus, Els Joglars, Dagoll Dagom and the three-man mime team El Tricicle; again check listings in the *Guia del Ocio*. Of special note is the beautiful 19th-century Mercat de les Flors, the wholesale flower market converted into a theatre at 59 C/ de Lleida, ✆ 93 426 1875 (Ⓜ Espanya), which offers a full range of events, from two-day theatre marathons to big-name international performances.

Music

The free monthly music calendar *Informatiu MUSICAL*, put out by the Amics de la Música de Barcelona (available at the tourist offices), lists daily performances of everything from the most classical to the most scurrilous country and western twangs. You can book tickets 24 hours a day for major classical music concerts before even leaving home (✆ 34 93 495 39 24) or within Spain (✆ 902 33 22 11).

L'Auditori, 140 C/ de Lepant (Ⓜ Marina) is spanking new, acoustically pure and architecturally sterile. Classical music concerts are held here on a regular basis.

La Boîte Mas i Mas, 477 Avinguda Diagonal, ✆ 93 419 59 50 (Ⓜ Verdaguer) leans towards soul and blues.

El Cangrejo, 9 C/ Monserrat, ✆ 93 301 85 75 (Ⓜ Drassanes), in the Barri Xinès, is where low-brow, sleazy kitsch can be enjoyed, with its surreal, campy cabaret reviews.

Centre Artesà Tradicionàrius, 6–8 Travessera de Sant Antoni (Ⓜ Fontana), in Gràcia, is the place for traditional Catalan music.

Club Apolo, 113 C/ Nou de la Rambla, ☎ 93 309 12 04 (Ⓜ Paral.lel) is a pop venue.

Costa Breve, 230 C/ Aribau, ☎ 93 414 27 78 (FGC Gervasi) brings in an eclectic, wide variety of music from acid jazz to African, rumba and 60s sounds.

La Cova del Drac, 33 C/ Vallmajor, ☎ 93 200 70 32 (FGC Muntaner) gets some big-name jazz performers at the weekend, while, during the week, pop, funk and ethnic fusion concerts can be heard.

Gran Teatre del Liceu, 51–9 Ramblas, *www.liceubarcelona.com* (Ⓜ Liceu), reopened in 1999, once again offers opera fans the chance to hear their favourite arias.

Harlem Jazz Club, 8 C/ Comtessa Sobradiel, ☎ 93 310 07 55 (Ⓜ Jaume I), in the Barri Gòtic, is a small club with live swing, Celtic, country and just about everything in between.

Jamboree, 17 Plaça Reial, ☎ 93 301 75 64 (Ⓜ Liceu) is a good club with a busy programme of live jazz. It doubles later on in the evening as a disco for soul and hip-hop fans.

Jazzsi Club, 2 C/ Requesens, ☎ 93 329 00 20 (Ⓜ Sant Antoni) is associated with one of Barcelona's best music schools and offers regular home-grown performances of jazz, rock and flamenco.

London Bar, 34 C/ Nou de la Rambla, ☎ 93 318 52 61 (Ⓜ Liceu) has been in operation since 1910 and is now a popular venue for blues, jazz and pop performances.

Luz de Gas, 246 C/ Muntaner, ☎ 93 209 77 11 (FGC Muntaner) is a large, happening club for jazz, rock, pop, salsa and funk, with live music most nights.

Magic, 40 Passeig de Picasso, ☎ 93 310 72 67 (Ⓜ Barceloneta), located in the Born area, is the place for good old rock and roll.

Palau de la Música Catalana, 2 Sant Francesc de Paula, ☎ 93 295 72 00 (Ⓜ Urquinaona) is magnificent and the place where lovers of classical music will really feel at home.

Palau Sant-Jordi, Montjuïc (Ⓜ Espanya) is where visiting rock and pop megastars perform.

Santa Maria del Mar, Plaça de Santa Maria, ☎ 93 310 23 90 (Ⓜ Jaume I), Barcelona's most beautiful church, is worth mentioning for its excellent, semi-regular concerts.

Savannah Músic Club, 16 C/ Muntanya, ☎ 93 231 38 77 (Ⓜ Sant Andreu), up on the northern side of town, showcases local performers and informal jam sessions.

Zeleste, 122 C/ Almogavers, ☎ 93 486 44 22 (Ⓜ Marina) is where the smaller-fry pop stars play.

After Dark: Bars and Cafés

Barcelona's nightlife cranks up after 11pm and at weekends lasts until a late breakfast, if you've got the energy (and money) to keep up. Note that bars officially close at 2 or 3am, but if the ambience is good the owner will close the door and let the party continue inside. Favourite spots for drinks and *montaditos* (tiny tapas on a slice of bread) are the Barri Gòtic, Gràcia, in the Eixample around the Passeig de Gràcia, and trendy Sant Gervasi (the district just south of Gràcia), where posing can get in the way of a good time. The Barri Gòtic is more relaxed, while the Passeig del Born by Santa Maria del Mar is a favourite hangout.

Barri Gòtic and La Ribera

Abaixadors Deu, 10 C/ Abaixadors (Ⓜ Jaume I), off Plaça de Santa Maria, is a hip and fashionable theatre café and nightclub, located on the first floor of an immense Modernista flat. It offers poetry readings, belly-dancing, classical recitals and jazz concerts, as well as late-night dinners.

L'Antiquari de la Plaça del Rei, 13 C/ Verguer (Ⓜ Jaume I), in the centre of things and popular, is a great place to sit out on a summer's night, or take in the café-concert from Thursday to Sunday.

El Born, 29 Passeig del Born (Ⓜ Barceloneta) is a friendly rendezvous, especially after midnight.

Café Royale, 3 C/ Nou de Zurbano (Ⓜ Liceu), off Plaça Reial, is sleek and relaxed, offering giant comfy sofas to sink into and soak up the eclectic, groovy rhythms.

Dot, 7 C/ Nou de Sant Francesc (Ⓜ Liceu), running towards Plaça del Duc de Medinaceli from Plaça Reial, is for those looking for the latest sounds in electronic dance.

Plàstic, 19 Passeig del Born (Ⓜ Barceloneta) is currently the trendiest bar by far in the Born. It's where shiny young things get warmed up for the long night ahead.

The Eixample

La Fira, 171 C/ de Provença (Ⓜ Hospital Clinic) is a bar of bizarre design, jammed full of fun-house paraphernalia, including a row of warped mirrors in the entrance hall that could throw you off balance as you exit.

Les Gens Que J'aime Pub, 286 C/ de Valencia (Ⓜ Diagonal) has dim lights, ancient velvet couches and an incurable romanticism.

El Otro, 166 C/ de Valencia (Ⓜ Hospital Clinic) is a relaxed hangout for a young, likeable crowd.

La Pedrera, 261–5 C/ de Provença (Ⓜ Diagonal) is the place to be on summer evenings, on Gaudí's remarkable roller-coaster roof terrace. Cocktails are served July to September and live music is performed.

Zsa Zsa, 156 C/ del Rosselló (FGC Provença) is for those looking for a modern, elegant place to sip a professionally made cocktail.

Sant Gervasi

Flann O'Brien's, 264 C/ de Casanova (Ⓜ Hospital Clinic) is a friendly place to hoist a pint and great for meeting fellow English-speakers.

Mas i Mas, 199 C/ Marià Cubí (FGC Muntaner) is a good place to rub elbows with uptown youth and get good tapas.

Universal Bar, 182 C/ Marià Cubí (Ⓜ Fontana) offers 'drinks and design' (only in Barcelona).

Gràcia and Tibidabo

Barcelona Brewing Co., 14 C/ de Sant Augustí (Ⓜ Diagonal) is the place for down-to-earth beer lovers: watch them make the contents of your beer glass.

Café del Sol, Plaça del Sol (Ⓜ Fontana) is the main grandstand for Gràcia's hipsters.

La Ñola, 39–41 C/ Planeta (Ⓜ Fontana), running off Plaça del Sol, is New Age and offers 'visual, olfactory, auditive, gustative and tactile experiences'.

Partycular, 61 Avinguda Tibidabo (no public transport) is a huge fun bar located in a mansion on Tibidabo, with outdoor bars in its gardens during the summer.

Zimbabwe, 13 C/ Mozart (Ⓜ Diagonal), off Plaça Rius i Taulet, plays non-stop reggae music.

Xampanyerias

Barcelona's popular *xampanyerias* serve Catalan champagne, cava, as well as the French stuff, and elegant titbits from bitter chocolate to raw oysters. Try out:

Casablanca, 6 C/ de Bonavista, in Gràcia (Ⓜ Diagonal).

La Cava del Palau, 10 C/ Verdaguer i Callís (Ⓜ Uriquinaona), near the Palau de la Música.

Languedoc Roussillon, 77 C/ de Pau Claris (Ⓜ Urquinaona), Barcelona's first oyster bar, featuring the fine bivalves from Bouzigue.

Xampú Xampany, 702 Gran Vía de les Corts Catalanes (Ⓜ Girona).

Discos and Clubs

Discos and clubs don't gear up for action until after midnight, and they stay open until 5am or later, especially on Friday and Saturday nights. Drinks and/or the cover charge generally cost a bomb.

Antilla Barcelona, 141–3 C/ d'Aragó, ✆ 93 451 21 51 (FGC Muntaner) is the hottest place for salsa in all its forms, with superb live bands.

Buenavista Club, 217 C/ del Roselló, ✆ 93 237 65 28 (Ⓜ Diagonal) plays great Cuban tunes.

Bikini, 105 C/ Déu i Mata, ✆ 93 322 08 00 (Ⓜ María Cristina), under the commercial centre of L'Illa on Avinguda Diagonal, is one of the most popular nightspots on the scene. In the 1950s, this was where young fiancés Juan Carlos and Sofia danced the cha-cha-cha.

Gràcia Llatina, 19 C/ de l'Or, ✆ 93 237 71 72 (Ⓜ Fontana) has the spiciest Cuban sounds.

KGB, 55 C/ de ca l'Alegre de Dalt, ✆ 93 210 59 06 (Ⓜ Joanic) is a classic neo-Barcelona design creation, this one with a Cold War spy theme. It's something of a traditional late-late last stand.

Lagota2, 5 Vía Laietana (Ⓜ Jaume I) is full of the Caribbean community dancing their socks off at the weekend.

Maremagnum, Port Vell (Ⓜ Drassanes) has a slew of latin bars on the first floor, including the **Mojito Bar**, ✆ 93 225 80 14, and the **Tropicana Bar**, ✆ 93 225 80 46.

Mirablau, Plaça Dr Andreu (by the funicular up to Tibidabo), ✆ 93 418 58 79, has tremendous views over the city to go with its cocktails.

Nitsaclub, in the Sala Apolo, 113 C/ Nou de la Rambla, ✆ 93 441 40 01 (Ⓜ Paral.lel) is a current favourite.

Otto Zutz, 15 C/ de Lincoln, ✆ 93 238 07 22 (FGC Gràcia) has the dress-code police guarding the door. It calls itself 'the New York-style disco where the beautiful people go'. It's a designer converted warehouse that opens at midnight, sometimes with good live music.

La Paloma, 27 C/ del Tigre, ✆ 93 301 68 97 (Ⓜ Universitat), near the Centre de Cultura Contemporani, is in an ornate 1902 dance hall and is one of the current favourites for serious dancing. Until about 1am it sports a live band playing anything from salsa to the bugaloo, and then, on Thursday and Friday nights, it becomes a hugely popular house, breakbeat and dance club.

Row, 208 C/ del Rosselló, ✆ 93 215 65 91 (Ⓜ Diagonal) is where the youthful, trendy crowd head for on Thursday nights, when it becomes a mecca for international dance DJs.

Torres d'Avila, in the Poble Espanyol, Montjuïc, ✆ 93 424 93 09 (Ⓜ Espanya), designed by Mariscal and Arribas, is where amazement at the design and bill go hand in hand (*see* p.67). In a town obsessed with design, it's not surprising to find this completely over-the-top latenight high-tech multi-space music bar.

Woman Caballero, Avinguda Marquès de l'Argenteria (Ⓜ Barceloneta) is in the basement of the Estació de França.

Gay Barcelona

To find out the latest places to go after dark, try the general **gay info hotline**, ✆ 900 601 601 (*6pm–10pm only*). Barcelona's gays and lesbians tend to share the same music bars and clubs.

Arena, 32 C/ de Balmes (Ⓜ Passeig de Gràcia) is one of the liveliest gay discos at the moment.

Café de la Calle, 11 C/ de Vic (Ⓜ Diagonal) is a favourite.

Café Dietrich, 255 C/ Consell de Cent (Ⓜ Universitat) is a very elegant spot with regular live music performances.

Free Girls, 4 C/ Marià Cubí (FGC Muntaner) is a disco-bar that is popular with a young lesbian crowd.

Punto BCN, 63 C/ Muntaner (Ⓜ Universitat) is a long-time favourite, with two floors.

La Rosa, 39 C/ Brusi (FGC Sant Gervasi) is popular with more mature women.

Salvation, 19–21 Ronda de Sant Pere (Ⓜ Urquinaona) is great fun.

Shopping

Barcelona's new slogan is 'the city of shops' and it claims to have the highest ratio to residents in Europe. It may be one of Spain's most expensive cities, but it is also her fashion and design capital, with a fantastic range of shops from the very chic to the refreshingly humble. There are roughly three main shopping areas in Barcelona: the **Barri Gòtic** for trendy streetwear, secondhand clothes, interesting junk, and antiques; the centre of the **Eixample** (around the Rambla de Catalunya and Passeig de Gràcia) for good-quality clothes and jewellery; and **Sant Gervasi** (south of Gràcia and west of Avinguda Diagonal) for designer boutiques.

Serious shoppers hit Barcelona in January, when everything's on sale; look out for the word '*rebaixes*' (or '*rebajas*' in Castilian). Most shops are *open Mon–Fri 10–2 and 4.30–8, Sat 10–2*, and there are still a traditional few that close in August.

Antiques and Bric-a-brac

There are dozens of tiny antique shops tucked in the maze of narrow sidestreets around the cathedral, particularly along Carrer Palla.

L'Arca de l'Àvia, 20 C/ de Banys Nous (Ⓜ Jaume I) has an exquisite, if expensive, selection of beautifully cared-for antique fabrics, clothes and bags.

Boulevard dels Antiquaris, 55 Passeig de Gràcia (Ⓜ Passeig de Gràcia) has plenty of overpriced antiques and bric-a-brac in its arcades.

Casa Usher, 533 C/ d'Aragó (Ⓜ Glòries i Clot) is the place for kitschy bric-a-brac, with a collection of film posters, lamps and other objects carefully resuscitated from the 50s, 60s and 70s.

Gothsland Galeria d'Art, 33 C/ Consell de Cent (Ⓜ Espanya) has to be the star attraction, specializing in Catalan Modernista and Noucentista arts and decoration. It has sculptures by, among others, Gargallo and Marés, as well as a fine selection of furniture and decorative pieces.

Urbana, 13 C/ Seneca (Ⓜ Diagonal) restores old furniture, much of it prewar. They have another branch at 258 C/ de Corsega which restores old fireplaces, balustrades and architectural fittings.

Books and Music

Besides chains like **FNAC** (there's a large branch in the Triangle mall on Plaça de Catalunya), which have some titles in English, you can find English-language newspapers and magazines in most of the kiosks along the Ramblas. FNAC also stocks mainstream music.

Altair, 69 C/ de Balmes (🚇 Passeig de Gràcia) stocks travel books.

BCN, 118 C/ de Roger de Llúria (🚇 Passeig de Gràcia) has TEFL texts, teaching aids and dictionaries, as well as a selection of paperbacks.

The Book Store, 13 C/ de la Granja (🚇 Fontana), in Gràcia, has secondhand books and a video section, as well as books in English.

La Casa, 6 Plaça Vicenç Martorell (🚇 Catalunya) is good for dance music.

Ethnomusic, 6 Carrer del Bonsuccés (🚇 Catalunya) is great for world music, including flamenco.

Llibreria Mallorca, 86 Rambla de Catalunya (🚇 Passeig de Gràcia) has an extensive selection of magazines and newspapers in English, as well as a travel section in English.

Llibreria Quera, 2 C/ de Petritxol (🚇 Liceu) specializes in maps and hiking guides.

Department Stores and Malls

In most cities these wouldn't be worth a mention, but Spain has some of the best chain stores around (Camper for shoes and Zara and Mango for clothes, to name just a few). The department stores are also good stand-bys for gifts and souvenirs.

Centre Commercial Barcelona Glòries 1, Plaça de les Glòries Catalanes (🚇 Glòries) has all the usual shops, plus restaurants, bars and a cinema.

El Corte Inglés, Plaça de Catalunya (🚇 Catalunya) is a huge upmarket department store.

L'Illa, 555–9 Avinguda Diagonal (🚇 María Cristina), between C/ Numància and C/ Entença, is the giant in the mall stakes, with branches of all the usual chain favourites, plus some swanky designer shops, as well as branches of El Corte Inglés and Marks & Spencer.

Maremagnum, Port Vell (🚇 Barceloneta/Drassanes) is a glassy, modern shopping mall complete with restaurants, discos and bars, and a number of shops selling souvenirs and gift items, but little else.

Marks & Spencer, Plaça de Catalunya (🚇 Catalunya) sell their products cheaper here than in the UK.

El Triangle, Plaça de Catalunya (🚇 Catalunya) is a new, uninspiring shopping centre redeemed by its enormous **FNAC**, with a massive range of books (some in English) and CDs. FNAC also books concert and performance tickets. Downstairs is the world's largest perfume emporium, **Sephora**, down the escalator through a bewildering forest of zebra-print trees. They have an exhaustive range of perfume and cosmetics at good prices.

Design and Household Goods

Galeries Vinçon, 96 Passeig de Gràcia (🚇 Diagonal) is one of Spain's top names in design and furniture, and is right next to La Pedrera; their annexe, **Tinc-Çon**, 246 C/ del Rosseló (🚇 Diagonal) has the finest designer linen and beds.

Modernista BD Ediciones de Diseño, 291 C/ Mallorca (Ⓜ Diagonal) has the best in old and new furniture designs in Domènech's Casa Thomas.

Insolit, 353 Avda Diagonal (Ⓜ Diagonal) has the surreal touch.

Neocerámica, 43 C/ Mandri (FGC La Bonanova) has the widest range of wall and floor tiles.

Riera, 91 Passeig de Gràcia (Ⓜ Passeig de Gràcia), and **Diagonal 421** (Ⓜ Diagonal) have the most stylish collection of (expensive) tableware from around the world.

Zeta, 22 C/ de Avinyó (Ⓜ Jaume I/Liceu) has some of the most innovative home-grown designs around.

Punto Luz, 146 Carrer de Pau Claris (Ⓜ Diagonal) is the place to go for extravagant light fittings.

Lulaky, 333 Carrer Consell de Cent (Ⓜ Girona) is the place for quirky modern decorative objects and kitchen utensils, designed for professionals and individuals.

Pilma, 403 Avda Diagonal (Ⓜ Diagonal) has the latest furniture designs and eminently desirable decorative objects for the home.

MDM, 405 bis Avda Diagonal (Ⓜ Diagonal) is one of the city's meccas for interior design, with an astonishing array of furnishings, including garden furniture, and gifts.

Fashion

The centre of the Eixample (around Rambla de Catalunya and Passeig de Gràcia) is full of designer clothes and jewellery. C/ Avinyó (Ⓜ Jaume I/Liceu) is home to a number of young designers with an edge. The other popular street for urban trendies is C/ Riera Baixa (Ⓜ Liceu/Sant Antoni) over in El Raval, with a mixture of music shops and vintage fashion.

Adolfo Dominguez, 32 Passeig de Gràcia (Ⓜ Passeig de Gràcia) is a Galician designer. He has been creating classic, well-tailored clothes for men and women for almost two decades.

Antonio Miró, 349 C/ Consell de Cent (Ⓜ Passeig de Gràcia) is good for Catalan designers, with super-chic clothes and beautiful accessories for men and women.

Atalanta Manufactura, 10 Passeig del Born (Ⓜ Jaume I) produces exquisite handpainted silk scarves while you watch.

Bad Habits, 261 C/ de Valencia (Ⓜ Diagonal) has cool, comfortable clothes with a confident twist, and a beautiful selection of shoes.

Camper, 249 C/ de València (Ⓜ Diagonal) is great for fashionable shoes at reasonable prices. There are branches elsewhere, including in the Triangle shopping mall (*see* 'Department Stores and Shopping Malls' above).

DKNY, 618 Avinguda Diagonal (Ⓜ Hospital Clinic) has Donna Karan's sleek streetwear line.

Emporio Armani, 490 Avinguda Diagonal (Ⓜ Hospital Clinic) stocks the usual gear.

Filis M. Sala, 3 C/ del Call (Ⓜ Liceu) is hard to beat for rhinestone tiaras and feather boas.

Gucci, 415 Avda Diagonal (Ⓜ Diagonal) sell their stylish and expensive clothes and accessories.

Jean-Pierre Bua, 469 Avinguda Diagonal (Ⓜ Diagonal) is a mecca for the truly fashion-conscious, with exclusive designs from Jean-Paul Gaultier, Vivienne Westwood, Yohji Yamamoto and others.

Josep Font, 106 Passeig de Gràcia (Ⓜ Diagonal) has sharp, spare designs in beautiful fabrics at his minimalist store.

Loewe, 35 Passeig de Gràcia (Ⓜ Passeig de Gràcia) is among the smartest international names, with luxurious leather clothes and shoes for men and women.

Loft, 22 C/ de Avinyó (Ⓜ Jaume I/Liceu) is good for clubwear and has labels such as Anglofilia, Gaultier Jeans and Box Office.

Mango, 65 Passeig de Gràcia (Ⓜ Passeig de Gràcia), with other branches, is a classic fashion chain.

Mathilde Peterschen, 7 C/ Vidrieria (Ⓜ Jaume I), on the southern continuation of C/ Montcada, has designer fashion for women, with a fantastic range of glamorous accessories, including beautiful brightly coloured bags.

El Mercadillo, 17 C/ de Portaferrisa (Ⓜ Liceu) is one of two small shopping malls stuffed with young fashion. It's grungier than its cooler neighbour, the **Gralla Hall**, one of the city's best spots for urbanwear, with units like Fantasy Shop, which has a good selection of designers including Dolce and Gabanna and Moschino.

Mies & Felj, 5 C/ Riera Baixa (Ⓜ Liceu/ Sant Antoni) has second-hand Levi's, and a delicious selection of 60s and 70s cocktail dresses.

Purificacion García, 4 Avinguda de Pau Casals (Ⓜ Hospital Clinic) offers sleek urban fashion for women.

So_Da, 24 C/ de Avinyó (Ⓜ Jaume I/ Liceu) is a café, fashion and music shop, with a sushi bar at weekends.

Toko, 14 C/ Llibreteria (Ⓜ Jaume I) is run by a charming Scottish lady, with pretty and inexpensive clothes mainly in natural fabrics and a good range of costume jewellery.

Tribu, 12 C/ de Avinyó (Ⓜ Jaume I/Liceu) is a hyper-trendy place for international and local designs in a very funky setting.

Trip, 9–11 C/ del Duc de la Victòria (Ⓜ Catalunya/Liceu) is a favourite with skateboarders.

Zara, 245 C/ de Valencia (Ⓜ Passeig de Gràcia), with other branches, has become a worldwide favourite for its funky clothes at affordable prices—even less expensive here than at home.

Zsu Zsa, 50 C/ de Avinyó (Ⓜ Jaume I/ Liceu) has sparky and original collections for young women.

Markets

Avinguda Pau Casals (Ⓜ Hospital Clinic) has a crafts market on the first Sunday of the month.

Els Encants, Plaça de les Glòries Catalanes (Ⓜ Glòries) is a fabulous, rambling flea market held every Mon, Wed, Fri and Sat from 9am to 8pm, although there's more choice in the morning. Saturdays tend to be jammed.

Mercat Abaceria Central, C/ Puigmarti (Ⓜ Diagonal) is a food market. Open Mon–Sat 8–3 and 5–8.

Mercat de la Boqueria (*see* p.80), on the Ramblas, is the most famous food market, though it is rather filled with tourists. Open Mon–Sat 8–3 and 5–8.

Mercat Concepcio, on the corner of C/ d'Aragó and C/ de Girona (Ⓜ Passeig de Gràcia), is a food market. Open Mon–Sat 8–3 and 5–8.

Mercat de la Llibertat, in Gràcia (Ⓜ Fontana), is in a lovely Modernista building. Open Mon–Sat 8–3 and 5–8.

Mercat de Sant Antoni, C/ del Comte d'Urgell (Ⓜ Sant Antoni) is a Sunday institution, with coins and secondhand books.

Moll de les Drassanes (Ⓜ Drassanes) has antiques and bric-a-brac on Saturdays and Sundays.

Plaça del Pi (Ⓜ Liceu) sees a lot of market action: there is an antiques market on Thursdays, art in the adjoining Plaça Sant Josep Oriol at weekends, and a monthly honey market on the first Friday and Saturday of the month.

Plaça Reial (Ⓜ Liceu) has a stamp and coin market on Sundays.

Plaça de la Seu, in front of the Cathedral (Ⓜ Jaume I), has antiques and bric-a-brac on Thursdays.

Rambla de Santa Monica (Ⓜ Drassanes) has a crafts market on Saturday and Sunday afternoons.

Museum Shops

Botiga Textil, 12 C/ Montcada (Ⓜ Jaume I), part of the Museu Téxtil i de la Indumentària, has some attractive modern silver jewellery along with well-priced throws and textiles by young designers.

Centre de Cultura Contemporani, 5 C/ Montalegre (Ⓜ Catalunya) has a good selection of books on all kinds of urban topics.

Museu d'Art Contemporani, Plaça dels Àngels (Ⓜ Catalunya) has an excellent range of books and gifts.

Museu d'Història de Catalunya, 3 Plaça Pau Vila (Ⓜ Barceloneta) has one of the nicest, with an unusual range of gifts (crockery, picture frames, vases and a delightfully kooky collection of bags and jewellery).

Palau de la Música Catalana has a very pretty gift shop (Les Muses del Palau, on Plaça de Lluis Millet, just outside the museum), with a range of ceramics and frou-frous with Modernista designs.

Souvenirs and Gifts

Almacenes del Pilar, 43 C/ de la Boqueria (Ⓜ Liceu) specializes in Spanish national costumes from all over the country.

Ceramiques Pahissa, 18–20 C/ Llibreteria (Ⓜ Jaume I) is the place to pick up a ceramic Catalan Christmas crapper (*cagoner*; *see* p.62), in a wide variety of personas and professions from fireman to nun.

El Corte Inglés, Plaça de Catalunya (Ⓜ Catalunya) has a delightfully tacky souvenir department.

La Cubana, 26 C/ de la Boqueria (Ⓜ Liceu) is the home of mantillas, shawls, gloves and fans. It has been in business for almost two centuries.

Dos i Una, 275 C/ del Rosselò (Ⓜ Diagonal) has upmarket designer gifts from household items to postcards and T-shirts.

Grafiques El Tinell, 1 C/ Freneria (Ⓜ Jaume I), just south of the cathedral, has exquisite old-fashioned handmade paper products, including stationery and engraved books.

Grau, C/ Freneria (Ⓜ Jaume I) sells exquisite red roses made of glass, and other fragile beauties.

Kitsch, 10 Plaçeta de Montcada (Ⓜ Jaume I) sells quirky papier mâché creatures, with a tall model of a flamenco dancer (La Rócio) with a steely eye at the entrance.

Toys and Magic

Casa Palau, 34 C/ de Pelai (Ⓜ Catalunya) is the place for classic toys like Scalectrix and train sets.

Festival, 127 C/ Gran de Gràcia (Ⓜ Fontana) sells all kinds of child-orientated toys.

El Ingenio, 6 C/ d'En Rauric (Ⓜ Liceu) has a bewildering range of fancy dress costumes, masks, decorations, puppets, tricks and jokes.

El Rei de la Màgia, 11 C/ de la Princesa (Ⓜ Jaume I) has a dusty Modernista façade and a hushed, magical world of pure theatre within.

Wine and Gastronomy

La Casa del Bacalão, 8 C/ del Comtal (Ⓜ Catalunya) stocks an excellent variety of salted cod (*bacalao*). The staff are quite happy to let you in on their recipe secrets.

Celler de Gelida, 65 C/ de Vallespir (Ⓜ Plaça del Centre) has been in the same family for four generations and has over 3,500 kinds of wine and liqueurs.

La Pineda, 16 C/ del Pi (Ⓜ Liceu) is a delightful old-fashioned delicatessen in the heart of the Barri Gòtic.

Vina Viniteca, 7–9 C/ dels Agullers (Ⓜ Jaume I) has an extensive cellar drawn from all over Spain, and informed, helpful staff.

Andrews, Colman, *Catalan Cuisine* (Grub Street, London, 1998). Food is an important part of Catalan identity, and this classic on the subject sheds light and humour to go with its delicious and sometimes surprising recipes.

Bassegoda Nonell, Joan, *Antonio Gaudí: Master Architect* (Abbeville, 2000). A new book by the director of the Catedra Gaudí, with concise text on Gaudí's life, vision and influences, accompanied by beautiful colour photos by Melba Levick.

Bergos Masso, Joan and Marc Llimargas, *Gaudí: The Man and His Work* (Bulfinch, 1999). Bergos worked with Gaudí for a decade, and wrote this biography of the architect in Catalan in 1954. Now translated into English, with beautiful illustrations.

Botey, Josep, *Inside Barcelona* (Phaidon, London, 1998). A coffee-table book with lush photos of many of the city's otherwise inaccessible interiors by Peter Aprahamian.

Burns, Jimmy, *Barça: A People's Passion* (Trafalgar Square, 2000). A complete history of the local obsession.

Carandell, Josep M., *Park Güell: Gaudí's Utopia* (Triangle Postals, Menorca, 1998; readily available in Barcelona). Just what were Barcelona's richest man and greatest architect up to in the Park Güell? Carandell lets the cat out of the bag.

Conversi, Daniele, *The Basques, the Catalans and Spain: Alternative Routes to Nationalist Mobilisation* (Hurst, London, 1997). On the dry and scholarly side, but a fascinating account of how Catalan nationalists evolved their pragmatic and generous solution to embrace everyone in Barcelona.

Fernández-Armesto, Felipe, *Barcelona: A Thousand Years of the City's Past* (out of print, 1991). An excellent thematic history of the city, by a non-Catalan historian, but impossible to find outside a good library.

García Espuche, Albert, *The Quadrat d'Or* (Ajuntament de Barcelona). Building-by-building account of Barcelona's Modernista treasures.

González, Antoni and Raquel Lacuesta, *Barcelona Architecture Guide 1929–2000* (Gustavo Gili, Barcelona, 1999). What happened after the Modernistas isn't always pretty, but it's nearly all here, illustrated with black and white photos.

Further Reading

Güell, Xavier, *Gaudí Guide* (Gustavo Gili, Barcelona, 1991). A good, no-nonsense and instructively illustrated account of Gaudí's work.

Hargreaves, John, *Freedom for Catalonia? Catalan Nationalism, Spanish Identity and the Barcelona Olympic Games* (Cambridge University Press, 2000). Detailed account of the complex nationalist politics behind the 1992 Olympics, and the very delicate manoeuvres that satisfied both Spain and Catalunya's aspirations for the games.

Hughes, Robert, *Barcelona* (Harvill, London, 1992). The best and certainly the fattest of the spate of books about the city that came out in 1992, a beautifully written, witty and wide-ranging history of the city from the beginning to the Modernistas and Gaudí.

Martrell, Joanot, *Tirant lo Blanc*, trans. by David H. Rosenthal (John Hopkins University Press, reprinted 1996). Written in Catalan in the late 1400s, this was the first European novel in prose, bawdily satirizing the conventions of courtly love. It was the chief inspiration for *Don Quixote*.

Mendoza, Eduardo, *City of Marvels* (out of print, 1989). A well-researched historical novel starring a French adventurer, an idealistic journalist, an arms dealer, a gypsy, a begger and many many more, with Barcelona between the World's Fairs of 1888 and 1929 as a background. His later Barcelona novels translated into English, *The Year of the Flood* and *The Truth About the Savolta Case*, are also sadly out of print; his non-fiction *Barcelona Modernista*, written with his sister Cristina Mendoza, is one of the finest guides to the subject and you may just find a copy in Barcelona.

Montalbán, Manuel Vázquez, *Barcelonas* (Verso, London, 1992). A quirky, personal and cynical overview of the city on the eve of the Olympics by the author of a series of excellent thrillers that take place in Barcelona, starring the foodie detective Pepe Carvalho. Several of these have been translated into English: *Southern Seas* (Pluto, London, 1986), *The Angst-Ridden Executive* and *An Olympic Death*.

Orwell, George, *Homage to Catalonia* (Harcourt Brace, 1987). An account of Orwell's first-hand participation in the Civil War, and the bewildering war within the war in Barcelona. A book that has inspired more than one reader to take up a career in journalism, and helps to explain why foreigners are more interested in the Civil War than today's Spaniards, who are more interested in forgetting.

Penrose, Roland, *Miró* (Thames & Hudson, London, 1985). A lavishly illustrated account of the life and work of Barcelona's greatest modern painter.

Permanyer, Lluis, *Barcelona: Architectural Details and Delights* (Harry N. Abrams, 1993). A lavish coffee-table book, with photos by Melba Levick. The same two collaborated to produce *Barcelona Art Nouveau* (Rizzoli

Bookstore, 1999), with beautiful photos of the exteriors and interiors of 46 Modernista landmarks.

Pomés Leiz, Juliet and Ricardo Feriche, *Barcelona Design Guide* (Gustavo Gili, Barcelona, 1999). Not only where to find the city's designers and architects, but a rating of the city's restaurants, hotels and bars, purely by their design qualities. Only in Barcelona.

Richardson, John, *A Life of Picasso, Volume I 1881–1906* (Jonathon Cape, London, 1991). A beautifully illustrated account of Picasso's Barcelona years—one of the very best artist biographies.

Rodoreda, Mercè, *The Time of the Doves,* the translation of *La Plaça del Diamant* (trans. David Rosenthal, Greywolf, 1986). Bittersweet story about the chains of the past, named after the square in Gràcia. This is the most widely read Catalan novel.

Tóibín, Colm, *Homage to Barcelona* (Simon & Schuster, London, 1991). An Irish journalist and long-time resident evokes the city in the 1970s and 80s, its history and art. This is a good introduction to Barcelona.

Castellano, or Castilian, as Spanish is properly called, was the first modern language to have a grammar written for it. When a copy was presented to Queen Isabel in 1492, she understandably asked what it was for. 'Your majesty', replied a perceptive bishop, 'language is the perfect instrument of empire'.

It's quite easy to pick up a working knowledge of Spanish; but Spaniards speak colloquially and fast. Expressing yourself may prove a little easier than understanding the replies. If you already speak Spanish, note that the Spaniards increasingly use the familiar tú instead of usted when addressing even complete strangers.

Pronunciation: Castellano

Vowels

a	short *a* as in 'pat'	u	silent after *q* and gue- and gui-; otherwise long *u* as in 'flute'
e	short *e* as in 'set'		
i	as *e* in 'be'	ü	*w* sound, as in 'dwell'
o	between long *o* of 'note' and short *o* of 'hot'	y	at end of word or meaning *and*, as **i**

Consonants

c	before the vowels *i* and *e*, pronounced as *th;* cinco is *theenco*
d	often becomes *th*, or is almost silent, at end of word; Madrid is *Madree*
g	before *i* or *e*, pronounced as **j**
h	silent
j	the *ch* in loch—a guttural, throat-clearing *h*
ll	like English *y*
ñ	*ny* as in canyon
q	*k*
r	usually rolled at the beginning of a word; always when rr
v	often pronounced as *b*
z	*th*, like a soft *c*, but *s* in parts of Andalucía

Language

Everyone in Barcelona speaks Spanish, but increasingly they prefer to express themselves in *Català*, or Catalan, a language closely related to Provençal or Occitan. Although Barcelona is officially bilingual, you'll find street signs and shops signs, and often museum descriptions exclusively in Catalan. You'll be able to decipher many of the signs if you can read French or Spanish—but just try to understand spoken *Català*, at least until you get the hang of the pronunciation.

Pronunciation: Catalan

You'll have to listen closely; Catalan, like French, but unlike Castellano, elides words together.

Vowels

a	short as in pat; *à* like *ah*	**ig**	tch at the end of a word
e	usually short *e* as in 'set'	**o**	short *o* of 'hot'; at end of a word, like 'to'
i	as *e* in 'be'	**u**	a bit like oo as in look

Consonants

c	soft before *i* and *e*; **ç** like s
g	before *i* or *e*, pronounced as a hard *sh;* **tg** like *dg* in budge
h	silent
j	as the French, *jambon*
ll	like the *lli* in million; pronounced the unique Catalan **l.l** as a single L
ny	like the Castellano *ñ, makes* a twang at the end of a word as in *seny*
q	*k,* but like *quick* before an *a* or *o*
r	rolled at the beginning of a word; always when **rr**; silent at the end of a word
x	usually soft sh as in shop; **tx** is like tch as match
z	like the English *zone*

Accommodation

English	Castilian	Catalan
Do you have a room	*¿Tiene una habitación?*	*Té alguna habitació?*
...for one person?	*...para una persona?*	*...per a una persona?*
...with 2 beds	*...con dos camas*	*...amb dos llits*
...with double bed	*...con una cama matrimonial*	*...amb llit per dues persones*
...with a shower/bath	*...con ducha/baño*	*...amb dutxa/bany*
...for one night/one week	*...para una noche/una semana*	*...per una nit/una setmana*
Do you have anything cheaper?	*¿Tiene algo más barato?*	*En té de més bon preu?*

Time

English	Castilian	Catalan
At what time..?	¿A qué hora ..?	A quina hora...?
When?	¿Cuando?	Quan?
At 2 o'clock	A las dos	A les dues
... half past 2	...las dos y media	...a les dues i mitja
... a quarter past 2	...las dos y cuarto	...a un quart de tres
... a quarter to 3	...las tres menos cuarto	...a tres quarts de tres
month/week/day	mes/semana/día	el mes/la setmana/el día
morning/afternoon/evening	mañana/tarde/ noche	el matí/la tarda/la nit
today	hoy	avui
yesterday	ayer	ahir
now/later	ahora	ara
later	más tarde	mès tard
tomorrow	mañana	demà

Days and Months

English	Castilian	Catalan
Monday	lunes	dilluns
Tuesday	martes	dimarts
Wednesday	miércoles	dimecres
Thursday	jueves	dijous
Friday	viernes	divendres
Saturday/Sunday	sábado/domingo	dissabte/diumenge
January	enero	gener
February	febrero	febrer
March	marzo	març
April	abril	abril
May	mayo	maig
June	junio	juny
July	julio	juliol
August	agosto	agost
September	septiembre	setembre
October	octubre	octobre
November	noviembre	novembre
December	diciembre	desembre

Numbers

	Castilian	Catalan		Castilian	Catalan
1	uno	un (a)	7	siete	set
2	dos	dos/dues	8	ocho	vuit
3	tres	tres	9	nueve	nou
4	cuatro	quatre	10	diez	deu
5	cinco	cinc	11	once	onze
6	seis	sis	12	doce	dotze

Numbers (*cont'd*)

	Castilian	Catalan		Castilian	Catalan
13	*trece*	*tretze*	50	*cincuenta*	*cinquanta*
14	*catorce*	*catorze*	60	*sesenta*	*seixanta*
15	*quince*	*quinze*	70	*setenta*	*setanta*
16	*dieciseis*	*setze*	80	*ochenta*	*vuitanta*
17	*diecisiete*	*disset*	90	*noventa*	*novanta*
18	*dieciocho*	*divuit*	100	*cien*	*cent*
19	*diecinueve*	*dinou*	101	*cento uno*	*cent un*
20	*veinte*	*vint*	200	*doscientos*	*dos-cents*
21	*veintiuno*	*vint-i-un*	500	*quinientos*	*cinc cents*
30	*treinta*	*trenta*	1000	*mil*	*mil*
40	*cuarenta*	*quaranta*			

Common Expressions

English	Castilian	Catalan
hello/goodbye	*hola/adios*	*hola/adéu*
please	*por favor*	*si us plau*
thank you (very much)	*muchas gracias*	*(moltes)gràcies*
you're welcome	*de nada*	*de res*
good morning	*buenos días*	*bon dia*
good afternoon	*buenos tardes*	*bona tarda*
good night	*buenos noches*	*bona nit*
What's your name?	*¿Cómo se llama?*	*Com se diu?*
Do you speak English?	*¿Habla inglès?*	*Parla anglés?*
I don't speak Spanish/Catalan	*No hablo Castellano/Catàlan*	*No parlo Castellano/Català*
I don't understand	*No entiendo*	*No entenc*
How do you say that	*¿Me lo puede decir en catalàn?'*	*Com es diu aix òen català?'*
excuse me/sorry	*perdón*	*perdoni/disculpi*
excuse me (listen!)	*oiga!*	*escolti*
Mr/Mrs/Miss	*Señor/Señora/Señorita*	*Senyor/Senyora/Senyoreta*
very good	*muy bueno*	*molt bé*
fine/ok	*vale*	*val/d'acord*
who?	*¿quién?*	*qui?*
what?	*¿qué?*	*qué?*
where?	*¿donde?*	*on?*
when?	*¿cuando?*	*quan?*
how?	*¿cómo?*	*com?*
why?	*¿porqué?*	*perqué?*
congratulations	*felicidades*	*felicitats*

Directions

English	Castilian	Catalan
How can I get to... ?	*¿Por donde se va a...?*	*Per anar a...?*
Where is... ?	*¿Dónde está...?*	*On és...?*
What time does it leave (arrive)?	*¿Sale (llega) a qué hora?*	*A quina hora surt (arriba)?*

English	Castilian	Catalan
From where does it leave?	¿De dónde sale?	De on surt?
I'd like a (return) ticket to...	Quisiera un billete (de ida y vuelta) para...	Voldria un bitllet (d'anar i tornar) a...
here/there	aquí/allí	aquí/allí
near/far	cerca/lejos	a prop/lluny
left	izquierda	esquerra
right	derecha	dreta
straight on	todo recto	tot recte
towards	hacia	cap a
corner	esquina	cantonada

Shopping and Sightseeing

English	Castilian	Catalan
I would like...	Quisiera...	Voldria...
Where is...?	¿Dónde está...?	On és...?'
Is there (any)...?	¿Hay	hi ha...? n'h'i ha de...?
How much is it?	¿Cuánto vale ?	Quant es?
I like/I don't like	Me gusta.../No me gusta...	m'agrada/no m'agrada
open/closed	abierto/ cerrado	obert/tancat
cheap/expensive	barato/caro	barat(a)/car(a)
entrance/exit	entrada/salida	entrada/sortida
good/bad	bueno(a)/malo(a)	bo(na)/dolent(a)
more/less	mas/menos	més/menys
with/without	con/sin	amb/sense
price	precio	preu
change/exchange	cambio	canvi
free	gratuito	gratuit
church/market/pharmacy	iglesia/mercado/farmacía	eglésia/mercat/farmacía
post office	correos	correus
toilet/toilets	servicios/aseos	lavabos/els serveis
men	señores/hombres/caballeros	Homes
women	señoras/damas	Dones

Eating Out

English	Castilian	Catalan
breakfast/lunch/dinner	desayuna/almuerzo/cena	esmorzar/dinar/sopar
fork/knife/spoon	tenedor/cuchillo/cuchara	forquilla/ganivet/cullera
Do you have a table?	¿Tiene una mesa?	Té una taula?
set meal	menú del día	menú del dia
bill/check	la cuenta	el compte/la nota

Pescados

Castilian

Castilian		
almejas		
anchoas		
anguilas		
atún		
bacalao		
boquerones		
bogavante		
bonito		
calamares		
cangrejo (de río)		
gambas		
langosta		
langostinos		
lenguado		
lubina		
mariscos		
mejillones		
merluza		
mero		
navajas		
ostras		
percebes		
pescadilla		
pez espada		
platija		
pulpo		
rape		
salmón (ahumada)		
salmonete		
trucha		
vieiras		
zarzuela		

Peix

Catalan

Fish

English

Castilian	Catalan	English
almejas	cloïsses	clams
anchoas	anxoves	anchovies
anguilas	anguiles	eels
atún	tonyina	tuna
bacalao	bacallà	salt cod
boquerones	seitons	fresh anchovies
bogavante	llamàntol	lobster
bonito	bonítol	tuna
calamares	calamars	squid
cangrejo (de río)	cranc (de riu)	crab (crayfish)
gambas	gambes	prawns
langosta	llagosta	lobster
langostinos	llanostins	giant prawns
lenguado	llenguado	sole
lubina	llobarro	sea bass
mariscos	mariscos	shellfish
mejillones	musclos	mussels
merluza	lluç	hake
mero	mero	perch
navajas	navalles	razor-clams
ostras	ostres	oysters
percebes	percebes	barnacles
pescadilla	llucet	whiting
pez espada	peix espasa	swordfish
platija	palaia	plaice
pulpo	pop	octopus
rape	rap	monkfish
salmón (ahumada)	salmó (fumat)	salmon (smoked)
salmonete	moll/roger	mullet
trucha	truita	trout
vieiras	vieires	scallops
zarzuela	sarsuela	fish stew

Carnes y Aves

Carn i Aviram

Meat and Fowl

Castilian	Catalan	English
albóndigas	mandonguilles	meatballs
asado	rostit/escalivat	roast
buey	bou	beef
cabrito	cabrit	kid
callos	tripa	tripe
cerdo	porc	pork
chorizo	xoriço	spiced sausage
chuletas	llonza/costella	chops
cochinillo	garrí/porcell	sucking pig
conejo	conill	rabbit

Castilian	Catalan	English
cordero	*be/xai/corder*	**lamb**
faisán	*faisà*	**pheasant**
fiambres	*carn freda*	**cold meats**
fricandó	*fricandó*	**fricasse**
hígado	*fetge*	**liver**
jabalí	*porc senglar*	**wild boar**
jamón de York	*pernil de York*	**baked ham**
jamón serrano	*jamón serrà*	**cured ham**
lengua	*llengua*	**tongue**
liebre	*llebre*	**hare**
lomo	*llom*	**pork loin**
morcilla	*botifarró*	**blood sausage**
parrillada	*graellada*	**mixed grill**
pato	*ànec*	**duck**
pavo	*fall dindi*	**turkey**
perdiz	*perdiu*	**partridge**
pinchitos	*broqueta*	**spicy kebabs**
pollo	*pollastre*	**chicken**
rabo de toro	*cua de toro*	**bull's tail**
salchicha	*salsitxa*	**sausage**
salchichón	*llomganissa*	**salami**
solomillo	*filet*	**sirloin**
ternera	*vedella*	**veal**

Note: *potajes, cocidos, guisados (guisats) estofados (estofats) fabadas* and *cazuelas* are various kinds of stew and casseroles.

Verduras y Legumbres *Verduras i Llegumes* Vegetables

Castilian	Catalan	English
alcachofas	*carxofes/escarxofes*	**artichokes**
ajo	*all*	**garlic**
acietunas	*olives*	**olives**
berenjena	*albergínies*	**aubergine (eggplant)**
cebolla	*ceba*	**onion**
champiñones	*xampinyons*	**button mushrooms**
col	*col*	**cabbage**
coliflor	*col-i-flor*	**cauliflower**
endibias	*endívies*	**endives**
espárragos	*espàrrecs*	**asparagus**
espinacas	*espinacs*	**spinach**
garbanzos	*cigrons*	**chickpeas**
guisantes	*pèsols*	**peas**
judías (verdes)	*mongetes (tendres)*	**beans (French)**
lechuga	*enciam*	**lettuce**
lentejas	*llenties*	**lentils**
patatas (fritas/salteadas)	*patates (fregides/saltat)*	**potatoes (fried/sautéed)**
pepino	*concombre*	**cucumber**

Verduras y Legumbres

Castilian

puerros
remolacha
setas
tomates
zanahorias

Verduras i Llegumes

Catalan

porros
remolatxa /bleda-rave
bolets
omàquets
pastanagas

Vegetables

English

leeks
beetroot (beet)
wild mushrooms
tomatoes
carrots

Postres

Castilian

arroz con leche
bizcocho
crema catalana
pastel/torta
galletas
helados
pajama
pasteles
queso
requesón (con miel)
turron
yogurt

Dolços

Catalan

arròs amb llet
bescuit
crema cremada
pastís/tarta
galetes
gelats
pijama
pastissos
formatges
mel i mató
turron
iogurt

Desserts

English

rice pudding
cake
creme caramel
pie/tart
biscuits (cookies)
ice creams
flan with ice cream
pastries
cheese
cottage cheese (with honey)
almond nougat
yogurt

Micellaneous

English	Castilian	Catalan
water (mineral/sparkling/still)	*agua mineral/con gas/sin gas*	*aigua mineral/amb gas/sense*
wine (red, white)	*vino (tinto,blanco)*	*vi (negre,blanc)*
beer	*cerveza*	*cervesa*
milk	*leche*	*llet*
juice	*zumo*	*suc*
bread/butter	*pan/mantequilla*	*pa/mantega*
eggs	*huevos*	*ous*
omelette	*tortilla*	*truita*
rice	*arroz*	*arròs*
sugar	*azucar*	*sucre*
oil/vinegar	*aceite/vinagre*	*oli/vinagre*
salt/pepper	*sal/pimienta*	*sal/pebre*
salad	*ensalada*	*amanida*

Main page references are in **bold**; page numbers of maps are in *italic*

Index

Also Available from Cadogan Guides...

Country Guides

Antarctica
Central Asia
China: The Silk Routes
France: Southwest France;
  Dordogne, Lot & Bordeaux
France: Southwest France;
  Gascony & the Pyrenees
France: Brittany
France: The Loire
France: The South of France
France: Provence
France: Côte d'Azur
Germany: Bavaria
Greece: The Peloponnese
Holland
Holland: Amsterdam & the Randstad
India
India: South India
India: Goa
Ireland
Ireland: Southwest Ireland
Ireland: Northern Ireland
Italy
Italy: The Bay of Naples and Southern Italy
Italy: Bologna and Emilia Romagna
Italy: Italian Riviera
Italy: Lombardy, Milan and the Italian Lakes
Italy: Rome and the Heart of Italy
Italy: Sardinia
Italy: Tuscany, Umbria and the Marches
Italy: Tuscany
Italy: Umbria
Italy: Venetia and the Dolomites
Japan
Morocco
Portugal
Portugal: The Algarve
Scotland
Scotland: Highlands and Islands
South Africa, Swaziland and Lesotho
Spain
Spain: Southern Spain
Spain: Northern Spain
Syria & Lebanon
Tunisia
Turkey
Yucatán and Southern Mexico
Zimbabwe, Botswana and Namibia

City Guides

Amsterdam
Barcelona
Brussels, Bruges, Ghent & Antwerp
Bruges
Edinburgh
Egypt: Three Cities—Cairo, Luxor, Aswan
Florence, Siena, Pisa & Lucca
Italy: Three Cities—Rome, Florence, Venice
Italy: Three Cities—Venice, Padua, Verona
Italy: Three Cities—Rome, Naples, Sorrento
Italy: Three Cities—Rome, Padua, Assisi
Japan: Three Cities—Tokyo, Kyoto and
  Ancient Nara
Morocco: Three Cities—Marrakesh, Fez, Rabat
Spain: Three Cities—Granada, Seville, Cordoba
Spain: Three Cities—Madrid, Barcelona, Seville
London
London–Amsterdam
London–Edinburgh
London–Paris
London–Brussels
Madrid
Manhattan
Moscow & St Petersburg
Paris
Prague
Rome
St Petersburg
Venice

Island Guides

Caribbean and Bahamas
Corfu & the Ionian Islands
Crete
Greek Islands
Greek Islands By Air
Jamaica & the Caymans
Madeira & Porto Santo
Malta
Mykonos, Santorini & the Cyclades
Rhodes & the Dodecanese
Sardinia
Sicily

Plus...

Bugs, Bites & Bowels
London Markets
Take the Kids Travelling
Take the Kids London
Take the Kids Paris and Disneyland
Take the Kids Amsterdam

Available from good bookshops or via, in the UK, **Grantham Book Services**, Isaac Newton Way, Alma Park Industrial Estate, Grantham NG31 9SD, ℗ (01476) 541 080, ℗ (01476) 541 061; and in North America from **The Globe Pequot Press**, 246 Goose Lane, PO Box 480, Guilford, Connecticut 06437–0480, ℗ (800) 243 0495, ℗ (800) 820 2329.